THE CHILDREN'S
PICTURE ATLAS
IN COLOUR

THE CHILDREN'S
PICTURE
ATLAS
IN COLOUR

HAMLYN

First edition 1965
Second impression 1966
Third impression 1967
Fourth impression 1968
Revised edition 1971

Published by
THE HAMLYN PUBLISHING GROUP LTD.
HAMLYN HOUSE • THE CENTRE • FELTHAM • MIDDLESEX
for Golden Pleasure Books Ltd.
by arrangement with GOLDEN PRESS, INC.
© Copyright 1960, Golden Press, Inc. All rights reserved.
Text © Copyright 1965, Golden Pleasure Books, Ltd.
ISBN 0 601 08280 X
Printed in Czechoslovakia by TSNP Martin
51087/5

CONTENTS

SPECIAL SECTION OF STATISTICAL MAPS
RICHARD EDES HARRISON

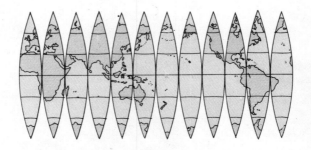

INTRODUCTION

Never before has the world presented greater contrasts than it does today, when modern jets land at airports only a few miles from villages that have developed little since the Stone Age.

Certainly there are no more hidden continents or mysterious islands to be discovered, and the frontiers of exploration now lie in Space or beneath the sea. And yet, though faster and faster aircraft are bringing the most distant parts of the world ever closer to us, this closeness only underlines the tremendous contrasts of the world, and the fascination of foreign lands, people, and customs. For the people of the world live their lives very differently, and in conditions that vary from the cold of the polar regions to the intense heat of deserts and tropical jungles. Some live securely in highly developed modern states, surrounded by modern aids and comforts. Others are faced with a permanent threat of starvation and disease. Some live in countries where the number of motor cars causes serious traffic-jams and delays. Others have never even seen a train.

It is these contrasts which this Atlas sets out to show: the deserts, jungles, cities, plains, and also — and just as important — the people of the world, where they are and what they do.

THIS IS EUROPE

Europe is part of the Old World. On its eastern side it is joined on to Asia, and it is often grouped with Asia in the term Eurasia. In fact Europe is sometimes spoken of as a peninsula of Asia. It has been the rule to trace the eastern boundary of Europe along the Ural mountains, but the Urals have never been an effective natural barrier — least of all today when the determined efforts of the U.S.S.R. to forge Siberia and European Russia into a single unit are making the Urals more and more meaningless as a frontier.

Unlike the solid mass of Asia, Europe is a peninsula thrust between the Atlantic and the Mediterranean, or, more accurately, numbers of peninsulas, with sea inlets between them—the Baltic, the North Sea, the English Channel, the Adriatic, and so on. This gives a very complicated coastline. In no other part of the world are sea and land so markedly intermixed as they are throughout Europe.

The fact that Europe lies in an area of moderate temperature makes the interplay of sea and land all the more important. The parallel of 50° North runs approximately through Penzance, Amiens, Frankfurt, and Prague. Only a very small part of Europe lies within the Arctic Circle, and even here, under the moderating influence of the North Atlantic Drift, the sea is ice-free throughout the year. Europe is the only continent with a mild climate. Its position on the globe and the influence of the sea mean that, except in the most eastern part of the continent, there are no great contrasts of heat and cold, no barren deserts. The whole of Europe, excluding European

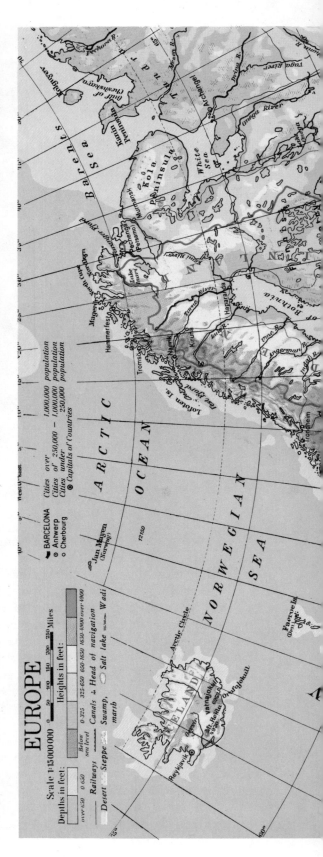

A group of happy Norwegian children, dressed in national costume, dancing in a meadow by the side of Hardanger Fiord.

Russia, has an area of 2,200,000 square miles, i.e. 4 per cent of the world's land surface. It is everywhere populated and exploited.

From North Cape in the extreme north of Norway to Cape Matapan at the southernmost tip of Greece the distance is only 2,400 miles, while from west to east, from Cape Finisterre to the mouth of the Danube, the distance is no more than 2,000 miles. Thus all parts of Europe are readily accessible. In addition there are numerous rivers which have played a considerable role in the development of the continent.

Its population of about 470 millions is 16 per cent of the world's total. That means there is an average of 21 persons per square mile compared with 17 in Asia and less than 3 per square mile in North America — making the smallest continent the most densely populated as, in fact, Europe's population exceeds that of Africa or the Americas.

The states of Europe vary between great modern industrial countries like Britain and Federal Germany, and tiny principalities like Monaco, Liechtenstein, Andorra, San Marino and, of course, the Vatican State.

MOUNTAINS AND PLAINS

Europe is not very mountainous. The average height of the continent is only 1,000 feet above sea level. The Alps, the dominant heights of Europe, are modest in extent compared with the Andes and the Rockies, and modest in height compared with the Himalayas.

They stretch for 750 miles from Nice in the south of France to Vienna in Austria, and altogether they include a dozen peaks over 12,000 feet. The Alps are less worn down by weather than older mountains, and beneath their jagged peaks are ice-bound hollows, and lower still, wooded slopes and deep valleys. The great valleys lead up to the famous passes: the Mont Cenis between France and Italy, the Great St Bernard and Simplon between Switzerland and Italy, the St Gotthard in Switzerland on the road leading to the Italian lakes, and the

Swedish National Travel Office

Falun in Sweden has one of the oldest copper mines in the world. Mining has been going on here since the year 1230.

Brenner Pass between Austria and Italy.

Other mountain ranges are less craggy. The Pyrenees run between France and Spain, and their highest peak, the Pico de Aneto, is only 11,168 feet in height. The Apennines run down the whole Italian Peninsula and continue in Sicily. The highest peak of these mountains, which are, in fact, an extension of the Alps, is Monte Corno in the Gran Sasso d'Italia (9,574 feet). On the flank of the

Ernst Kleinberg - Shostal

Many Italian towns have remained almost unchanged through the centuries: San Gimignano.

Müller - Miny

A characteristic Greek landscape scene: small villages scattered at the foot of mountains.

Apennines are famous volcanoes: Vesuvius near Naples, Etna in Sicily, and Stromboli, a small island north of Sicily.

An extension of the Alpine system runs through the Balkans into Greece. On the other side of the Danube is a more detached extension, the Carpathians. The Carpathians are the largest mountain system in Europe after the Alps, covering 72,000 square miles, though not rising above 9,000 feet. This range flanks the Great Plain of Hungary.

In other parts of Europe the mountains are not disposed in elongated ranges but in great masses such as the Massif Central in France, the Vosges on the left bank of the Rhine, the Grampians in Scotland, and the mountains of Scandinavia. Such mountains are lower and less dense than the ranges. They rise in great rounded masses, worn down by the weather, and some of their lower slopes are heavily wooded. Often coal seams are found beneath the foothills. Bordering them are often great plains, like that of Lorraine, which adjoins the Vosges.

The two important plains in Western Europe are the sharply marked Plain of Lombardy, watered, for the most part,

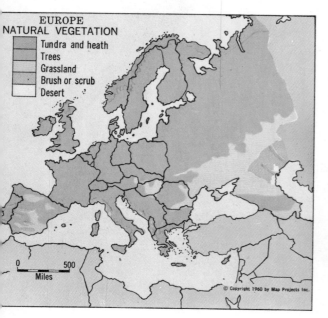

EUROPE
NATURAL VEGETATION

Tundra and heath
Trees
Grassland
Brush or scrub
Desert

0   500
Miles

© Copyright 1960 by Map Projects Inc.

by the Po; and, less clearly marked, the plain which gradually develops from the lesser uplands of Western Europe and sweeps across northern France and Germany, extending over Denmark, Finland, and the lowlands of Sweden.

There are also two important plains in Eastern Europe. The Great Plain of Hungary, and the North European Plain, which is an extension of the one that runs through France and Germany. Bohemia (the western part of Czechoslovakia) is an intermediate zone, being an undulating plateau over 1,000 feet above sea level surrounded by mountains of a little more than 4,000 feet in average height.

To understand the great variety of the European landscape we must keep in mind the manner of its formation. The Alps are among the youngest mountains in Europe. They were thrust up between 50 and 70 million years ago, and that is not long enough for the rocks to have been worn smooth by wind and weather, or the peaks to be rounded. Masses like the Grampians on the other hand were thrust up more than 400 million years ago. Once they possessed the forbidding craggy outline of the Alps, but over the ages they have been steadily weathered and scarred by deeper and broader valleys.

Amongst the agents in this weathering process the glaciers have played a major part, particularly those of the great Ice Ages, the last of which occurred some 20,000 years ago. Ice caps formed in Northern Europe, notably in Scandinavia and north-western Britain, and extended at their maximum to the Thames valley in the west and across the German and Polish plains to Bohemia and the Carpathians in the east. To the

Amleto Fattori, Filmeco, Rome, Italy

Fishing is very important to the economies of the countries of Southern Europe. Tunny fishing off the coast of Sardinia.

south the glaciers flowed outwards on both sides from the Pyrenees and the Alps. These glaciers acted like giant files, scraping the land they flowed over. When the ice eventually receded, it left behind deposits and depressions, the latter of which, filling up with water, remained as lakes. The lakes of the Alps, Finland, and Norway were formed in this way.

Ray Gardner - Philip D. Gendreau

'The Glory that was Greece' — ruins of the Temple of Apollo at Delphi.

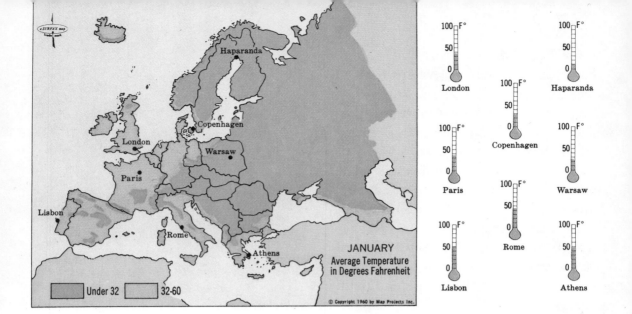

JANUARY
Average Temperature
in Degrees Fahrenheit

London Haparanda Copenhagen Paris Warsaw Rome Lisbon Athens

Under 32   32-60

© Copyright 1960 by Map Projects Inc.

THE CLIMATE, COASTS AND SEAS

The nature of the coasts varies greatly in Europe. In mountainous regions the coast rises steeply, as in Portugal, Italy, and Norway. Where there are plains, on the other hand, the coast consists of a gently shelving and easily eroded beach which often needs to be protected by breakwaters. The Atlantic Ocean washes the coasts of Europe from Gibraltar to Scandinavia, and the warm North Atlantic Drift is felt as far as the north of Norway.

The Mediterranean is made up of a series of deep basins in which there are numerous islands, the most important being the Balearic Islands (Majorca, Minorca, Ibiza), Corsica, Sardinia, Sicily, Crete, and Cyprus. The Mediterranean is so enclosed by the land that it is practically tideless. Consequently coastal erosion by the sea proceeds much more slowly. As the Mediterranean is warm, the water evaporates quickly, making it more salty than other seas. It has been

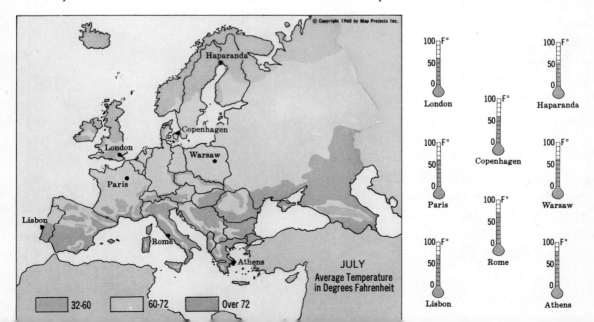

JULY
Average Temperature
in Degrees Fahrenheit

© Copyright 1960 by Map Projects Inc.

London Haparanda Copenhagen Paris Warsaw Rome Lisbon Athens

32-60   60-72   Over 72

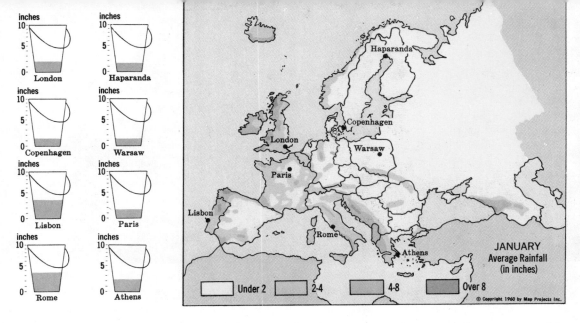

JANUARY
Average Rainfall
(in inches)

Under 2   2-4   4-8   Over 8

© Copyright 1960 by Map Projects Inc.

calculated that if the Straits of Gibraltar were stopped up, the Mediterranean would dry out completely in less than 8,000 years.

The climate of Europe is much less variable than that of other continents. This is partly due to its position about half-way between the Equator and the North Pole. But in this area, often called the temperate zone, the prevailing wind is from the west. The west wind brings moisture and, because of the warm Gulf Stream and North Atlantic Drift, warmth. Thus, the summers are less hot and winters less cold on the western side of the land mass than on the eastern side of Eurasia.

In this way the sea exercises an influence far into the interior of Europe, particularly in the north. In fact, we can distinguish three climatic zones. In Western Europe, where the influence of the sea is greatest, we have the true maritime climate. In central Europe and farther east the influence of the sea progressively diminishes, and there is what is called the continental climate. In the south the influence of the sea is only felt in winter, and that is the season of rains. During the summer, depressions do not penetrate

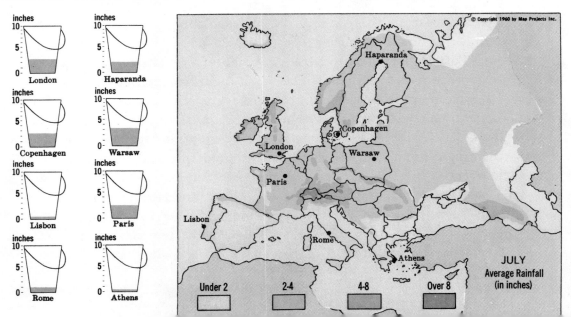

JULY
Average Rainfall
(in inches)

Under 2   2-4   4-8   Over 8

© Copyright 1960 by Map Projects Inc.

Mild winters, sunny summers, and the Mediterranean make the towns of the French and Italian Rivieras ideal holiday resorts.

into the Mediterranean regions, and the summers are hot and dry. This is called the Mediterranean climate.

The maritime climate, extending over nearly all of Western Europe, is characterised by abundant rain, which falls at frequent intervals throughout the year (though slightly more often in autumn), by constant changes in the weather, and the absence of clearly marked seasons and extremes of heat and cold. With this climate rivers such as the Thames and Rhine have streams which are more or less uniform, as rainfall is fairly evenly spread over the year.

The continental climate extending over Central and Eastern Europe, is characterised by more uneven rainfall, which reaches its maximum in brief summer storms, and by the sharp contrast between summer and winter, divided by a very short spring and autumn. In these conditions such rivers as the Vistula flow very unevenly, being frozen during the winter and at their height in spring, when they are swollen by the thaw and heavy rains. Pine forests or grassland are the

typical vegetation of this particular kind of climate, especially in the great steppes of Eastern Europe.

The Mediterranean climate, extending across Southern Europe, is characterised by hot summers and mild winters (though sudden cold spells do occur), and by definitely seasonal rainfall — occurring in heavy downpours, chiefly in winter. The summer is extremely dry. Dryness and heat together account for the arid appearance of the plains and low plateaus of the Mediterranean regions. The influence of this kind of climate on the rivers, on vegetation, and on agriculture is decisive. The flow of rivers is extremely variable. Vegetation is chiefly characterised by protection against drought. Trees are evergreen with small waxy leaves, — olives and ilexes, for instance. They very rarely grow to a great height but form thick undergrowth. The maquis in Corsica is an example.

The Rhine rises in the Swiss Alps. Its winding course stretches in all some 850 miles. After flowing for a considerable distance in Switzerland, it turns northwards, and for a while forms the frontier between Germany and France, then flows on through Germany, and finally crosses into Holland. Here it empties into the North Sea, forming a large delta with several arms.

The flow of the Rhine is steady, making navigation possible. Thanks to great improvements during the last 100 years or more, big lighters can be towed as far as Basle, thereby giving Switzerland an outlet to the sea. The Rhine is linked by canal to the Rhône, which flows into the Mediterranean. Another canal joins it to the Marne, a tributary of the Seine, which flows into the Channel; the Seine in turn is similarly joined to the Loire. Lastly, one of the tributaries of the Rhine, the Main, is joined by canal to the Danube, and thus to the Black Sea. These important rivers and their connections thus make up a great system of international inland waterways, which link the North Sea with the Mediterranean and the Atlantic with the Black Sea.

The Rhine flows through some of the most productive industrial regions in all Europe, and carries more traffic than any other river in the world.

The Danube is a still longer river than the Rhine, flowing some 1,700 miles from its source in Germany to the Black Sea, yet from the viewpoint of navigation it is much less important. This is for two reasons. First, it flows through a less populated, much less industrialised part of Europe in a direction unfavourable for trade. Secondly, the flow varies greatly with the seasons. In the spring, when the snow melts, the current is so strong that it is a hard task for tugs to tow lighters upstream. The river is also often frozen over in winter.

EUROPE
MAIN RAILROADS
© Copyright 1960 by Map Projects Inc.

EUROPE
MAIN
AIR ROUTES
© Copyright 1960 by Map Projects Inc.

EUROPE
MAIN ROADS
© Copyright 1960 by Map Projects Inc.

EUROPE

Miles

© Copyright 1960 by Map Projects Inc.

UNION OF SOVIET SOCIALIST REPUBLICS

CASPIAN SEA

IRAN

IRAQ

BLACK SEA

Sea of Azov

TURKEY

SYRIA

LEBANON

CYPRUS

ROMANIA

BULGARIA

Bosporus

Dardanelles

GREECE

Aegean Sea

Rhodes

Crete

WHITE SEA

Lake Ladoga

FINLAND

Gulf of Finland

Gulf of Bothnia

POLAND

HUNGARY

YUGOSLAVIA

Adriatic Sea ALB.

Ionian Sea

SWEDEN

Baltic Sea

Berlin

GER. DEM. REP.

CZECHOSLOVAKIA

AUSTRIA

SAN MARINO

ITALY

Sardinia

Tyrrhenian Sea

Sicily

NORWAY

VESTERALEN ISLANDS

Arctic Circle

GER. FED. REP.

SWITZ. LIECHT.

MONACO

Corsica

BALEARIC ISLANDS

MEDITERRANE

MALTA

TUNISIA

NORWEGIAN SEA

ICELAND

FAEROE ISLANDS

SHETLAND ISLANDS

ORKNEY ISLANDS

NORTH SEA

DENMARK

GREAT BRITAIN

NETH.

BELG.

LUXEMBOURG

FRANCE

ANDORRA

SPAIN

ALGERIA

NORTH IRELAND

IRELAND

English Channel

Bay of Biscay

PORTUGAL

Strait of Gibraltar

MOROCCO

ATLANTIC OCEAN

PEOPLES OF EUROPE

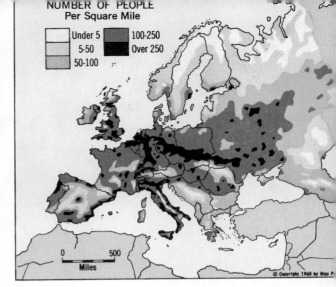

The ancient Bronze Age peoples of Europe were pushed to the west by invading tribes from the east who usually had more unified civilisations and more powerful iron weapons.

The Celts are an example of such early inhabitants. Their descendants in our day include the Bretons (Brittany), the Irish, Welsh, Scots, and the people of the Isle of Man and Cornwall. These Celtic people all live on islands or peninsulas in Western Europe, where they were forced by stronger tribes from the east.

Each of these groups of Celts had its own language. Some of these languages have disappeared, while others, such as Breton, Welsh, and Gaelic, may still be heard.

The Romans, in the days of their greatness, ruled and colonised much of Europe, especially the south and west. The French, the Spanish, Portuguese, Italians, and Romanians speak languages of Latin origin.

In Britain the invading Angles, Saxons, and Danes wiped out almost all trace of the Roman tongue and culture. Similar invasions wiped out Latin in other parts of Europe where Rome had ruled peoples of different languages and cultures.

Many of the 'Barbarians' that invaded the Roman Empire were of Germanic stock. They are represented today by the English, Dutch, German, and Scandinavian peoples.

After the Germanic invasions, tribes that spoke Slavic languages came from Asia and settled in Eastern Europe. Descended from them are the Russians, Poles, Czechs, Slovaks, Serbs, Croats, Slovenes, and Bulgarians.

Thus we see that today the three great language and cultural groups of Europe are the Romance (derived from Latin), the Germanic, and the Slavic.

The influence of the culture of ancient Rome is still shown in the alphabet we use: all the countries of Western Europe use the same alphabet that the Romans did. When the Slavs invaded Europe,

In their remote mountain villages Bulgarian women still wear traditional national costume.

Paul Hufner - Shostal

The streets of Copenhagen are full of bicycles — one Dane out of every two owns one.

Roman culture had lost much of its influence. But it was still strong enough to give its alphabet to the most westerly Slavs: that is, the Poles, Czechs, and Slovenes.

The tribes of the east, however, did not adopt the Roman alphabet. In the ninth century the monk Cyril invented an alphabet based on Greek as well as Roman letters. This Cyrillic alphabet is the one used today by the Serbs, Croats, Bulgarians, and Russians.

There are also several smaller groups of European peoples. The modern Greeks long ago drove out or conquered the original inhabitants and settled in Greece.

These traditional round loaves of bread are sold in the street markets of Spain.

They still live there and on the nearby Aegean Islands. In ancient days far-flung Greek colonies were scattered over the Mediterranean Sea, especially in Sicily and Italy. The name 'Naples' (*Napoli*) comes from two Greek words meaning 'New City'.

Today there are many descendants of the Greeks scattered from Spain to Istanbul. But the language and way of life of these early Greek settlers have been assimilated with those of the populations that came after them.

Other smaller groups are the Finns and the Hungarians. The Finns, whose culture now is very like that of the Scandinavians, have a quite different language. It is related to Estonian and to Hungarian. Both of these peoples also have their own language and way of life.

Besides the Hungarians in Hungary, groups of Hungarians are found also in Yugoslavia and in Romania. The Turks, who once conquered all Europe as far as Vienna, are now confined to an area around Istanbul in the south-east of Europe. They have their own language and culture. So have the Albanians who live in the rugged uplands north-west of Greece.

Most Europeans are fair-skinned. Many of those who live in the north are tall and have blue eyes and light hair. Southerners tend to be shorter with dark eyes and hair.

Thousands of years have gone by since the first men came into Europe. In that time tribes have conquered tribes and nations have conquered nations. Victors and vanquished have mingled and intermarried. And the blood of Greek and Roman, Celt, German, and Slav is now widely spread throughout the continent.

The Houses of Parliament and Big Ben: the political hub of the British Commonwealth.

THE PRINCIPAL CITIES OF EUROPE

London, the greatest city in Europe, was originally built by the Romans at the lowest crossing point of the Thames. No other city can approach the variety of London, a quality stemming from the fact that it is not only a great centre of population and the cultural centre of the British Isles, but also the political hub of Britain and the Commonwealth, and a great industrial city and port as well.

Most of London has been built over the last 100 years, but there are many historic buildings, including the Tower, Westminster Abbey, St Paul's Cathedral, etc. Perhaps the most famous physical feature of London is its parks, which bring something of the countryside right into the very heart of the enormous urban area.

London is the leading industrial concentration in Britain; 21 per cent of all British workers are employed in the London area, chiefly in light industry. The great Port of London is the busiest port in Britain, handling half of all the raw materials imported from abroad and half of all British exports.

Well over 7 million people live within Greater London, which stretches 21 miles from north to south and 15 miles from east to west. However, in the heart of this great expanse is the original City of London, measuring a single square mile. This tiny area is one of the greatest commercial and banking centres of the world, the home of the Bank of England, the Stock Exchange, and many great banks.

Copenhagen is not only the capital of Denmark, it is also the largest and most important city in the whole of Scandinavia. Copenhagen is one of the most beautiful cities in Europe, famous for its canal and the many statues and historic buildings. It is often referred to as the 'Paris of the North'.

Copenhagen's most celebrated citizen was Hans Christian Andersen, and the world-famous statue of his Little Mermaid looks out over the city from the calm waters of the harbour.

Rotterdam is situated 19 miles inland, connected with the sea by a deep-water canal called the New Waterway. At present Rotterdam handles more than three-quarters of Holland's trade, and forms — together with its satellite ports, Schiedam, Vlaardingen, and Hoek van Holland (the Hook of Holland) — the chief port in all Europe, and second largest in the world after New York. But when Europoort, at present being constructed along the New Waterway, is completed, the Rotterdam area will almost certainly handle more goods than any other port in the world.

Fox Photos Ltd

The statue of Hans Christian Andersen's famous Little Mermaid, Copenhagen.

About 20,000 ships call every year at Rotterdam, where many shipping companies have their headquarters. Rotterdam is also the terminus for large passenger liners setting sail to America, Africa, and the Far East.

Though Paris is a great political and economic centre, its chief claim to fame is in the field of culture, of which it can be truly stated to be the capital of the world. The art collections of the Louvre and the Museum of Modern Art are unrivalled, and students and artists of all kinds flock to this beautiful city from every country.

Much of the inimitable atmosphere of Paris comes from the river Seine which runs through it, and among the most famous landmarks are the Gothic cathedral of Notre-Dame, the enormous palace of the Louvre, the church of Sacré-Coeur in Montmarte, the Arc de Triomphe commemorating Napoleon's victories, and the Eiffel Tower. The tree-lined boulevards of Paris are some of the most famous and beautiful streets ever built.

Built on seven hills on the banks of the Tiber, Rome is the capital of Italy and also embraces the independent Vatican City, the centre of the Roman Catholic Church.

Rome — the Eternal City — is richer in historical remains than any other place in the world. Contrasting with such buildings as the Forum and Colosseum of classical days are the many splendid palaces and churches of the Renaissance, the most outstanding of which is St Peter's. This was chiefly the work of Michelangelo, who also painted the ceiling of the Sistine Chapel in the Vatican. The work was started in 1508 and took four years to accomplish. It is generally regarded as one of the greatest artistic works of all time.

No capital city is more important than Moscow, the capital and greatest city of the Soviet Union. The administrative

Educational Productions Ltd

Europoort, Rotterdam. When finally completed this will form the most important dock area in the world.

and governmental departments are concentrated within the Kremlin, the historic centre of the Russian State. It was from the Kremlin that Ivan the Terrible united the whole of Russia, becoming the first Czar. He and his successors imported architects from Italy, Germany, Holland, and England to design and build palaces and churches and monasteries. Despite

Moscow. The great Kremlin, the palace of the Czars and now the centre of the Soviet State.

A general view across Rome — the Eternal City.

this, the Kremlin is essentially Russian — blending European with Asiatic.

Most of residential Moscow is modern, and today the city is also a great centre of industry.

Apart from the historic legacy of the Czars, Moscow has one world-famous landmark that is twentieth-century and entirely Soviet — the Tomb of Lenin in Red Square, which is the great shrine of modern Russia.

Courtesy of TWA - Trans World Airlines

The famous thirteenth-century Gothic cathedral of Notre-Dame in Paris.

Wolfgang Linke

An example of the effect of glaciers on landscape: endless lakes and low islands in Finland.

NORTHERN EUROPE

Of the four Scandinavian states the two largest, Norway and Sweden, form a long peninsula attached in the north to Finland and Russia. Denmark, another peninsula, is attached to Germany. Iceland is an island formerly belonging to Denmark. The shores of these countries are washed by four seas: the Baltic Sea, the North Sea, the Atlantic Ocean, and the Arctic Ocean.

The outstanding physical feature consists of the Kjolen mountains (*kjolen* meaning keel), which are not very high, mainly between 3,000 and 8,000 feet. During the great Ice Ages these were deeply scored by glaciers, which cut out fiords — deep inlets, shallow at the seaward end — and innumerable islands, along the Atlantic coast.

Great areas of northern Scandinavia are covered by ice and snow, and only in the south can much farming be done. Crops ripen owing to the fact that the continual daylight of the summer months

compensates for the absence of hot sunshine. The chief crop is hay, which is dried on long trellises in the fields.

Of the four Scandinavian states, Sweden, with an area of over 170,000 square miles, and nearly 8 million inhabitants, is much the largest, the most densely populated, and the richest. Agriculture is able to supply most of the country's food requirements and one-third of the working population are employed in it.

Industry is very varied, including the mining of iron, copper, and other metals, and the exploitation of the country's timber, much of which is exported in the form of pulp for paper-making. The energy needed for industry is derived from hydro-electric power-stations. Exports include machinery and ball-bearings made from high quality steel.

The chief trading port is Göteborg at the northern end of the Kattegat from which ships sail through the Skagerrak to reach the North Sea.

The capital, Stockholm, besides being the political and administrative centre, has, like London, acquired a considerable amount of industry, particularly in the new electrical products.

Norway has a population of almost 4 million, fewer than either Sweden or Denmark. Though there is a broad area in the south-east where farming is possible, over 70 per cent of the total area is barren, and 20 per cent of the remainder forest. On the other hand the Atlantic coast is deeply indented, there being some 12,000 miles of fiords, and consequently Norway is essentially a maritime country.

Of the working population 4 per cent is engaged in fishing, either for cod and herring off the coast, or for whales in the

Philip D. Gendreau

Customers making up their minds in the old Fish Market in Copenhagen.

Antarctic. Norway possesses the third largest merchant fleet in the world, after Britain and the United States. Fish-products and the products of Norway's forests, particularly wood-pulp, are principal exports. Norway is not rich in minerals, but there is a certain amount

Richard Tegstrom

A Lapp woman working on reindeer hide from which boots will be made.

Wolffe Tietze

Another example of the effects of glaciation. Sogne Fiord, Norway. The fiords were formed when valleys carved by glaciers were filled with sea water at the end of the Ice Age.

of heavy industry, particularly in electro-chemical machinery. Mining and manufacturing employ 34 per cent of the working population. These industries provide products for the home market as well as important exports.

In the far north of Norway occurs the phenomenon of the Midnight Sun — in summer the sun does not set for eleven weeks. This region is inhabited by the Lapps, who live off their large herds of reindeer.

Oslo, the capital, with a population of under half a million, is beautifully situated at the head of a fiord, 80 miles from the sea. Besides being an administrative and commercial centre, it is an industrial town, with shipbuilding yards and factories producing a wide range of goods, including textiles, paper, sail-cloth, hardware, etc.

Roy Pinney - Photo Library

Göteborg is an industrial and shipbuilding town as well as being Sweden's chief port.

Stockholm, Sweden, is built on islands. Men fish with these round nets even in the heart of the city.

The whaling industry is still important, though today the catching of whales is strictly controlled.

Denmark stands at the entrance to the Baltic, and provides a stepping-stone between northern Europe and Germany. With an area of over 16,000 square miles it has a population of 4.8 million people, about a quarter of whom live in the capital.

Denmark is flat, its soil is rich, and it is accordingly above all an agricultural country. The surplus produce — butter, milk, eggs, and bacon — is exported to nearby industrial countries. There are few countries in the world where the soil is so intensively cultivated or where stock-breeding and dairy production have reached so high a standard. This is partly due to the very high standard of education of those who work on the land, and also to the advanced system of co-operative marketing. Denmark produces one-third of the butter sold in the world.

Industry is developing in spite of the need to import a large proportion of raw materials needed. The Danes too are a seagoing people, with a considerable merchantile marine.

Copenhagen, the capital, is situated on the low-lying eastern shore of the island of Zealand. It is an old town which has suffered much destruction in the course of its long history, but it has always been quick to recover. More than either Stockholm or Oslo it is the centre of the Scandinavian world.

Finland has always been a border

Hydro-electric plants use the steep mountain streams of Scandinavia to generate electricity for homes and factories.

A hillside farm in Norway.

country between two worlds. From the Middle Ages to 1808, Finland was under Swedish domination. Then the country came under Russian rule, and did not become entirely independent until 1917.

Finland is mainly a country of forests and lakes. The climate is more continental than that of Sweden, which means that

Denmark exports cheese and other dairy products all over the world.

Dairy farming is important all over Scandinavia. This farm is in Finland.

it is necessary to grow spring wheat.

More than a tenth of the country is occupied by lakes, some of vast size. At the turn of the century, lakes and marshland occupied a quarter of the country, but the marshes are progressively being reclaimed. Finland is the most forested country in Europe, and the greater part of its industry is concerned with wood-products, such as paper and plywood, prefabricated houses, etc. Finland is also famous for high-quality domestic goods, such as furniture, glass textiles, etc. In the last twenty years minerals have been discovered, and industry based on them now exists. Helsinki is the capital, and the other large towns are Tampere and Turku. The lakes, linked by canals, provide a great system of inland waterways. The Finns have an extensive fishing industry, but, unlike their Scandinavian neighbours, have never gone in much for shipping.

The whole country lying within a few degrees of the Arctic Circle, Iceland may be regarded as the most northerly country of Europe. It is a mountainous country with few trees and with an ice-field covering one-eighth of its surface. It is chiefly famous, however, for its many volcanoes and hot springs or geysers. Today the power of these geysers has been harnessed and one Icelander in four has his house heated from this source; while, in greenhouses similarly heated, bananas grow. Hot springs are found in every part of the island. Sulphur springs and lakes of boiling mud are also common in the volcanic districts. Earthquakes are frequent.

With little arable land, the Icelanders are chiefly occupied by sheep breeding and fishing. Two-fifths of the population

Ewing Krainin - Photo Researchers

The Town Hall, Copenhagen. The kiosks sell ice cream, sweets, and newspapers.

of about 200,000 is concentrated in the capital, Reykjavik, a port in the southwest of the island, where an aluminium plant began production in 1969.

Patrick Morin - Monkmeyer

The fisheries form the basis of Iceland's economy. The men catch the fish and women workers do the sorting and cleaning.

Fasoloi

Patrick Morin - Monkmeyer

Two Danish children play in a public garden in Copenhagen.

These Icelandic children are the descendants of Viking settlers.

Joe Barnell - Shostal

Finnish lumbermen collect logs on Lake Päijänne, one of the 'Finger Lakes' of Finland.

Cattle grazing beside a Scottish loch: some of the finest cattle in the world are bred in Scotland.

WESTERN EUROPE — THE BRITISH ISLES

Great Britain is the economic hub of north-west Europe, and the economy of the Scandinavian countries is closely linked with it. Great Britain is also the centre of the British Commonwealth, and no other European power has so many economic contacts all over the world — some 200 million people outside the British Isles speak English.

In few other countries is there such a variation of landscape as in the British Isles: the flat broad Fens of Lincolnshire, the mountains and moors of Scotland, the orchards of Kent.

Looking at a map of the island it would be impossible to guess the outline of its three great divisions — England, Scotland, and Wales — the boundaries being cultural rather than physical. The only considerable physical difference is that Scotland and Wales are much more mountainous than England.

Scotland is sharply divided into the Highlands and the Lowlands. The Highlands of Scotland are famous as areas of great natural beauty and for the cattle bred there. The Highlands include Ben Nevis, which at 4,406 feet is the highest mountain in Great Britain. However, most of the population, industry, and agriculture of Scotland is concentrated in the Lowlands.

Wales presents an almost solid block of mountains, whose highest peak, Snowdon, is 3,560 feet high. The only other regions in Great Britain which are extensively hilly are Cumberland, Derbyshire, Devon, Cornwall, and parts of Yorkshire. Dartmoor in Devon is a last example of the landscape of Britain before it came to be cleared and levelled and farmed.

The south and east of England consist of plains interspersed with modest ranges of hills like the North and South Downs, the Cotswolds, and the Chilterns.

London reflects the whole history of England; it is immense and was for long the largest city in the world. The population of Greater London is at present almost 8 million. The London of the City and the West End is known to all. What is less known is that the Port of London is one of the largest in the world. The Royal Albert and King George V Docks can accommodate the largest cargo steamers, while passenger liners dock at Tilbury, also included in the Port of London.

No place in Britain is more than 100 miles from the sea, and this fact has done more than any other to shape British history, in the same way as it has always been the principal influence on the climate. The climate of Britain is well-known: frequent rather than heavy rainfall, no great extremes of temperature, a tendency to fog and cloud. All this is the result of the fact that the sea is

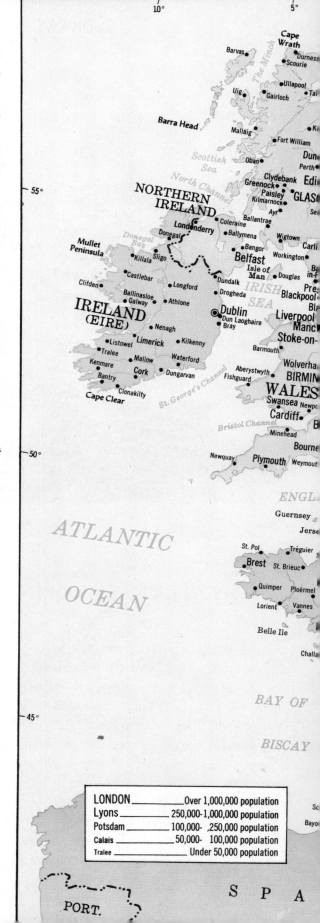

LONDON	Over 1,000,000 population
Lyons	250,000-1,000,000 population
Potsdam	100,000- 250,000 population
Calais	50,000- 100,000 population
Tralee	Under 50,000 population

WESTERN EUROPE

0 — 50 — 100 — 150
Miles

◉ National Capitals

© Copyright 1960 by Map Projects Inc.

so close to all parts of the British Isles.

Historically, the sea has brought the various races that became the British — Celts, Romans, Angles, Saxons, Danes, and Normans — and the sea also inspired Englishmen to rove the world, establishing trade, creating colonies, and building empires. Britain has a coastline of 5,000 miles — twice as long as France.

Today most of the former British Empire has achieved independence — generally within the Commonwealth.

But the maritime tradition continues, and the British merchant fleet is the largest in the world, with a tonnage of almost 21 million tons.

Out of all British workers, only 3 per cent are employed on the land or in fishing, compared to France's 20 per cent, and 23 per cent in Italy. Of all the agricultural land of Britain, about a third is under the plough, mostly in the lowlands of the south and east. The rest consists of pastures, moorlands, etc. In any case

Atomic Energy Authority

Britain is a leader in the peaceful uses of atomic energy. This is the nuclear power station at Bradwell.

A chequered pattern of small fields, gently rolling hills — the unmistakably English countryside of Cornwall.

In the past the hop fields of Kent attracted many hop pickers at harvest time — mainly from London. However, most of the work is now done by machinery.

the moist climate makes the country unsuitable for growing wheat except in the south-east. Accordingly many farmers go in for dairy-farming, poultry, and vegetables. Though British farming is excellently organised and highly productive, Britain can only supply two-thirds of her own food needs.

British fishermen bring in over a million tons of fish a year, much of it from the shallow Dogger Bank in the North Sea and the waters round Iceland. The principal fishing ports are Hull, Grimsby, Aberdeen, Yarmouth, Lowestoft, and Fleetwood.

The principal industrial regions of Great Britain are: (A.) The Midlands, Yorkshire, and Lancashire. The northern part specialises largely in textiles: wool in Leeds, Bradford, Halifax, and Huddersfield; cotton in Manchester and other Lancashire towns. However, with the advent of artificial fibres, more and more textile mills are being converted to other light industries. Heavy industry exists too, shipbuilding for instance, at Birkenhead and Barrow-in-Furness, and steel-

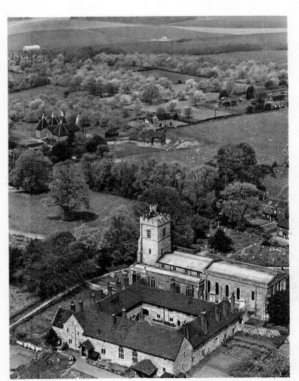

Lush green meadows and a fine old church in the south of England. The park-like landscape is the result of centuries of skilled farming.

Aerofilms Limited

London. The Royal Albert Dock (left) and the King George V Dock (right).

works at the latter, as well as near Rotherham in Yorkshire. Round Birmingham, further south, in the midst of what is known as the Black Country, engineering and hardware manufacture are centred. A vast range of goods, especially metal goods, are produced in this great manufacturing area and in the neighbouring towns of Wolverhampton and Walsall. Coventry, on the other hand, specialises in cycles and motor-cars, while Sheffield is famous for its cutlery. Liverpool serves as the chief port for this region, though the Manchester Ship Canal enables sea-going ships to reach Manchester, 30 miles inland.

(B.) South Wales. This area is chiefly famous for its coalfields, which produce hard, smokeless coal of the highest quality, and for its great steel industry, located at Port Talbot, Cardiff, and elsewhere. The tinplate industry of Swansea and Llanelly consumes much of the steel and also uses imported tin ore. This

Courtesy of TWA - Trans World Airlines

The sentry at the Horse Guards in Whitehall always attracts a crowd.

John Herdman

A piper leading a wedding procession in Scotland.

area also has several large oil refineries.

(C.) The north-east region of Newcastle and Teesside is famous for iron and steel manufacture, shipbuilding, and an important chemicals industry.

(D.) The Clyde. A wide range of manufactures is concentrated in Glasgow and its neighbouring towns, including textiles

Keystone Press

Bond Street, London, is one of the world's great shopping centres.

The Llandarcy oil refinery, Wales. Crude oil is one of Britain's biggest imports.

(cotton and wool), chemical products, and iron and steel, while shipbuilding is the main industry along the Clyde estuary from Glasgow to Greenock.

(E.) London. Until recently there was relatively little industry in London. Its importance was in the first place political and administrative, but it has always been a commercial centre. It has also for long been a world-famous financial centre, that is to say a great centre of banking, insurance, and the buying and selling of shares at the Stock Exchange. In recent years, however, it has grown rapidly as an industrial centre. Many new light industries, the manufacture of radios and refrigerators, for example, have taken root there. But even engineering, so long centred in the north, is now developing on the banks of the Thames, as in the motor-car works at Dagenham, and there is also the production of cement.

Coal mining is a traditional occupation in Wales. Welsh coal is of very high quality. This mine is in the Rhondda Valley.

IRELAND

Ireland, with its soft, humid climate, is traditionally a country of grassland, peat-bogs, and potato fields. The island is divided into the Republic of Ireland (Eire) and Northen Ireland (Ulster), which is part of the United Kingdom.

The Republic of Ireland is much the larger of the two territories. But Northern Ireland is far more densely populated: $1\frac{1}{2}$ million people in 5,461 square miles compared to Eire's 3 million in 26,600 square miles.

Until recently there was very little industry in Eire, but there has been an increase in the interest from other European countries, notably West Germany, and today there is a growing

Peat from peat bogs is a very widely used fuel in Ireland. Ten years are all that are needed to form peat from decaying vegetation.

volume of industry in the Irish Republic.

In Northern Ireland, which is part of the United Kingdom, industry is highly developed, much of it being concentrated round Belfast, the capital. The principal industries are shipbuilding, linen, and artificial textiles.

There is a great contrast between Dublin and Belfast. Dublin is still an essentially eighteenth-century city, and was, of course, the capital of Ireland before its division in 1920. Belfast, on the other hand, grew to importance during the nineteenth century. Both are famous university towns.

Dublin, capital of Eire.

Windmills, are a traditional feature of the Dutch landscape, though they are rapidly being replaced by modern pumping machinery. The pumps are necessary in order to prevent flooding.

THE BENELUX COUNTRIES

The three Benelux countries, Belgium, the Netherlands (Holland), and Luxembourg, have a total area of only 35,000 square miles, but they are the most densely populated countries in Europe with, in all, 22 million inhabitants. If they are taken as one unit they constitute the fourth richest economic power in the world.

Since 1948, when a customs union was formed, the Benelux countries have been moving steadily towards full union, thereby setting an example to the other members of the European Common Market.

Holland and Belgium are often bracketed together as the Low Countries. A good deal of the coastlines of both countries can be as much as 10 feet below sea-level, the sea being kept at bay by sea-walls or dykes. About a quarter of Holland's arable land has been reclaimed from the sea — these reclaimed lands are called polders. The centre part of the Belgium-Holland coast is occupied by the extensive deltas of the Rhine, the Meuse, and the Scheldt.

In the southernmost region of the Benelux group we find the hills and forests of the Ardennes, whose average height is less than 1,600 feet.

Luxembourg has for long been an independent Grand Duchy. It consists of a plateau furrowed by valleys and wedged in between France, Germany, and Belgium. With an area of 1,000 square miles it has a population of about 335,000. It is rich in iron ore and the mining and smelting of this metal is, with agriculture, the chief industry.

The capital, in which over a fifth of the population lives, is also called Luxembourg. Besides being the seat of government it is the seat of the High Authority of the European Coal and Steel Community, a body which co-ordinates the production and marketing of coal and steel in Luxembourg, Belgium, the Netherlands, West Germany, France, and Italy.

Rosignoli

Belgium. This tree-lined canal runs from Bruges to Damme.

A barge with a cargo of flowers passing a tulip field in Holland. The flowers are of secondary importance, whereas the bulbs are a major source of revenue.

Malak - Annan Photo Features

Eighteenth-century houses on the waterfront of Amsterdam, the biggest city in Holland.

Rotterdam is an international centre for diamonds. Great skill is needed to cut and polish them.

BELGIUM

Belgium only became an independent country in 1830. The kingdom is a union of two peoples: the Flemings from the north (Flanders), and the Walloons from the southern provinces. The Flemings speak their own language, Flemish, while the Walloons are French-speaking.

The capital, Brussels, with over a million inhabitants, is situated in the middle of the country, where the two groups meet.

Belgium is above all an industrial and commercial country. Industry goes far back into the past, beginning with the old linen weavers of Flanders, and the armourers of Liège.

Like England, Belgium has its Black Country, which is centred on a line running from Mons through Charleroi, Namur, Huy, Seraing, to Liège. Alongside the pits of the coalfields are great blast furnaces and steel-works, chiefly at Charleroi and Liège. There are also glass-works and vast chemical factories. On the Campine coalfields are zinc and glass-works, cement-works, brick-yards, and factories for the making of chemical fertilisers.

Weaving is still a great industry in Flanders — though today all kinds of fibres are used, not only the traditional linen.

Belgium is intensively cultivated and crop yields are high. The principal crops are wheat, rye, oats, barley, sugar-beet, flax, potatoes, and hops. Even so, Belgium like England, has to import great quantities of foodstuffs. The greater part of Belgium's trade passes through Antwerp, one of the best equipped ports in Europe.

The famous weekly cheese market at Alkmaar, Holland, always attracts plenty of attention from visitors.

The rich alluvial farmland of the lower Seine consists of soil washed down by the river.

THE NETHERLANDS

Hard-working, conscientious, and business-like, the Dutch are equally at home on land and sea, and signs of their energy and enterprise are everywhere apparent. On the two great estuaries of the Scheldt, and the Maas, on the Waal, and inland on the innumerable canals, a constant traffic may be seen which exceeds that of the railways. Rotterdam and Amsterdam are ports of world-wide fame, providing evidence that this small country is of greater importance in the business world than many a big one.

Dutch agriculture, like Belgium's, is intensively developed and the yield per acre high, and, in fact, farming here plays a decidedly bigger part in the nation's economy than it does in Belgium. The soil of the polders is very rich. The two principal occupations are dairy-farming and market gardening and flower growing. A considerable amount of butter and cheese is exported, and large quantities of bulbs.

With a population of over $12\frac{1}{2}$ millions and an area of some 13,000 square miles (960 per square mile), Holland is quite incapable of producing all the food she needs.

Over the centuries the Dutch have fought a running battle with nature in order to reclaim more and more land from the sea, and then to defend what they had reclaimed. In particular, during this century, the map of Holland has undergone a marked change owing to one of the greatest enterprises ever undertaken by civil engineering, the reclamation of a large part of the former Zuider Zee. The idea, already projected in the sev-

Mont Blanc, the highest mountain in Western Europe, has several glaciers.

enteenth century, was put into operation a generation ago. This large but shallow gulf, covering an area of 2,000 square miles, was enclosed by a dam $18\frac{1}{2}$ miles long across the entrance, making it into an inland lake. By pumping the water out three huge polders have already been formed, adding some 300,000 acres to Holland's soil. That, however, is not the end of the story. During the next generation, another two great polders are to be reclaimed, making a total area of over half a million acres, or nearly 850 square miles. The name Zuider Zee has now been dropped, the remaining water being called Ijssel Meer. The Ijssel Meer is a fresh-water lake vital for irrigation.

The Delta project to dam the Scheldt and Lower Rhine estuaries is even more exciting. Under this, four massive dams and three secondary dams will close all but two of the deep-sea inlets of the Delta. The two left will serve the ports of Antwerp and Rotterdam. A great adjustable storm-barrier has been built near Capelle-on-the-Ijssel, north-east of Rotterdam, with sluice gates that can be lowered when the waterlevel is very high. The principal dams across the Haringvliet will also have adjustable sluices, and a small lock. The sluices are necessary to allow the tide waters to pass through the dams.

In addition three huge sluices are being built on the lower Rhine, which will control the distribution of fresh water, some of which will be directed into Lake Ijssel, which is part of the former Zuider Zee. Fresh water has been mentioned several times: it must be remembered that land reclamation by itself is valueless unless there is fresh water available for irrigation, since wherever land is below sea-level, as it always is in reclaimed areas, the ground-water will always be salty, and therefore useless for crops.

When the project is fully completed in 1978 the coastline will have been shortened by 435 miles, the danger of floods in the south-west of Holland will have been removed, and the area's fresh-water supply assured. Also, once the roads along the dams have been completed, the area, formerly rather isolated, will be opened up for development.

If her industry is prosperous, Holland is, still more, a commercial country. The Dutch have always been a great maritime nation and trade was greatly furthered by Holland's long rule over the greater part of the East Indies. Moreover, the Rhine, which reaches the sea in Holland, is itself a great commercial highway.

Amsterdam, the capital, and Holland's oldest and second largest port, is peculiar in that it is not the seat of government. The political and administrative centre is The Hague. Amsterdam is a world-famous centre of the diamond trade. Rotterdam is the principal port of the Netherlands and the second largest in the world behind New York.

Its rise dates from the great development of the industry of the Rhineland and the great increase of traffic on the Rhine towards the end of the nineteenth century. Besides being a port for merchandise it is frequented by great passenger liners plying between America, Africa, and the Far East. One quarter of the ships entering Rotterdam sail under the Dutch flag: the Netherlands' merchant navy has a total tonnage of 500,000 tons.

FRANCE

Of all the countries of Europe, France is the one which presents the greatest variety of scene and climate.

There are three main areas: the first comprising two high mountain ranges — the Pyrenees in the south, and the Alps, running down from Mont Blanc (in Savoy) to the Mediterranean coast along the Italian frontier. There are also lower mountain ranges — the Vosges, between France and Germany — and the Jura Mountains, running into Switzerland. There are broad lowlands in the north and west, and between the heights and the lowlands, a plateau, that reaches its greatest height in the Massif Central, and rises in its highest peaks to over 5,000 feet. Uranium is being worked in the Massif Central.

With an area of over 200,000 square miles, France is the largest country of Western Europe and a great agricultural

A small farmhouse in the Tarn gorge in southern France.

E. W. Mercier

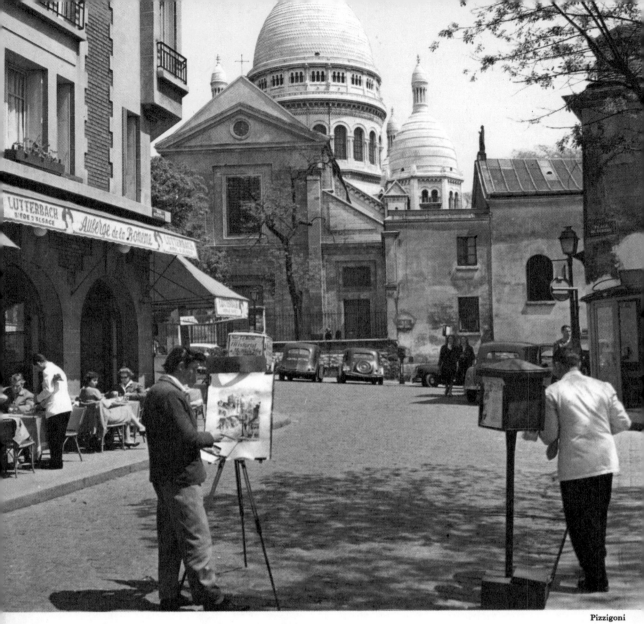

Crowned by the Sacré Coeur the hill of Montmartre is a favourite part of Paris with tourists.

country. Farming is second only to manufacturing in the number of people it employs. Much of the mountainous country is forested, but many of the lower slopes are used as pastures. In the lowlands, all branches of farming prosper. On the arable land, a great deal of wheat is grown. Vines are cultivated all over France but the most important areas are the regions of Champagne, Burgundy, and Bordeaux, all world-famous names.

Paris, built on the banks of the Seine, is the principal city of France, one of the great capitals of Europe, and probably the most important single cultural centre in the world. Paris has many historic buildings — the cathedral of Notre-Dame, the Law Courts, the Louvre etc., but much of the city is of nineteenth-century origin: including the famous Boulevards and the even more famous Eiffel Tower. The growth of Paris was restricted for many years after 1840 by a ring of fortifications round the city. Since their demolition at the end of the First World War, the city has expanded rapidly, so that many of the population of more than 8 million live in fairly modern suburbs. Few other major European states are centred so completely round their capitals as France is. Paris is really the only great city in France, and something of a gulf has always existed between the Parisians and the people from the provinces.

Lucien Hervé

The UNESCO headquarters in Paris is a fine example of modern architecture.

David Forbert - Shostal

The grape harvest. The vine has one great advantage over other crops, in that the best wine always comes from very poor quality soil.

The fields of Alsace along the banks of the Rhine.

INDUSTRY AND TRADE

Most of France's industry is concentrated in the northern half of the country. Sixty-five per cent of France's coal comes from the extreme north-west near the border with Belgium. In addition to coal-mining there are great steelworks in Douai and Valenciennes, and a new one in Dunkirk. Manufactures include agricultural machinery, railway equipment, chemicals, and the products of the traditional textile industry. Lille is the biggest town in the region with a total population of 881,439, and is the chief commercial centre.

The mines of Alsace-Lorraine in the north-east make France the biggest producer of iron-ore in Europe. There is

also considerable production of coal. Other natural resources of this region include potash in Alsace and salt deposits in Lorraine. Iron and steel is the most important industry in Lorraine, textiles in Alsace. The food-processing and brewing industries of this region are also very important. The chief town is Strasbourg with a population of 334,000.

The Normandy region, situated between Dieppe and Cherbourg, is the centre of the French oil-refining industry. There are many petrol refineries round Rouen and Le Havre, particularly the latter. Le Havre is the chief port of the region and oil amounts to nine-tenths of its imports. It is also an important shipbuilding town, and its other industries include the manufacture of machinery, boilermaking, etc., and dyestuffs. Rouen, though far up the Seine, is a port of considerable importance, added to which it also has a large textile industry.

The Paris region, though without any natural resources, has, like all capitals, attracted a considerable amount of industry: in particular cars, light engineering, and consumer goods.

The chemical industry is very highly developed in the Lyons region, where four-fifths of French synthetic fibre is produced. The area is also a traditional centre of the silk industry. Other industrial towns in the Lyons region are Saint-Étienne: coal-mining, machinery, and electrical equipment; Le Creusot: armaments; Clermont-Ferrand: rubber; and Chalons-sur-Saône: copper castings.

France is the biggest producer of aluminium in Europe, and the mining and processing of bauxite (aluminium ore) is concentrated in the Marseilles region. The production of aluminium requires an enormous amount of electricity, consequently after the initial stages the aluminium is transported to factories in the Alps, and, to a lesser extent, the Pyrenees, where there is hydro-electric power.

Marseilles is the greatest port of France. It is also a port of call for many passenger liners travelling through the Mediterranean. Among its other industries, besides its part in the aluminium industry, there is every kind of shipbuilding and repair, iron and copper ores are smelted, and one of the oldest manufactures is soap.

Bordeaux is another important port, and from it large quantities of wine are shipped. Industries include the making of sulphur-phosphates and oil refining.

At work on a locomotive. France has over 25,000 miles of railways.

David Forbert - Shostal

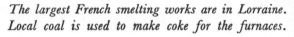

The largest French smelting works are in Lorraine. Local coal is used to make coke for the furnaces.

Philippe Doumic - Shostal

TWA — Trans World Airlines

Medieval barons in castles like this one overlooking the Rhine, were able to enforce the payment of tolls by passing ships.

A.F.M.

The Black Forest is a favourite holiday resort with Germans and foreign tourists alike.

WEST GERMANY

With a total area not far short of 100,000 square miles and a population of 60 million, Western Germany has a fairly dense population. It is largely Protestant, though there is a majority of Catholics in Bavaria.

The northern part of the country is flat, and, in fact, on the North Sea coast rather like Holland. However, south of Brunswick, the Harz mountains rise to more than 3,000 feet; further south are the mountains of the Black Forest with the Feldberg, 4,700 feet, while on the Austrian frontier, the Bavarian Alps rise, in the Zugspitze, to 9,800 feet, this being

A.F.M.

A vineyard in the Rhine valley near the Lorelei rock, famous in legend.

The Zugspitze, Germany's highest mountain, towers over this Alpine village.

A. Modl

Rosignoli

Even in modern Germany old methods still survive — a Rhineland farmer ploughing with oxen.

A. F M.

The town of Heidelberg on the Neckar. Heidelberg is the home of one of the world's greatest universities.

Germany's highest mountain. Chief rivers are the Rhine (which has already been dealt with) and its tributaries the Main, Neckar, and Moselle. The other chief rivers are the Elbe, which serves the port of Hamburg and flows into the North Sea, and the Danube, which rises in the Black Forest and empties into the Black Sea. Of the many lakes, the largest, Lake Constance, is bounded by Germany, Switzerland, and Austria. There are many fine forests in Germany.

Tom Hollyman - Photo Researchers

Bright lights and bustling traffic in the Kurfürstendamm, one of the principal streets in West Berlin.

Tom Hollyman - Photo Researchers

After the destruction of the Second World War, West Berlin has been rebuilt in modern style.

INDUSTRIAL GERMANY

Western Germany has shown an extraordinary power of recovery after the destruction of the Second World War. For 50 miles along the valley of the Ruhr, mines, blast-furnaces, and factories are in full production. On the Rhine a steady stream of lighters, many of them of 1,000 tons and more, are towed up and down the river. Hamburg, which suffered enormous destruction, is now restored, and once again in full activity as one of the greatest ports of Europe.

The chief industrial region of Federal

Wolff & Tritschler - Shostal

Motor cars are one of West Germany's greatest exports.

Dr. Stodter, Düsseldorf

This steel works at Essen in the Ruhr is only a small part of one of the greatest concentrations of industry in the world.

Pixfeatures

Huge blocks of steel in the smithy. German industry is the basis of her prosperity.

Germany is the Ruhr. It employs 2 million workmen. 125 million tons of coal are produced yearly. Steel is produced at Dortmund and Duisburg, while the most important manufacturing town is Essen, where a host of factories produce a vast range of products from iron and steel manufactures to synthetic rubber and synthetic fibres.

The Saar is very like the Ruhr on a smaller scale, though the actual quantity of coal present is roughly the same. Amongst its many manufactures, two outstanding products are glassware and pottery.

The Rhineland contains a whole series of towns including Cologne, best known for machinery, chemicals, and aluminium ware. Frankfurt and its neighbouring towns are best known for dye-stuffs, chemicals, machinery and cars; and Mannheim-Ludwigshafen, for chemicals and agricultural machinery.

Besides these industrial regions, there are large industrial towns in all parts of Western Germany, and outstanding amongst them are Augsburg, Nuremberg, Hanover, Brunswick, Bremen, and Hamburg. The last-named, besides being a great port and trading centre, is in the front rank for shipbuilding. Its wide range of factories includes many in the food industry.

With all this, agriculture is still the industry employing the most labour in Western Germany. In the north-west, there is a great deal of dairy-farming, and fruit-farming. In central Germany and

Pixfeatures

The high production levels in German industry are partly due to the use of very modern machinery.

Pixfeatures

An early stage: molten steel is poured into the casts.

A German autobahn, one of a great system of arterial motorways.

the south are fertile farmlands producing rich crops of wheat, barley, oats, maize, sugar-beet, and potatoes. Famous wines come from the vineyards of the Rhine and Moselle valleys. Yet, even with highly mechanised farming and the extensive use of fertilisers, Western Germany is quite unable to feed herself. She has not enough land, less than half as much as France, and has a greater population to support.

A view of Hamburg, the largest port in Germany and one of the most important in Europe.

VEB Leuna-Werke "Walter Ulbricht", Merseberg, DDR

The Leuna works, in Merseberg near Leipzig, East Germany, make chemicals out of coal.

EAST GERMANY

The German Democratic Republic (East Germany, the D.D.R.) has an area of 41,000 square miles and a population of over 17 million. Two-thirds of East Germany is devoted to agriculture, which is concentrated in two regions: the northern plain, most of which is only moderately fertile; and Thuringia and Lower Saxony, which is rich farming land.

There is little coal in East Germany but, on the other hand, the country has two rich fields of lignite (brown coal). One lies in the basin of the Lower Saale in the Leipzig region, and the other in the basin of the Upper Spree.

The end of the Second World War saw East Germany in a very bad position with regard to industry, whose principal centres had always been in the western part of the country. As it was, lignite and potassium salts (potash) were the only raw materials available in bulk. Nevertheless, great efforts were made at industrial redevelopment, and production is now three times higher than pre-war.

Lignite is the most important of East Germany's resources. In fact the country is the world's chief supplier, mining 242 million tons a year. Lignite is used both for domestic heating and to fuel the

The celebrated Frankfurterallee (formerly the Stalinallee) in East Berlin. It is entirely new.

D.D.R.'s vital power stations. Coke, made by a special process (itself an East German invention) from lignite, is used in the metallurgical industry, and lignite is also the raw material in the manufacture of synthetic fibres and other products of the important chemical industry.

Though there is little iron-ore in East Germany, steel production, which had to start from scratch in 1945, is now about 4½ million tons a year. The chief steel works are at Kalbe and Eisenhattenstadt. Dependent on them are the great mechanical engineering works at Magdeburg and Schmalkalden and the shipbuilding yards of Rostock and Wismar. Other important industries are the mining of uranium at Erzgebirge, the manufacture of optical instruments, and the world-famous porcelain of Meissen.

The capital of East Germany is East Berlin, with more than a million inhabitants. East Germany's second most important city is Leipzig. The annual Leipzig Fair is over 800 years old and one

The Spree at Berlin, with the industrial district on the left.

H. Smotkine

Rich cornfields near Magdeburg, East Germany.

of the most important events in the European trade calendar. It attracts visitors from all over the world and is East Germany's principal commercial contact with non-communist countries.

H. Smotkine

A panoramic view over East Berlin, with the Frankfurterallee in the distance.

AUSTRIA

The Federal Republic of Austria is all that is left of what was once a great empire. Hence its capital, Vienna, has a population of $1\frac{3}{4}$ million, whereas there are only 7,3 million people in the whole country.

The eastern extension of the Alps occupies most of the country, with great facilities for winter sports and mountaineering. The highest peak is the Gross Glockner, 12,450 feet, and there are other peaks scarcely less high.

Austria can produce only three-fifths of her food. The rest has to be paid for through exports, and by economic aid from abroad. A considerable advance has been made in industry, which is based primarily on timber and its products. Over two-fifths of Austria's 32,500 square-miles are forested; Austria comes third

The cathedral of St Stephan towering above the roofs of Vienna. Situated on the Danube, Vienna is a world-famous name in the realm of music.

after Finland and Sweden in its production of timber. The most important industry derived from wood is papermaking. There is little coal, but a certain amount of lignite. Oil-wells have been working since 1936, and Austria is the fourth largest producer of oil in Europe behind Russia, Romania, and West Germany. Austria is rich in iron-ore and its export, combined with that of metal manufactures, is almost as important to the economy as that of the products of timber. Industry, chiefly centred in Vienna, Linz, and Graz, includes the manufacture of machinery, chemicals, and textiles. Austria is also one of the world's chief sources of high-quality graphite.

Great use is made of water-power, more than five-sixths of the country's electricity being hydro-electric. The rivers so far exploited for this purpose are the Inn, the Salzach, the Enns, and the Danube.

Until 1918 Austria was the centre of a great empire, but today her chief claim to fame is in the field of culture. Vienna, one of the most beautiful cities

The Viennese specialise in the very finest cakes and pastries; their cream cakes are esteemed all round the world.

Switzerland. The little church of the village of Engadine, dwarfed by the Alps.

in Europe, is famous for its university and as a musical centre. The town of Salzburg, the birth-place of Mozart, is equally famous in the world of music, and, like Vienna, is the home of an international music festival, held annually.

SWITZERLAND

Switzerland has an area that is about half the size of Scotland, with a population of only 6 million. Yet her central position, standing as she does between Germany, France, and Italy, makes her a country of considerable political importance.

The Swiss are strictly neutral, which is to say they do not take sides in international politics, being neither a member of N.A.T.O. nor even of the United Nations. On the other hand the International Red Cross was founded by a Swiss, and has its headquarters in Geneva. The Swiss have a 'citizens' army', which means that, though every man has to do a short period of military service, there is no standing army.

The country is divided into three main areas. South and east are the Alps, on the west the low mountains of the Jura, and between them a broad plateau which

Children playing on board one of the river craft that ply the Danube.

Courtesy of TWA - Trans World Airlines

The steep valleys of the Swiss Alps were cut out by glaciers.

is the country of the lakes. The whole area contains four river basins: those of the Rhine, Rhône, Inn, and the Ticino (a tributary of the Po). The largest lakes are those of Geneva, Neuchâtel, Zürich, and Constance. The Alps are, of course, much the most important feature and attract large numbers of visitors.

Four different languages are spoken in Switzerland, reflecting the different nationalities that have formed the Federal Republic. Nearly three-quarters of the population of 6 million speak German. About a fifth, living in the west, speak French, 5 per cent Italian, and 1 per cent Romansch.

The Federal capital is Berne, but three other towns are bigger: Zürich, Basle, and Geneva. Zürich, a large commercial and industrial town, has a population of 432,500. Basle, on the Rhine, is a commercial as well as a great banking centre, and Geneva is the economic centre of the south-west.

INDUSTRY AND TRADE

Few countries can depend so much on the outside world as Switzerland. Not only does she depend on imported food and raw materials, but the tourist industry brings in much revenue.

Nevertheless, Switzerland is primarily an industrial country, and much of her industry, like watch-making, demands delicate workmanship. Her factories produce machines, precision instruments, electrical equipment, optical apparatus, cottonstuffs, and paper. Fast-flowing Swiss rivers provide abundant hydro-electric power. More than half the working population is employed in industry, which is concentrated in the cantons of Zürich, St Gall, and Basle.

Though Swiss agriculture is able to

Ernst A. Heiniger

Cattle browsing in the high Swiss pastures. The cowbells mean they can be easily found. Dairy produce and chocolate are important Swiss exports.

produce little more than half the country's needs, the pastures are so good that large quantities of dairy produce are exported. Another important export is the famous Swiss chocolate.

Courtesy of TWA - Trans World Airlines

The Swiss Alps. Collecting hay for winter fodder.

The map legend reads:

ROME	Over 1,000,000 population
Seville	250,000-1,000,000 population
Salonika	100,000- 250,000 population
Burgos	50,000- 100,000 population
Portimão	Under 50,000 population

SOUTHERN EUROPE

0   100   200
Miles

⊙ National Capitals

© Copyright 1960 by Map Projects Inc.

SOUTHERN EUROPE:
PENINSULAS AND ISLANDS
SPAIN AND PORTUGAL

In no other part of the Western Hemisphere are the links with the past so strong and so fundamental as they are in Southern Europe. For it was in these countries, bordering the Mediterranean and Aegean seas, that western civilisation was born and developed thousands of years ago. Here classical culture faded and here too, in Italy and Spain, it was reborn again and spread throughout the world.

Southern Europe consists largely of three peninsulas, the Iberian Peninsula (Spain and Portugal), Italy, and Greece, together with the islands that belong to them. The Balearic Islands belong to Spain; Sardinia and Sicily belong to Italy. Crete and the host of islands of the Aegean and Ionian Seas belong to Greece. To these must be added Corsica, which is French, and Malta and Cyprus, both formerly British Crown Colonies and

now independent members of the Commonwealth of Nations. All three peninsulas are largely mountainous: with the Pyrenees, the central Cordilleras, and the Sierra Nevada in Spain, the Apennines in Italy, and the Pindus mountains in Greece. Spain is the second most mountainous country in Europe, more than half of it being over 1,000 feet above sea-level. The chief plains of Southern Europe are those of Andalusia in southern Spain, Lombardy in northern Italy, and Thessaly in Greece.

The Mediterranean climate is too dry to be favourable for many types of farming. Formerly Southern Europe was thickly forested, but during the centuries the trees have gradually disappeared.

When there are no trees to retain the moisture and to hold back the soil the heavy southern rain washes the soil away. This erosion has turned vast fertile areas into barren land.

But despite this, in Southern Europe more than half the working population lives on the land, though often poorly. On the other hand the soil and climate are ideal for vines. The best wine is always made on poor soils. Spain alone has nearly 4 million acres of vineyards. Most of the Iberian wines are for home consumption, but the best and most famous are an important export: Port from the Douro valley in Portugal, Sherry from the Jerez region of southern Spain, and Madeira from the island of that name.

Another plant that thrives in the south is the olive. The old twisted trees, with their quivering grey-green leaves, may be seen all over the hills that fringe the northern shores of the Mediterranean. Olive oil is widely used in cooking, and large quantities are exported. Oranges and lemons are widely grown, and Spain exports large quantities of chestnuts to other European countries and to America. Other products of the south are almonds, figs, and dates.

Wheat is the biggest crop in Spain and Portugal, next coming maize, barley, oats, rye, and rice. Barley can grow in land too dry for wheat. Oats and rye are often grown in the mountains. Rice is grown on low land capable of being flooded.

In both Portugal and, more particularly, Spain, there are large plantations of cork-oak, from whose bark comes most of the cork used in the world. And pigs graze freely in the woodlands. With less well-watered pastures than in the north, the Mediterranean countries tend to breed sheep and goats rather than cattle. Goats have a lot to do with the absence of trees in Southern Europe. Though they can thrive and produce milk in almost any country, they help to destroy forests by eating the young saplings of trees.

Some cattle are reared in the south, but not so much for dairy-farming as for other purposes. Bulls are bred for the bull-rings of Spain and Portugal; and oxen, donkeys, and mules are widely

Madrid, capital and largest city of Spain.

used on the land and for transportation.

Fishing is a resource of great value to countries with poor agriculture. On the Atlantic side, Spain and Portugal are very active in this field. In Portugal, fish is the most important item of diet and the largest of her exports. Her fishing fleet consists of nearly 18,000 vessels, many of which, however, are very small. Sardines and tunny-fish are tinned at the factories of Setubal. These are caught close to the coast but Portuguese fishermen sail as far as Newfoundland to fish for cod. The Spanish fishing industry is less developed, and most of the fishing is done in the Bay of Biscay, chiefly for tunny-fish.

Of the many kinds of fish found in the Mediterranean the tunny is the only one to be fished on a big scale. The others are generally consumed locally.

Harry Edwards - Shostal

Avila in Spain is still encircled by its medieval defences.

In Andalusia, in the south of Spain, plantations of olive trees cover the hillsides.

Josef Muench

MODERN INDUSTRIES

Many articles of everyday use are made, as in the past, by hand. In Portugal piles of hand-made pottery can be seen in any market. Artisans can still be seen painting magnificent tiles, and women can be seen lace-making. Madeira is famous for its embroidery. Except in northern Spain (in Barcelona and Bilbao, for instance) modern industry has hardly been established. The chief reason for this is the lack of raw materials, particularly coal. Industries are traditional: such as the production of olive oil, the making of wine, and weaving.

The tourist industry is a great source of revenue to both Spain and Portugal. The principal areas are the Costa Brava, the Costa del Sol, and the Balearic Islands (Spain), and Madeira and the Azores (Portugal).

The political, administrative, and cultural centre of Spain is Madrid, a city of nearly 3 million inhabitants. It has also, in the last twenty years, become an industrial centre, producing electrical

Courtesy of TWA - Trans World Airilnes

Lisbon, a fine capital, is one of the most ancient ports in Europe.

equipment, machinery, and chemicals. Barcelona, the second town in Spain, with a population exceeding 1 million, is the capital of the province of Barcelona. It stands in a luxuriant plain, beautifully situated between the mouths of two rivers. It is a town that has developed rapidly, and now possesses a variety of industries, such as textiles, chemicals, and cement.

Lisbon, the capital of Portugal, has about 1,335,000 inhabitants, over a tenth of the population of the country. It stands on the northern banks of the Tagus, about 9 miles from the mouth. Above the mouth, the river is greatly enlarged for 10 miles or more, making a magnificent harbour. Lisbon is, accordingly, an important port of call for ocean liners. The town also has an important airport. Industries include shipbuilding, chemicals, textiles, and food products. Except for the old Moorish quarter, the town was largely destroyed in the great earthquake of 1755. It was then replanned and rebuilt and, climbing up the slopes of a low range of hills, has long been regarded as one of the most imposing cities of Europe.

Johnson Motor Company

A Portuguese sardine fishing boat. Its catch is drying on the beach.

The bark of cork-oaks being loaded on to an ox cart.

THE AZORES

The Azores, a little group of islands lying more than 1,000 miles out in the Atlantic, have always been looked on as a province of Portugal and as part of Europe. It was at Flores in the Azores that Sir Richard Grenville took on the whole Spanish fleet, and in the Second World War aircraft based on the Azores provided air-cover for the Allied North Atlantic convoys.

The Rock of Gibraltar rises over 1,000 feet, above the Mediterranean. Gibraltar is a famous British base.

GIBRALTAR AND MALTA

The rocky promontory of Gibraltar, though geographically part of Spain, is a British Crown Colony. It has been a British base for nearly two and a half centuries. 'The Rock', as it is often called, is over 1,000 feet high and thrusts out for $2\frac{1}{2}$ miles into the Mediterranean. It commands the Strait of Gibraltar and has a very important naval dockyard. Many ships entering the Mediterranean call at Gibraltar for fuel and other supplies. Famous features of Gibraltar are the Barbary Apes who live on the Rock. The tradition is that if they were to leave, Britain would lose Gibraltar.

Malta is a fully independent island country, 17 miles long and 8 miles wide, lying between Sicily and the north coast of Africa. A member of the Commonwealth, Malta was once the home of the Knights of St John and has a long history as a naval base, owing to its strategic position in the Mediterranean. The fortress-town of Valletta is Malta's capital city.

St Peter's Square with Michelangelo's great cathedral, Rome.

ITALY

Of the countries of Southern Europe, Italy, with its population of about 54 million, is the most densely populated, the most industrialised, and the most advanced in agriculture. With an area of 116,000 square miles, Italy presents four dominant geographical features: (1.) The Alps, that stand between her and the rest of Europe. (2.) The Plain of Lombardy, lying within the general confines of the continent. (3.) The relatively narrow, mountainous peninsula jutting 500 miles into the Mediterranean. (4.) The islands of Sicily and Sardinia.

By virtue of her central position and her road and rail communications with Austria, Germany, Switzerland, and France, Italy is, of the southern countries, much the most closely integrated into Western Europe. The best example of this integration is provided by Italy's prominence in the European Common Market.

The great Autostrada del Sol linking Italy and France is symbolic of Italy's development. This section of the road runs through the St Bernard Pass.

Venice is built on islands in a lagoon. Canals take the place of streets, gondolas of taxis.

THE LAND

Of the Italian Alps, the best known are the Dolomites, which are among the most picturesque of the whole Alpine system. The great Plain of Lombardy is watered, for the most part, by the Po, whose valley is the most fertile part of Italy. Further east it is watered by the Adige and by a succession of shorter rivers flowing into the Gulf of Venice. In the foothills of the Alps are five famous lakes: Lake Maggiore, Lake Lugano, Lake Como, Lake Iseo, and Lake Garda. The climate along the Po is not unlike the climate along the middle course of the Danube, though rather warmer. The winters are cold: the average temperature at Milan being 34°F. The summers are warm and moist.

The staple food crops are maize, rice, and, in particular, wheat — which is chiefly used to make the various kinds of pasta. Pollenta, made from maize (corn) flour, is the other basic Italian food.

Little bread is eaten. With one or two exceptions, like Parmesan cheese and Bel Paese, most of the dairy produce is consumed locally. Vines are cultivated all over Italy, largely for wine, the best-known variety being Chianti from Tuscany, though the best wines come from

This photograph was taken during the construction under Mont Blanc of the road tunnel linking Italy and France.

A rice-field of the Po valley in Lombardy in northern Italy.

An orange grove on the slopes of Mount Etna in Sicily.

Piedmont in the north. Oranges and lemons are widely grown in the southern-most part of Italy, and in Sicily; olives somewhat further north. Mulberry trees are also grown in the north where their leaves, fed to silk-worms, support the local silk industry. Sheep-farming is common in the uplands.

Italy is much the most densely populated of the three southern peninsulas, with a population of approximately 54 million. The population is moreover increasing rapidly at a rate of 400,000 a year. The most thickly populated districts are the Plain of Lombardy, Campania (the area round Rome), Apulia (in the south-east), and Sicily.

Turin is an important centre of Italian industry, particularly the manufacture of motor vehicles, one of Italy's chief exports.

INDUSTRY

Industry furnishes the greater part of the national income. This is remarkable as, except for water power from the mountains and oil from Sicily, Italy has practically no natural sources of energy. Coal from her own mines supplies only one-tenth of her needs, and to this must be added a rich supply of natural gas. For her textile industry, wool and silk are the only products that do not come from abroad. Thus a long list of imports, including rolled iron and steel, coal, and cotton, have to be paid for by exports, shipping and tourism. Manufactures include motor vehicles, machinery, footwear, and textiles.

The greater part of heavy industry is in the north, centred on the towns of Milan, Turin, Brescia, Genoa, and Savona. The chief industrial towns of the south are Naples, Terni (north of Rome), and Piombino. However, efforts are being made to bring more industry to the hitherto impoverished south: the most notable development being the opening of a great new steel works at Taranto. Most of the Italian textile industry is concentrated along the northern edge of the Lombardy plain below the Alps.

Although great cities like Turin and Milan and great ports like Genoa are vital to the country's expanding economy, to most people Italy still means the past much more than the present or future; Venice with its canals and palaces, Florence of the Medicis, Naples with the ruins of Pompeii nearby, and above all, Rome, a thriving modern city of 2 million people, yet with the Colosseum and the Forum, the great church of St Peter's, and many other links with history.

Terry S. Lindquist - FPG

The glass-blowers of Murano have been celebrated for their skill since the thirteenth century.

GREECE

Greece is mainly an agricultural country, but farms are small and the farmers are poor. Vineyards occupy much of the land, especially in the south, and, though much wine is made, large quantities of grapes are dried and sold in the form of currants and sultanas. One of the main agricultural regions is the Macedonian plain in the north, where tobacco, the chief export crop, and cotton are grown. In view of the geographical position of Greece and her many islands, it is not

Philip D. Gendreau

A Greek shepherd boy carrying a lamb on his shoulders.

Herbert Lanks - Monkmeyer

A shepherd and his flock in Greece, where much of the countryside is wild and unproductive.

surprising that the Greeks are a maritime nation. They now have the sixth largest merchant navy in the world.

The population of Greece exceeds $8\frac{1}{2}$ million, with over $1\frac{3}{4}$ million in the capital, Athens. Salonika (Thessaloniki) is the chief town of the north, and is a port of considerable importance.

Greece possesses many monuments from her classical past, the outstanding ones being the Parthenon and two other temples on the Acropolis on the outskirts of Athens. The Parthenon, the most famous of all Greek temples, was long left to fall into ruin. Many of its carved figures, which had fallen, were rescued by Lord Elgin. These are the world-famous Elgin marbles now in the British Museum. Piraeus, the port of Athens, handles a considerable amount of shipping. A steadily growing industry, spread over Athens and Piraeus, includes ship-building, the manufacture of textiles and chemicals, and food processing.

The Island of Cyprus lies about 60 miles from the coasts of Syria and Turkey and was, until recently, a British Crown Colony. It is now, however, a republic, an independent member of the Commonwealth. The total population of Cyprus is about 614,000, nearly 80 per cent of whom are Greeks and 20 per cent Turks. The capital is Nicosia.

High on the Acropolis above modern Athens stands the Parthenon, dreaming of another age.

Ewing Krainin - Photo Reseachers

Bratislava on the Danube is one of the most important towns of Czechoslovakia.

CENTRAL AND EASTERN EUROPE

Central and eastern Europe consists of Poland, Czechoslovakia, Hungary, Yugoslavia, Albania, Romania, Bulgaria, the U.S.S.R, and the European section of Turkey.

The dominant physical features of this area are the mountains of the Balkans and the Carpathians. The mountains of the Balkans are an extension of the Alps, while the Carpathians are the largest mountain system in Europe after the Alps.

The Carpathians flank the Plain of Hungary; the other great plain of Eastern Europe is the North European Plain that extends from France and Germany across Poland and into Russia. An intermediate zone is formed by the undulating plateau of Bohemia.

Within the Bohemian mountains (generally referred to as the Bohemian Diamond), is a huge area of high rolling country with very fertile soil. The heights are covered with forests, and there are rich deposits of minerals.

The Carpathians flank the great Hungarian Plain; many oil wells are sited in the outer ring, and the lower slopes are well-forested. Above the forests are pastures to which flocks are moved in summer. These mountains are covered

Sheaves of hemp, which grows abundantly in Yugo-slavia. The fibre is used to make coarse textiles.

in snow but there are no glaciers.

Of the two Plains already mentioned, the North European Plain is composed of loose, mainly sandy materials, mostly brought down from Scandinavia by the glaciers of the Ice Ages, which also scatter-ed great blocks of granite torn from the Scandinavian mountains. The plain is drained by two great rivers: the Oder and the Vistula, which empty into the Baltic.

The Hungarian Plain is the basin formed by the lower reaches of the Danube, which bisects it from north to south. The plain is made up of marshes and great areas of alluvial material washed down from the Alps and Carpa-thians by the Drava, Tisza, and Mures. In the centre, where the climate is dry, dust blown by winds has settled into thick layers of fine yellow-grey loess.

A characteristic Serbian church.

POLAND

The bulk of Poland consists of plains and plateaus drained by the Vistula and the Oder. It is backed in the south by the Bohemian mountains and the Carpa-thians, rising to over 8,000 feet.

The plains and the plateaus fall into three groups. In the south, the Plateaus of Silesia and Little Poland and the Plain of Silesia make up a fertile farming region, and there are also rich deposits of coal, iron, zinc, lead, copper and rock salt. The second group consists of the central plains, Greater Poland, and Mazovia. The soil is less fertile, but there are min-erals below: lignite and rock-salt. The third group consists of the northern plains and the Baltic ridges. sandy hills alternate with lakes and peat bogs.

The Baltic coast of Poland runs for 300 miles, from the German to the Russian frontier. The Baltic is shallow, not very salty compared with other seas, and practically tideless. There are two deltas, one made by the Oder, which has the port of Stettin, now called Szcze-cin. This delta is crossed by a number of channels and is sheltered on the sea-ward side by low islands, the passages between which give access to the sea. The eastern delta is that of the Vistula.

Though the Vistula is the national river of Poland, it plays a relatively small part in the economy of the country. Its winding track and the fact that for many months in winter it is ice-bound make it unsuitable for traffic. There are two ports serving the Vistula basin: Danzig, the old port, and Gdynia, an entirely new port created in 1919. Since 1945 these two ports, which are less than 15 miles apart, have been working in partnership.

An aerial view of Warsaw, the capital of Poland. The town has been carefully reconstructed after the devastation it suffered during the Second World War.

POLISH INDUSTRY

The Silesian coalfield makes Poland the second greatest coal-producing country in Europe, after the U.K., and sixth in the world. Thanks to her coal, Poland, formerly a predominantly agricultural country, has turned resolutely to industry.

The seams of coal are very thick, some being 20, 30, and even 60 feet in depth. They are, therefore, very easily worked. Mechanisation has been easy to introduce. The Upper Silesian coalfield, situated around Katowice, has attracted heavy industry into the same area, and there is another big plant in eastern Cracow. However, Poland is not rich in iron-ore, and heavy industry has to rely on ore imported from Sweden and the Ukraine.

Besides having at its disposal oil, lignite, and coal, the chemical industry has access to enormous reserves of salt and sulphur.

Amongst other industries, the manufacture of textiles takes a leading place. There are cotton mills at Lodz and Warsaw, and wool is woven in Lower Silesia.

The concentration of Polish industry in two chief regions has led to a very uneven distribution of population. The Upper Silesian region, which in area is only 4 per cent of the country, contains 13 per cent of the population. The other two industrial areas, Lower Silesia and Lodz, employ between them 60 per cent of the industrial workers.

EASTERN EUROPE

BALTIC SEA

GERMAN DEMOCRATIC REPUBLIC

Gulf of Danzig

EAST PRUSSIA

Masurian Lakes

POMERANIA

MASURIA

POLAND

WARSAW

UNION OF SOVIET SOCIALIST REPUBLICS

ERZGEBIRGE

Giant Mts.

CZECHOSLOVAKIA

Bohemian Forest

Prague

CARPATHIAN MOUNTAINS

AUSTRIA

BUDAPEST

HUNGARY

Danube

TRANSYLVANIA

ROMANIA

MOLDAVIA

JULIAN ALPS

SLOVENIA

CROATIA

YUGOSLAVIA

SERBIA

BOSNIA

HERZEGOVINA

DINARIC ALPS

DALMATIA

ADRIATIC SEA

ISTRIA

ITALY

MONTENEGRO

North Albanian Alps

ALBANIA

Korab 9,066

Tirana

WALACHIA

BUCHAREST

TRANSYLVANIAN ALPS

Ploesti

Danube

BALKAN MOUNTAINS

BULGARIA

Sofia

Thracian Plain

Rhodope Mountains

BLACK SEA

Constanta

TURKEY

GREECE

BUDAPEST _____ Over 1,000,000 population
Lodz _____ 250,000-1,000,000 population
Cluj _____ 100,000- 250,000 population
Novi Sad _____ 50,000- 100,000 population
Mohacs _____ Under 50,000 population

0   50   100   150
Miles

⊙ National Capitals

© Copyright 1960 by Map Projects Inc.

POLISH FARMING

Paul Hufner - Shostal

The new steel works at Nowa-Huta, Poland, are designed to produce 2 million tons of steel a year.

Before the Second World War 70 per cent of the total population of Poland lived on the land, which was very unevenly divided, with the great estates on the one hand and the small-holdings on the other. This sort of division always produces considerable extremes of poverty and wealth but it never leads to efficient farming.

The Land Reform Act of 1944 created 800,000 new holdings, and enlarged 250,000 existing ones. Today, the fertile soil and efficient farming methods enable Poland to supply all the country's food. It produces nearly 8 million tons of rye, 4 million of wheat, and 48 million of potatoes in a year, besides large quantities of sugarbeet. 12 per cent of the industrial population work in food processing and 33 per cent of the total population are farmers.

R. Guerand

The flower market at Cracow, one of the oldest towns in Poland.

R Guerand

A farming village on the flat plains of Poland.

WARSAW

The development of Polish industry has, of course, drastically affected the distribution of population. Whereas before the Second World War the Poles were essentially a peasant people, 50 per cent of a total population of about 32 million now lives in towns. Already 23 Polish towns have a population exceeding 110,000. The capital, Warsaw, has a population of a little over 1.2 million. It lies on the left bank of the Vistula, and is built on a high plain and on the terraces which lead up to it. Bridges across the river connect it with its huge suburb of Praga on the other bank.

The town was virtually reduced to rubble in the course of the Second World War, 80 to 90 buildings out of every 100 being destroyed, but the most historic part of the town has been very carefully and skifully restored, while the rest of the buildings are modern.

The old quarter in Prague.

CZECHOSLOVAKIA

Geographically Czechoslovakia can be divided into three parts: Bohemia, centred on Prague, the capital; Moravia, drained by the Morava River, a tributary of the Danube; and Slovakia in the Carpathian Mountains.

Bohemia consists of an undulating plateau drained by the Upper Elbe and its tributaries, surrounded by mountains very rich in coal, lignite, graphite, and uranium.

The broad plain of Moravia consists of rich farm land in the south, while the north forms the southern end of the Silesian coalfield.

Slovakia shares with Poland the highest range of the Carpathians, the High Tatra, whose highest peak rises to over 8,700 feet. The mountains, which supply abundant water-power, are well forested, and also rich in iron ore and non-ferrous metals.

John Strohm

Czech schoolchildren comparing their collections of stamps.

R. Guerand

Folk dancing is very popular in Czechoslovakia.

Eastfoto

A foundry at Ostrava, close to the Silesian coal-fields.

INDUSTRY IN CZECHOSLOVAKIA

The prosperity of the country depends, in the first place, on the old-established industries of the western part, but recently a determined effort has been made towards the industrialisation of Slovakia.

The most important concentration of industry is around the coalfields of Ostrava (in Silesia) and Kladno (near Prague, in Bohemia). The principal Czech iron and steel works are at Vítkovice, Kunčice, and Třinec in Silesia, and Kladno. To these must be added the opencast lignite works in north Bohemia. Graphite is mined in south Bohemia. Certain sands

John Strohm

Old and new methods combine to thresh corn in Czechoslovakia.

Eastfoto

Eleven bridges span the Vltava (Moldau) at Prague. Once called the 'golden city of a hundred spires' historic Prague is now a great industrial city.

provide the raw material for the famous Bohemian glass made in the Riesen Gebirge or Giant Mountains. China-clay is used for the manufacture of porcelain.

The old-established Škoda works at Pilsen, now called the Lenin Works, have been completely reconstructed since 1945 and employ some 40,000 workers.

Lignite is the basis of the chemical industry centred on Ústí and Most in north Bohemia, and the old textile industries are still active, cotton being produced in the Liberec region, wool and rayon at Brno (Brunn).

Since 1945 the government has been developing industry in Slovakia to take advantage of the abundant water-power and mineral wealth — including iron, copper, pyrites, and lead — and the fact that the area is relatively over-populated.

Slovakia produces 80 per cent of the minerals mined in Czechoslovakia. A factory has been constructed to make aluminium goods from Hungarian bauxite, and large iron and steel and chemical works have been constructed south of Košice, the chief town of the region.

AGRICULTURE

In the past Czech farming was of two very different kinds. In Bohemia and Moravia, fertile soil, and advanced farming methods resulted in a high yield per acre. In Slovakia on the other hand, before 1939 the land was in the hands of great landowners, who used obsolete farming methods. Since 1945 a scheme of land reform has broken up the estates, and formed many state-owned collective farms.

The principal crops are wheat and rye, but barley, oats, and maize are also grown, and some fodder crops.

Prague, with a population of more than a million people, is a city of great architectural beauty. It stands on both sides of the river Moldau (Vltava). On the left bank is the upper town, built round the fourteenth-century castle and the cathedral. The lower town on the right bank is a thriving industrial area producing all kinds of goods and equipment. As with other great capitals, industries tend to have their head offices there.

Budapest is really two towns: Buda, the old fortified city, and the industrial and residential area of Pest, on the other bank of the Danube.

HUNGARY

Hungary consists of a vast area of lowlands, flanked on the west by the Alps, and on the east by the Carpathians. West of the Danube, much of the ground is hilly. In the north are the hills of the Bakony Forest, on the southern edge of which is Lake Balaton, and further south are the Mecsék Hills, also forested. Lake Balaton is the largest lake in Hungary, about 4 miles wide and nearly 50 miles long. Much of the forest land is of oak or beech. These hills are of industrial interest, as beneath them are lignite, oil, and bauxite.

In general the climate is continental, with a long severe winter, during which Lake Balaton is frozen over. The summer is hot, in the south-east, very hot.

AGRICULTURE AND INDUSTRY

Wheat is the most important crop, though actually slightly more land is devoted to maize — which covers an area not far short of $3\frac{1}{2}$ million acres. Half the arable land of the country is taken up by these two crops. A variety of other crops is grown and there are extensive vineyards around Tokay (Tokaj) and Lake Balaton in the north.

The raising of cattle, sheep, and pigs is important to Hungarian agriculture.

Until 1914 Hungary had hardly any factories. The mining of lignite, coal, iron, and bauxite was developed between the two wars. But it is only since 1945 that industrialisation has been really pushed along. Besides the production of iron and steel, Hungary has a big aluminium industry, for the country has some of the largest reserves of bauxite in Europe. Hungary specialises in the manufacture of precision instruments.

The principal industrial centres are

The final touches being put to rolling stock in a Hungarian factory.

Eastfoto

AFM

All the cotton used in the textile mills of Hungary has to be imported.

Dubrovnic is one of the most beautiful towns in Yugoslavia.

Pécs (close to the coalfield beneath the Mecsék Hills), Miskolc (engaged in iron smelting), Szeged (a textile centre near oil and natural gas deposits), Debrecen, and above all Budapest (which is at the end of an oil pipeline from Lipse).

With a population of 1,990,000 Budapest is one of the great cities of Central Europe. It is, in fact, composed of two towns, lying on opposite sides of the Danube: Buda, the upper town on the right bank, and Pest, the lower town on the left bank. Today, as in the past, the two are very different in character — Buda remains a historical town of palaces, churches, museums, and parks. Pest is residential and, in the suburbs, industrial. As a centre of industry Budapest, like Prague, is active in almost every field.

YUGOSLAVIA

Because of its popularity with tourists Yugoslavia is, of all the Eastern European countries, the one best known to people from the West. Yugoslavia is composed of mountain groups. In the northwest, in Slovenia, are the Julian Alps, with Triglav (9,396 feet) the highest peak.

In the south-west, running parallel to the coast, is a long, mountainous range which includes the Dinaric Alps. To the east, in Serbia and Macedonia, there is a series of mountainous blocks enclosing river basins. These basins, connected by the Morava and the Vardar, form a line of communication with Salonica (Thessaloniki) in Greece. Belgrade in the north gives access to the Hungarian Plain.

As well as being an important port, Dubrovnic, on the Dalmation coast, is also a popular holiday resort.

YUGOSLAV ECONOMY

Yugoslavia is composed of the six republics of Serbia, Croatia, Slovenia, Montenegro, Bosnia-Hercegovina, and Macedonia. 53 per cent of the population are settled on the land. Maize and wheat are the chief cereals grown in the Danube basin, and other crops of the plains and foothills are sugar-beet and grapes. The

Ox-drawn ploughs at work in Yugoslavia.

mountains provide valuable timber and grazing for large herds of cattle. Both the Dinaric and Transylvanian Alps have fine oak forests.

Mines are plentiful. There is iron-ore in the valleys of Bosnia, bauxite on the Dalmatian coast. Elsewhere there is copper, lead, zinc, and mercury. Coal is rare, but lignite plentiful. To harness the water power available, hydro-electric power-stations are rapidly being built. The chemical industry is fairly well developed.

Fine new factories are being built, including a splendid one at Ljubljana for the manufacture of turbines and similar products. A plastics industry has been started at Split. Furniture and metal construction units are being manufactured in the neighbourhood of Titograd. There are carpet looms at Sarajevo and Skopje, and immense and ultra-modern iron and steel works at Zenica in Bosnia.

ZAGREB AND BELGRADE

Zagreb, capital of Croatia, and the second town in the country, is Yugoslavia's chief industrial and economic centre. Its character is very western, an inheritance from the days when it was part of the Austrian Empire. It consists of two parts, the old Upper Town and the modern Lower Town. The latter, with its rich buildings and neo-classical monuments, stretches down to the Sava. The chief industry is the weaving of cotton stuffs. Zagreb is one of the most important railway centres of South-east Europe, where lines from Milan, Vienna, Prague, and Budapest all converge.

Paul Byers - FLO

The open-air market in Belgrade. These peasant women wait for customers for their knitting.

Jerry Cooke - Photo Researchers

The start of another day for these Yugoslav workers.

Agence Rapho

The bustling city of Zagreb is the chief industrial and economic centre of Yugoslavia.

Belgrade, the capital, is built on a spur of land at the confluence of the Danube and the Sava, which is also a point at which the Danube curves to the east. In such a position, it is obvious that Belgrade was first of all a fortress. It has certainly suffered many attacks and much devastation, the most recent being during the last war when it was largely destroyed. As a result it has little to show of old architecture. It is a modern town, grey and sombre in its buildings.

De Biasi - AFM

The Danube at Belgrade.

Rice is an important crop in Albania, and even the children help out in the fields. Only 15 per cent of the total area is cultivated in Albania.

ALBANIA, A MOUNTAINOUS LAND

Albania is an inaccessible country of mountains, running north-west to south-east, reaching over 8,000 feet, and torrential rivers, running through deep gorges that only here and there broaden into valleys.

With abundant rainfall the country is rich in forests. The crops grown depend on the height of the land. In the valleys and on the lower slopes the vegetation is typically Mediterranean, the crops being maize, tobacco, olives, and oranges.

Higher up are the grazing lands, and then, higher still, uninterrupted forests of oaks, chestnut trees, walnuts, etc. Mineral wealth includes oil, copper, coal, chrome, iron lignite, and salt.

The production of timber and rearing of sheep and goats are the mainstay of Albania. Hitherto a backward country, it has, under the communist regime, made strenuous efforts at modernisation, though the changes hardly amount to a complete transformation. With Chinese help, chemical and engineering industries are being built up. Other industries include food processing and textiles. Until 1947, Albania was the only European country without a single railway. The first line was opened in 1950. Now there are four lines in operation totalling about 100 miles. The Tiranë-Durrës line is of particular service to the textile industry.

Tiranë and Shkodër (Scutari) are the two chief towns. Tiranë, the capital, with a population of 169,000, stands in the shelter of wooded hills. It is famous for its mosques, a survival of the days when Albania was under Turkish rule.

Breton- Rapho

The Athene theatre at Bucharest.

ROMANIA

The southern Carpathians and the Transylvanian Alps form the backbone of Romania, rising, in the Fagaras range, to over 8,000 feet. These ranges form a birch- and fir-clad screen between Transylvania and the hills of the south and the Danube plain. Transylvania itself consists of hills, usually covered with orchards, and broad fertile valleys.

On the other side of the backbone, beneath the wooded foothills, stretch the plains with their fields of wheat and maize, amongst which, here and there, are large prairies not unlike the Russian steppes. Crops, however, are at the mercy of the very uncertain rainfall. In the plains the winters are severe, the summers are very hot with occasional rain-storms.

A hand-loom at work. The handicrafts of Albania are still very much alive.

Breton - Rapho

Stock-farming depends largely on the high pastures, flocks being taken up in the summer and brought down again to the villages during the long winters.

Oil is the great source of Romanian wealth. There are four principal fields: three in Wallachia, at the foot of the Carpathians, and the fourth in Moldavia. Natural gas, found in Transylvania, is another very important natural resource.

One of the lakes at Bucharest. The Institute of Science is in the distance.

Most of the petrol refineries are in the neighbourhood of Ploesti, north of Bucharest and a pipeline has been laid from there to the port of Constanta on the Black Sea and to Giurgiu on the Danube. Romania has little coal and the exploitation of water-power is only beginning.

There are scattered deposits of iron-ore, but only in meagre quantity. However, Romania is pushing ahead with industrialisation and mechanisation. Iron-ore and coke are imported from Russia, and tractors and agricultural machinery are being manufactured, as well as railway equipment and motor-cars. The chemical industry is also progressing.

The chief industrial centres are: Bucharest (the capital), Cluj, Orasul and Brasov (in Transylvania), Craiova (in Wallachia), and Resita and Timisoara (in the Banat).

Virtually all of modern Bucharest has been built since the end of the Second World War. There are big parks, broad avenues, and newly planned quarters with fine buildings. The factories produce agricultural and electrical equipment.

The population of the city has risen from 340,000 in 1914 to about 1½ million.

The Château of Sanaia was built in the late nineteenth century by King Carol. It is situated at the foot of the Transylvanian Alps.

Marilyn Silverstone - Palmer Photo Agency

Harvesting in Bulgaria. Before long this work will be done by machinery.

BULGARIA

Bulgaria is one of the least well-known of the countries of Eastern Europe.

Along the frontier with Romania in the north, lies the broad plain of the Danube where maize and wheat are grown. On the coast is the port of Varna.

The wooded Balkan mountains, which rise to over 7,000 feet, run right across the country south of the Danube plain.

South of this chain are the central lowlands, through the western half of which flows the river Maritsa. Here the produce is more varied than in the north. Tobacco, cotton, and rice are grown, and flowers. The biggest town here is Plovdiv, better known as Philippopolis, the centre of the textile industry. In the west of the country lies Sofia, with a population of over three-quarters of a million.

To the south and south-west of Plovdiv are two other ranges: the Rhodope mountains which rise to over 9,000 feet, and the highest mountains in Bulgaria —

the Rila mountains, which reach 9,000 feet. In the valleys tobacco and sugar beet are grown.

Bulgaria depends almost entirely on agriculture. The produce of the collectivised farms feeds over 80 per cent of the population. The commercial crops are: cotton, roses for attar of roses, fruit, and tobacco, which accounts for half of the exports.

Efforts to promote industry have been handicapped by the absence of raw materials. Oil, a few beds of lignite and some lead, zinc, and copper are all Bulgaria has. Nevertheless an industrial centre has been developed at Dimitrovgrad on the Maritsa using lignite for the production of electricity, and an atomic power station is being built with Soviet aid at Lozlodni, on the Danube. Cement and chemicals, including artificial fertilisers, are produced. Steel works have been started south-west of Sofia. However, the principal industry is weaving — much of which is done by hand at home.

Paul Hufner - Shostal

Making attar of roses. It takes 200 lbs of petals to make ½ oz of essence.

TURKEY IN EUROPE

Although Turkey used to be a great European power her European possessions have shrunk, and most of her territory today is in Asia Minor.

Turkey in Europe has an area of about 9,000 square miles. It includes eastern Thrace, a pastoral land of sheep and goats, with, in the valleys, an occasional crop of tobacco, rice, or maize. The only real asset lies in the city of Istanbul, formerly Constantinople, which controls the entry to the Black Sea.

This former capital of Turkey, which, before that, under the name of Byzantium, was the capital of the Eastern Roman Empire, has had a long and tumultuous history. Long after the Byzantine Empire had declined, Constantinople, with its magnificent defences, held out against the Turkish advance into Europe, but finally fell in 1453. The town stands on a hilly promontory, which encloses its splendid harbour, the Golden Horn. The town is full of historical remains, the most famous being the great mosque of Santa Sophia, once the most famous church in Christendom.

There is little industry in Istanbul, but trade is brisk and tourists are plentiful.

Situated on the European side of the Bosphorus, Istanbul is famous in history under its earlier names: Constantinople and Byzantium.

Tomas Berner - Shostal

GERMANY

CZECH.

AUST

HUNGARY

CARPATHIAN

ROMANIA

MTS.

POLAND

SWEDEN

FINLAND

BARENTS SEA

NOVAYA ZEMLYA

KARA SEA

BALTIC SEA

Gulf of Bothnia

Gulf of Finland

Murmansk
Monchegorsk
Kirovsk
Kandalaksha

Kem
Belomorsk

White Sea

Archangel

Ust-Tsilma

Pechora R.

Vorkuta

Novy Port

Usa R.

Kaliningrad
Memel
Klaipeda
Liepaja
Ventspils
Parnu
Viljandi
Tallinn
Tartu
Narva
Luga
Pskov
LENINGRAD
Vyborg
Tikhvin
Lake Ladoga
Lake Onega
Kondopoga
Medvezhyegorsk
Onega
Nyandoma
Velsk
Kotlas
Veliki Ustyug
Syktyvkar
Ukhta

Kaunas
Riga
Jelgava
Siauliai
Panevezys
Daugavpils
Rezekne
Borovichi
Chudovo
Volkhov
Novgorod
Staraya Russa
Cherepovets

Vilna
Grodno
Vitebsk
Polotsk
Orsha
Kalinin
Rybinsk
Sokol

Bialystok
Brest
Baranovichi
Minsk
Mogilev
Smolensk
MOSCOW
Vologda

Vologda

LVOV
Vladimir-Volynski
Lutsk
Pinsk
Mozyr
Gomel
Bryansk
Tula
Yaroslavl
Kostroma
Ivanovo
Dzerzhinsk
Gorki

Yavorov
Borislav
Kovel
Korosten
Bobruisk
Novozybkov
Orel
Serpukhov
Ryazan

Chernovtsy
Vinnitsa
Kiev
Nezhin
Romny
Lgov
Mtsensk
Yelets
Mereta
Muroz
Arzamas

Kishinev
Zhitomir
Kirovograd
Krivoi Rog
Poltava
Kursk
Kupyansk
Voronezh
Michurinsk
Tambov
Penza
Saransk
Alatyr
Kanash
Kazan

Ismail
Odessa
Dnepropetrovsk
Kharkov
Belgorod
Liski
Usman
Serdobsk
Balashov
Ulyanovsk
Ruzaevka
Syzran

Simferopol
Nikolayev
Zaporozhe
Donetsk
Gorlovka
Shakhty
Millerovo
Borisoglebsk
Balakovo
Volsk
Pugachev

Sevastopol
Crimea
Kerch
Sea of Azov
Rostov
Volgograd
Saratov
Uralsk

Yalta
Krasnodar
Shakhty
Tikhoretsk
Kotelnikovski
Krasnaya Sloboda
Nikolayevsk
Novouzensk
Sorochinsk
Buzuluk
Abdulino
Belorets
Zlatoust

BLACK SEA
Tuapse
Batum
Poti
Maikop
Stavropol
Armavir
Salsk
Stepnoi
Elista
Astrakhan
Chkalov
Orsk
Aktyubinsk

Petrozavodsk

CAUCASUS MTS.
Grozny
Mozdok
Budennovsk
Kizlyar
Derbent

Tiflis
Gori
Kirovabad
Kuba
Sumgait

Batumi

Erivan
Nakhichevan
Agdam
Kirovabad

Baku
Salyany
Lenkoran

TURKEY

IRAN

CASPIAN SEA

Krasnovodsk

Kizyl-Arvat

KOPET DAGH
(mts)

Ashkhabad
Mary
Bairam-Ali
Kushka

Termez

AFGHANISTAN

Ural R.

Guryev
Dossor

Emba R.

Emba

Chelkar

UST URT
(plateau)

ARAL SEA

Aralsk
Novokazalinsk

Karsakpai

Nukus
Tashauz
Khiva
Turtkul
Syr Darya R.

KYZYL KUM DESERT

Borisovka
Kyzl Orda

Bukhara
Kagan
Katta Kurgan
Samarkand
Karshi

Kushka

Dushanbe

Amu Darya R.

Leninabad
Dzhizak
Kanibadam
Fergana
Kokand
Kyzyl-Kiya

Tashkent
Chirchik
Chust
Dzhalal-Abad

Achisai
Turkestan
Arys
Chimkent
Dzhambul

PAKISTAN

KASHMIR

UNION

OF

SOVIE

URAL

MTS.

Krasnovishersk
Berezniki
Solikamsk
Kizel
Lysva
Kushva
Krasnouralsk
Kirovgrad
Nizhni Tagil
Kamensk-Uralski

Serov
Perm
Sverdlovsk

Glazov
Kudymkar
Kirov
Ishevsk
Sarapul

Sharya
Kotelnich
Slobodskoi

Yaransk
Cheboksary
Chistopol
Melekess
Bugulma
Buguruslan

Ufa
Chelyabinsk
Magnitogorsk
Kustanai
Troitsk
Dzhetygara

Shadrinsk
Kurgan
Petropavlovsk
Ishim

Tyumen
Tobolsk

Ob R.

Tara

Omsk
Tsil-Kul
Kuibyshev
Barabinsk

Kolpashevo

Tomsk

Shchuchinsk
Kokchetav
Stepnyak
Atbasar

Akmolinsk
Pavlodar

Kargat
Novosibirsk
Kamen
Slavgorod
Aleisk
Barnaul

Yaya
Taiga
Topki
Belovo
Kemerovo
Sarala
Chernogorsk
Abakan

Temir-Tau
Semipalatinsk
Ust-Kamenogorsk
Leninogorsk
Zyryanovsk
Gorno-Altaisk

Karaganda

Balkhash

Ayaguz

Zaisan

Bisk
Temir Tau

Lake Balkhash

Chu R.

Frunze
Tokmak
Alma Ata
Przhevalsk

TIEN SHAN
(mts.)

SINKIANG

CHI

Irtysh R.

Tobol R.

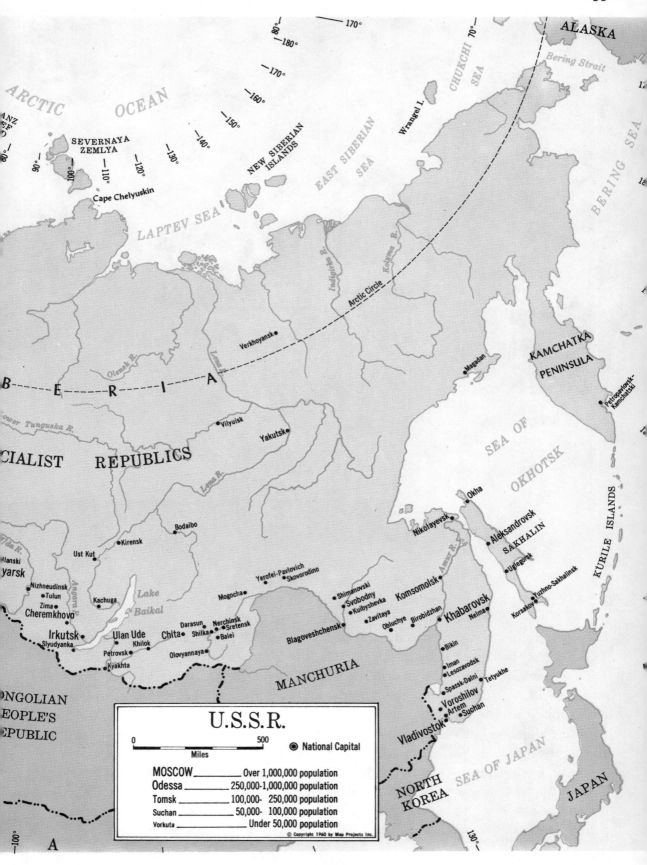

ALASKA

ARCTIC OCEAN

FRANZ JOSEF L.

SEVERNAYA ZEMLYA

Cape Chelyuskin

NEW SIBERIAN ISLANDS

EAST SIBERIAN SEA

CHUKCHI SEA

Bering Strait

Wrangel I.

LAPTEV SEA

BERING SEA

Olenek R.

Lower Tunguska R.

Indigirka R.

Kolyma R.

Arctic Circle

Lena R.

S I B E R I A

Verkhoyansk

KAMCHATKA PENINSULA

Magadan

Petropavlovsk-Kamchatski

Vilyuisk

Yakutsk

CIALIST REPUBLICS

Lena R.

SEA OF OKHOTSK

Okha

Bodaibo

Vida R.

Kirensk

Ust Kut

Nikolayevsk

Aleksandrovsk

SAKHALIN

KURILE ISLANDS

yarsk

Nizhneudinsk

Tulun

Zima

Cheremkhovo

Angara R.

Kachuga

Lake Baikal

Yerofei-Pavlovich

Skovorodino

Mogocha

Shimanovski

Svobodny

Kuibyshevka

Zavitaya

Komsomolsk

Uglegorsk

Yuzhno-Sakhalinsk

Korsakov

Irkutsk

Slyudyanka

Ulan Ude

Khilok

Petrovsk

Chita

Darasun

Shilka

Nerchinsk

Sretensk

Balei

Obluchye

Birobidzhan

Khabarovsk

Nelma

Olovyannaya

Blagoveshchensk

Kyakhta

MANCHURIA

Bikin

Iman

Lesozavodsk

Spassk-Dalni

Voroshilov

Artem

Suchan

Tetyukhe

ONGOLIAN EOPLE'S EPUBLIC

Vladivostok

NORTH KOREA

SEA OF JAPAN

JAPAN

U.S.S.R.

0 _____ 500

Miles

◉ National Capital

MOSCOW _____ Over 1,000,000 population
Odessa _____ 250,000-1,000,000 population
Tomsk _____ 100,000- 250,000 population
Suchan _____ 50,000- 100,000 population
Vorkuta _____ Under 50,000 population

© Copyright 1960 by Map Projects Inc.

A

John Strohm

Russia's future lies with children like these 'Young Pioneers' hiking through Moscow.

THE SOVIET UNION,
THE WORLD'S LARGEST STATE

The Union of Soviet Socialist Republisc, generally denoted by its initials, U.S.S.R., is the largest state in the world. It covers one-seventh of the world's land surface. It stretches from the middle of Europe, to the extreme eastern tip of Asia, which is only a few miles from the western tip of North America. The distance from west to east is such that sunrise on the frontier with Poland is eleven hours later than sunrise at the other end of the country. Travelling across the country the clocks have to be put on or back ten times. In the south the frontiers are formed by the Black Sea, Turkey, Iran, Afganistan, China, and Outer Mongolia; in the west by Norway, Finland, the Baltic Sea, Poland, Czechoslovakia, Hungary, and Romania; in the north by the Arctic Ocean, and in the east by the Bering, Okhotsk, and Japan Seas, which lead to the Pacific. From north to south the landscape varies from tundra to sub-tropical deserts.

THE PHYSICAL GEOGRAPHY OF SOVIET RUSSIA

Russia is out of reach of the warming influence of the North Atlantic Drift. Almost all the water that washes her coasts is cold, and freezes in winter. Thus Russia has the severest of continental climates. Winter and summer are sharply contrasted and follow each other abruptly, as both spring and autumn are very short. In winter frost comes early and lasts for a long time. The summer is hot and stormy. The climatic differences between the various areas do not consist of how hot or how cold it may become so much as how long or how short each season may be. Beyond 50° North, winter is longer than summer. The greatest cold is encountered at Verkhoyansk, where the temperature falls to over 94°F below zero. At the other extreme are the torrid steppes and deserts east of the Caspian Sea. The shores of the Baltic, however, are less continental in climate, and Murmansk and Petsamo, though well within the Arctic Circle, are just reached by the warm surface currents of the Arctic Ocean and are open all the winter. Other exceptions are the warm coasts of the Black Sea and the maritime provinces bordering on the Sea of Japan.

Though for the most part very low-lying, Russia has some great mountains on her periphery. The Caucasus, which lie between the Black Sea and the Caspian, are considerably higher than the Alps, having half a dozen peaks over 16,000 feet — Elbruz, the highest, being 18,540 feet. Still higher are the Pamirs in Tadzhik at the north-western end of the

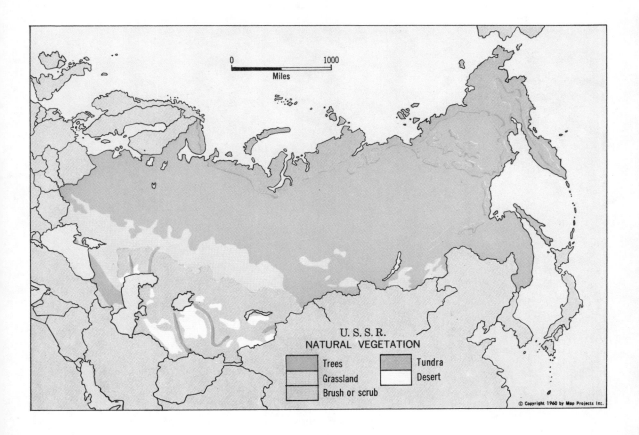

U.S.S.R.
NATURAL VEGETATION

Trees   Tundra
Grassland   Desert
Brush or scrub

© Copyright 1960 by Map Projects Inc.

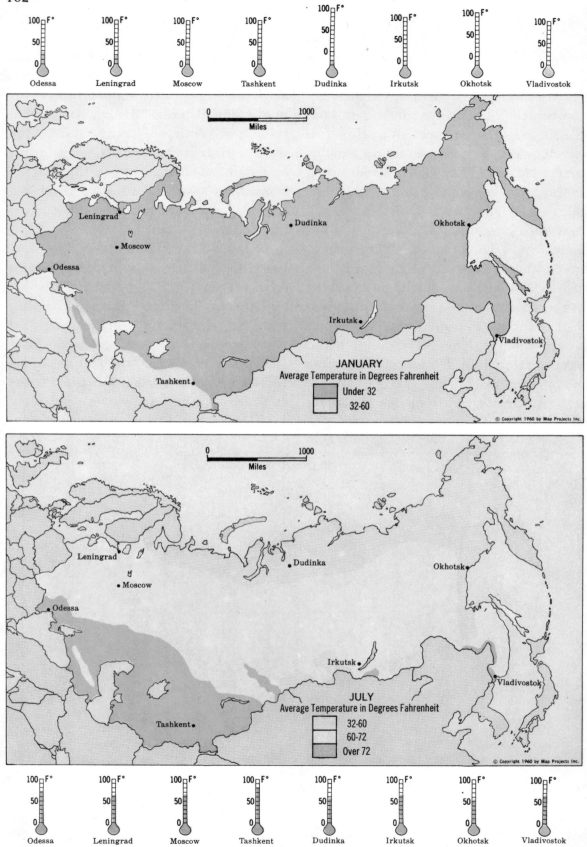

JANUARY
Average Temperature in Degrees Fahrenheit

Under 32

32-60

© Copyright 1960 by Map Projects Inc.

JULY
Average Temperature in Degrees Fahrenheit

32-60

60-72

Over 72

© Copyright 1960 by Map Projects Inc.

Himalayas, whose heights rise to over 20,000 feet, and Communism peak, which reaches 24,500 feet, and continues eastward into the Tien Shan. Starting east of Lake Balkhash is a long mountainous area which includes the Sayan, Yablonovy, and Stanovoy mountains, the three ranges of eastern Siberia — Verkoyansk, Cheriky, and Kolyma — and finally the Kamchatka Mountains which run through the peninsula on the eastern side of the Sea of Okhotsk. Along the southern part of the Pacific coast, the Sikhote Alin range sweeps south towards Vladivostok.

By far the greater part of Russian territory consists of an immense stretch of plains or low plateaus, hardly interrupted by the gentle slopes of the Urals, reaching 5,500 feet. This area is drained by a number of great rivers, the Dnieper,

the Volga, the Ob and Irtysh, the Yenisei, and the Lena, all of which have slow currents. In the south the dryness is an obstacle to normal river drainage. As a result we find the great inland seas, the Caspian, the Sea of Aral, and Lake Balkhash.

Vegetation varies with the latitude. In the extreme north the peaty soil is frozen in winter and produces only a scanty growth of moss and lichens. This is called tundra. South of the tundra is an enormous area of coniferous (evergreen) forests. In eastern Siberia, the forests are almost continuous down to the frontier with China. South of the forests, chiefly in the west, is the steppe. As we move towards the hotter regions, the steppe gradually gives place to scrub, in which are large patches of desert.

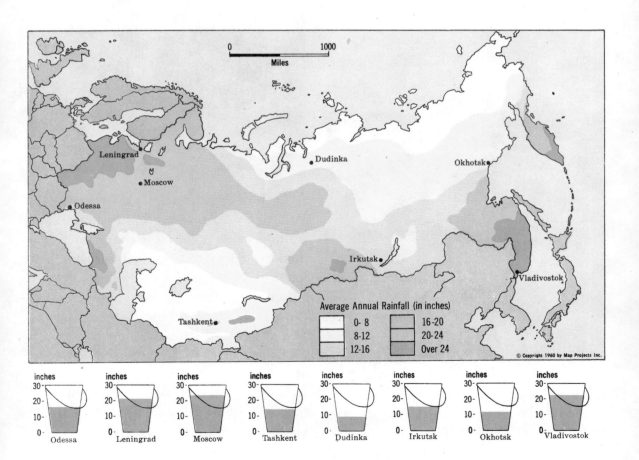

THE POLITICAL AND ECONOMIC STRUCTURE OF RUSSIA

More than 100 nationalities live within the Soviet Union, each maintaining its own language and culture. In the interior are Finno-Ugrians, Mongols, Tunguses; on the borders are Balts, Caucasians, Kazakhs, Kirghiz, Uzbeks, Turkomans, and many others. But in spite of their differences and the great variety of the country they live in there is a remarkable uniformity in their manner of life.

By dint of great efforts and sacrifices, Russia has succeeded, since the Revolution of 1917, in nationalising her production, and in completely reorganising the structure of the country. This is particularly remarkable when the damage by the Second World War is taken into account. The whole economic life of the country rests on a system of planned socialism. The land and all its resources, the railways and other means of transport, the banks, factories, and most of the shops are all owned by the State, which represents the workers of the country. The State co-ordinates their activities and plans development. Agricultural production is controlled by worker co-operatives. Industrial production is supervised by regional controllers. Factories making the same class of goods are grouped together in local combines.

John Strohm

Women shovelling wheat with wooden shovels.

Technical advances are very rapid, and the distribution of the population is undergoing a constant change with the opening of new mines, the building of new factories, the cultivation of new lands. Thousands of people are moving away from their original homelands, and particularly great is the movement towards the towns, whose population is increasing at the rate of 2 million a year. Already Russia has become the second industrial power of the world, and is challenging the United States for first place.

C. R. Twidale

Part of the enormous forests of Siberia. Russia has encountered great difficulties in opening-up the virgin lands of Siberia.

Much of the heavy work in the Soviet Union, such as road maintenance, is done by women.

Russia is fast building new towns and rebuilding old ones. This new housing estate is in Leningrad.

THE PEOPLES OF SOVIET RUSSIA

The Soviet Union seeks to combine the idea of unity on all major questions with the largest possible amount of decentralisation. The population of over 237 million is divided up between 15 different Socialist Republics. Each linguistic minority not only maintains its own language, but has a government of its own.

The largest of the Republics is Greater Russia (the Russian Socialist Federal Soviet Republic), totalling an area of over 6 million square miles, and a population of some 128 million. This is itself organised on a federal basis and, though the most Russian part of the country, nevertheless includes 15 autonomous republics in which languages other than Russian are spoken.

The Ukrainians form the next most important national group. They make up

Professor Sokolov is one of the foremost agricultural experts in the Soviet Union.

Peasant women from one of the huge Soviet Republics that are part of Asia.

John Strohm

*Managers of a state farm in the Ukraine sitting
down to a fine meal.*

John Strohm

*A peasant home in Byelorussia, which lies between
Poland and Moscow.*

a fifth of the total population, and live
in the Ukraine Soviet Socialist Republic
which lies to the north of the Black Sea.
With the most fertile soil in the Soviet
Union, the Ukraine is often spoken of
as the granary of Russia. The other
Republics vary in size and importance.
The Russians, Ukrainians, and White
Russians are Slavs, but there are numerous other national and racial groups,
like the Mongol-featured Turko-Tartars

from Central Asia, the Tadzhiks from the
Pamirs, the Kerilians, Estonians, Georgians, Armenians, and many others.

Fifty years ago Russia was a country
of peasants, traditionally attached to the
land, mostly illiterate, and so poor as to

John Strohm

*A group of villagers from a collective farm in
Byelorussia.*

Robert Lackenback - Jim Quigney Associates

*This gentle buffalo in Georgia is not at all concerned
by the boy sitting on his back.*

G. Sanger

Soviet Information Bureau

A turbaned Uzbek in the streets of Taskhent, the capital of the Uzbek Republic.

Hunters, wearing their national costume, in the extreme east of Siberia.

D. Lex

This village street scene is typical of hundreds on the fertile plains of the Ukraine.

A long queue of people from all over the Soviet Union forms every day to visit Lenin's tomb in Red Square, Moscow. This is the shrine of Russian communism.

THE PRODUCE OF THE LAND

Agriculture utilises well over 2 million square miles, that is to say more than one-quarter of the Soviet Union.

The bulk of arable land is in the temperate area, and the crops are mostly cereals. But it also extends into sub-tropical regions, where cotton, rice, oranges, and grapes are grown.

The steppes of Central Asia provide good grazing ground for sheep. For the rest there are the forests, which cover an area nearly twice as great as all the arable land of the country.

Cotton and flax are grown in enormous quantities, and even hemp, the smallest of the fibre crops, amounts to about one-quarter of world production. The yearly production of timber is over 350 million cubic yards.

be the virtual slaves of the great aristocratic landowners. Today, over half the population live in cities, and no state in the world has a more efficient system of education than the U.S.S.R.

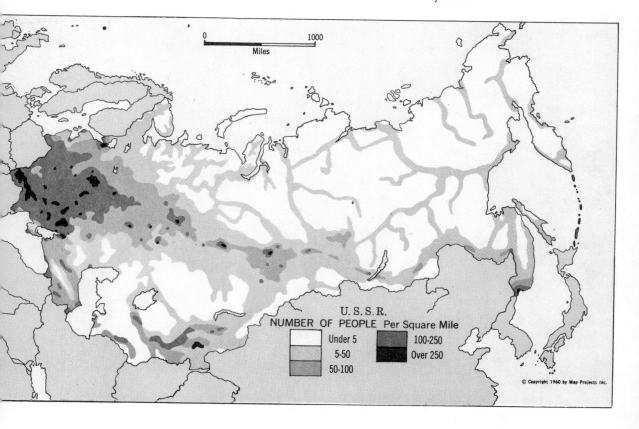

0   1000
Miles

U.S.S.R.
NUMBER OF PEOPLE Per Square Mile

Under 5   100-250
5-50   Over 250
50-100

© Copyright 1960 by Map Projects Inc.

There are two kinds of farm in the Soviet Union — both for the breeding of dairy and stock cattle and arable farming. There is the Collective Farm and the State Farm. Collective farms are often very large, combining all the land of one or several villages. The Uzbeks, for example, have one collective farm with an area of some 150,000 acres, on which cotton is grown. It employs the workers of 3,500 families, distributed among over 70 villages. Collective farms are planned and run by the people who work on them, though plans have to be approved by the elected local authorities.

The bulk of production is sold to the state at a pre-arranged price. The remainder is sold locally for whatever price it may fetch. Of the money earned by a collective farm, part goes in tax, part is to pay expenses, and the remainder — the profit — is divided amongst the farm workers. The more skilful or experienced farm workers earn more than the others. Managers or specialists earn two or even three times more than the ordinary labourers do.

Each worker on a collective farm has his own house and, round it, a small quantity of land for his own use. What is not needed by himself and his family, he can sell at the market of the collective farm, keeping the proceeds.

Apart from the collectives about one-fifth of the land farmed in Russia is under direct state ownership. Here decisions come from above. The manager is appointed by the authorities, and the labourers receive a fixed wage. State farms are generally bigger than the collectives and are run very much on factory lines.

The chief crops are wheat, rye, maize, sugar-beet, and potatoes. Oats and barley

John Strohm

Stacking the straw on a collective farm in the Ukraine. This is rich farming land.

are grown on land unsuitable for other cereals. Cotton and fruit are grown on irrigated land in Central Asia.

The only sub-tropical regions of Soviet Russia are the coasts of the Black Sea and the valleys and foothills of the

In the Kirghiz Republic in Central Asia much of the newly irrigated land is devoted to cotton.

U.S.S.R. Magazine - Sovfoto

Part of the enormous wheatfields of the Ukraine.

Cattle grazing on 'the roof of the world'. This valley in the Pamirs is 12,000 feet above sea level.

U.S.S.R. Magazine - Sovfoto

Sunflowers are an important crop in the Soviet Union. They are used both as food and as a source of vegetable oil.

A wheatfield on the enormous plains of Siberia. Despite every effort production from these pioneer lands has so far proved disappointing.

Marilyn Silverstone - Palmer Photo Agency

There are large herds of goats in the Caucasus.

INDUSTRIAL PRODUCTION

All industry is nationalised. Mines, oil-wells, power-stations, and factories, are all in the hands of the state, which represents the sovereign people.

The government decides what shall be produced and in what quantity. It decides when to open a new mine, when and where to build a new factory. Every detail has to fit in with a plan, usually a Five Year Plan. Before a plan is finally decided there are long discussions between experts and representatives of the workers take part in them too. Once decided upon, the plan is very strictly enforced.

Each undertaking works as a separate economic unit, selling its produce to meet its expenditure. To co-ordinate their man-

Caucasus. In them tea is grown, vines, citrus fruits, and various crops. On the dry plains east of the Volga in Central Asia, herds of cattle are kept, and flocks of sheep and goats.

Flax is grown in White Russia and in the neighbourhood of Moscow, while sugar-beet is grown in the Ukraine, the Caucasus, Central Asia, and the Far East. Vines are grown everywhere in the south.

Science is playing an increasing part in Soviet agriculture. Soviet scientists have succeeded in developing certain crop varieties which can grow and ripen in a very short season of 90 days. This is vital if Siberia, Russia's great Arctic 'frontier', is to be developed as the Soviet people hope.

Inside a Soviet textile factory. Many textile plants have been built recently in Central Asia.

Today, the Soviet Union's production of steel is second only to the United States.

ufacture, factories of the same sort are often grouped together. Another sort of group combines industrial undertakings that are dependent on one another — as blast furnaces are dependent on mines, and as the manufacture of machinery is dependent on steel production.

The Soviet's first concern after the Revolution of 1917 was to 'electrify the land' and develop heavy industry: iron and steel production, shipbuilding, heavy machinery, etc. The manufacture of consumer goods had to take second place, though greater emphasis is now being placed on them. It must be remembered that fifty years ago Russia was a very backward country, not only politically and in the standard of general education and living, but industrially.

Today Soviet Russia is second only to the United States in industrial production. She has acquired that position by virtue of her vast stores of raw material, including fuel, and by the determined effort she has made to achieve it.

Russia possesses coal, oil, natural gas, and water-power.

The most important coalfields are the Donbas, or Donetz Basin (in the southern Ukraine), the Kuzbas or Kuznetsk Basin (the Upper Yenisei Valley), the Karaganda Basin in the Kazakh Republic, the Irkutsk in central Siberia, and the Basins of the Far East.

In coal production, as in industry, Russia comes second only to the United States. She produces four times as much as in 1939, ten times as much as in 1928. In oil production, she also comes second after North America.

John Strohm

A new dam being built across the Volga at Volgograd for what will become the largest hydro-electric power-station in the world.

Modern Russian farm machinery on display in Moscow.

Here are other examples of advanced Russian farm equipment.

The chief source used to be the Caucasus, the principal regions being Baku, Grozny, and Maikop, but about three-quarters of Russian oil now comes from the Ural-Volga area, the so-called 'Second Baku', where there are four important oilfields. Stores of natural gas are being very actively exploited in various regions.

Less advance has been made in the building of hydro-electric power-stations. The great rivers of European Russia have rarely enough fall for the development of much power. But power-stations have nevertheless been built, the largest being on the Svir and the Volkhov, both in the neighbourhood of Leningrad, on the Kama, further inland, and on the Dnieper.

A craftsman at work in the Tadzhik Republic, Central Asia.

Selling kvass in Moscow. Kvass is a kind of beer made from fermented black bread.

A laboratory in a Russian school. Education has played an important part in the development of the Soviet Union into a great modern state.

Further east, big dams have been built on the Volga at Kuybyshev and on the Angara (which flows out of Lake Baikal) near Irkutsk. But as the rivers of Russia and Siberia are frozen in winter, heating systems have had to be installed, using either natural gas, oil, coal, or peat.

Russia possesses ample quantities of most of the important metals. From the Urals come iron, copper, zinc, lead, bauxite, gold, and platinum; from the Ukraine iron, manganese, and bauxite. From the Caucasus come manganese, zinc, and lead. From the Kazakh Republic come copper, lead, and zinc. Central Siberia produces zinc, lead, tin, and bauxite. The iron ore from Krivoi Rog in the Ukraine is of a very high grade. The manganese production of Georgia and the Ukraine constitutes 40 per cent of world production.

The most important iron and steel works are in the Donbas (in the southern Ukraine), at Magnitogorsk (in the Urals), and in the Kuzbas in western Siberia.

The resources of the Donbas are enormous. Besides the coal of the Donetz basin there is the iron ore of Krivoi Rog and the Kerch Peninsula in the Crimea, and bauxite, lignite, etc., all organised into a complementary industrial area. The principal towns are Donetsk (formerly Stalino): coking plant, steel works, etc.; Makeyevka: blast-furnaces and chemical industries; Lugansk (Voroshilovgrad), locomotives, heavy machinery; Zaporozhe, aluminium; Krivoi Rog, iron mines, smelting.

The Urals extended for over 1,500 miles and on their flanks is an oil-bearing basin that has only been partially prospected. There are more than 1,000 veins of iron-ore. One of them, called Magnet Mountain, is linked by rail to Magnitogorsk, which contains the largest steel works in the world. New mining and manufacturing towns have sprung up with the development of this area. Sverdlovsk, with 981,000 inhabitants, specialises in the manufacture of machinery and machine tools; Chelyabinsk in special steels and ferro-alloys, tractors, and motor-cars; Nizhni Tagil has large steel works, and manufactures railway equipment.

The smelting works of the Urals have no local coal available, but a deposit of natural gas has been located along the River Ural.

Apart from these two great industrial concentrations, the principal industrial towns of European Russia are Leningrad, electrical machinery; Moscow and Gorki, motor-cars; Kharkov and Volgograd, formerly Stalingrad, tractors, locomotives, and turbines.

A chemical industry based on coal has been built up at Novomoskovask (formerly Stalinogorsk). At Baku and Kuibyshev, the chemical industry is based on oil, while in other areas it is based on wood, cellulose, or phosphates. The raw material for the manufacture of synthetic rubber at Yaroslavl is alcohol.

The Middle Volga is a traditional centre of textile manufacture. Moscow is the principal region for the manufacture of cotton stuffs, and weaving has also been introduced in Tashkent in the cotton-growing Uzbek Republic.

The processing of food is steadily increasing, with the development of towns. Sugar-refining is done in the Ukraine and Kazakh Republics: a fish-tinning industry exists on the Lower Volga and on the coast of the Sea of Okhotsk. Meat

Paul Hufner - Shostal

This textile factory in Taskhent, capital of the Uzbek Republic, is one of the largest in the U.S.S.R.

tinning is a growing industry in Moscow.

Naturally there is a multitude of other industries in a country so vast as Russia. Almost every kind of industry is rapidly developing, and more new factories are built every year.

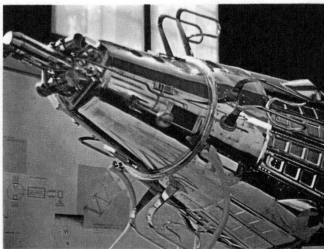

John Strohm

The nose-cone of a Russian Sputnik. Russia has scored many outstanding successes in the field of space exploration.

Cattle grazing on stubble on a Siberian collective farm. The Russians are making great efforts to increase their herds.

SIBERIA

With an area not far short of 6 million square miles, Siberia is three times the size of Western Europe. A large part of it consists of fertile steppes, a continuation of the steppes of European Russia, but a much greater part makes up the largest forested area of land anywhere outside the tropics. Siberia has its coalfields and the greatest hydro-electric power-station of the country. For the Russian millions, Siberia represents the wide open spaces, just as North America did to the Europeans of the nineteenth century.

The population of this vast area is only about 70 millions, but it is increasing at the rate of 3 million a year. The towns are expanding rapidly. Omsk is a good example. Founded in the eighteenth century, this town, lying on the River Irtysh, had a population in 1939 of 281,000 which has now more than tripled. The town still contains many one-storied houses built of wood, yet great buildings of reinforced concrete are going up, while on the outskirts is a constantly growing forest of chimneys. Industry includes flour-milling and meat-packing, the tanning of leather, petrol refining, and the manufacture of agricultural machinery and railway equipment.

We have already spoken of the Kuzbas, the great industrial centre of western Siberia whose coalfield is the richest of the Soviet Union. That coalfield has become a centre of iron and steel production (using iron ore from the Altai), and a general centre of heavy industry. The chief towns are Novokuznetsk (formerly Stalinsk), Kemerovo, Leninsk, and Novosibirsk.

Another industrial concentration is centred on the coal basin of Karaganda, lying some 200 miles north of Lake Balkhash. It includes smelting works, though the iron ore has to come from as far away as the northern part of the Kazakh Republic. Non-ferrous metals, including copper from the Lake Balkhash region, are also worked.

Another concentration is in central Siberia in the neighbourhood of Lake Baikal and the River Angara, which runs northward from it. Lake Baikal is longer than the Adriatic and its area is sixty times that of Lake Constance. The Angara is a great river, with rapids at several places, so that dams and hydro-electric power-stations have been built. In this industrial region an important coalfield near Irkutsk is being worked, while bauxite and other non-ferrous metals are being mined on the further side of Lake Baikal. The Amur River in eastern Siberia is also the centre of an industrial area. For a considerable distance this great river forms the frontier with Manchuria, then it flows northward to the Sea of Okhotsk. The area's industries are served by the coalfields of the Bureya Mountains, Vladivostok, and the Island of Sakhalin; and by the ores of the Sikhota Alin range. Heavy industry is concentrated in Komsomolsk, Ussuriisk, and Vladivostok. Other industries depend on local timber and fish.

Jerry Cooke - Photo Researchers

The dam across the Angara river, here seen under construction. It supplies electricity to Siberia's new industries.

Jerry Cooke - Photo Researchers

Siberian villages usually have a frontier atmosphere.

SOVIET COMMUNICATIONS

It has already been pointed out that one of the cardinal facts of Soviet industry is that it is spread over such an enormous area. The huge distances involved demand a highly organised system of transport, which thus becomes one of the nation's major problems.

The magnitude of these problems is illustrated by the fact that a train takes about nine days to travel the whole length of the Trans-Siberian Railway, a distance not far short of 6,000 miles. Siberia has many great rivers, which would provide excellent transport were it not that, firstly, they nearly all flow northwards into the Arctic Ocean, whereas east-west transport is desired, and secondly that they freeze in winter. Even the Lower Volga, one of the most southerly stretches of river, is frozen over for three months in the year. The more northerly rivers are ice-bound for much

longer. In the more western areas canals have been constructed between rivers. There is one between the Dnieper and the Bug, and the Volga is linked to the Sea of Azov on the one hand, and to the Neva on the other, which in turn is linked to the White Sea. The cost of building these canals is enormous and frost greatly reduces their use since canal water, being almost stationary, freezes more rapidly than running water. In Russia inland water transport carries little more than 5 per cent of the goods traffic, while the railways carry 81 per cent of this traffic.

Road transport is more hampered by spring than by winter. When the thaw comes the roads become muddy, and transport is apt to be bogged down.

There remain the railways. The construction of railways in Russia only began seriously in 1880. The highest point in

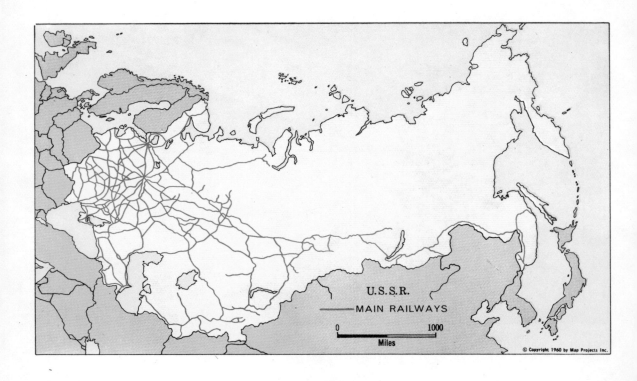

U.S.S.R.

MAIN RAILWAYS

0   1000

Miles

© Copyright 1960 by Map Projects Inc.

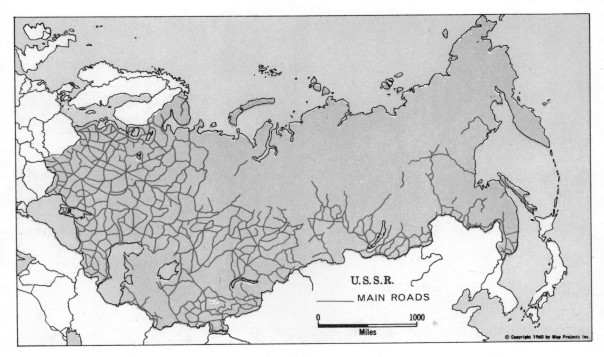

pre-Revolution days was the construction of the Trans-Siberian railway, begun in 1892. This railway, which took ten years to build, is 8,750 miles long — the longest railway in the world. Its construction marked a vital stage in the development and colonisation of Siberia.

However, in 1917, the Soviet government inherited one of the poorest railway systems in the world, and the progress of railway construction across the U.S.S.R.'s great distances remained slow

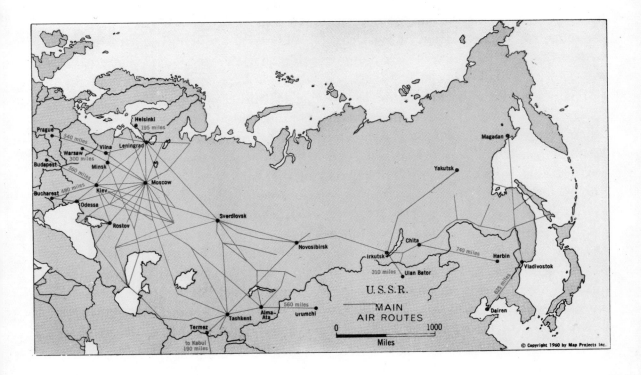

The fortress of St Peter and St Paul, Leningrad.

Homer L. Dodge - FPG

until 1930, when the Turksib railway, running between Turkestan and Siberia, was constructed. The railway allows the exchange of the coal, cereals, and wood of the north against the cotton and oil of the south.

Joining up with the Turksib, transverse lines were constructed to connect further industrial areas. The Karaganda railway linked the coalfield of that name with the industrial concentration of the Urals, with branches to connect the copper mines of Lake Balkhash.

Today a southern branch of the Trans-Siberian Railway links Magnitogorsk and other Ural industrial centres with the Kuzbas, passing through the northern part of the Kazakh Republic. A line linking the Russian and Chinese systems, the Trans-Mongolian, branches off from the Trans-Siberian at Ulan Ude, south of Lake Baikal, and runs to Peking, thus providing an outlet for the Angara industrial area. A second line, from the Turksib, will eventually join the Chinese railway now being constructed through the Sinkiang-Uighur Autonomous Region.

PRINCIPAL TOWNS

In 1917 only 16 per cent of the population lived in towns. The proportion has now risen to just under 50 per cent. There are 160 towns with more than 100,000 inhabitants, and 32 of them with more than half a million. This sudden advance is largely due to the development of Russian industry.

Three types of towns are distinguishable. Firstly, the small country towns that provide market facilities for the agricultural population. Secondly, the commercial and industrial towns, usually situated beside rivers. Lastly, there are the administrative towns: the capitals of the various republics, and the headquarters of regional authorities.

In some cases industrial towns are old towns that have become industrialised. These include Perm (formerly Molotov), Volgograd (formely Tsaritsyn and Stalingrad), Sverdlovsk (formerly Ekaterinburg). In other cases new towns have sprung up in open country, their sites being determined by the presence of coal

Novosti Press Agency

The University of Moscow.

or other minerals. Such are Magnito-gorsk in the Urals, Chelyabinsk and Makeyevka in the Donbas, and Novo-kuznetsk in the Kuzbas.

Minsk, the capital of White Russia, stands in an area of half-drained marsh-land, between the Niemen and the Upper Dnieper. At the beginning of this century, it looked like a vast, untidy, over-grown village. During the Second World War, four-fifths of it was de-stroyed, but today it is a city of broad streets in the centre, flanked by modern houses and flats. Immense new factories are making heavy machinery, tractors, lorries, trailers, and a wide range of

A group of women asphalt a road in Volgograd. Women can do this work just as well as men.

An Uzbek man, squatting on the ground in oriental style, enjoys a melon in the market of Samarkand.

miscellaneous products, including chemical products.

Gorki, formerly Nizhni Novgorod, lies on the Volga at the confluence with the Oka. It is typical of the Russian river towns that mark the various stages of Muscovite expansion, when markets were set up on the rivers at a time when they were the only highways. Once important as a meeting place for the trade of Europe and Asia, its importance as a market declined after the opening of the Suez

Leningrad is Russia's most important port. It was first built in 1703 by Peter the Great, who wanted Russia to have an outlet to the Baltic.

Harrison Salisbury - Photo Library

A power-driven barge on the Volga. The Volga is the longest river in European Russia.

Most of the Siberian towns are new. Krasnoyarsk is built on the river Yenisei at the point where it is crossed by the Trans-Siberian railway. It lies in a huge clearing of the forest, and is a picturesque town, backed by rocky hills which supply the setting for a school of mountain climbing.

Though dating from the eighteenth century Omsk has only expanded in recent years, with the agricultural development of the northern part of the Kazakh Republic. Its industries are mostly concerned with foodstuffs.

Novosibirsk is the giant amongst the Siberian towns, with a population of

Canal. However, more recently the town has become an active manufacturing centre, in particular for tractors and motor cars.

Kiev has now been entirely rebuilt, after the damage of the last war. There are 800 completely new streets. Extending to the north-west are the industrial quarters, in which mechanical engineering takes a prominent place. Kiev, with its university and several scientific research organisations, has considerable status as a cultural centre.

Leningrad (formerly Petrograd and St Petersburg) is a historic town. Though it has ceased to be the capital of the country, it has become a great commercial and industrial centre. It has excellent communications. Nine railways start from it. Its port, Kronstadt, is the largest of the Soviet Union. Canals link it both to the White Sea, in the extreme north, and inland to the Volga. Its many industries include the manufacture of all equipment needed in the building of power-stations.

J. Sauger

The atmosphere in the market of Taskhent is decidedly oriental. Though integral parts of the U.S.S.R., the various Republics all retain their own individual character.

Julien Bryan - Photo Researchers

St Basil's Cathedral in Red Square was built by Ivan the Terrible. The story goes that he had the architect blinded so he could never design anything more beautiful.

1,079,000. It is built at the point where the Trans-Siberian railway crosses the river Ob and is the natural centre of communications for the coalfields of the Kuzbas. A large hydro-electric power-station, recently constructed, has added to its importance. The town is also a great cultural centre, a witness to the extent

Siberia has developed as a civilised area.

Vladivostok is Russia's most important Pacific port. It stands on a gulf in the extreme south, almost on the border of Manchuria. It lies in roughly the same latitude as Marseilles, but its climate is very different. The average temperature throughout the year is only a few degrees above freezing point, the Gulf itself never freezes, but thin ice forms along the shore and remains for four months in winter. With the constant growth of Siberia, the importance of Vladivostok is bound to increase.

Moscow, the Soviet capital is both a historic and modern city. The historic buildings of old Moscow date from the fourteenth century. Many of the most famous lie within the Kremlin, including the great palace of the Czars, built of white stone with great gold cupolas, and outside the Kremlin walls, in present-day Red Square, is the Cathedral of St Basil's built by Ivan the Terrible. Moscow ceased to be the capital of Russia in the seventeenth century, but since the Revolution has once again become the centre of the Russian State.

The rest of the city is of recent construction: big blocks of flats, and government offices, theatres, museums, hotels. big stores, and the huge University.

Special residential suburbs have been built round the old town. An impressive underground railway was opened in 1935, and every quarter is served by buses or trolleybuses.

Practically every branch of industry is represented in Moscow. Prominent amongst them are mechanical engineering and light industry, such as textiles, printing, etc. Two thirds of the products of light industry consumed in Russia

Agence Rapho

The beautiful city of Leningrad was built by Peter the Great to be his capital. At that time it was called St Petersburg.

are manufactured in or round Moscow.

Eleven railways radiate from Moscow, and with canals in every direction, Moscow is truly the heart of European Russia.

The Oriental appearance of the old towns is generally matched by that of their Moslem inhabitants.

Bukhara, with a population of 60,000 is one of the oldest towns of the Uzbek Republic. It was already a very prosperous place in the ninth century, being one of the halts on the caravan route which led to India and China. On a hill in the centre of the town is the old palace of the Khan. For ages the religious centre

U.S.S.R. Magazine - Sovfoto

A mosque in Samarkand in the Uzbek Republic.

U.S.S.R. Magazine - Sovfoto

Lake Ritsa, in one of the upper valleys of the Caucasus, in Georgia, is very popular with Russian holidaymakers.

of Central Asia, Bukhara has innumerable mosques.

Baku, which stands on a promontory on the western shore of the Caspian, is a town of nearly 1¼ million inhabitants. Once a Moslem town, it is now the great oil centre of the Caucasus. So rich is the land in oil, that it used to spout out spontaneously and sometimes these fountains used to burst into flames. Because of this, Baku was once regarded as a Holy City by the Parsees or fire-worshippers.

Samarkand is another of the oases once used by caravans. It was taken by Alexander the Great in 329 B.C. In the Middle Ages it was a great Moslem centre. Genghiz Khan sacked the town in 1220. It became Tamerlane's capital in 1370, and he made it into a fine town

U.S.S.R. Magazine - Sovfoto

Fishing boats on the Caspian Sea. It is from the roes of sturgeon caught here that caviar is made.

with mosques, palaces, and gardens. To-day it has some factories producing textiles and machinery.

Tashkent, the capital of the Uzbek Republic, is the biggest Soviet town of the east. It stands in a wide oasis, watered by the Syr Darya and by numerous canals. It is a double town. On the one hand is the old town, with narrow, dusty streets; beside it, a new town that sprang up when the railway was built in 1898. The new town is well-planned with imposing buildings and monuments. Tashkent is an important educational centre, particularly in technology, and it has become a great industrial town, producing farming machinery, mining equipment and electrical goods for Central Asia. Tashkent is the seat of the Central Asian University. The Soviet Union's cotton research institute is situated there.

Jerry Cooke - Photo Researchers

Russia's new housing programme is being pushed forward as fast as possible. All houses and flats are built by the local authorities; there is no private housing.

Snow-capped Fujiyama, Japan's highest mountain, is a national symbol for Japan's people.

THIS IS ASIA

Asia is the largest of the seven continents, and in it live well over 1,500 million people, more than half the population of the globe. Within its boundaries there is a greater diversity of race, territory, and climate than in any other. Looking at the map of the world it is at once obvious that Europe is really no more than a peninsula of Asia. Asia covers an area greater than that of Europe and Africa together, or the two Americas combined. It covers almost one-third of the earth's land surface.

A space-man, looking down on Asia, would see strikingly different landscapes. Asia has more mountains than any other continent. Plateaus and mountain ranges criss-cross the whole of Central Asia. The plateaus are higher than most mountains, and the peaks themselves tower many thousands of feet higher still. Those peaks are covered with ice and snow even in summer, and they rise not merely into but right above the clouds. There are half a dozen peaks five miles high, the highest being Mount Everest which is over 29,000 feet above sea-level. It is easy to understand why this region came to be called 'the roof of the world'.

There are also thousands of miles of desert. A desert belt stretches from the Red Sea to Mongolia. Some deserts, like the Arabian, are hot all the year round, while in others, such as the Gobi Desert of Mongolia, great extremes of cold may be encountered.

Deserts and steppes cover between them more than a third of Asia. Water is so scarce that few people can live there, and these few are nomads who drive their flocks from one grazing land to another.

Immense, dark, evergreen forests cover most of Northern Asia. In this vast area there are relatively few people, mainly trappers and lumbermen. In the extreme north the forests end, giving place to tundra, a belt of which skirts the Arctic Ocean. Here the ground is frozen hard most of the year, and nothing can grow except for a few mosses and lichens. Only a very few wandering tribes live here with their large herds of reindeer.

South of the coniferous forests are thousands of square miles of arable and grazing land used for growing wheat and rearing cattle.

Further south still, are the rainy tropical zones, and here, in the steaming jungle, live tigers, elephants, monkeys, and a host of tropical birds. Many millions of people live in these hot areas, most of them crowded into tiny villages along the banks of rivers, where they cultivate the rich soil. All over the world it is the general rule that the greatest numbers of people are found near water.

In Eastern Asia too, millions of people live on small farms close to the rivers. Some live actually on the water itself — in boats or house-boats. There is greater

Utilising every inch of land, Philippine farmers grow rice on carefully terraced hillsides.

A. Kolb, Hamburg

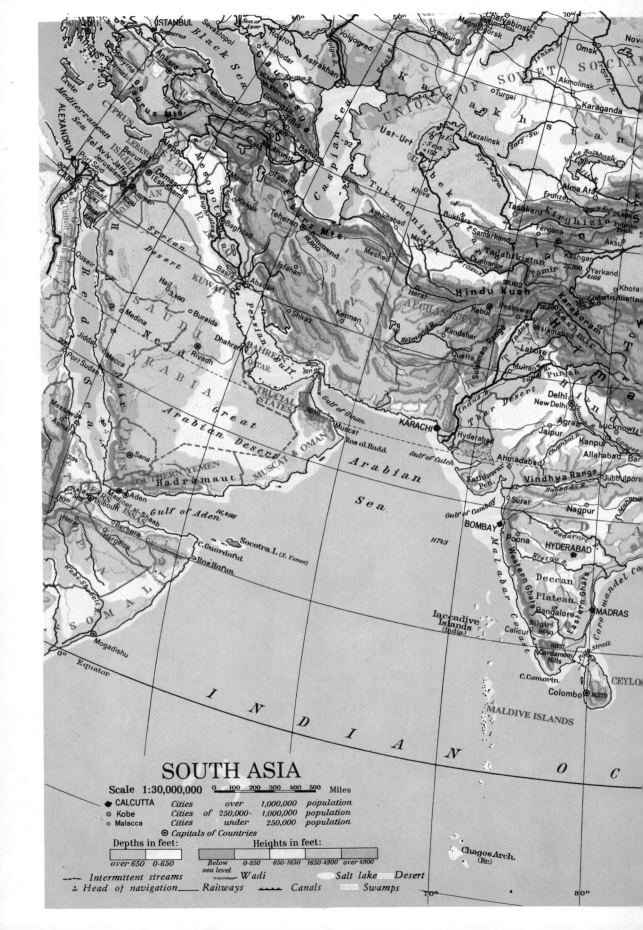

ISTANBUL Sevastopol Sea of Azov Rostov Volgograd Magnitogorsk Chelyabinsk Nov
Bosphorus Black Sea Krasnodar Astrakhan Orenburg UNION OF SOVIET Omsk
ATHENS Smyrna Ankara Trebizond Caucasus Kuma R. Volga R. Ural R. Akmolinsk Karaganda
Crete Taurus Mts. Georgians Baku Turgai Kazalinsk Lake Balkhash
CYPRUS Mt. Ararat Erivan Tabriz Caspian Sea Ust-Urt Syr Darya SOCIALIST
Mediterranean Sea Beirut LEBANON SYRIA Mosul Elburz Mts. Teheran Ashkhabad Khiva Bukhara Tashkent Alma Ata Poleda Peak
ALEXANDRIA Tel Aviv-Jaffa Damascus Kirkuk Teheran Kerman Meshed Turkmenistan Samarkand Fergana Kirghizia Aksu
CAIRO Jerusalem ISRAEL Baghdad Isfahan Herat Hindu Kush Kashgar Yarkand Khota
Suez Canal Basra Abadan Shiraz AFGHANISTAN Kabul Peshawar Karakoram Godwin Austen
Port Said Kuwait Buraida Dhahran BAHREIN Riyadh QATAR Quetta Suleiman Range Kandahar Lahore Kashmir
Quseir SAUDI Nejd Gulf of Oman Multan Punjab Islamabad
Jidda Mecca ARABIA TRUCIAL STATES Muscat Karachi Thar Desert Delhi New Delhi Agra Lucknow
Medina Great Arabian Desert Ras al Hadd MUSCAT & OMAN Hyderabad Jaipur Kanpur Allahabad
Port Sudan YEMEN Sana Hadramaut Arabian Gulf of Cutch Ahmadabad Vindhya Range Jubb
Massawa SOUTHERN YEMEN Aden Sea Kathiawar Pen. Narbada R. Surat
Asmara Djibouti Gulf of Aden Surat Nagpur Deccan
ISSAS Socotra I. (S. Yemen) BOMBAY Poona HYDERABAD
Hargeisa C. Guardafui Ras Hafun 11743 Malabar Coast Deccan Plateau Bangalore Nilgiri Eastern Ghats Coromandel Co
SOMALI Mogadishu Laccadive Islands (India) Calicut Western Ghats MADRAS
Equator Cardamom Hills C. Comorin CEYLON
Colombo
INDIAN MALDIVE ISLANDS
OCE

SOUTH ASIA

Scale 1:30,000,000   0 100 200 300 400 500 Miles

◆ CALCUTTA   *Cities*   *over*   1,000,000   *population*
⊙ Kobe   *Cities of*   250,000-   1,000,000   *population*
○ Malacca   *Cities*   *under*   250,000   *population*
⊙ *Capitals of Countries*

Depths in feet: Heights in feet:

over 650   0-650   Below sea level   0-650   650-1650   1650-4900   over 4900

---- *Intermittent streams*   *Wadi*   *Salt lake*   *Desert*
⌐ *Head of navigation*   *Railways*   *Canals*   *Swamps*

Chagos Arch. (Br.)

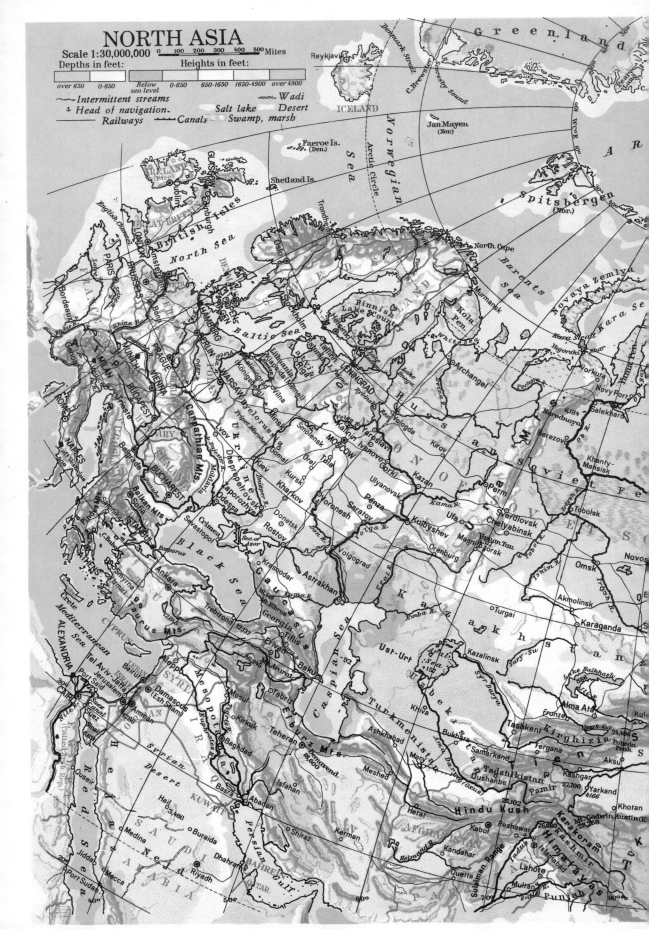

NORTH ASIA

Scale 1:30,000,000

0 100 200 300 400 500 Miles

Depths in feet: Heights in feet:

over 650 | 0-650   Below sea level | 0-650 | 650-1650 | 1650-4900 | over 4900

- Intermittent streams   Wadi
- Head of navigation.   Salt lake   Desert
- Railways   Canals   Swamp, marsh

Greenland

ICELAND   Reykjavik

Jan Mayen (Nor.)

Denmark Strait   C. Brewster   Scoresby Sound

Faeroe Is. (Den.)

Arctic Circle

Norwegian Sea

North Cape   Spitsbergen (Nor.)

Shetland Is.

IRELAND (Eire)   GLASGOW   Trondheim

Dublin   Edinburgh   Oslo

GREAT BRITAIN   British Isles   North Sea   Murmansk   Barents Sea   Novaya Zemlya

English Channel   Stockholm   Finnish Lake Country   Kola Pen.   Vaigach   Kara Strait   Kara Sea

LONDON   Amsterdam   SWEDEN   Baltic Sea   Helsinki   White Sea   Yugorski Shar   Yamal Pen.

PARIS   BRUSSELS   COPENHAGEN   Tallinn (Reval)   LENINGRAD   Archangel   Pechora R.   Yorkuta   Novy Port   Salekhard

HAMBURG   BERLIN   Riga   Lake   Vologda   6,184   Narodnaya   Berezovo   Khanty-Mansisk

FRANCE   Bonn   Königsberg   Vilna   MOSCOW   Kalinin   Yaroslavl   Kirov   Perm   URAL   SOVIET FEDERAL

Bordeaux   MUNICH   PRAGUE   WARSAW   Byelorussia   Minsk   Smolensk   Ivanovo Gorki   Perm   Sverdlovsk   Tobolsk

Geneva   VIENNA   Lvov   Pripet Marshes   Orel   Tula   Ulyanovsk   Kazan   Ufa   Chelyabinsk

ALPS   BUDAPEST   Moldavia   Kiev   Kursk   Penza   Kuibyshev   Magnitogorsk   Ob R.   Omsk   Novosibirsk

ROME   HUNGARY   Carpathian Mts.   Dnepropetrovsk   Kharkov   Voronesh   Saratov   Yablori Tau   Orenburg   Irtish R.   Akmolinsk

NAPLES   Belgrade   Zaporozhye   Donetsk   Rostov   Volga R.   Volgograd   Emba R.   Turgai   Karaganda

Balkan Mts.   BUCHAREST   Odessa   Sea of Azov   Krasnodar   Astrakhan   KAZAKHSTAN

Sofia   Crimea   Kuma R.   Caspian Sea   Ust-Urt   Aral Sea   Lake Balkhash

Pindus Mts.   ISTANBUL   Sevastopol   Caucasus   Tbilisi   Kazalinsk   Bary-Su   Alma Ata

ATHENS   Ankara   Black Sea   Elbrus   Georgia   Baku   UZBEK   Syr Darya   Frunze   Kirghizia   Issyk-Kul   Pobeda Peak

Crete   Smyrna   Trebizond   Erivan   Ararat   Khiva   Tashkent   Fergana   Aksu

Mediterranean Sea   Taurus Mts.   Tabriz   Turkmenistan   Bukhara   Samarkand   Kashgar   Yarkand

CYPRUS   Aleppo   Mesopotamia   Elburz Mts.   Ashkhabad   Mary   Amu Darya   Tadzhikistan   Pamir   Khotan

ALEXANDRIA   Beirut   Mosul   Teheran   Meshed   Dushanbe   Karakoram   Kashmir

Tel Aviv-Jaffa   Damascus   Kirkuk   Isfahan   Herat   Hindu Kush   Mt. Godwin Austin

CAIRO   Jerusalem   SYRIA   Euphrates   Baghdad   AFGHANISTAN   Peshawar   Himalayas

Amman   IRAQ   Basra   Abadan   Kabul   Islamabad   Lahore

Suez   Syrian Desert   Shiraz   Kerman   Kandahar   Sulaiman Range   Multan

Sinai   SAUDI   Kuwait   Persian Gulf   Quetta   Punjab

Port Said   Hail   BAHREIN   QATAR

Red Sea   Medina   Buraida   Dhahran

Jidda   Mecca   NEJD   Riyadh

SAUDI ARABIA

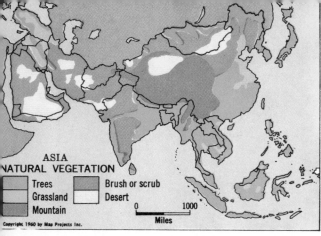

ASIA
NATURAL VEGETATION

- Trees
- Grassland
- Mountain
- Brush or scrub
- Desert

0   1000
Miles

Copyright 1960 by Map Projects Inc.

of South-East Asia it rains most of the year. These islands are covered with hot, tropical jungles. In some islands, where the jungle has been cleared, rubber, coffee, sugar, tea, and spices are grown.

Asia has both the highest mountains and the lowest depressions in the world. We have already seen that the continents of Asia and Europe belong to a single land mass which is sometimes called Eurasia. Asia alone measures about 18 million square miles, which is over a third of the earth's land surface. From north to south it stretches from a point within 5 degrees of the North Pole to 10 degrees south of the Equator, while from Cape Baba in Asia Minor to Cape Dezhnev on the Bering Strait it occupies 163 degrees of lontigude, which is nearly half the way round the world.

crowding in the towns than anywhere else in the world; while, in contrast, Central Asia is very bare and supports only the scantiest population.

In the islands of Japan farms extend high up the sides of mountains, for the population is so dense that every inch of soil must be used to produce food. Even so, not enough is produced.

On many of the innumerable islands

The glacier-gouged Karakoram Mountains in Central Asia contain some of the world's highest peaks.

K. Paffen

Many seas and oceans wash the vast coastline of Asia. To the north lies the cold Arctic Ocean. The Black Sea, the Mediterranean, and the Red Sea wash the south-western shores, while to the south lies the Indian Ocean, which in the north, divides into the Arabian Sea and the Bay of Bengal. To the east lies the Pacific, whose inshore branches are the South China Sea, the East China Sea, the Yellow Sea, and the Sea of Japan. Still further north is the Sea of Okhotsk and lastly, the Bering Sea.

The heart of Asia is a mass of great mountain ranges and high bleak plateaus. There are no fertile lowlands in Central Asia comparable to the Basins of the Mississippi, the Amazon, or the Congo. Central Asia is not only high, cold, and bleak, but it is very, very hard to reach. The mountain ranges and plateaus of Central Asia make up the largest mountainous area in the world. Together with the deserts that lie between many of them they make Central Asia an extremely inhospitable region for any outsiders to approach.

Aramco - Photo Researchers

Encroaching sand dunes threaten to cover this date-palm oasis in the deserts of Saudi Arabia.

Some of the world's greatest water systems have their sources in these mountains. Melting snows from the slopes of the Hindu Kush, the Pamirs, the Elburz, the Karakoram, the Altyn Tagh, the Tien Shan, and the Himalayas, pour downwards to form great rivers. Rising in the more northern mountains the Ob, the Yenisei, and Lena Rivers flow northwards to empty into the Arctic Ocean. Few people are able to live in the cold,

Wheat is raised on the treeless, hilly steppes of the Anatolian Plateau in Turkey.

H. Spreitzer

Courtesy of TWA - Trans World Airlines

Ceylon's warm, wet climate and rich soils favour rice cultivation.

Southern China has rugged terrain. Farms are crowded into the valleys between the craggy hills.

Van Bucher - Photo Researchers

Monsoon rains feed the waterways along which nine-tenths of Thailand's people live.

northern plains watered by these rivers. Other great rivers flow eastward and southward from these ranges. These are the Indus, the Ganges, the Irrawaddy, the Mekong, the Brahmaputra, the Salween, the Yangtze, and the Hwang Ho. Millions of Asians make their homes in the hot, fertile valleys through which these rivers flow on their way to the Indian Ocean or the Pacific. In Western Asia the Tigris and Euphrates rise in the highlands of Turkey and flow down into the Persian Gulf. Today, as in ancient times, this river system, provides water for irrigation.

Some of the rivers of Asia never reach the sea. Instead, flowing across hundreds of miles of steppes or desert they empty finally into salt swamps or into inland seas and lakes such as the Caspian Sea, Lake Balkhash, and the Aral Sea.

Tropical vegetation does well, bricks and mortar less well, in this village in Bengal.

140

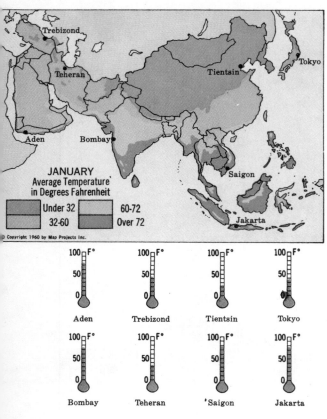

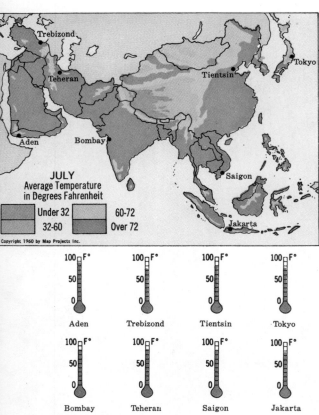

CLIMATE

Stretching as it does some 5,000 miles from the Arctic Ocean to the Equator, the continent is naturally affected by great extremes of climate. Asia contains some of the coldest and hottest, wettest and driest places in the world.

The enormous area of Central Asia is over a thousand miles from the nearest sea and surrounded by high mountain chains. The warm moist air from the sea has to pass over these, and in doing so becomes chilled and loses its moisture. The only winds that do not pass over heights come from the icy polar regions. The climate of this central region is thus a severe one: the winters long and cold, the summers, except on the plateaus, hot and short. There is little rainfall except in the mountains, so that much of the region is desert.

Northern Asia has much the same climate as Central Asia, except that it has more rainfall. Winters are extremely cold. Verkhoyansk, a village in Siberia, is the coldest inhabited place in the world, the temperature having once fallen to - 94° F.

In Southern Asia the climate is quite different. Here it is hot all the year round, except in the mountains. In the plains the temperature may reach as much as 125°F. Instead of summer and winter, there is merely a rainy season and a dry one.

The rainy season usually lasts from June to October, inclusive, and during that period it rains heavily every day. This region has the heaviest rainfall in the world. Some areas of India get more than 300 inches of rain during the wet season.

The rainy and dry seasons are caused by winds called monsoons, *monsoon* being a word of Arabic origin meaning season. The monsoons blow over all South and South-East Asia, which is sometimes called 'the monsoon region of the continent'. In winter, the monsoons blow from Central Asia towards the southern and eastern edges of the continent. Winter monsoons are dry because they blow from the land, and cold because they blow from the mountains. The summer monsoons blow inland from the sea, bringing moisture as far as they reach.

The monsoons that bring the rain are a vital factor in the lives of the millions of people living in Southern and Eastern Asia. With its coming they plant the crops on which their existence depends. Drought quickly brings people to the verge of starvation. Sometimes the monsoons are late, so that crops cannot be planted in time to ripen, sometimes the rains cause floods. In either case, the result is disastrous.

South-West Asia, is an extremely dry area, with long, very hot summers. Winters are relatively mild except in the highlands of Persia. In parts of South-West Asia, winter is the rainy season, and the season for crops — moisture being more important than temperature.

Climate largely determines the way people live. In northern Siberia, for instance, the almost permanently frozen soil makes any sort of farming impossible. Therefore people must depend for their living on hunting and fishing.

In Burma the climate is warm and rainfall is abundant. In the rainy seasons floods are frequent, so the people living near rivers build their houses on piles to raise them above flood level. The warm moist climate is ideal for growing rice, and rice-growing is the chief occupation.

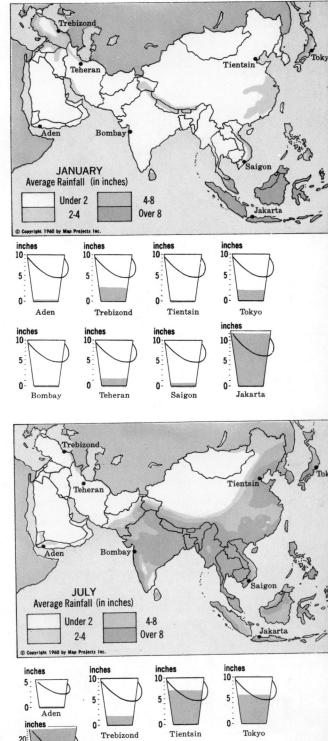

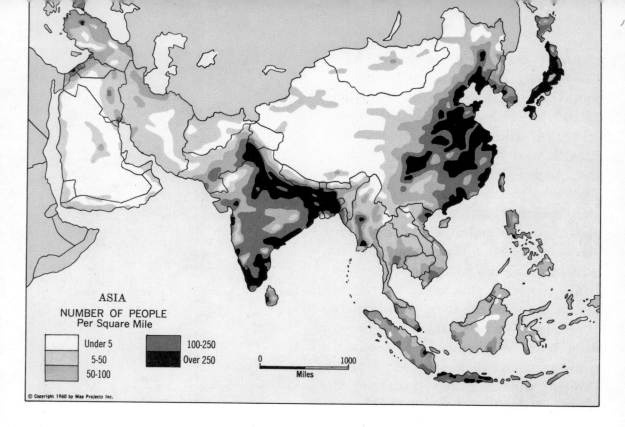

ASIA
NUMBER OF PEOPLE
Per Square Mile

Under 5		100-250
5-50		Over 250
50-100		

0   1000
Miles

PEOPLES OF ASIA

With all the other contrasts presented by Asia — contrasts of climate, landscape, animal and plant life — it is only to be expected that the continent would present us with a wide variety of people. In fact, almost every racial type known in the world can be found within Asia.

There is every variety of skin colour: white, yellow, brown, black, and every intermediate shade. Within each of the colour groups there is every type of figure and feature. Thousands of years of mixing between the racial groups has created every possible combination of physical characteristics.

Even more significant are the cultural differences between the various peoples of Asia. They differ in their habits and customs, their religions, their languages, their sense of values, their arts, and their degree of education. And these differences, like the physical ones, cut across the racial lines.

In South-Western Asia, for example, most of the people are Caucasian in origin, that is, theoretically white. Yet

Turbaned Afghan men in Kabul, the capital of Afganistan.

Maynard Williams - Shostal

These men are Jordanian Arabs. Arabs are the largest group of people in South-West Asia.

there are the greatest differences both in their appearance and the way they live. Arabs, Turks, Persians, Kurds, and Israelis, all speak different languages, dress differently, follow different religions, and obey different moral codes. The Turks, Persians, and most of the Arabs are Moslems. Some of the Arabs are Christians, the Israelis are Jews. Within each religion there are many sects. Even when there is a common language, as with the Arabs, there are great differences between the desert nomads, who are shepherds, the settled farmers of the more fertile regions, and the townsmen.

There are still much wider differences

With great toil the people of Israel have turned barren desert into flourishing farmland.

A. L. Goldman - Rapho Guillumette

An Arab rug merchant squats by his wares in the market-place of Kuwait on the Persian Gulf.

J. P. Charbonnier - Photo Researchers

between the people of Southern Asia. In India alone fourteen major languages are spoken, and if every different dialect is counted the number rises to 845. In religion most Indians are Hindus, but there are also Moslems, Sikhs, Jains, Buddhists, Christians, Parsees, and others. Such cultural differences are carried on by tradition — local customs being handed down from generation to generation.

Yet another reason is the influence of surroundings: the climate, the landscape, the nature of the soil, and the natural resources. It is obvious that people who live in cold dry prairies or deserts, as the Mongolians do, will live differently from those in a wet, tropical island like Java.

The broad rolling grasslands of Mongolia are ideal for herding livestock. To follow their herds and live on the meat and milk they produce is the traditional way of life of the Mongolians. The people of Java can stay in the same place and raise good crops on their fertile soil. They have solved the problem of growing crops in mountains by building terraces.

But Java is very crowded, and there is barely enough land to grow food for all the people and fodder for all the animals. The Javanese live chiefly on rice, they get most of their protein from fish.

Israel, to which large numbers of Jews from all over the world have returned, was formerly a land of deserts or swamps.

Hindu pilgrims bathe in the Ganges River at Benares in order to acquire spiritual merit.

Valentina Rosen

Ed Lettau - Shostal

A Pakistani snake-charmer practises his traditional, and dangerous, art.

The Philippine government is trying to put education within the reach of all children.

Harrison Forman - Shostal

The Philippine government is trying to put education within the reach of all children.

Great efforts have been made to drain the swamps and irrigate the deserts, so that food can be produced for the settlers on the land and for those who are now creating industries.

Because the distances in Asia are so great, and the facilities for travel so limited, communities have tended to develop in isolation, with the result that each area developed a language or dialect of its own. Often two dialects of the same language are so different that the people who speak the one are unable to understand the other. A Chinese from Canton, for example, may not be able to understand his countryman, even though he comes from a village only fifty miles away.

The fact that so many Asian people speak different dialects or languages from their neighbours has created many difficulties for their governments. In an

George Holton - Photo Library

Tibetan porters can carry loads of more than 300 lbs on their backs over country far too steep for any animals.

An old lady of Peking tends her young grandchild. In China, 55,000 babies are born every day.

The face of this Chinese engineer reflects his country's determination to advance industrially.

attempt to overcome this problem some countries have chosen one dialect or language to be the official one. In China, for example, the Mandarin dialect is taught to all schoolchildren. In the Philippines, where the people speak various Malay dialects, the official one is Tagalog.

Daily life in Asia is deeply affected by religion, both by its commandments and by its general influence on the outlook of the people. For instance, Hindus, because they hold the cow sacred, are forbidden to eat beef or injure cattle in any way. Some Hindus will not eat any kind of meat nor kill any living creature, even if it be a harmful one.

Asia is the great breeding ground of religions. The two great religions born in the heart of Asia are Hinduism and Buddhism. Hinduism is the religious and social system adopted by the majority of the inhabitants of India. Formerly it was chiefly responsible for the division of Indian society into castes though, in fact, the caste system is not a fundamental part of the Hindu religion. It was forbidden for Hindus to marry outside their own religious caste. Their caste also prescribed the sort of work they did, the food they might eat, and the clothes they could wear. The caste system was abolished in the Constitution of 1950.

Unlike other great religions like Chris-

This Mongol woman's ancestors once ruled a mighty empire that covered most of Asia.

tianity, Islam, or Buddhism, the Hindu religion did not have any one founder. It gradually grew over a period of 5,000 years, absorbing and assimilating all the religious and cultural movements of India. As a result there is no one great holy book like the Bible or the Koran. Hinduism, the oldest of the world's great religions, has influenced and in turn been influenced by many differing beliefs during its history — Buddhism being the most important. To many people Hinduism seems to involve the worship of literally thousands of different gods and goddesses, but, in fact, Hindus regard these as just different names for the same all-embracing God.

Buddhism has the greatest number of followers of any of the world's religions. Its founder was Gautama, the Buddha, who was born in India in 536 B.C. From India Buddhism has spread, in various forms, to Tibet, China, Japan, Ceylon, and South-East Asia.

Buddhism originally grew out of Hinduism, and there is quite a large degree of similarity between them. The other great influence on Buddhism was the Taoist doctrines which came from China, though these have had the greatest influence on Japanese Buddhism.

Another group of religions arose in the south-western fringes of Asia. Christianity, an offshoot of Judaism, was born in Palestine. It spread from there to Greece and Rome and to the whole of Europe and to all the New World. Mohammedanism, or Islam, was started by an Arab prophet, Mohammed, in the seventh century, but its original stock was of much the same origin as Judaism and Christianity. In all these three religions, Adam was the first man, and

Ewing Krainin - Photo Researchers

This Javanese man's red fez shows that he is a Moslem, as are nine out of ten Indonesians.

the Koran (the Bible of Islam) in many respects overlaps the Old Testament. Following the Arab conquests, Islam spread right across North Africa, while

Ernst A. Heiniger

A Japanese father gives his child a lesson in the tricky technique of handling chopsticks.

An early morning market scene in the north of Laos.

Smiling Malayan children lead a carefree life.

in Asia it spread to Syria, Arabia, Iraq, Turkey, Iran, Afghanistan, Turkestan, and what is now Pakistan. It even reached the East Indies.

Until the communists came to power in China, most of the Chinese worshipped the spirits of their ancestors. This led them to feel great reverence for the past and for traditional ways of doing things, and often made them unwilling to adopt

A straw coolie hat shields this Vietnamese girl from the sun.

newer and more advanced methods.

Mankind has lived in Asia from a very early period. Some of the oldest known fossils of prehistoric man have been found on the island of Java, in the East Indies, and near Peking in Northern China. The world's oldest civilisations are those of Asia. Chinese civilisation is nearly 5,000 years old, that of India almost as old.

Anthropologists, whose business it is to study mankind, tell us that the oldest civilisation of all, and the source of all other civilisations, was located in the region called Mesopotamia, which lies between the Tigris and the Euphrates, the two great rivers of South-West Asia.

Asia has greatly influenced the nations of the West, its greatest influence being, of course, religious. Nowadays we tend to think of Asia as being rather a backward area. But it was not always so. The great civilisations of Asia — particularly China and India — were highly developed while Europe was still primitive and barbaric. It was from Sanskrit,

Herbert Knapp

This saffron-robed Thai youth is a Buddhist monk.

Jack Scheerboom

The Hindu-festival 'Under Red Curtains'.

the classical language of India, that Greek, Latin, and in fact most of the languages of Europe were evolved. Many inventions of great importance such as paper-making, printing, and gun-powder have come from China. The scientific knowledge of the Greeks and Romans was preserved for hundreds of years during the Dark Ages by Arab scholars. Incidentally, it was a search for a sea route to the spice markets of India that led Columbus to discover America.

Michel Serraillier - Rapho Guilluinette

A Kashmiri merchant serves his customers.

Jack Scheerboom

A tea-ceremony in Japan.

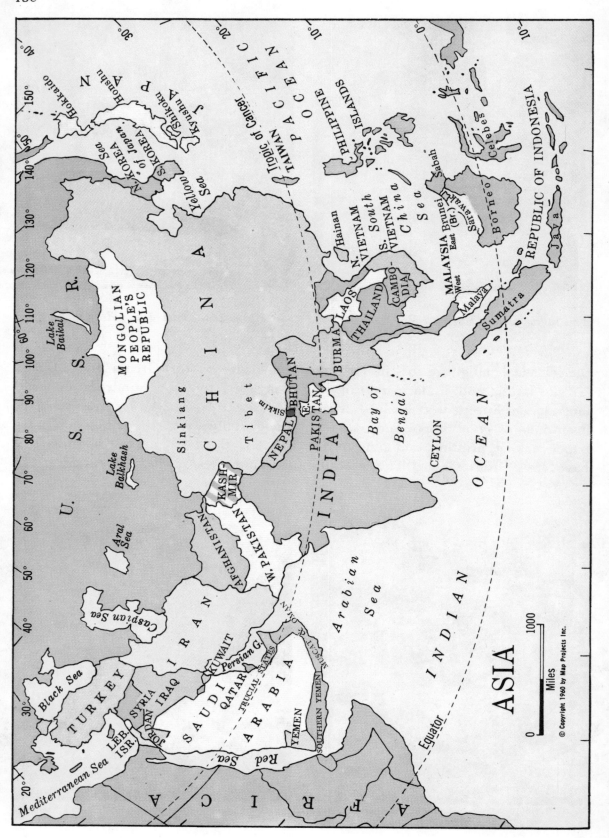

ASIA

© Copyright 1960 by Map Projects Inc.

Miles

0   1000

COMMUNICATIONS

There are more than thirty countries in Asia today. The names and forms of government of many have changed since 1945. Some, like Israel, did not exist and others were under colonial rule.

In Western Europe it is easy to get quickly from one place to another over long distances because of the abundance of good roads, railways, and air services. In Asia travel is altogether different. In many places high mountains, plateaus, deserts, and jungles make it extremely difficult, if not impossible, to build roads or railways. Even where technically possible, the great distances involved make it very expensive.

In Asia there are few international railways. Millions of Asiatics have never seen, let alone travelled on, a train.

There are exceptions. In India the British built a fairly extensive and efficient railway system. And Japanese railways are among the most modern in the world.

For the most part, serviceable roads are even rarer than railways in Asia. This situation is changing, but changing slowly, and progress is inevitably uneven. Sometimes roads have been built where not even a track existed before. But enormous areas of Asia are very thinly populated, and there is little use in spending an enormous amount of money, time, and labour building a road nobody will use.

Fortunately, there has been a rapid development of air services in recent years. Several major airlines link Asia with Europe and America. There are now important airports at Tokyo, Hong Kong, Singapore, Manila, Bombay, Calcutta, Rangoon, and Ankara. And the Chinese

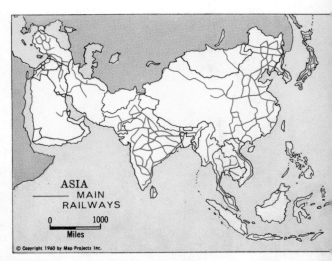

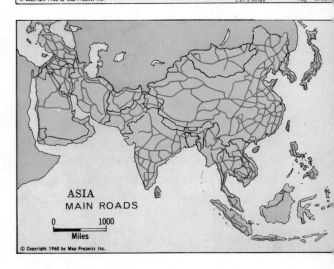

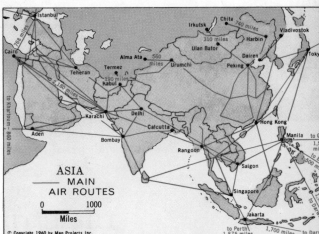

are developing air services to the immense central area of Asia, which is the part of the continent that is most lacking in communications.

TWA - Trans World Airlines

Bombay, India's second largest city, is a bustling, modern metropolis.

THE CITIES OF ASIA

The cities of Asia, like the landscape, climate, and people, vary very widely. Some are more than 1,000 years old, and their older quarters have remained unchanged through the centuries. Others contain the most modern buildings. Many European and American firms, besides those from the country concerned, have offices in these rapidly developing towns. And often, today, they are crowded with visitors from abroad.

Tokyo, the capital of Japan, is the largest city in the world. Besides being a great cultural and political centre, it is a great industrial one, whose exports are shipped to all the world from its great port, Yokohama, on the other side of Tokyo Bay. Industries include shipbuilding, textiles, and the manufacture of motor-cars, toys, cameras, optical goods, etc. Many airlines run services to Tokyo and thousands of tourists go there every year, particularly during the cherry-blossom season.

Peking, the capital of the Chinese People's Republic, is one of the oldest cities of China. Its main industries produce steel, machinery, and textiles.

Shanghai is the largest town and seaport in China. It stands on a small river which discharges at the seaward end of the estuary of the Yangtze Kiang, and, as a port, it serves the millions of Chinese in the farms, villages, and towns of the crowded Yangtze Valley. At the beginning of this century it was entirely dominated by the offices, warehouses, and banks, of the great European trading and finance companies. Now all that has been swept away. Shanghai has the largest textile industry in China, and its other industries include shipbuilding, machinery, and food-processing.

Tientsin is another important Chinese port. Lying some seventy miles southeast of Peking, it is the commercial centre of north China. As a manufacturing town it is second only to Shanghai in the production of textiles. As a great railway centre it is the gateway to the inland region including the Chinese capital.

Shenyang (formerly called Mukden) is the chief town of Manchuria. It is one of the important manufacturing towns of China. Coal and iron are found in the vicinity, and supply the raw material for a number of industries, amongst which is the manufacture of motor-cars.

Hong Kong is a British Crown Colony on a small island off the coast of China. It is one of the busiest towns in the world. Ships from all over the world use its fine deep-water harbour. The mainland of China is only a mile away, and ferries daily bring thousands of people over to work in Hong Kong. Hong Kong lives on foreign trade. But there are many related activities such as insurance, banking, warehousing, and ship-repair.

Calcutta is India's second largest town. Situated on the Ganges Delta, about eighty miles inland from the Bay of Bengal, it is a leading manufacturing centre and the most important town on the east coast of India. One of its chief products is hessian, which is a coarse canvas made from the jute grown in the

Wendy Hilty - Monkmeyer

Minarets tower over Bagdad, capital of Iraq and formerly of a great empire.

Hamilton Wright Organization Inc.

Hong Kong has modern office buildings and residences, but many poor live in slums.

neighbourhood. But many other products including tea, coffee, rubber, cotton, and hemp are shipped from Calcutta.

Bombay is on the west coast of India. The largest town of India, it is situated on an island a short distance from the mainland, with which it is connected by bridges. Bombay has one of the finest harbours in the world. It became an important cotton centre during the American Civil War, when England was unable to get cotton from the Southern States of America. It is now the leading town in India for the manufacture of cotton stuffs. With the opening of the Suez Canal, Bombay became the nearest Indian port to Europe, and its importance has grown steadily.

Karachi, former capital of Pakistan, has grown rapidly, and now has a population of 2.7 million. Its enormous airport is of great importance, for through it pass the main routes from Europe to India, the Far East, and Australia. Karachi is also a thriving port whose most im-

Ray Halin - Shostal

Saigon, the capital of South Vietnam, shows both European and Oriental styles.

portant exports are wheat and cotton. Islamabad is now Pakistan's official capital.

Singapore lies at the southern tip of the Malay peninsula. It is the world's fourth largest port, whose principal exports are rubber and tin. Trade is done with Great Britain and the Commonwealth and the United States, on one hand, and with Indonesia and South-East Asia on the other. Singapore is now a fully independent island nation within the Commonwealth, and its great port thrives

Ewing Krainin - Alpha

The bright lights of the centre of Tokyo. Tokyo is the second largest city in the world.

Van Bucher - Photo Researchers

The streets of Jakarta, capital of Indonesia, are filled with busy traffic of all kinds.

commercially and as a British base.

Jakarta, a seaport on the north coast of Java, is the capital of the Republic of Indonesia and its largest town. The name Jakarta means 'important city'. During the Dutch rule of the East Indies it was called Batavia. The products of the Indonesian islands are shipped all over the world from Jakarta.

Manila is the largest and most important town in the Philippine Islands. In addition to Filipinos, the population includes large numbers of Chinese, who have settled there and become naturalised. There are also quite a number of people of Spanish extraction, for the islands were ruled by Spain until the Spanish-American War of 1898. The leading exports are copra, sugar, timber, rope, and coconut oil. Iron and chrome and precious metals are mined.

Baghdad, the capital of Iraq, stands on the Tigris river, 350 miles north of the Persian Gulf. It was once the chief town of the caravan route from Europe

Paul Hufner - Shostal

Small barges transport much of the merchandise handled in Shanghai's busy harbour.

to the Far East. The discovery of oil in Iraq has made Baghdad a town of great activity. It has a population of 1,745,000. The old part of the town lies on the right bank of the Tigris, while the modern avenues are on the left bank.

John Strohm

The Palace of Rest and Culture in Peking. Many former palaces are now used as places of recreation.

Ray Halin - Shostal

Manila's location on a protected bay has helped it become one of the Orient's great ports.

SOUTH-WEST ASIA

The most important difference between the Middle East on the one hand, and Southern and South-East Asia on the other, is the climate. Although part of the Middle East (the extreme south-west) is influenced by the monsoons, the bulk of the area has a Mediterranean climate, with dry summers and even a permanent drought in some areas, causing large expanses of desert. The greater part of the Arabian peninsula, Iraq, Syria, and Jordan, receives less than 10 inches a year. Only in the Yemen, in the south-west corner of the peninsula, is rainfall more abundant (20 inches), due to the monsoon which strikes the mountains there.

Iran and Afganistan, shielded by mountains both from the monsoon and Mediterranean air currents, are semi-deserts and life is largely confined to the oases.

Rainfall is much greater in the coastal regions of the Mediterranean and the mountains behind them. Jerusalem gets 25 inches a year, Beirut 36 inches. It is much the same on the coast of Asia Minor, Izmir (Smyrna) receiving 20 inches, while Trebizond, on the Black Sea, has 36 inches. However, in these regions irrigation is often necessary in summer as the soil becomes very parched. On the Black Sea coast, although most of the rain falls in winter, meterological conditions are more complex, and summer rain occurs also.

Because of these conditions the population is very unevenly spread. The people are largely concentrated in the more humid coastal areas. Iran has a population of about 25.7 million. The two

Shepherds still water their flocks at the wells of Jericho, as they did in Biblical times.

great sallt deserts of Dasht-i-Kavir and Dasht-i-Lut are almost completely uninhabited. Although Turkey in Asia has a fairly good climate, its average population density is only 88 to the square mile.

South-Western Asia is occupied principally by three great races: the Persians or Iranians, the Arabs, and the Turks, united by a common religion, Islam, which originated among the Arabs.

Besides these three races there are a few small minorities that must be mentioned. The Kurds of Iraq, numbering no more than 1 million, are one of the most ancient peoples of Asia Minor, speaking an Indo-European language. Israel is peopled by Jewish colonists and refugees from many countries, but particularly from Central Europe and the Middle East. The Maronites of the Lebanon are a religious group rather than a racial one, being one of the Christian communities left in the wake of the Crusaders which have managed to survive in spite of all since the Middle Ages.

The disruption of the Ottoman Empire after the Turkish defeat in the First World War, left the map of the Middle East much as it is today, and was shortly followed by an event of the utmost economic importance: the discovery of oil. The oilfields of South-West Asia lie in what were the most poverty-stricken areas of this part of the world, areas which

A Turkish woman gathers rose petals, the essence of which will be extracted for perfume.

A Syrian village clings to the side of an eroded mountain for protection against raiders.

Primitive methods of harvesting characterise most agriculture in South-West Asia.

suddenly discovered there was a fortune beneath their feet.

Turkey covers a total area of 300,000 square miles of which all but 9,000 are in Asia.

Asia Minor is extremely mountainous.

Israel's farmers use modern machinery, when the wheat crop is being harvested.

It consists of a central plateau averaging over 3,000 feet in height. Of its lakes, many of which are salt, the largest is Lake Tuz, south of Ankara. To the south and east of Lake Tuz are the Taurus Mountains, including Asia Minor's highest peak, Mount Ararat, 16,945 feet high. The plateau is fringed on the north by a range of mountains sometimes called the Anti-Taurus. They are only high in the east, near the Georgian frontier, where they rise to a height of over 12,000 feet. There are deltaic plains along the Black Sea, the most important of which belongs to the low valley of the Sakarya, to the east of the Sea of Marmara. Two famous rivers, the Tigris and Euphrates, rise in the mountains of eastern Turkey.

Turkey has about 33.3 million inhabitants. Agriculture is the chief occupation of the country, employing over 70 per cent of the total population. For the most part land is divided into small-holdings. In recent years a large-scale effort has been made to launch irrigation schemes and arrest the exhaustion of the soil. Modern methods of farming and stock-breeding have also been introduced, and seem to have given excellent results. The agricultural produce of Turkey is very varied; wheat and barley, rice and cotton, tobacco and tea, olives, and linseed and other oil seeds.

Large crops of olives are obtained in western and southern Anatolia. Turkey is one of the world's greatest producers of raisins, and a large quantity of dried figs is also exported. The production of fresh fruit and nuts is abundant.

In recent years industry has thrived. Deposits of bituminous coal, lignite, oil, iron, chromium, bauxite, manganese, and sulphur are being exploited. There are industries for the production of sulphuric acid, cement, cotton goods, and paper. Sugar, tobacco, etc., are processed.

Starting south of Iskenderun, a mountain range runs along the coast from Turkey through Syria, Lebanon, Israel,

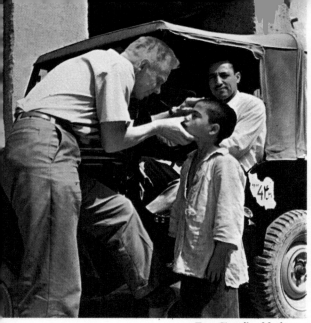

Tony Chapelle - Monkmeyer

Doctors from all over the world help in the fight against disease in the Middle East.

and Jordan. Its greatest height, Dhor-el-Khodib, is a little over 10,000 feet. South of Tyre, the mountains move back from the coast leaving room for several coastal plains, including the famous Plain of Sharon. East of the mountains is the long depression which contains Lake Tiberias, the River Jordan, and the Dead Sea. Further east is another mountain range which joins the coastal range south of the Dead Sea and with it runs down to the Gulf of Aqaba.

The Republic of Lebanon is only about 4,000 square miles in area with 2,179,000 Arabic-speaking inhabitants, a small majority of whom are Christians.

Agriculture is the chief occupation, though cultivation is limited by the mountainous nature of the country and by soil erosion. The chief products are wheat, maize, barley, olives, potatoes, sugarbeet, tobacco and fruit — particularly grapes and citrus fruits. Except for food-processing and petrol refining, there is very little industry, owing to the lack of raw materials. Oil from Iraq and Saudi Arabia is refined at Tripoli and Saida (Sidon).

Israel has an area of about 8,000 square miles and was cut out of Palestine to make a national home for the Jews. Since 1948 more than a million Jews have emigrated to Israel. It includes the Negev, an arid area running as far as the Gulf of Aqaba, giving the Israelis an outlet to the Red Sea. The Negev represents more than half the total area of Israel. Since 1967, Israel has been engaged in an on-going war with neighbouring Arab countries.

Economic development is handicapped

Israeli schoolchildren learn about farming in the fields of their kibbutz.

Jerry Cooke - Photo Researchers

Jaffa oranges and grapefruit are among the chief exports of Israel.

Jerry Cooke - Photo Researchers

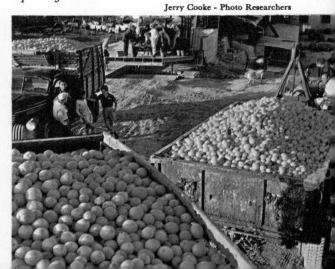

The Euphrates River supplies water for irrigation, as shown in this Syrian cottonfield.

Mechanised farming is little known in Asia. Animals are the chief source of power.

by an adverse balance of trade. The principal unit of agriculture is the collective farm or *kibbutz*. But there is also the *mofhav* (co-operative) and some private farms. There is extensive use of irrigation. To provide energy fuel has to be bought from abroad, and as the Suez Canal is closed to Israel, a port has been built at Eilat, on the Gulf of Aqaba. Oil imported there is piped via Beersheba to Tel Aviv. From Beersheba, a railway runs up to Lod (Lydda) and on to Tel Aviv. The Negev is rich in minerals, and chemicals are manufactured from the

Dates are an important source of food in South-East Asia. They are also a valuable export.

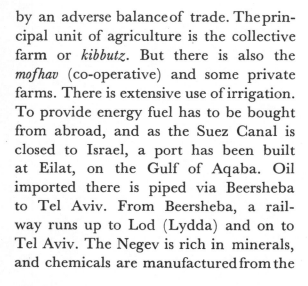

salts found in the water of the Dead Sea. Other industries are concerned with food-processing. Tel Aviv was founded in 1909 by Zionists. Together with Jaffa, it had a population of 388,000 in 1968. Haifa comes next with 210,000 inhabitants. Jerusalem was divided into two parts, one part belonging to Jordan, the other to Israel, until the Israelis took over the whole of the city by force in 1967. Jerusalem is the capital of Israel, with about 332,300 inhabitants. Jerusalem is regarded as a sacred city alike by Christians, Jews, and Moslems.

The total area of the Hashemite Kingdom of Jordan is 37,000 square miles. But of this only 5,000 square miles in the west is really habitable, the remainder being largely desert. The population in 1966 was 2,100,800, consisting of farmers in the western part of the country, semi-nomads in the western sectors of the plateaus, and complete nomads living entirely on their herds. What little industry there is is limited to food-processing. Except for phosphates and potash, no mineral wealth has been discovered in the country, though it has not yet been thoroughly prospected.

Amman, with 330,000 inhabitants, is

Kurd nomads wander the mountains of the Iran-Iraq border, seeking grass and water.

This Jordanian goat-herd keeps a protective eye on his herd as it crosses the desert.

about twenty miles east of the Jordan. The only other towns of any importance lie west of the Jordan. Besides part of Jerusalem, they include Nablus, Jericho, and Hebron.

Iraq has an area of over 170,000 square miles. Nearly half of it, lying west of the Euphrates, is part of the Syrian Desert. The Tigris and Euphrates together form a great river basin, a good deal of which is marshy. Where they flow into the Persian Gulf, a great delta has been formed which is divided between Iran, Iraq, and the small state of Kuwait. In the north-east is a range of mountains along the Turkish and Persian frontiers which, from a height of 2,000 to 6,000 feet, is covered with forests of oaks. This area and the upper Tigris basin are the only regions with an adequate rainfall.

Agriculture depends, as it always has, on irrigation. The Tigris and Euphrates each have two seasons of spate a year. They rise with the winter rains and again when the snows melt in their upper reaches in spring. There are two harvests a year: autumn-sown wheat and barley; and maize, millet, rice, sesame, and cotton sown in the spring. Moreover Iraq is the greatest date-producing country of the world. Other agricultural produce includes oranges, vegetables of all sorts, and leguminous plants.

The country is backward in industry, although factories are being established with Soviet aid. Manufactures include textiles, both cotton and wool, shoes and leather goods, and food-processing. There are deposits of various metals — iron, copper, etc. — but prospecting has hardly started. Since 1927 oil has been the great source of wealth. The wells are at Kirkuk, Khanaqin, and near Basra.

Jerusalem, sacred to three religions, spreads out below the Mount of Olives.

Because of physical conditions, Syria is an even poorer country. Except for the coastal plains and one or two other fertile areas, most of Syria consists of either mountains or deserts.

Agriculture is chiefly concentrated in the coastal plains. Receiving a fair amount of rain, they produce wheat, barley, grapes, and other fruit. There is also a certain amount of fertile volcanic soil in the Jebel Druse and Hauran areas immediately north of the Jordan frontier, and at the foot of the mountains there is a series of oases bordering the desert. The finest of these is that of Damascus, which owes its fertility to the waters of a small river coming down from the mountains. Besides growing cereal crops in considerable quantities, Syria is able to export cotton and wool. Sheep are kept largely for the sake of their wool.

Under government supervision, industry has made considerable progress since 1930. Textiles are manufactured of cotton, wool, silk, and rayon. There is also a certain amount of food-processing and

As they have done since Biblical days, fishermen still fish the Sea of Galilee (Lake Tiberias).

Philip D. Gendreau

Shrines dot the Mount of Olives, where Jesus kept vigil in the Garden of Gethsemane.

manufacture of leather goods. Damascus still pursues her ancient manufacture of damascene jewellery (inlaid gold and silver work), and woven damask with figured designs in light and shade. The country has only small deposits of minerals, and so far no oil has been found, though there is natural gas in the Jezirah.

The great square-cut Arabian peninsula, with an area of a million square miles, consists of a vast plateau sloping gradually down from a line of mountains along the Red Sea coast towards the Persian Gulf and the Gulf of Oman. The mountains, which average some 5,000 feet in height, rise in the Yemen to over 12,000 feet. The only other mountains of any importance run along the coast of the Gulf of Oman, reaching nearly 10,000 feet in the Jabal Akhdar.

Most of this area is extremely dry. The only part to receive a fairly adequate rainfall consists of the Yemen and the Hadhramaut, the latter being a coastal strip running half-way along the south coast, traditionally famous as a land of

Aramco - Photo Researchers

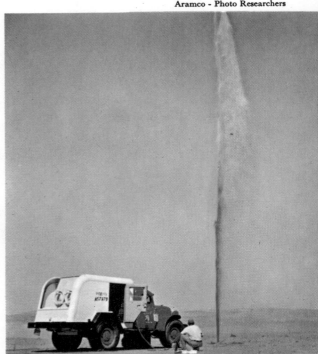

Geologists explore for oil in Saudi Arabia. Echoes from explosions help them to locate deposits.

A pipeline to a prospective oil well stretches through the desert. Oil is piped from the fields to the Mediterranean for shipment to other countries.

prosperity. Another prosperous region is along the coastal plain at the foot of the mountains in the Batina district of Oman. Inside these areas a region of dry steppes runs all round the peninsula, particularly in the Hejaz, in the west, and in the Syrian Desert, which extends into Iraq,

The ungainly camel is familiar in all desert areas — even those occupied by oil wells.

John Strohm

Jordan, and Syria. The real desert is in the stony central part of Nejd, and in the sandy desert to the east and south-east.

On both steppe and desert, life is concentrated in the oases, some of which are thriving, particularly those of the Hejaz and the Hasa on the northern half of the Persian Gulf.

The kingdom of Saudi Arabia is the dominant power of the Arabian peninsula, not because of its population, which is no more than about 7 million, but because of its enormous area of 770,000 square miles, and because, in the west (the Hejaz), it includes the Moslem holy places — Jidda, Medina, and above all Mecca — which give Saudi Arabia a certain moral authority. The country derives a handsome income from the oil extracted in the Hasa.

Kuwait, which has a common frontier with Iraq, enjoyed British protection from 1899 to 1961, when Britain recognised its independence. The sheikhdom is prosperous and its port, which bears the same name, and which lies on a sheltered bay, has long been a thriving market, exporting the products of the hinterland: horses, sheep, and wool. When oil was added to the list, the wealth of the country soared. Production is now more than 100 million tons a year. The town of Kuwait now has a population of about 295,000. Recently the only terminal in the world fully capable of loading the new mammoth tankers came into use on an island off the Kuwait coast.

Bahrein has a population of 143,000. It was once famous for pearl fishing, but the industry has declined in recent years. On the other hand the soil is rich and agriculture prosperous. Oil was discovered in 1932 and since then Bahrein has become one of the world's richest oil-producing countries.

The area to the east and south-east is divided into two sections. The larger one is the Sultanate of Muscat and Oman, with an area of about 82,000 square miles. The other, the Trucial States, formerly called the Pirate Coast, is on the Persian Gulf. It consists now of seven sheikhdoms. The Sultanate has a population of 750,000. Agriculture flourishes in the coastal plains and in the oases of the interior, and produce is considerable. Another resource is fishing, and trade is carried on with India. The capital is Muscat, which has lost much of its trade to the neighbouring town of Matrah. Oil production began in 1967. The Trucial States area takes its name from a truce established in 1853 between the recognised ruling sheikhs.

The Southern Yemen People's Republic has a population of about 1½ million, divided into a number of governments and native sultanates, one of the most important being that of Hadhramaut.

The town of Aden, with about 250,000 inhabitants, is an immense warehouse and trading centre for south-west Arabia. It is also an industrial centre and a fuelling and victualling station for ships. Since 1945 it has had an oil refinery. Its airport is one of the most important halts on the route to the East. The capital of Southern Yemen is Madinet al-Shaab.

In Yemen the soil is fertile on the coastal plains and in the mountain valleys. Commercial crops are cotton, coffee, tobacco, grapes and qat, a narcotic shrub. The capital is Sana, a town of 100,000 inhabitants, standing in the mountains at a height of 7,500 feet. From it a road runs down to Hodeida, the principal port, while another runs down to the more southerly port of Mocha, which gives its name to a famous variety of coffee. It has been estimated that the total capacity of the oil wells of Saudi Arabia together with those of Kuwait and Bahrein constitute 30 or 40 per cent of the oil reserves so far discovered in the world.

The kingdom of Iran, a country with an area of 630,000 square miles, is, like Afghanistan, much more truly part of the

An up-to-date oil refinery at Abadan (left). Oil is very important to the Iranian economy. (right) A crew of Arab workmen laying an asphalt road across the Arabian desert.

Iranian Oil Participants Ltd.　　　　　　　　　　　　　　　Aramco - Photo Researchers

continent of Asia than the countries we have been dealing with. Lying between the Caspian Sea and the Persian Gulf, it consists of a central plateau surrounded by high mountains. The most important of these are the Zagros Mountains in the west and south-west and the Elburz Mountains in the north, whose highest peak is Demavend, 18,900 feet. In the east, the Iranian plateau is separated from Afghanistan and Pakistan by the heights of Khurasan and Baluchistan.

The climate is characterised by sharp contrasts of heat and cold, severe snowy winters being followed by hot, dry summers. Grazing on the plateaus is poor. In the Azerbaijan region of the Zagros Mountains fertile basins alternate with great mountain blocks. These basins, particularly that of Lake Urmia, provide excellent arable land giving a high yield of wheat and barley, or, on some parts, cotton.

Of the country's 25.7 million inhab-itants, 70 per cent live on the land. Large quantities of wheat are grown, as well as other cereals, such as barley and rice. Sufficient rice is grown to provide a surplus, which is exported to Oman. Fruit is grown in great variety, and considerable amounts are exported. Sugar-beet, tobacco and tea are now being grown. Of industrial crops, cotton is much the most important, about 80,000 tons a year being produced. The only important industry is the manufacture of textiles. Persian rugs, and carpets, the most famous produce of the country, are still being made by hand in the traditional way in the neighbourhood of Tabriz, Hamadan, Sultanabad, Kashan, Shiraz, and Kerman. In spite of a decline in world demand, they still form one of the country's leading exports.

The country's chief source of wealth, however, is oil, found at the northern end of the Persian Gulf, and refined at Abadan. Production is more than 130

This neat community at Dhahran, Saudi Arabia, houses the employees of a large oil company.

Courtesy of TWA - Trans World Airlines

million tons. No other export bears any comparison with that of oil.

Tucked away between Iran, Pakistan, and the south-western corner of Siberia, Afganistan is a completely inland country, covering an area of some 250,000 square miles. It is a very mountainous country, and the frontiers are, to a considerable extent, formed by mountains. But in the extreme north the frontier with Siberia follows the course of the Amu Darya (Oxus). On the Pakistan frontier is the famous Kojak Pass on the route from Kandahar to Quetta, and the still more famous Khyber Pass on the route from Kabul to Peshawar. The spine of the country is the Hindu Kush.

In a country so mountainous and so far from the sea, great varieties of temperature are only to be expected. At Kandahar, in the south, for instance, it varies from a maximum of 110°F. in summer, to a minimum of 14°F. in winter. Rain falls mainly between December and April. What rain there is in summer is confined to occasional monsoon storms.

A recent estimate gives the population as around 16 million, all Moslems.

Except for soldiering, the only occupation of the people is agriculture. Some Afghans are settled, living in village communities in the valleys and the lower foothills of the mountains. Crops consist of wheat, barley, maize, millet, fodder crops, sugar-beet, sugar-cane, rice, cotton, and a wide range of fruits. Still more Afghans are nomads, shifting their tents from the lower plains frequented in winter to the higher grazing grounds in summer. They breed horses, donkeys, camels, and, most of all, Karakul sheep, which go to export as 'Persian' lambskins.

Industry is in its infancy. There is a certain amount of weaving of cotton and wool, and some leather-working and food processing. Mineral deposits are rarely exploited, with the exception of the coal in the Hindu Kush. Some oil has been found in the northern region, and natural gas is piped to the U.S.S.R.

John Strohm

Iranian children start their study of foreign languages at a very early age.

Child labour is common in the Near East. This Iranian girl strings tobacco for drying.

Davis Pratt - Rapho Guillumette

Houseboats are a familiar sight in Kashmir, a fertile land of many beautiful lakes.

The Himalayas, the world's highest mountains, form the boundary between India and Tibet.

SOUTHERN ASIA

The peninsular part of India, the Deccan, consists of ancient plateaus joined on to the main body of Asia by plains formed long ago by two great rivers. These are: in the west, the Indus which has a length of 1,900 miles; in the east, the Ganges, with a length of 1,560 miles. The latter joins the Brahmaputra, and the united rivers form an immense delta occupying the greater part of the province of Bengal — a very fertile area, but greatly overpopulated. The ridges of the Deccan are called *ghats*. The two main ridges, called the Western Ghats and the Eastern Ghats, look down on the Arabian Sea and the Bay of Bengal respectively. North of the plain is a hilly region, and north of that again the great barrier of the Himalayas. This, the greatest mountain range in the world, has formidable glaciers. In their long course of fifty miles and more, these

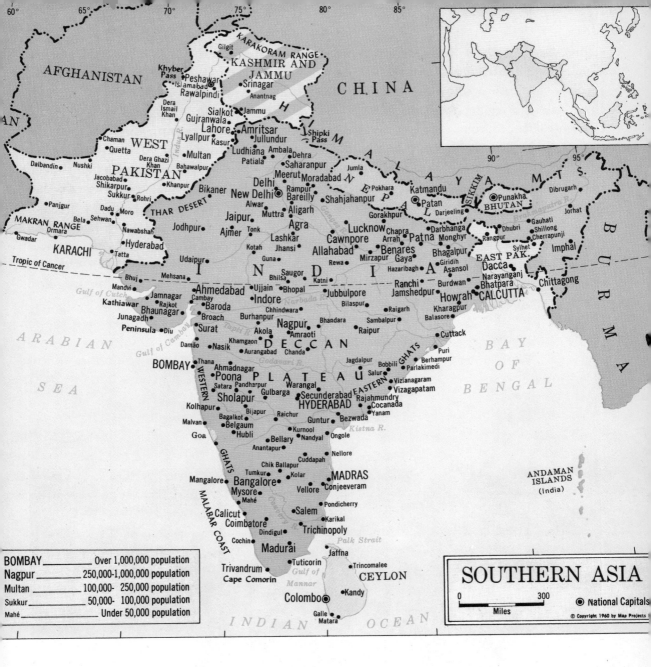

SOUTHERN ASIA

0   300
Miles

◉ National Capitals

© Copyright 1960 by Map Projects

BOMBAY	Over 1,000,000 population
Nagpur	250,000-1,000,000 population
Multan	100,000- 250,000 population
Sukkur	50,000- 100,000 population
Mahé	Under 50,000 population

glaciers, like rivers, receive tributaries. The lower Himalayan slopes are forested. In depressions are the mountain states of Kashmir, Nepal, and Bhutan. Sheltered by the high mountains, these states have a prosperous agriculture.

In the Near and Middle East, the climate is similar to that of the Mediterranean countries, while India and South-East Asia are dominated by the monsoons. Here, unlike the Mediterranean area, winter is the dry season, because then the Asiatic continent is the centre of a high-pressure zone, and winds blow outwards towards the sea. In summer the pressure over the southern part of the continent is low, and moisture-laden winds blow in from the Indian Ocean or the

China Sea. In their more exposed position, both India and South-East Asia receive enormous quantities of rain from the time the monsoon breaks, in May or June, throughout the summer. In some areas, for instance, this rule is broken, and on the Coromandel Coast of Madras or the east coast of Annam, much rain falls in the winter.

In India, the west coast of the Deccan, Bengal, and Assam in the extreme northeast receive the heaviest rainfall — 40 inches or more in three months. One place in Assam holds the world record. Valleys sheltered from moist winds, like the valley of the Indus and the interior of the Deccan, are relatively dry, and here the soil is unproductive and the population thin. An area in the south of the Indus Basin is almost a desert. In South-East Asia, too, the rainfall varies considerably.

The most rainy parts of India and South-East Asia are covered with tropical forests. Where these have been cleared, the combination of heat, moisture, and

Whole families spend long hours in the rice-fields.

Vidyavrata - FLO

The Ganges, India's sacred river, begins its 1,600 mile trip through India high in the Himalayas.

Courtesy of TWA - Trans World Airlines

This Calcutta temple was built by Jainists, who refuse to inflict pain on other living creatures.

Valentina Rosen

A Hindu farmer and his family outside their home. Seven out of ten Indians are farmers.

good soil makes the plantations extremely productive, particularly for the growing of rice, which is the staple crop of the monsoon area of Asia. Abundance of food leads to density of population, and the

warm plains and deltas, like Bengal and Lower Burma, are very crowded, while the hills and plateaus are more thinly populated.

Hinduism is one of the two chief

Kulwant Roy

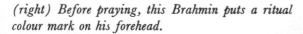

(right) Before praying, this Brahmin puts a ritual colour mark on his forehead.

Wolfe Worldwide Films, Los Angeles 24, Calif

(above) The sacred cows of the Hindus are permitted to roam freely through the streets in India.

Kulwant Roy

Kulwant Roy

This Sikh, with traditional beard and turban, is a member of India's presidential guard.

A farm woman from northern India displays her favourite piece of jewellery — a nose ring.

religions of Southern Asia. To the Hindus God is seen as something (rather than somebody) essentially nameless and formless. The many gods of Hindu mythology are, in fact, considered different names applied to something which is really without a name. Thus, Brahma is the creator, Vishnu the preserver, and Siva

This humble village near Delhi is typical of many Indian villages.

C. J. Coulson - Shostal

the destroyer in a kind of Trinity. It is within the power of every individual to reach, by a sort of personal deliverance, the divine goodness. After death, life begins again, the soul entering into another human or animal body. Accordingly, all living creatures are sacred, and it is a crime to kill even a cow or a snake. All meat-eating is thus forbidden to the followers of this religion. At least once in his life every believer should bathe in the purifying waters of the Ganges at Benares, which is the Holy City of the Hindus.

The second of the two principal religions of this area is Islam. Unlike the Hindus, the Moslems eat meat, with the exception of pork. That is a cause of antagonism between the followers of these two religions, especially the eating of beef, for cattle are particularly sacred to the Hindus. Another serious division is that the Moslems have no caste system. It was these deep divisions which led to the separation of the Moslems in the state of Pakistan when the British made India independent.

The famous warrior race of the Punjab, the Sikhs, have their own religon — Sikhism. Sikhism was founded in the fifteenth century by Nanak, who preached simplicity and equality and rejected idolatry and the Hindu caste system. He was followed by ten *gurus* (spiritual leaders or 'teachers'), the most famous of whom was Gobind Singh (1666—1708) who welded the sect into a nation of warriors. They took the name of Singh ('lion'). When British India was partitioned in 1947 the Punjab, and with it the Sikh people, was divided fairly equally between India and Pakistan.

Religious differences have been further aggravated by differences of language

Vidyavrata - FLO

The weight of the men as they run up and down the pole operates this water well.

Ferreira - FLO

This boy uses an age-old method of ploughing. Children provide India with much of her labour.

or dialect. Including minor ones, there are 200 of them. There are several Dravidian languages of some importance, but the most important of all are those derived from the Aryan or Indo-European stock. The chief of these are Hindustani and Bengali. But English, so long used in the administration of the country, has been accepted as the common language amongst educated Indians and Pakistanis, although the Indian government has recently made Hindi the official language.

To the north of India, and the north-east of West Pakistan, lies Kashmir, a province claimed by both powers. The population is largely Moslem, but India has refused to surrender it or to allow the issue to be arbitrated upon by the United Nations. Division does not seem to provide a solution, since both powers claim the same part, the famous Vale of Kashmir, a fertile valley surrounded by snow-capped peaks.

The principal countries of Southern Asia, India, Pakistan, and Ceylon, when combined together cover an area of over 1 million square miles, and have between them a population of over 644 million people. When independence was granted in 1947, the Moslem areas elected to separate, even though it meant forming a state in two separate parts, East Pakistan being nearly 1,000 miles from West Pakistan, The latter consists of Baluchistan, Sind, and almost the whole of the Punjab. The main city, Karachi, stands north-west of the Indus delta. East Pakistan contains most of Bengal and part of Assam. The two parts are very ill-balanced, since East Pakistan, with one-sixth of the area of West Pakistan, has a slightly larger population.

Pondicherry and the other small

Tony Chapelle - Monkmeyer

Indian women are at home in the fields. A small sickle is used for harvesting wheat.

Harrison Forman - Shostal

Indian women study hard to prove themselves worthy of their new equality with men.

This Indian woman is a toxicologist, one who studies poisons and their antidotes.

Harrison Forman - Shostal

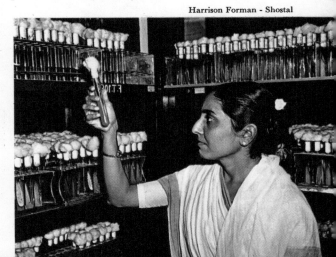

Kulwant Roy

Metal windmills, only recently used in Indian irrigation, dot the countryside near Delhi.

French possessions on the Indian coast were handed over to the Indian government in 1954. Portugal declined to do

Kulwant Roy

New power plants like this one in India will supply power for factories and homes.

likewise, and Goa was seized by India in 1961.

Ceylon, an island of 25,000 square miles, with a population of about 11.7 million, became independent in 1948. Colombo is the chief town and capital, with 511,600 inhabitants. It exports the chief products of the island: tea, rubber, coconut oil, cocoa and copra, and is one of the most important ports of call on the sea route from Europe to India, the Far East, Australia, etc.

India, Pakistan, and Ceylon, though all three are independent republics, are members of the British Commonwealth.

By far the largest part of the population live by farming — often on a very small scale. Families are large and grouped into villages containing a few hundred people. From an early age the children work in the fields beside their parents.

Farming methods are still generally very primitive. There is often little or no machinery and a great shortage of fertilisers and manures. Carts, ploughs, weeders, etc. are drawn by bullocks, and they also provide the power to work the chain pumps for irrigation. To nourish the soil, leaf-mould is used, with household refuse, and even silt scraped up from the bottom of irrigation tanks. The soil, nevertheless, gets poorer and poorer, for the manure of the great herds of cattle, instead of going back on the land, is dried and used for household fuel.

Irrigation, which has been in use from ancient times, even in the rainy districts, enables more than one crop a year to be raised. The water is generally drawn up from wells, but in the southern provinces and Ceylon irrigation tanks form a familiar feature of the landscape. In the Punjab, the great alluvial plain swept

Singhalese women pick tea. After picking the leaves must be dried before they are shipped.

out by the five rivers that flow into the Indus, a whole network of canals was constructed by the British to water the vast dry patches between the rivers. A dam constructed across the Indus at Sukkur, in northern Sind, has enabled an enormous region that was once desert to be reclaimed.

Of the cereals grown, rice is by far the most important. It is found chiefly in Bengal and Assam, and in the coastal plains. With the first rains the peasants spread the grain, which is quickly buried in the wet soil. Each parcel of land has a low dyke to prevent the water running off. The water is not allowed to run off until the rice begins to ripen. After harvesting, the sheaves are beaten against packing cases to separate the grains. In its rough state, before polishing, rice is

An elephant pulls a plough in Ceylon. Elephants are the tractors of Southern Asia.

New wells, like the one above, have been dug under the supervision of agricultural experts, as seen below.

called paddy, hence the phrase 'paddy-fields'.

In the drier areas of India, such as the interior of the Deccan, millet is the most important crop. Wheat is grown in the irrigated areas of the Punjab, and is the only cereal to be exported. Other food crops are chick-peas, groundnuts, and a rather poor quality sugar-cane. None of these is exported.

Tea is one of the great export crops of India and Ceylon. A great deal is grown in the Deccan, but particularly famous teas are those of Assam and Ceylon, as well as those of Darjeeling in the extreme north of Bengal. Hundreds of thousands of tons of tea are exported, the United Kingdom being the principal consumer.

Of the crops for industrial use, the most important are cotton and jute. Much of the cotton is grown on volcanic soil in the north-west of the Deccan, but Pakistan also produces considerable quantities. The great produce of Pakistan is jute, which is grown over a considerable part of Bengal. Today most of the jute and cotton of India and Pakistan is processed by local industry before being exported.

India is making great efforts with Five Year Plans to modernise the country and raise the standard of living of the Indian people. Her output of food grains in 1967 - 8 was 90 million tons, compared with 50 million tons in 1949 - 50. This increase was largely the result of the additional irrigation of nearly $16\frac{1}{2}$ million acres. The irrigation of a further 51 million acres is planned.

In addition, India has made rapid progress in developing her electrical and industrial capacity, as well as raising the welfare standards of her people. However, despite all India's efforts, the surface of the problem has hardly been scratched, as yet.

The division of India and Pakistan left India with very nearly all the existing industries and mineral resources, while Pakistan was, at the outset, an almost purely agricultural country. Since then, however, Pakistan has made considerable progress in building hydro-electric power stations and developing the textile industry (using jute and cotton), and the food-processing and chemical industries. Great efforts have also been made to increase food production. However, despite all Pakistan's efforts the production of crops is only just over 25 million tons compared with 12 million at Partition. Consequently Pakistan has to import large quantities of rice and wheat to feed her 109.5 million people.

Pakistan's first large oil deposits have been located in the Dum Duma area of upper Assam. Coal production has been increased to about 950,000 tons compared with 240,000 in 1948; and natural gas is also being exploited, although only on a comparatively small scale.

Iron and steel have been produced in India for many years. The Tata steel works in Jamshedpur, in Bihar, are amongst the largest in Asia, and impor-

John Strohm

Education has improved in Pakistan, but many schools still work with inferior materials.

tant reserves of coal and iron ore are in the neighbourhood. There are also iron and steel works near Calcutta. India also has deposits of manganese, copper and bauxite. Industry includes engineering and food processing, and the

Hand-made clay bricks are still common building material over a large part of India.

Vidyavrata - FLO

Textiles are one of India's greatest industries, yet much weaving is done with handlooms.

Vidyavrata - FLO

manufacture of cement, glass and chemicals, though textiles are the most important products. With industrial development, towns have grown. In India 17 per cent of the population live in towns, in Pakistan no more than 10 per cent. Calcutta, in West Bengal, is a great industrial town with a population of over 4½ million, and also a great port lying on a busy navigable river, the Hooghly. It is well supplied with railways, and is one of the busiest urban centres in the world. It is the second largest town in the Commonwealth. Its exports include jute and hessian, tea and oilseeds.

Bombay is on the west coast of India. Actually it is on an island, but it is linked to the mainland by bridges. It has one of the finest harbours in the world and has a population, with suburbs, of

The Bhakra dam provides a new source of irrigation and hydro-electric power for India.

Kulwant Roy

S. F. Dorsey - House of Photography

East Pakistan is a hot, damp lowland. Tropical plants like coconut palms and jute do well here in this particular type of climate.

nearly 5 million. Bombay rose to being a great cotton centre during the American Civil War, when England was unable to get cotton from the United States. It now has the biggest textile mills in India. As a port it benefited greatly from the opening of the Suez Canal.

Madras, on the east coast of India, is, with a population of nearly 2 million, the largest town in southern India. Its industries produce textiles and machinery. Hyderabad, in the Indian province of that name, has a population of 1½ million, and is an important university and commercial town. Lastly Delhi, with 2.8 million inhabitants, is the capital of the Republic of India. In the colonial era it was the seat of the Viceroy.

Islamabad is the capital of West Pakistan but Karachi is the leading town. As a city and a port Karachi has grown rapidly, and now has a population of 2.7 million. Its enormous airport is of great importance, for through it pass the main routes from Europe to India, South-East Asia, the Far East, and Australia. Karachi has a pleasant dry climate and is much preferred by tourists to either Bombay or Calcutta. Its chief exports are wheat and cotton.

Lahore, in the Punjab, is the chief university town of Pakistan, and also

Despite modernisation, demonstrated by the Jamshedpur steel works, age-old customs still prevail.

a banking and commercial centre. It has a population of 1,674,000. The most important town in East Pakistan is Dacca, and it serves as capital of the area. It has a population of over 741,000, including the suburbs, and it is the centre of the rice- and jute-growing area of the Ganges — Brahmaputra delta.

Colombo is the chief town and capital of Ceylon, with 511,600 inhabitants. Situated in the south-west of the island, it exports tea, rubber, coconut oil, and copra, its imports being, sugar, cotton goods, fuels, and fertilisers. It is one of the most important ports of call on the sea route from Europe to the Far East, Australia, etc.

Despite the progress it has made, this area suffers greatly from the blight of tropical diseases. The health of these countries is undermined by cholera and, still more, by malaria. The great poverty of the mass of the people, and also to some extent the caste system of India, makes it very difficult to combat disease. The birth-rate is high, but so is mortality, especially infant mortality. These remarks apply to India and Pakistan much more than to Ceylon, which has a much lower death-rate. A great deal of progress has been made in both countries, however. In India, for example, the death-rate has been reduced by half during the last thirty years.

North-east of India are three independent mountain states. The largest one, Nepal, has a population which totals 9.5 million.

Nepal is the usual starting point of climbing expeditions into the Himalayas, and the home of the famous Ghurkas. The second of the three states is Bhutan, with a population of about 800,000. Life in these countries is concentrated in the valleys, where rice, maize, vegetables, and fruit are grown. The great valley of Nepal also produces sugar-cane and potatoes.

The capital of Nepal is Katmandu, and the population is made up of the Newari people who are related to the Tibetans, and the Gurkhas themselves, the ruling group whose language is derived from Sanskrit. A great deal of foreign currency comes into Nepal from the large numbers of Gurkha soldiers serving in the British and Indian armies. The first road from India to Katmandu was only completed in 1953.

Bhutan is one of the most isolated countries in the world and is rarely visited by outsiders. It has an area of 18,000 square miles. The capital and only important town is Punakha.

The third and smallest of these states is the Himalayan kingdom of Sikkim. It has a population of only 162,000 and is under Indian protection. The capital is Gangtok

Kulwant Roy

Hundreds of men have been working on the Bhakra Dam project for more than 10 years.

and its people, who are also related to the Tibetans, live by agriculture, in the valleys, and by yak-breeding.

George Holton - Photo Library

This expedition, in search of the 'abominable snowman' of the Himalayas, camps at 15,000 feet.

George Holton - Photo Library

The Sherpa tribe lives in the mountains. They are used to high altitudes and make good guides.

Fields of rice, Asia's chief food crop, stretch for miles across the fertile lowlands of Thailand.

SOUTH-EAST ASIA

Burma was split off from India in 1937 to become a separate British colony. Ten years later, the country became an independent federal republic with an area of 262,000 square miles, and about 26.4 million inhabitants who speak a language nearer to Chinese than to any Indian language. A high range, the Arakan Yoma, runs up the west coast, and its northerly extension, the Chin Hills, separates the country from India. In the east is a racial group, the Shans, about a million strong, who belong to the Thai race and speak Thai dialects, and are thus related to the Siamese. They occupy plateaus which belong to the vast mountain ranges of the Yunnan province of China, across which runs the Salween River.

Between Arakan Yoma and the Eastern heights is the enormous basin of the Irrawaddy and its tributary, the Chindwin. A much smaller basin is that of the Sittang which runs parallel to the Irrawaddy. On the whole, the central area is fairly low, except for a range of hills, the Pegu Yoma, between the last two rivers.

SOUTH-EAST ASIA

0   100   200
Miles

⊙ National Capitals

© Copyright 1960 by Maj. Projects Inc.

SINGAPORE	Over 1,000,000 population
Rangoon	250,000–1,000,000 population
Haiphong	100,000– 250,000 population
Ipoh	50,000– 100,000 population
Cha Mai	Under 50,000 population

The sun gleams off the brilliant gold-leaf-covered Buddhist temples in Rangoon, Burma.

Agriculture is the chief occupation of Burma. The central plain is rather dry, because the moist south-west monsoon is cut off by the Arakan Yoma. Crops needing little moisture are grown there, such as millet, sesame, and groundnuts. Where there is irrigation rice can be grown as well as cotton and sugarcane. Large numbers of cattle are raised, many of which are used for haulage. In this area the peasants own their land. It is otherwise in the deltas, where they have to pay rent. There the abundant rain brought by the south-west monsoon makes rice-growing easy, and large quantities of it are exported. But though much money is made by this crop, little of it finds its way into the pockets of the peasants, who have had to borrow money from the bank, generally an Indian bank, in order to finance all their operations.

Burma was occupied by the Japanese from 1942 - 5. The independence granted in 1947 was followed by disturbances and civil war, and even by the invasion of bands of Chinese Nationalists.

The port of Rangoon, capital of Burma, stands on one of the mouths of the Irrawaddy, not far from the sea, and is very active as a port, particularly from May to December, when the rice is being exported. Another great export is teak, which comes from the tropical forests of the Pegu Yoma and from the whole region drained by the Chindwin. Elephants carry the trees down to the river, where they are floated down to Rangoon or shipped down on rafts.

Burma has mineral resources, but little has been done so far to exploit them.

Kofod - Monkmeyer

A passer-by drops some money into the begging-bowl of a Buddhist monk.

Herbert Knapp

Teak logs, which must be dried by the sun before they can float downstream, are put in piles.

The most important is oil, which is found in the central plain. Production had reached a considerable volume by 1939, but had to start again from scratch after the war. Between 1951 and 1968 it increased from 100,000 tons to over six times that amount.

Burma produces gold and precious stones, such as rubies, sapphires, and jade. Her other mineral resources include tin, tungsten, copper, nickel, lead, and coal.

Siam changed its name to Thailand in May, 1949. It is a country of some 200,000 square miles with a population of over 33.6 million. A range of low mountains running down the centre of the country divides it into two great basins. The western basin is the most populous, drained by the Menam and its tributaries. The eastern basin is

Teak logs float down a Thai river from the highlands to the coast, where they will be sold.

A. Kolb, Hamburg

Fujihira - Monkmeyer

Rice paddies must be ploughed to stir up the mud before seeds are planted.

drained by the Mun which flows towards Laos to join the Mekong on the frontier.

The principal crops are teak, rice, and rubber. Thailand also ranks third among the world's producers of tin.

Bangkok, the capital, is both the chief port of Thailand and, with a population of 2,318,000, the largest town in South-East Asia. It lies on the east bank of the Menam about 20 miles from the coast, and is built on the banks of the innumerable canals and branches of the river, which earn it the nickname of the 'Venice of the East'. There are, in all, 300 Buddhist temples in Bangkok. In one of the most famous, the Temple of the Emerald Buddha, the statue of the Enlightened One sits on a throne of pure gold, and its ornaments of gold and precious stones are changed with the seasons, each time with great religious ceremony.

The Khmer Republic was (formerly Cambodia) a French Protectorate but became independent in 1955. It has an area of about 67,000 square miles, with

South-East Asia's chief beast of burden, the water buffalo, is a playmate for this Thai boy.

Thomas d'Hoste - Shostal

This crude water-scoop makes the task of hand irrigation somewhat easier.

A Vietnamese beats bundles of rice stalks against a frame to separate grain from straw.

a total population of about 6.5 million.

The centre of the country consists of the great basin drained by the Mekong and its tributaries. The chief tributary in Cambodia is the Tonlé Sap, which broadens out into a great lake in the western half of the basin. In the dry season it has an area of about 1,000 square miles, while in June the water rises till the lake covers nearly three times that area, flooding all the neighbouring fields and forests, and encouraging the cultivation of rice. Mineral resources are confined to some precious stones and deposits of iron ore between the Tonlé Sap and the Mekong.

Pnom Penh, the capital, stands at the junction of the Mekong and the Tonlé Sap River. It has a population of over half a million. The old town is very beautiful, with a royal palace whose silver pagoda is famous. There are also many museums. As a religious centre, it attracts big crowds. There is a troupe of dancers, who maintain the ancient traditions of their art, give religious performances at every festival. There is also a Buddhist university.

Pnom Penh is a river port and a busy commercial centre. The river is navigable all through the year. The town is a great market for rice, maize, and dried fish and cotton. River steamers ply between Pnom Penh and Saigon, and launches go upstream far into Laos. Most of the external trade is done by Chinese. A railway runs down to the port of Saigon and another runs through Battambang to Bangkok.

Laos is a very mountainous country with deep valleys carved by the rivers. In the north, where the mountains are most rugged, the only fertile soil is close to the Mekong, as at Luang-Prabang and

Many people in Thailand live on sampans. Here, a family is about to have a main meal.

The canals of Thailand are crowded with floating markets, from which sampan dwellers buy supplies.

Vientiane. The country's agriculture depends entirely on the south-west monsoon which, between May and October, brings anything from 40 to 80 inches of rain to all areas.

Rice and maize are the two most important crops and fish provides an important part of the Laotian diet. The forests, though rich in teak, are not much exploited: and the deposits of tin and iron ore are very little worked.

There are no big towns. Vientiane, the administrative capital, has only 162,000 inhabitants, while Luang-Prabang, the royal capital, has about 22,000.

In 1968 the population was estimated to be 2,800,000. Two-thirds of these are Laotians who are racially akin to the Thais and the Shans of Burma and, like them, Buddhists. The remainder of the population consists of primitive tribes who live in the mountains. They clear a bit of the forest, grow crops for a few years, and then move on.

Vietnam extends for over 1,000 miles down the east coast of the Indo-Chinese peninsula. In the extreme north it is 320 miles wide, but the rest is a relatively narrow strip. It is about fifty miles wide for a considerable distance, broadening in the south to about double that width.

Most of Tonkin, in the north, is occupied by mountains, which are an extension of the southern Chinese ranges. The valley and delta of the Red River are teeming with human activity.

Vietnam has a typical monsoon climate, but the temperature varies considerably with the latitude. In the south it is always hot, while in the north there are marked warmer and cooler seasons. Rain falls over the whole country from May to October, except in central Vietnam, where it is a little later. It varies from about 60 inches in the south to 100 in the north. The more rainy areas are thickly forested and, particularly in the south, are frequented by wild life. Fish abound in lakes, rivers, and even rice-fields, and contribute considerably to the people's diet. Sea fishing also thrives.

The population is nearly 37 million and is densest in Lower Tonkin which is one of the world's great rice-growing areas. Other crops are grown, however, including sugar-cane, maize, and tobacco.

Rice must be sown, transplanted, cultivated, and harvested by hand — a laborious process.

H. Verstappen

This mother and her son are typical of the handsome tribes from the mountains of Vietnam.

Fujihira - Monkmeyer

CENTRAL
AND EASTERN ASIA

Central and Eastern Asia comprise the great continental mass of China, the Korean peninsula, and the Japanese archipelago. It includes part of the Asian Highlands (Tibet and Mongolia), a number of plateaus and plains (Northern China and Manchuria), and regions of steep but not very high mountains (south China, Korea, Japan, and Formosa).

There is a certain uniformity derived from the climate which is dominated by the monsoons; the winter monsoon, which blows towards the Pacific and the summer monsoon, which blows landwards. There is also some cultural unity from the influence over the whole area of Chinese civilisation, together with the use of similar writing and, above all, from a general observance of Buddhism.

Apart from Mongolia, whose inhabitants are nomad herdsmen, the civilisation of these countries is predominantly agricultural. In consequence the mountains are almost completely empty. The whole population is crowded on to the plains, on which the bigger towns have become industrial centres. The total population of this area amounts to over 900 million people: nearly one-third of the world's population.

Few countries in the world possess a written history so old, so continuous, and so authentic as the Chinese. Chinese civilisation is indeed one of the oldest in the world, and until last century China was regarded by the people of the West as a civilisation rather than a state: a collection of peoples, observing the same administrative traditions without any real

PEKING ———— Over 1,000,000 population
Inchon ———— 250,000-1,000,000 population
Taejon ———— 100,000- 250,000 population
Turfan ———— 50,000- 100,000 population
Yungsin ———— Under 50,000 population

EASTERN ASIA

0   Miles   400

⊙ National Capitals

© Copyright 1960 by Map Projects Inc.

H. Harrer, Liechtenstein-Verlag, Vaduz

The Potala, in Lhasa, is 400 feet high and 1,200 feet long. It is the most important monastery in Tibet, though the Dalai Lama, the head of the Tibetan religion, now lives in India.

national cohesion. That view is no longer possible. China is now very definitely a state. It is moreover the most populated state in the world, with about 730 million inhabitants determined to make their country, a land of enormous resources, one of the great economic powers of the world.

China is a single whole. Nevertheless, in its immense area of 3,760,000 square miles, we are forced to distinguish and consider separately: (1) the China of Central Asia, which is a great mass of mountains and plateaus, steppes, and cold, almost uninhabited deserts; and (2) the China of Eastern Asia which is real, living China.

Chinese Central Asia consists of Tibet, Sinkiang (Eastern Turkestan), and Mongolia. This is a region of mountains, plateaus, and deserts. It covers an enor-

mous area but has a very small population.

In this area we find some of the highest mountains of Asia, the highest plateaus, and the most extensive deserts. The Tien Shan and Altai Mountains close the region on the north. Across it run the Kunlun Mountains which separate Tibet from Sinkiang. West is the plateau of the

On ceremonial days, Tibetan lamas march in processions. This temple is a starting point.

Colin Wyatt - Photo Researchers

Pamirs. The Himalayas in the south divide Central Asia from India.

Two vast deserts, the Gobi and the Takla Makan, extend over thousands of square miles. Mountains and deserts form barriers which isolate this region from the rest of the continent. Central

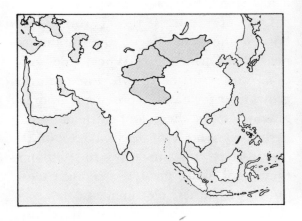

Van Bucher - Photo Researchers·

Asia's transition from old to new is seen in these Buddhist monks waiting to board a plane.

Asia is much too far from any ocean to receive the mild moist wind that brings rain.

The Chinese province of Tibet is the highest country in the world. Several of its summits are 20,000 feet in height. The plateau of Tibet itself is more than 16,000 feet above sea-level.

Few people can live at such a height and in so cold an atmosphere. The few who do are practically cut off from the rest of Asia. Until recently there were

An oasis in Sinkiang is a pleasant contrast to the surrounding mountainous country.

Eastfoto

no lines of communication apart from one or two narrow caravan tracks, but the Chinese have built two great roads to Lhasa, the capital of Tibet. And more recently still these have been extended towards the Indian frontier.

Most of the Tibetans live in the southern part of the country, where melting snows swell the rivers which irrigate the soil. Making the most of their livestock, they have learnt to scrape a living from their inhospitable land. Leather, skins, wool, and felt, provide clothing and shelter. Milk, butter, cheese, and meat are the chief items of food. Dried dung provides them with fuel.

In a few special areas, Tibetans grow barley and wheat, using the method known as dry farming. The national dish is *tsamba*, a sort of porridge made of barley or wheat, with the addition

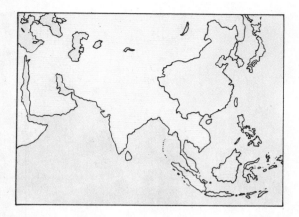

Sinkiang or Eastern Turkestan is a high plateau surrounded by still higher mountains. As a result most of the area is a desert. Winters are bitterly cold, summers unbearably hot. In the course of the year the rainfall is no more than 6 inches. The melting snows of the mountains feed a few rivers that cross the desert.

One of these is the Tarim. Oases border the foothills of the mountains near the Tarim river. Wheat and some other crops can be grown. Enough grass grows near the oases to provide temporary grazing for the sheep and cattle of nomad herdsmen who visit the villages of the oases from time to time to exchange their wool, skins, meat, butter, and cheese, for flour, leather, clothing, and tea.

of butter, and flavoured with tea. The pastures on the rolling plateaus and mountainsides enable them to rear sheep, cattle (yaks), and hardy ponies. Accustomed to the high altitude, the yaks draw the plough and serve as beasts of burden.

The religion of the people is Lamaism, which is a local form of Buddhism. Thousands of young men go into monasteries, where they study for years to become Buddhist monks or lamas.

Mongolia is another plateau country surrounded by high mountains, but the plateau is lower in this case, being for the most part 3,000 to 5,000 feet high. Mongolia occupies part of the great Gobi

Towns in Outer Mongolia are small. This desolate country is inhabited primarily by nomads.

Ergy Landau - Rapho Guillumette

A Mongol tribesman leads a nomadic life. His yurt, or portable home, is made of wool felt.

A family group in Outer Mongolia. They are Buddhists and speak the Mongol tongue.

desert, where explorers have discovered the relics of many prehistoric animals.

It was from here that Genghis Khan and his Mongol hordes advanced in the thirteenth century to conquer practically the whole of Asia. Today there are oil wells in the Eastern Gobi.

Most of the Mongolian plateau is covered with grasses. The nomad tribes wander from place to place with their sheep, goats, camels, and horses.

The whole life of the nomad herdsman is concentrated on his herd. He lives on meat, butter, milk, cheese. Sheep skins can be worn, and all skins turned into leather. Wool can be pressed into felt for boots, or woven into blankets. As we have seen already, dried dung provides fuel.

Horses, camels, and yaks are used for transport. They carry tea from China and *tsamba* from Tibet.

Because they depend on their flocks, the life of many Mongols is a continual search for pastures.

Roads in remote parts of China are apt to be no more than winding footpaths.

The nomads rather despise those who farm the land and remain fixed in the same place. Life on horseback, looking after their herds, is for them a much more noble occupation. When pastures give out, they pack up their tents and move elsewhere with their herds, families, and all they possess.

The Mongolian tent, or *yurt,* is round. The lower walls are vertical; above them the roof slopes gently upwards to a slightly rounded point. The *yurt* is made of thick sheep's and goat's wool felt stretched on a flexible framework of laths. Although easily transportable, these tents are strong and capable of standing up to the worst blizzards. They are easily pitched and struck, and are thus ideal for nomads.

In winter it is often difficult for the herds to graze. Freezing blizzards form a thick surface of ice on top of the snow, preventing the animals from reaching the dry grass beneath. In recent years the Mongolian People's Republic has built thousands of shelters to protect the herds from the cold and bitter winds. But most of the tribes build corrals, like those used in America, to protect their herds from the winter winds and the wolves. The walls of the corrals are of

China is the world's largest rice producer. The grain which feeds her people is raised in paddies.

The Great Wall of China was built in the third century B. C. as a defence against Mongol invaders.

bricks formed out of dried cow dung.

Nevertheless many herds are obliged to winter out of doors, and the 13,000 wolf skins brought in each year give an idea of the number of wolves that prey on livestock, particularly sheep. A certain amount of hay is now grown, reducing the number of animals that die of starvation, and Mongolia may one day become the great ranching country of Eastern Asia.

Caravan routes have crossed eastern Asia since the earliest times. They run east — west and north-east — south-west into India.

Turning to the railways, two lines will eventually link China with Soviet Russia: (1) the Trans-Mongolian, which is completed and runs from Peking to Ulan Ude, passing through Ulan Bator. (2) the line from Lanchow on the Hwang Ho to Kazakhstan through Urumchi and the Dzungarian Gates, which has not yet been completed.

China proper, sometimes referred to as the Eighteen Provinces, extends from the plateau of Central Asia to the Pacific.

Northern China and south China are divided by the Tsinling mountains which are an eastward extension of the great Kunlun Mountains of Central Asia.

Although Peking is in the same latitude as Nepal, the climate of north China is severe: with cold, dry, windy winters

A technician records data on the health of a worker in a Peking textile mill.

A ceremony to mark the opening of a new sports stadium in Peking.

and hot, rainy summers. In the west are the Taihang Mountains in Shansi, and, in the east, the immense plain of China and Manchuria. Almost everywhere the land consists of yellow loess to a depth of 1,000 feet. This loess is soil which has been blown in fine particles from the desert of Central Asia and is very fertile, excellent for the cultivation of wheat. It breaks away very easily, and silts up the rivers and estuaries. That is why the coast of China is flat and not indented. The peninsula of Shantung is the only one of note north of Shanghai. Under the loess are valuable mineral ores, besides which there are the coalfields of Shansi and Shantung, as well as the one at Fushun in Manchuria.

South China is much more hilly. In the west are the mountains of Szechwan and the plateaus of the Yunnan. In the east is a hilly country ending in a rocky, indented coast. Here the summers are hot and the winters mild. Rain falls throughout the year, but chiefly in summer under the influence of the monsoon. The vege-

The farmer who owns a water buffalo is lucky indeed. The animal can be used to help with the ploughing.

Heavy use of fertiliser, spread by hand, has kept the soil of southern China fertile for centuries.

tation is luxuriant and crops are of the tropical type, including rice, cotton, opium, and tea. Mulberry trees, on which the silk industry depends, are common. With a hot, moist climate, it is often possible, particularly on the deltas, to grow two crops of rice a year.

The plain of Manchuria is drained by the Sungari, a tributary of the Amur. The great rivers of China are the Hwang Ho or Yellow River, in the north, the Yangtse Kiang, in the centre, and the Si-Kiang or Western River in the south.

The Hwang Ho is about 2,900 miles long and drains a basin whose area is 28,000 square miles. Winding through the immense plains of yellow loess, it picks up great quantities of alluvium, hence its name, the Yellow River. It often overflows causing disastrous floods, during which it often changes its course.

The Yangtse with a length of about 3,400 miles is the longest river in Eastern Asia and one of the greatest in the world. Though only about 500 miles longer than the Hwang Ho, it drains a basin two-and-a-half times the size. It is navigable for

John Strohm

The life of a Chinese farmer is hard. It will take time before machines are widespread.

1,660 miles, and, with its tributaries, contains over 10,000 miles of navigable waters. It is thus the chief highway into central China, particularly into Szechwan, which is the most populated province of all. Nearly half of the total population of China lives in the Yangtse basin. Less irregular and less dangerous than the Hwang Ho, it is capable nevertheless of very serious floods. One, in 1931, flooded over 100,000 square miles and drowned 3 million people.

Before leaving this area, another water highway should be mentioned. This is the Yun-Ho, or as it is generally known in Europe, the Grand Canal. It is a magnificent artificial river running from Hangchow, south-west of Shanghai, first to the Yangtse, then to the Hwang Ho and then, beyond that river, to Tientsin, where it joins the Pai Ho, which links it with Tungchow in the neighbourhood of Peking.

The Si-Kiang is the most important river in the southern Provinces, with a length of over 1,000 miles. It is navigable to Canton, which is not far from the coast, and thereafter for over 100 miles by shallow draft vessels.

John Strohm

Most Chinese must do all their work by hand. The tools which are available are very primitive.

The population of China is formed of Chinese proper or Hans, mingled with a considerable variety of races. In Central Asia, which is very thinly populated, the racial minorities — Mongols, Tibetans, etc. — prevail, while in the densely populated areas the population is largely Chinese. In some areas the density of population rises to as much as 1,500 per square mile.

The population of China is already more than 730 million and is increasing at a rate of 10 million a year.

The chief agricultural areas of China are: (1) the loess plains (or yellow country) of Northern China. On these immense and monotonous stretches, broken only by the few trees round villages, wheat, maize, soya beans, potatoes, and groundnuts are grown, as well as a plant called kaoliang which is a sort of sorghum. (2) The Manchurian plains in the northeast are used for growing wheat, soya beans, kaoliang, tobacco, and sugar-beet. (3) The plains of the middle and lower Yangtse are of great fertility owing to irrigation. Here the farmers grow wheat and reap two harvests of rice a year; they grow tea, tobacco, oil-seeds, and cotton,

the last being the most important crop of all. (4) The Red Basin (region of Chungking) where the crops are rice, colza, fruit, and vegetables, and where pigs are reared on a big scale. (5) The delta of the Si-Kiang, in southern China. The climate here is sub-tropical; the summer months are long and hot, and during them the monsoon brings torrential rains. There is no frost in winter. Tea is grown here, sweet potatoes, the mulberry trees necessary for silk production, and all sorts of sub-tropical fruit and vegetables. The principal crop however is rice. At least two crops a year can be obtained.

In fifty centuries of farming, the Chinese peasants have learnt how to put their land to good use. In particular they have learnt that, in food value, rice gives better yields per acre than any other crop.

The Chinese peasant, his wife, and his sons all work together in the rice fields. They sow the rice, flood the paddy fields, tend the plants, and pick the rice by hand. Here and there buffaloes may be seen at work, but for the most part every operation is performed by hand.

The government has now introduced a

Farmers on a commune near Peking. China has made great strides in agriculture.

John Strohm

A Chinese farmer winnows grain. He is separating the good grain from the chaff.

John Strohm

Planting in a garden near Peking, children learn to work with hands as well as heads.

An interior view of a general shop typical of those found on Chinese communist communes.

major system of land reform under which the property of the landowners has been broken up into small lots, rarely more than three acres, and distributed amongst the peasantry. However, so enormous is the population that there is still insufficient production of food-stuffs. In times of floods or droughts there is a great threat of famine.

In an effort to increase production the government is trying to organise farming on a communal basis. A number of villages, which may be anything from thirty to eighty, are grouped together in a single community of anything from 20,000 to 70,000 people.

These communes, as they are called, began experimentally at first in the vast corn-land of Honan. From there the system spread until it was gradually introduced into all the provinces. At present all but one per cent of the peasantry are working in communes. The commune is an organisation with many functions, economic, administrative, social, educational, and even military. In return for pooling his land the peasant receives both food and clothing. The communes organise schools, canteens, public laundries, day nurseries, and medical centres.

Agricultural machinery is being employed by some communes. As a result the old-fashioned Chinese farming landscape, with its tiny fields, is rapidly disappearing.

An aerial view shows the years of work that have gone into this large open-cast coal mine.

These Chinese boys are pictured with oxen. But animals are not common on Chinese farms.

Sampans are widely used as permanent homes in the overcrowded river cities of China.

PEOPLE OF THE SAMPANS

In south-eastern China there are millions of people who live all their lives and work on rivers and canals. No other region in the world has such a network of navigable waterways. In addition to the rivers, there are thousands of miles of canals; in fact in this part of China waterways take the place of roads.

Every village and every town is either on a river or on a canal. Many of the great towns of China, like Wuhan and Canton, are inland river towns, some of them deep in the interior. In many of them there is such a network of canals that boats are used instead of motor vehicles or trains for transportation.

The little ships used by the Chinese are called junks. Smaller boats of all sizes are called sampans. Neither junks nor sampans have changed appreciably through the centuries. Many of the sampans can only carry two or three people and a very small quantity of goods, while junks can carry substantial cargoes from one seaport to another.

Both junks and sampans are used to ferry people from place to place in towns like Canton. They also take people from the mainland to their work in Hong Kong. Many more are used as homes for people who can find no other lodging.

Some junks are used as ferries. Although they look awkward, they are very seaworthy.

Many junks are used for fishing on the open sea. They come back loaded with fish, shrimps, oysters, and edible seaweed.

Fishing is also done on the inland waterways. Some of the fishermen use cormorants, which they have trained to catch fish for them. By putting a straw noose round its neck, the fisherman prevents it swallowing its prey. He also holds a string tied to one of the bird's legs. The cormorant is an excellent diver, and as soon as it has caught a fish, the fisherman pulls on the noose to prevent it swallowing, and with the string hauls the bird, and the fish, on board.

Some people spend all their lives afloat. The boats may be secured to the river bank or to other boats that are lying alongside. Small children and the families' chickens are often tethered to pre-

Ruth V. Bair

A sampan on a Chinese river is home to this family. They eat, sleep, and live on board.

vent them from falling overboard. Often even vegetables are grown on board. In Canton more than a tenth of the population lives afloat. In Hong Kong there are 100,000 sampan dwellers.

Some boats on the Yangtze River near Shanghai are houseboats. Others are commercial vessels.

Camera Clix

The Ming Tombs dam project will provide hydro-electric power for the Peking area.

THE INDUSTRIALISATION OF CHINA

The government of China is doing its utmost to transform an agricultural country into a great modern industrial power. China has set to work to build dams and hydro-electric power-stations, to construct railways and build factories. Emerging from its age-old lethargy, China will be a major force in world economy.

Nothing could be more impressive than the great dams that are now being constructed across the Hwang Ho and the Hwai Ho, which are destined not merely to produce electricity but also to conserve flood waters for use in the dry season.

Parallel with the constant harnessing of rivers to provide electricity, is the continual development of coal-mining. Production of coal and lignite rose from 63 million tons in 1952 to over 400 million tons in just over ten years. Oil production is just beginning to be developed on a similar scale. Production of iron and steel has also risen enormously:

more than 35 million tons of pig-iron are produced (3 million in 1954), and 11 million tons of steel (2½ million in 1954).

The north-eastern region (Manchuria), is one of the principal industrial centres of China. There are large deposits of coal, magnesite, and aluminium, processed by huge blast furnaces, steel mills, and rolling mills. Manufactures include machine tools, textiles, and chemicals.

New industrial regions have sprung into existence. One is on the coalfield of the province of Shansi. Others are at Chungking in Szechwan, at Canton, in the south, and, in the north-west, at Lanchow.

For 1,000 miles from its mouth the Yangtse is navigable by sea-going ships, and when the water-level is high in summer, ships of as much as 10,000 tons can steam up to the industrial centre of Wuhan. The canals and rivers of southern China are also navigable, though on a different scale, being frequented by junks and sampans, which manage to carry considerable quantities of goods.

Since 1949, however, it is in railway development that progress has been most striking. This is particularly so in north China, where they were most needed, since the Hwang Ho is not navigable.

The railways in this region may eventually join up with two lines to Soviet Russia. The first of these, the Trans-Mongolian, already runs from Peking across the Gobi desert to Ulan Bator, and then on to join the Trans-Siberian at Ulan Ude. The Trans-Mongolian reduces the journey by rail from Peking to Europe by nearly 2,000 miles. The second runs from Lanchow in a north-westerly direction, and will be taken across Sinkiang and through the Dzungarian Gates to join the Turksib, the railway from Turkestan to Siberia. A branch from this line runs southward across the Tsinling mountains to the rich agricultural province of Szechwan. One-third of this line runs through tunnels.

The railways of Manchuria are better organised than in any other part of China. They were originally constructed by the Russians, then taken over by the Japanese. They link up both with the railways

John Strohm

Another long day's work begins in this productive steel mill in Anchang, Manchuria.

Eastfoto

Oil tanks in the Yumen oilfields dot the Gobi desert, China's new industrial frontier.

of Korea and Siberia as well as with those of the rest of China.

Roads are chiefly used for local traffic. But two arterial roads run to Lhasa.

Many women are labourers in Manchuria. Here we see one at work in a busy cable factory.

Most of the construction of the Ming Tombs dam has been done by men, rather than by machines.

John Strohm

TAIWAN AND KOREA

Because of its growing textile industry, more flax is being cultivated on Taiwan.

The island of Taiwan or Formosa lies 100 miles off the south-east coast of China. It is now the last stronghold of what is called the Nationalist government of China. Before the Second World War, China was in the throes of a war with Japan, as well as being torn by years of civil war between the government on the one hand and the communists and various private war-lords on the other.

The civil war continued after the end of the Second World War and in 1949 the communists under Mao Tse-Tung succeeded in driving the Nationalists off the mainland. The Nationalist leader, Chiang Kai-Shek, withdrew his army to Taiwan, where they have remained.

Taiwan is one of a chain of west Pacific volcanic islands which include Japan. It is about 235 miles long and 90 miles broad at its widest, its area being a little greater than that of Holland.

Less than one-quarter of the land is available for farming, as the bulk of it is occupied by a great mountain range running the whole of its length. It has forty-eight peaks over 10,000 feet in height. On the eastern side the mountains drop abruptly to the Pacific. The narrow plain along the west coast is rarely more than 25 miles in width.

The climate of Taiwan varies with the seasonal winds. During the summer the south-west wind brings heavy rain to the south and to the coastal plain in the west, while the northern part of the island is clear and dry. From October to March the north-east wind brings heavy rains to the northern and eastern parts, while the south and west are dry.

Sometimes, in the late summer, violent typhoons occur, causing terrible damage

Sugar cane is an important crop. Here it is harvested by a roadside in south-west Taiwan.

Children at a co-operative school in Taiwan (Formosa) follow their teacher in a medley of songs.

to homes, farms, and often entire villages. Torrents of rain flood the mountain streams, bringing down tons of stones, gravel, and sand, which are deposited on the fields.

About nine-tenths of the inhabitants of Taiwan are Chinese, but the original inhabitants were primitive, brown-skinned Malays. Until recent years some of these tribes still practised head-hunting. Now only about 200,000 of them are left. They live in the hills, having been crowded out of the fertile plains by the Chinese.

At present the population of Taiwan is about 13.3 million, many of them having fled from China with Chiang Kai-Shek. Taipei is the capital, and there are some other towns, but most of the population live in small farming villages surrounded by rice fields. Whether in town or village, the Chinese live as they did in China.

Fishing is important to the economy of Taiwan. This is a good catch off the coast at NanFanAo.

Thomas Benner -Shostal

This village nestles at the foot of bare hills. De-forestation has ruined much of the land in Korea.

They do the same work and observe the same manners and customs. Rice is the chief crop and more than half the land farmed is devoted to it. Sugar-cane is another important crop, together with tropical fruits, jute, and soya-beans.

There are many small factories on the island, making textiles, chemicals, pottery, steel and machinery. Food processing is also done, but the most important industry is sugar refining. There is a small amount of coal mining. The forests of Formosa, which cover more than two-thirds of the island, are of considerable

value, and three-quarters of the world's supply of camphor comes from here.

Korea is a peninsula jutting out from the coast of Manchuria towards the southernmost islands of Japan. It is separated from Japan by the Sea of Japan, from China by the Yellow Sea, and from Manchuria and Siberia by the Yalu and Tumes Rivers.

It is a very mountainous country. As a result a limited area is sufficiently flat and fertile to be used as arable land. The best farmland is along the coasts, though there are fertile valleys in the mountains.

Korean farmers carry huge loads of rice on their backs from the fields to the threshing floor.

The chief crop of Taiwan is rice, grown in flooded fields.

Ewing Galloway

Keystone Press

North and South Korea differ considerably. The mountains in the north are higher and more rugged and are heavily forested. The climate is more severe, the winters being bitterly cold. North Korea is also more industrialised and has almost all of the mineral deposits of the peninsula. The Japanese, who governed Korea from 1895 to 1945, built many factories, railways, and hydro-electric power-stations there. South Korea is more agricultural. The climate is considerably warmer, the winters being quite mild. On the coastal plains rice is the chief crop. After the rice is harvested, the fields are drained and replanted with barley, cotton, wheat, or other crops. But the surrounding hills and mountains are almost devoid of vegetation. There is serious soil erosion.

South Korea is densely populated, the bulk of its 31 million inhabitants living in the farming villages along the crowded coastal plains.

Korean family life is mostly centred on the courtyards of the houses. Here the rice is dried and threshed; here the women make their *kimchi*. This is the

Edmund N. Paige - Shostal

This old man wears the traditional black horsehair hat and white clothing of Korea.

national dish of Korea and is made of pickled radishes and spices.

Each courtyard has its vegetable garden and a few fruit trees. Rice is grown on the level ground outside the village. On the hillsides, the crops are wheat, barley, millet, rye, and vegetables.

Old people are greatly honoured in Korea. White clothes, common among all ages, are the rule with the elderly, who also affect tall, very black horsehair hats, and, very often, beards as well.

The Spring and Autumn pavilions built on a beautiful lake and surrounded by willows in the port of Kaohstung, in the south of Taiwan.

Keystone Press

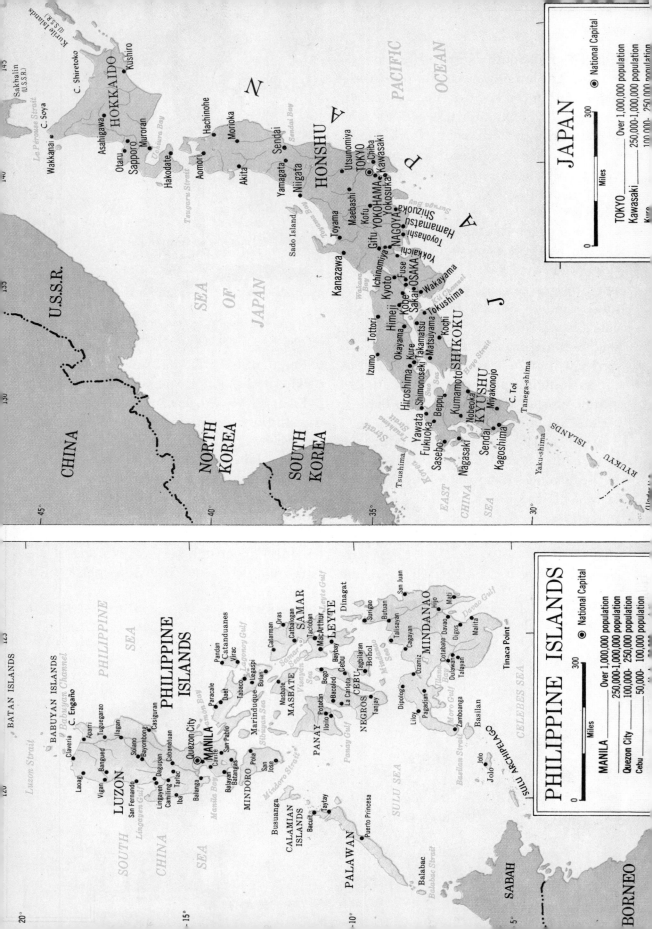

JAPAN

● National Capital

0   Miles   300

TOKYO	Over 1,000,000 population
Kawasaki	250,000-1,000,000 population
Kure	100,000- 250,000 population

Kurile Islands (U.S.S.R.)

Sakhalin (U.S.S.R.)

La Pérouse Strait

C. Soya

Wakkanai · C. Shiretoko

Kushiro

HOKKAIDO

Asahigawa

Otaru   Muroran

Sapporo

Hakodate

Tsugaru Strait

Uchiura Bay

Hachinohe

Aomori

Morioka

Akita

Yamagata   Sendai

Niigata

Sendai Bay

Sado Island

HONSHU

Utsunomiya

Toyama   Maebashi   Kofu   TOKYO   Chiba

Kanazawa   Gifu   Ichinomiya   YOKOHAMA   Kawasaki

  Yokosuka

Kyoto   Fuse   NAGOYA   Yokkaichi   Shizuoka

Ichinomiya   Kobe   OSAKA   Toyohashi   Hamamatsu

Wakasa Bay

Tottori   Sakai   Wakayama

Izumo   Himeji

Okayama   Takamatsu   Tokushima

Hiroshima   Kure   Matsuyama   SHIKOKU

Shimonoseki   Kochi

Yawata   Beppu

Fukuoka   Kumamoto   Miyakonojo

Sasebo   Nobeoka   KYUSHU

Nagasaki   Sendai   C. Toi

  Miyazaki   Tanega-shima

Kagoshima

Yaku-shima

RYUKYU ISLANDS

Suruga Bay

Eki Channel

Kii Channel

Hayo Strait

Inland Sea

Korea Strait

Tsushima

Tsushima Strait

PACIFIC   OCEAN

SEA OF JAPAN

EAST CHINA SEA

U.S.S.R.

CHINA

NORTH KOREA

SOUTH KOREA

45°

40°

35°

30°

120°   125°   130°   135°   140°   145°

PHILIPPINE ISLANDS

● National Capital

0   Miles   300

MANILA	Over 1,000,000 population
Quezon City	250,000-1,000,000 population
Cebu	100,000- 250,000 population
	50,000- 100,000 population

BATAN ISLANDS

BABUYAN ISLANDS

Babuyan Channel

C. Engaño

Claveria   Aparti

Laoag   Tuguegarao

Vigan   Bangued   Ilagan

Solano

San Fernando   Bayombong

Lingayen Gulf   Dagupan   Cabanatuan

Lingayen   Camiling

LUZON   Tarlac

Iba   Cabanatuan

Balanga   Quezon City

Manila Bay   MANILA

Cavite   Balayan   San Pablo

Batangas   San Jose

MINDORO   Pola

Marinduque

CALAMIAN ISLANDS

Busuanga

Taytay

Bacuit

PALAWAN

Puerto Princesa

Balabac

Balabac Strait

Tablas   Pandan   Catanduanes

Daet

Paracale

Tabaco   Legaspi

Bulan

Masbate   MASBATE

Calamian   Oras

Catbalogan   SAMAR

Tacloban

Bogo   MacArthur

Iloilo   Baybay   LEYTE

PANAY   La Carlota   Cebu   Tagbilaran

Pototan   Bacolod   CEBU   Bohol

NEGROS   Tanjay

Catanan

Dinagat

Surigao

Butuan

Talisayan

Cagayan

Oroquieta   Hilo

Dipolog   Ozamiz   MINDANAO   Davao

Pagadian   Cotabato   Digos   Mati

Liloy   Dulawan   Malita

Zamboanga   Talayan

Basilan   Davao Gulf

Jolo   Tinaca Point

Jolo

SABAH

BORNEO

PHILIPPINE SEA

SOUTH CHINA SEA

SULU SEA

CELEBES SEA

SULU ARCHIPELAGO

Luzon Strait

Lingayen Gulf

Manila Bay

Mindoro Strait

Tablas Strait

Sibuyan Sea

Samar Sea

Leyte Gulf

Visayan Sea

Panay Gulf

Mindanao Sea

Moro Gulf

Basilan Strait

Illana Bay

20°

15°

10°

5°

120°   125°

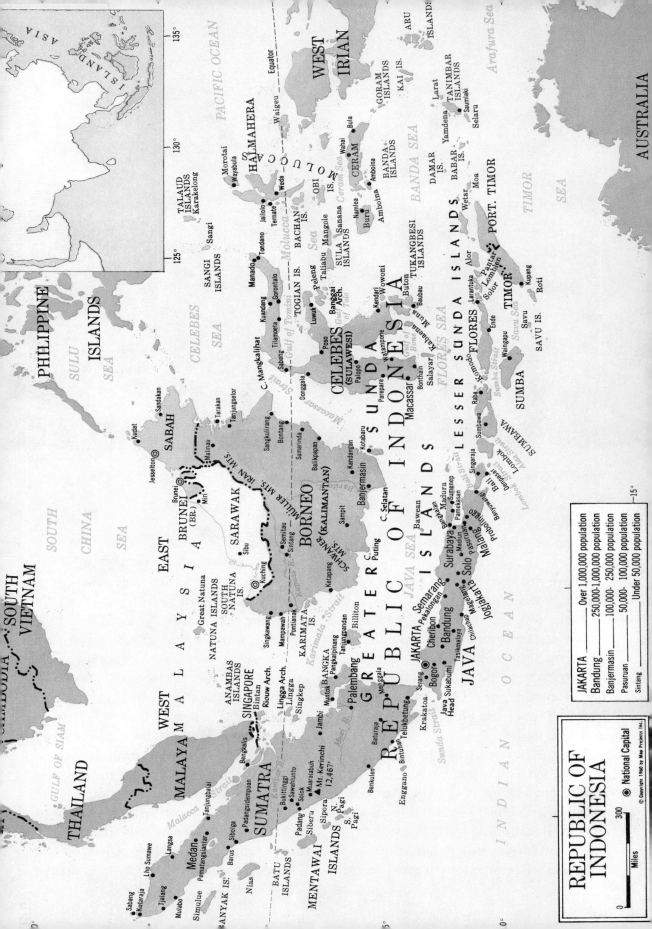

REPUBLIC OF INDONESIA

ASIA

ISLANDS

135°

130°

125°

PACIFIC OCEAN

Equator

WEST IRIAN

Waigeu

Morotai
Wayabula

HALMAHERA

GORAM ISLANDS

KAI IS.

Jailolo
Ternate
Weda

MOLUCCA

Bula
CERAM
Wahai

TANIMBAR ISLANDS
Larat

DAMAR IS.
Yamdena
Saumlaki
Selaru

BANDA SEA

BACHAN IS.

Sula
Sanana
Mangole

OBI

Namlea
Buru
Amboina

BANDA ISLANDS

Amboina

Tondano

Sangi

SANGI ISLANDS

TALAUD ISLANDS
Karakelong

Manado

Kuandang

Gorontalo

TOGIAN IS.

Peleng
Luwuk
Banggai Arch.

Taliabu
Mangole

SULA ISLANDS

Wowoni
Kendari

Buton
Baubau

TUKANGBESI ISLANDS

Muna

PORT. TIMOR

Wetar
Moa
Babar IS.

TIMOR

Kupang
Roti

Arafura Sea

SEA

AUSTRALIA

PHILIPPINE ISLANDS

SULU SEA

CELEBES SEA

C. Mangkalihat

Tanjungselor
Sandakan
Tarakan

SABAH

Kudat
Jesselton

Brunei
BRUNEI (BR.)
Miri

SARAWAK

Sibu

Kuching

Malinau
Sangkulirang
Bontang
Samarinda
Balikpapan

IRAN MTS.
MULLER MTS.

SCHWANER MTS.

BORNEO (KALIMANTAN)

Banjermasin
C. Selatan

Kandangan
Kotabaru

Semitau
Sintang
Kapuas R.
Ketapang
Sampit
C. Puting

Singkawang
Mampawah
Pontianak
Tanjungpandan

KARIMATA IS.

Billiton

BANGKA
Muntok
Pangkalpinang

Poso
Parepare
Palopo
Watampone
Donggala
Sabang
Tilamceta

CELEBES (SULAWESI)

Macassar
Bonthain
Salayar

Gulf of Tomini
Gulf of Todo

Gulf of Bone

FLORES SEA

SUNDA

SUNDA ISLANDS

LESSER SUNDA ISLANDS

Raba
Sumbawa
Bima

FLORES
Ende
Larantuka
Alor
Solor
Pantar
Lomblen

Komodo

Maumere

Waingapu

Savu
SAVU IS.

SUMBA

Kadakena

Singaraja
Bali
Denpasar

Bali Strait
Lombok
Sumbawa

Lombok Strait
Alas Strait

Sumba Strait
Savu Sea

Saru Sea

JAVA SEA

Bawean

Surabaya
Madura
Bangkalan
Sumenep
Pamekasan
Madiun
Malang
Probolinggo
Pasuruan
Banjuwangi

Semarang
Solo
Pekalongan
Magelang
Jogjakarta

Madura
Tjilatjap
Tasikmalaja

JAKARTA
Cheribon
Bandung
Bogor
Serang
Sukabumi

Java Head
Krakatoa

Sunda Strait

INDIAN OCEAN

REPUBLIC OF INDONESIA

GREATER SUNDA ISLANDS

JAVA

Palembang
Telukbetung
Menggala

Jambi

Tanjungpandan

Lingga Arch.
Lingga
Singkep

Rouw Arch.
Bintan

SINGAPORE

ANAMBAS ISLANDS

NATUNA ISLANDS

Great Natuna

SOUTH NATUNA IS.

SOUTH CHINA SEA

WEST MALAYA

EAST MALAYSIA

THAILAND
GULF OF SIAM

SOUTH VIETNAM

CAMBODIA

Medan
Lho Sumawe
Langsa
Pematangsiantar

Sabang
Kutaraja
Mulabo
Simulue
Tjalang

Barus
Sibolga
Padangsidempuan

Nias

BATU ISLANDS

MENTAWAI ISLANDS

Siberut
Sipora
N. Pagi
S. Pagi

Padang
Solok
Sawahlunto
Bukittinggi

Mt. Kerinchi 12,467'

Muaralabuh

Bengkulen

Baturaja
Bintuha

Benkulen

Enggano

Tanjungbalai

Bengkalis

Malacca Strait

Kampar R.
Indragiri R.
Hari R.
Musi R.

SUMATRA

ANYAK IS.

15°

0°

REPUBLIC OF INDONESIA

JAKARTA	Over 1,000,000 population
Bandung	250,000–1,000,000 population
Banjermasin	100,000– 250,000 population
Pasuruan	50,000– 100,000 population
Sintang	Under 50,000 population

◉ National Capital

0   300   Miles

© Copyright 1960 by Map Projects Inc.

Nagasaki, a leading Japanese port, was the first Japanese city which was opened to traders from Europe.

ISLAND ASIA

There are thousands of islands off the east and south-east coasts of Asia. Most of them are grouped in curved chains which are festooned from the continent. There are three main goups, each composed of several large islands and a number of smaller ones. They form the countries of Japan, the Philippines, Malaysia, and Indonesia.

Some of the islands can be seen on maps of Asia, but others are too small to be shown on any general map. And many islands which look close together on a map may be hundreds of miles apart.

These islands, which skirt the eastern edge of Asia, are the tops of great volcanic mountain ranges, which were thrown up many thousands of years ago.

On the seaward or Pacific side of these island mountain ranges, is a series of ocean deeps or trenches. Some of the greatest ocean depths are found here. Near these islands depths have been recorded of over 5,000 fathoms (30,000 feet).

The three island groups we are considering stretch in latitude from 45 degrees north to 10 degrees south of the Equator. This is a distance of more than 4,000 miles. But in spite of being in such very different latitudes the islands in these three groups have much in common.

Having what is called a maritime

climate, they experience fewer extremes of temperature than do the inland areas of continents. They have plenty of rainfall, though the rainy season falls at different times. All three groups are affected by severe storms called typhoons, sometimes accompanied by tidal waves that cause considerable loss of life and destruction of property.

Being so mountainous, these islands have only a relatively small area of arable land. They are, moreover, densely populated. Accordingly, every manageable slope is cut into terraces so that the maximum amount of land may be cultivated. Though the people, and the crops they grow, differ from place to place, much the same primitive methods of farming are still used. Most of the work is done by hand. Most of the slopes that cannot be tilled are heavily forested. The timber grown is often of great economic value.

Being for the most part close together, and also close to large continental countries, these islands are well placed for trade.

Some very primitive tribes still live in the interior forests of New Guinea, Borneo, and the Philippines. But there are also people who have had a high level of culture and civilisation for thousands of years.

Most of these islands have, at one time or another, been colonies of European powers, who have left their imprint on them. As a result, besides Asiatic races found on them — Japanese, Chinese, Indians, Malayans, and Arabs — there are also people of Spanish, Portuguese, Dutch, British, and American descent.

Japan's total area amounts to only 142,000 square miles: only a little greater

Ernst A. Heiniger

Japanese farm workers, one wearing a thatched grass raincoat, cultivate hillside rice paddies.

Tidy rice-fields and trees are typical in mountainous central Honshu, Japan's largest island.

Joe Barnell - Shostal

Japan's fishermen supply a major part of the nation's food, as well as a leading export item.

Girls carry seaweed to be dried and processed. Seaweed is important in the Japanese diet.

than that of Italy and Switzerland put together. The population however has risen to 100 million, which means an average density of 704 per square mile. In the past the over-population of Japan was a contributory cause of her drive to acquire additional territory; and since 1945 it has led her to redouble her efforts in the industrial field. It is only through

exports that Japan can maintain her population.

Along the Japanese islands there runs a mountain range which sends out lateral branches. High peaks are separated by comparatively low valleys, which lie at the height of the original uplands, above which the peaks have been thrust by volcanic action. Volcanic craters and

The silk industry is an old one in Japan. Here newly woven cloth is washed in a stream.

This bicycle factory in Tokyo is an example of Japan's newer industries.

cones are abundant. Fujiyama, the sacred mountain, which last erupted in 1709, is the highest in the country, being 12,395 feet above sea-level. It is generally considered one of the most beautiful mountains in the world. Japan also suffers repeated earthquakes, the worst of recent years being in 1923. The country has a remarkably indented coast. If the coastline could be stretched out, it would reach nearly half-way round the world.

Japan lies on about the same latitude as the Mediterranean. The climate is maritime. Rainfall is heavy, giving rise to luxuriant vegetation. 60 per cent of the land is covered by forest — oaks, maples, and beeches — in the north; sub-tropical forest in the south. The crops in the south include rice, tea, and cotton.

Owing to the mountains, only one-seventh of the islands of Japan, amounting to 21,000 square miles, is capable

David Forbert - Shostal

Kimonoed girls pick tea from well-trimmed bushes in Shizuoka Prefecture, central Honshu.

of cultivation. To make up for this, the Japanese work with the utmost diligence to get the maximum yield from the land, employing every artifice, including the massive use of fertilisers. The very small

Shipbuilding is an important industry to an island nation. This yard is at Nagasaki.

David Forbert - Shostal

Steel mills, like this one at Yawata, have become common sights in present-day Japan.

David Forbert - Shostal

A. Kolb, Hamburg

Bundles of Manila hemp await shipment to the factory. Hemp is a major export of the Philippines.

Ed Drews - Photo Researchers

Philippine mahogany is a beautifully grained wood which is in demand for fine furniture.

Primitive Igorot tribesmen of northern Luzon still grind their grain in crude mortars.

Harrison Forman - Shostal

size of the fields makes them suitable for this intensive cultivation. In spite of all efforts, however, the country cannot produce enough food for its population. Rice, which forms the major part of Japanese diet, is naturally the chief crop. It occupies practically all the plains, pushing other crops up the hillside. The low dykes which separate the rice-fields are themselves planted with vegetables: particularly soya-beans, or sometimes with mulberry trees. The upper, non-irrigated fields are planted with a variety of crops so that both sowing and harvesting can be done progressively. With good organisation sometimes as many as four crops a year can be raised on a piece of land.

Steps have been taken to mechanise farming, in so far as it is possible. A good deal of ploughing, harrowing, and harvesting is now done by machinery. Sowing, transplanting, and harvesting of rice is still done by hand, but the threshing and husking are done by machinery. Imports of rice have been considerably reduced, but a certain amount is bought from Asiatic countries, which take Japanese manufactured goods in exchange.

Fishing is a most essential industry to the Japanese. It employs over 500,000 people, and the catch amounts to 5 million tons a year. On the other hand, except for some dairy farming, there is very little livestock in Japan. Very little meat is eaten, barely seven pounds per head per year.

A third of the national income of Japan comes from her factories: 22 per cent of her population is employed in manufacturing, 20 per cent in commerce and 22 per cent in agriculture.

Industry in Japan exists on two levels.

On the one hand there are a multitude of small factories and even smaller workshops, supplemented by an appreciable amount of manufacture which is actually done at home in and around the big towns. Many part-time workers are engaged in this cottage industry, as it is called, particularly women and girls.

On the other hand there are the large organisations, the gigantic trusts, the *Zaibatsu*: grouping shipyards, steel-works, refineries, factories of every sort, railway companies, and big general stores.

Japanese industry suffers under the double handicap of being ill-provided with both sources of energy and raw materials. On the other hand she has a large supply of cheap, skilled labour.

Coal is poor both in quality and quantity. Only a third of it can be used for making coke. The output of oil is small. Water-power is the only abundant source of energy, but even that is only available during the rainy season (the monsoon), so that hydro-electric power stations have to be duplicated by those burning coal or oil. However copper and sulphur are fairly abundant and forests furnish all the cellulose necessary for the manufacture of plastic goods and synthetic fibres. Three gold veins are to be exploited in north-east Japan.

Accordingly Japan has to buy many raw materials from the under-industrialised countries of Asia.

Japanese industry produces a wide range of manufactures including textiles, chemicals, and a wide range of consumer goods, particularly radio sets, optical equipment and cameras, which are sold all over the world. Added to those are the products of heavy and processing industries. Japan leads the world in shipbuilding.

The Philippines consist of more than 7,000 islands of varying size, forming

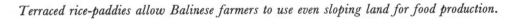

Terraced rice-paddies allow Balinese farmers to use even sloping land for food production.

Wolfe Worldwide Films, Los Angeles 24, Calif

a state that, in all, covers an area of 115,000 square miles. The two largest islands are Luzon, in the north, and Mindanao in the south. The capital is Quezon City, but the actual seat of government is in Manila, which, with a population of 1,402,000, is the only really large town in the archipelago. Both these towns are on Luzon which contains half the total population.

The islands are mountainous, and most of the mountains volcanic. Off the eastern shores, running north and south, is the deepest ocean trench in the world. At its deepest it is nearly 5,800 fathoms. The climate is tropical, moist and warm, becoming cooler in the mountains.

Over half of the population of the Philippines are employed in agriculture, which provides two-fifths of the national income.

19 per cent of the land is cultivated, if we include fruit farming and the growing of coconuts. The development of trade with the United States has greatly encouraged commercial crops. In addition to Manila hemp, and copra and coir (the two products of the coconut), there are plantations of sugar-cane and tobacco. Copra and sugar are the chief exports.

These commercial crops take up 40 per cent of the arable land, with the result that home-grown food is not sufficient for the population, and a certain amount of rice has to be imported.

Industry is for the most part on the artisan level and is at present chiefly concerned with the processing of agricultural produce, such as sugar-refining, tinning pineapples, and the making of rope and cigarettes.

After Malaysia the Philippines are the

Gilloon Photo Agency

Dyak women doing their housework near a 'long house' in Indonesia.

second biggest producer of iron ore in South-East Asia. The principal mines are in the north east of Mindanao and the south of Luzon. The Philippines come fourth amongst the countries of the world

Rice and cassava, grown in the coastal plains, are the principal food crops of Indonesia.

Bill Stapleton - Rapho Guillumette

in the production of chromium. There are also some gold mines.

In Manila there are some foundries and a certain amount of mechanical engineering.

The 3,000 islands of Indonesia compose the greatest archipelago in the world, and cover an area of more than half a million square miles with a total population of about 118 million. Running right across the Equator and enjoying an almost constant temperature, a little under 80° F., they have a luxuriant vegetation of palm trees, bamboos, lianas, and banana trees.

Java is much the most important of the Indonesian islands. Though only one-tenth of the area of Indonesia, it has a population of 72.6 million, which is over 60 per cent of the total population. A population averaging over 1,200 to the square mile, in a country lying on the Equator, is remarkable, but there are various factors to explain it. The soil is extremely fertile, formed, as it is in many places, by volcanic ash, and irrigation schemes have not been difficult to introduce. To the traditional crop of rice, which the Javanese have for long been expert in growing, the Dutch added plantations of sugar-cane, coffee, tea, tobacco, and hevea, the tree which produces rubber. There is also oil in the eastern part of the island. Main towns are Jakarta, Surabaya, and Bandung.

Sumatra, lying to the north-west of Java is a very much bigger island, but has only 18.3 million inhabitants. Chains of mountains run all along the south-west coast, some of the heights reaching 10,000 feet, while on the other side of the island marshy plains, mangrove-covered, slope down towards the South China

Gilloon - Photo Agency

These cowboys of Jesselton, Sabah, are very colourful individuals.

Sea. The population, living chiefly in the mountains, consists for the most part of Moslems, only the Bataks having been converted to Christianity. The big towns, however, are on the coastal plains, Medan

A fishing boat from a coastal village drops anchor off a tiny island in the Java Sea.

Van Bucher - Photo Researchers

Latex from Malayan rubber plantations is shipped to all parts of the world.

Sheets of crude rubber — latex coagulated by adding acid — are dried on heavy racks.

and Palembang in the north-east and Padang on the south-west coast. Rice is the chief food crop, while rubber, coffee, tea, and tobacco are exported.

The small island of Bali has an area of 2,200 square miles and a population of about 2 million. The people are the most expert rice-growers in the archipelago, and coffee, and sugar-cane are also grown. Unlike their Javanese neighbours, the Balinese have remained faithful to their Hindu faith.

These mountainous islands are remarkably volcanic. Altogether there are 100 active volcanoes.

This Malayan hut is built on stilts as a protection against floods and wild animals.

On the foothills of the volcanic mountains are grown cinchona, tea, and coffee, as well as tobacco, oil-palms and heveas in Sumatra, coconut palms in New Guinea, and sugar-cane in Java. Indonesia comes second in the world's leading producers of rubber and quinine. But the plantations have never reached the degree of productivity of the intensively cultivated small-holdings, where the work is closer to the traditions of the people.

Coal is rare, but oil fairly abundant. Indonesia produces 20 million tons a year, which is about 75 per cent of the total production of Eastern Asia, leaving out China. The chief oil-fields are in Sumatra, Java, and South Borneo.

The federation of Malaysia, with an area of 127,281 square miles, consists of Malaya, Sabah (previously called North Borneo), and Sarawak. Its total population is about 8½ million. All the territories share the same characteristics of a hot, wet equatorial climate; a soil rich in mineral wealth; and a largely uncleared jungle.

Malaya produces more of the world's

Ewing Krainin - Photo Researchers

A worker shaves off some of the bark from a rubber tree to permit the latex to seep out.

are on the west coast of the peninsula under the gravel beds of rivers. The metal has to be separated from mud and sand and melted into ingots, which are then exported from Penang on the west coast, or Singapore. Rice, copra, palm oil, and pineapple are important crops and timber is a significant export. Industries are now fast growing-up around the towns and cities, notably near Kuala Lumpur.

Separated from the mainland by the Strait of Johore is the island and town of Singapore. This independent island has a population of almost 2 million.

Sabah or North Borneo is about three-fifths the size of Malaya, but the population is only about 578,000. It is largely jungle-covered and undeveloped. However, it has the only railway in the Borneo territories, which runs from Jesselton to Weston on Brunei Bay.

supply of rubber than any other country. In 1967, 980,000 tons of it were exported. Next in importance as an export is tin, of which Malaya produces nearly a third of the world's supply. The chief deposits

The Hong Fatt tin mine, more than 400 feet deep, is one of Malaya's largest mines.

British Information Service

Millions of Africans live in villages like this one in Zambia. The round huts have grass roofs.

THIS IS AFRICA

The continent of Africa is washed by the waters of the Atlantic Ocean, the Indian Ocean, and the Red and Mediterranean Seas. From the extreme north in Tunisia to the Cape of Good Hope in the south, it stretches for 5,000 miles.

The total area of the continent approaches 12 million square miles. This makes it the second largest of the world's seven continents, the largest being Asia. The land of Africa is nearly one-fifth of all the land in the world. It is so big that Western Europe, the United States, China, and India could be put into it.

Apart from the coastal regions, most of the continent was unknown until about 100 years ago. Many men had tried to penetrate into the interior, but the nature of the country made it difficult. Even the coastal parts were often inaccessible, for the smooth coastline offered few natural harbours, and ships found it difficult to get through the rough surf to approach the shore. Few of the rivers provide waterways into the interior, for as a rule they reach the coast over waterfalls and rapids from a high plateau.

Inland, too, the way was blocked. In some places there were great expanses of sun-scorched desert, in others, dense jungle made travel equally difficult. The going was nowhere easy, and in many places virtually impossible.

Yet some daring explorers were ready to brave all the dangers and difficulties. They crossed blazing deserts and treacherous swamps; they cut their way through the thickest jungles. And they brought back stories of strange people, unknown animals, mighty rivers, lakes, plains, and forbidding mountains. Only now are we really beginning to know about Africa, to appreciate its beauty, to discover its tremendous natural resources, and to study the manners and customs of its 300 million people.

Laying a pipeline to carry crude oil to the refinery at Hassi Messaoud.

The greater part of the continent consists of a vast plateau which is lower in the north than in the south. In the extreme north-west are the Atlas Mountains, ranges of fold mountains that form part of the mountain system of southern Europe. At the narrowest part of the Strait of Gibraltar, where Africa approaches Europe, the continents are only nine miles apart. South of the Equator the plateau, which rises to a high ridge called the Drakensberg in the south-east, descends abruptly on all sides to narrow coastal plains.

Africa is a continent of great physical variety. The western half of Central Africa is covered by a vast tropical rain-forest. Rivers and narrow tracks are the only routes through the crowding trees and dense undergrowth. The branches of the taller trees intermingle to form a green canopy over all.

Rimmed around the edges of the tropical rain-forest is the savanna. This is made up mainly of grasslands with shrubs and scattered trees stretching for hundreds of miles between the jungles and the arid areas that lie to the north in the Sahara and south-west in the Kalahari and Namib deserts. Near the forest, the savanna has tall grasses, shrubs, and trees. As it approaches the desert, it becomes treeless — the broad sweep of the plains of short grass being broken only here and there by stunted bushes. Most of the big game of Africa lives among the tall grass and long trees of the savanna: antelopes, zebras, giraffes, elephants, and lions.

North of the tropical jungles the savanna reaches into the Sudan. It stretches from the Atlantic, past the Upper Niger almost to the Red Sea and Ethiopia.

South of the savanna, in South Africa, is another area of grasslands known as the 'veld', a Dutch word meaning 'field'. The veld is bounded on the west by a very dry region known as the Kalahari Desert. The Kalahari is, however, a mere baby compared to the enormous Sahara which flanks the northern savanna.

The Sahara is the biggest desert in the world. From the Atlantic to the Red Sea it stretches for 3,000 miles. From north to south it is 1,000 miles wide, and it separates North Africa from the rest of the continent. The Sahara occupies nearly a third of the entire continent.

Grassland covers a little more than two-fifths of the continent, forest a little less than one fifth. The remainder is desert. Within the broad areas of forest, savanna, desert, and coastal strips, there are many striking features. In East Africa, the land rises into highlands with extinct volcanoes towering above them. Even though they are almost directly on the Equator, Mount Kilimanjaro (more than 19,500 feet) and Mount Kenya (17,000 feet) are capped perpetually by a mantle of snow. Nearby is the East African Rift Valley, a deep valley running north and south, stretching for thousands of miles.

From a geological point of view Africa is considered unique amongst the continents because it consists of a single great shield of ancient rock. It is thought by some that the oldest rock of Africa was formed over 300 million years ago. Geologists have also observed that the rock-structure of Africa is very much like that of eastern Brazil, India, and the western part of Australia.

Those who study maps have for long been fascinated by the idea that these parts of the earth, now so widely separated, may once have been part of the same land mass. The eastern bulge of Brazil, for instance, would seem to fit fairly neatly into the Gulf of Guinea, which forms the great inward curve of the West African coast. Similarly, though less obviously, the western coasts of India and Australia can be made to fit on to the east coast of Africa. It is believed by scientists that, about 260 million years ago, all these lands were part of the same continent, to which they have given the name 'Gondwanaland'. According

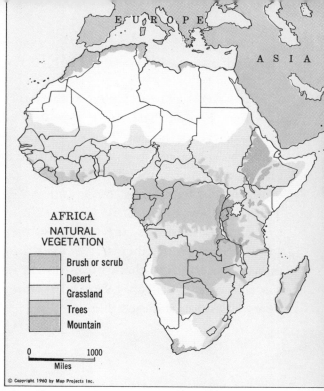

to them continental drift resulted in Gondwanaland being broken up into several land masses. The separate land masses were the rudiments of the continents we know today.

Ethiopia, a land of rugged highlands and mountains, is surrounded by hot, dry lowlands. Because of its height, Ethiopia receives considerable rainfall, enough to support lush forests and meadows.

W. Kuls

RIVERS OF AFRICA

Great rivers pour down from the heart of Africa. Five of them drain almost two-thirds of the continent. For hundreds of miles the rivers move sluggishly through marshlands or tropical forests fed by thousands of tributaries, large and small. Then as they begin their descent from the central plateaus the rivers gather speed. Some hurl themselves over immense waterfalls, others rush down in a series of short steep rapids. In either case navigation is impossible.

The longest river is the Nile — the longest not only of Africa, but of the whole world, if measured from its first source. From its head waters at Lake Victoria to its mouth in the Mediterranean, the Nile is over 4,000 miles long. It is actually two rivers. The White Nile begins with the jungle rainwater draining into Lake Victoria, which lies at the junction of Uganda, Kenya, and Tanzania. It flows northward through the Sudan, and is joined at Khartoum

Conzett and Huber

Only a few stunted trees can live amid the sprawling sand-dunes of the Sahara desert. Yet water can make the desert bloom.

A contrast to the arid Sahara: the lush vegetation of the Nigerian jungle.

by the Blue Nile. The Blue Nile rises in Lake Tana, high in the mountains of Ethiopia. The Nile continues northward, then turns sharply to the southwest to sweep in a great curve round the Nubian Desert. Then it drops sharply in a succession of rapids and flows through Egypt to the Mediterranean. The Lower Nile is as much as ten miles wide. Below Cairo it is broken up into many branches by the delta it has formed at its mouth.

The next longest river is the Congo.

The two Niles — the Blue and the White — flow into each other at Khartoum to form Africa's greatest river. Egypt's flourishing agriculture depends on the water of the Nile for irrigation.

Conzett and Huber

Kilimanjaro, Africa's highest mountain, rears its snow-covered summit nearly four miles into the sky.

In the course of its 2,900 miles, it drains $1\frac{1}{2}$ million square miles of Central Africa. In its descent from the central plateau, it passes over several series of rapids and two waterfalls. The Congo is the only river in Africa to cross the Equator twice. In some places it is so wide that it splits into many arms. There are more than 400 islands in the river.

The third river is the Niger, 2,600 miles long. For many years explorers sought to trace the courses of this mysterious river which, they believed, flowed westward into the Atlantic.

Actually it rises in mountains 200 miles from the Atlantic and starts to flow eastward. It then swings in a wide northerly loop into the Sahara Desert, where its flood-waters make it possible to grow rice and cotton in the area round Timbuktu. Then the Niger turns to the south, to the Gulf of Guinea, where its delta spreads across 200 miles of marshy coast.

The first white man to see the Niger was the Scottish explorer Mungo Park.

The Zambezi, about 2,200 miles in length, forms the border between Zambia and Rhodesia, then crosses Mozambique to discharge into the Mozambique Channel, between Madagascar and Africa. Like the Congo, it drains a huge area of the central plateau. Near the town

A rainbow arcs across clouds of spray from the thundering waters of Victoria Falls, where the Zambezi River plunges 347 feet into a narrow, rocky gorge.

Mountain craters reveal the volcanic origin of the Canary Islands, off Africa's north-west coast.

Algeria. A deep well enables crops to be grown where once there was only barren desert.

of Livingstone, the Zambezi plunges over the Victoria Falls at a rate of 47 million gallons of water every minute. Because of the booming sound it makes and the clouds of spray thrown upwards, the native tribes called the Victoria Falls the 'Smoke that Thunders'.

Leaving Central Africa, the chief river of the south is the Orange. It flows for 1,300 miles, almost completely crossing the Republic of South Africa, to discharge into the Atlantic some 400 miles north of the Cape. It flows through parts of the Kalahari Desert, but this stretch is generally dry, and so the river is useless either for navigation or irrigation, except in isolated schemes. There are several diamond deposits near its mouth.

The waters of the Atlantic and Indian oceans meet at Africa's southern tip, the Cape of Good Hope, once called the Cape of Storms. Today many South African coastal areas are popular beach resorts.

Courtesy of the South African Tourist Corporation

A herd of zebras drinks at a South African waterhole. They keep a wary lookout for prowling lions.

THE ANIMALS OF AFRICA

Africa has a richer variety of animal life than any other part of the world. Many of them are well-known: lions, elephants, gorillas, zebras, camels, giraffes, etc. But many are less familiar. The aardvark, for example, with its long ears, thick tail, sharp claws, and long snout is somewhere between an ant-eater and an armadillo. With its claws the aardvark tips open the tall mounds which are termite nests and scoops up thousands of the insects with its long sticky tongue.

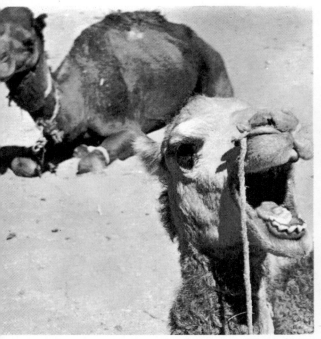

Kerwin B. Roche - House of Photography

Raymond Bricon

Gatti - FPG

The evil-tempered camel snarls and groans at its master. But it carries huge loads across the desert.

Giant anthills like the one shown provide food for the termite-eating aardvark.

Alfred G. Milotte

Buffalo are among Africa's most feared animals because of their strength and wicked, curving horns.

M. M. Schechter

A lioness stalks warily through the African bush. The African lion is known as the 'King of Beasts'.

Some animals live in particular areas. The Congo is the home of the gorilla. The lemur, a small monkey, swings in the forests of Madagascar. The grey parrot, the variety that can learn to talk, lives mostly in West Africa. The jackass penguin, whose cry sounds like a donkey's bray, waddles about on the coasts of South Africa. An interesting desert animal is the fennec, a tiny fox that

Giraffes' spots protect them from their natural enemies by acting as camouflage and blending with the vegetation.

Alfred G. Milotte

The speedy cheetah pauses to scan the plains for a possible victim for his next meal.

A hippopotamus grazes on dry land. Hippos are hunted for their hides.

lives in the Sahara, hiding by day and hunting lizards at night. The biggest concentration of game is on the high open plains of East Africa. Here the visitor can sometimes see as many as 10,000 animals in a day. Even this figure is tiny compared with what it was a century or so ago. Today many species are threatened with extermination.

Among the most interesting features of Africa are the great National Parks and Game Reserves. Here animals are free to roam, and hunting is prohibited. Since they are never shot at, the animals have lost their fear of man, and a lion will often walk right up to a parked car,

Ostriches are raised on farms for their feathers.

A tick-bird perches on the back of an impala, a graceful antelope of the African savannas.

'Rhinoceros' is Greek for 'horn-nosed'. When a rhino twitches his ears, he is about to charge.

African waters teem with crocodiles. They can lie motionless for hours then move with lightning speed.

indifferent to the occupants within.

Although millions of wild animals are still at large in Africa, experts estimate that nearly all the larger ones that have not sought the protection of the parks will be wiped out in the next twenty years by disease, by hunters, or simply the advance of civilisation. More and more ranches — even towns — are being developed where lions used to prowl. Thousands of square miles have been flooded by the building of new dams, as happened, for example, when the Kariba dam was built.

An elephant herd plunges into a stream to bathe. An elephant can eat 1,000 pounds of food a day.

Raymond Bricon

The proud Tuareg live in the Sahara.

THE PEOPLES OF AFRICA

The peoples of Africa fall into five main groups:

(1) Arabs, living mostly in Egypt and North Africa.

(2) Hamites, who occupy Ethiopia and most of the Sahara.

(3) The 'true' Negroes who live in West Africa and the Sudan.

(4) Isolated aborigines: the Bushmen of the Kalahari Desert, the Hottentots of South-West Africa, and the Pygmies of the Congo.

(5) The Bantus, Negro people who live in Central and Southern Africa.

To these must now be added some 5 million settlers of European stock, most of whom live either along the north coast of Africa or in the southern part. Inter-marriage has created a still more complicated racial pattern.

Charles Erikson - Shostal

A Libyan boy cradles his pet, a baby gazelle, in his arms. This tiny antelope lives in the desert.

Nigeria. The armour worn by the Emir of Kano's guard once belonged to the Crusaders.

Barefoot boys pass in front of the Coptic cathedral in Addis Ababa, Ethiopia's capital.

About 90 million (mainly in the north and east) are Moslems. About 30 million have been converted to Christianity. That leaves well over 100 million who are either Africans worshipping tribal gods, or Indians, who are Hindus.

Within the population of about 300

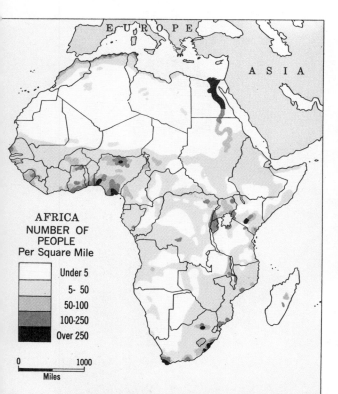

AFRICA
NUMBER OF
PEOPLE
Per Square Mile

Under 5
5- 50
50-100
100-250
Over 250

0   1000
Miles

Berbers, the chief native race of North Africa, are noted for their skill as horsemen. These men are armed with antique brass-bound muskets.

Bernheim - Conant, AMNH-FLO

It may hurt a bit, but these youngsters are proud of the anti-tuberculosis vaccinations.

million there are many different colours and races, and there are innumerable tribal groups. At least sixteen separate major languages are spoken, within each of which are many varieties of dialect and pronunciation.

Today, anthropologists, who study the

Paul Hufner - Shostal

A water seller fills a drinking cup. Water sellers are very important people in the dry regions of North Africa.

Mud houses are typical of northern Ghana.

Stephanie Dinkins - House of Photography

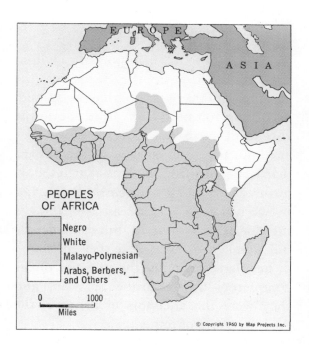

PEOPLES
OF AFRICA

Negro
White
Malayo-Polynesian
Arabs, Berbers,
and Others

0   1000
Miles

© Copyright 1960 by Map Projects Inc.

Villagers in the Sudan build their circular huts round a central clearing.

evolution of the human race believe that the earliest men developed in Africa. Bones of ape-like creatures with some human characteristics have been found

Egyptian steelworkers watch the tapping of the furnace in Egypt's first steel plant.

in different parts of East Africa, and it may be they are the long-sought 'missing links' of our evolutionary history.

Except for the area along the Mediterranean coast, very little was known of Africa until about 200 years ago, but we know now that important civilisations flourished in the heart of the continent 1,000 years ago, having spread, according to one theory, from the fertile regions of north-east Africa.

About the year 3,000 B.C. the Sahara dried out into the desert that it is today, forming an almost impassable barrier between the Mediterranean area and the interior of the continent. But some people did manage to cross it, either in search of new land or under the pressure of the conquerors from Europe or Asia, and they were the ancestors of many of the African tribes of today.

Watusi tribesmen are the world's tallest people. Warriors like these may reach a height of 7 feet.

A boatman crosses the Uélé River in the Congo.

Two warriors of the famed Masai tribe.

FPG

Two Pygmy children.

Tom Larson - American Museum of Natural History

A woman of a Bushman tribe tends her children.

Wolfe Worldwide Films, Los Angeles, 24, Calif.

In her best clothes, an Ndebele girl grinds corn.

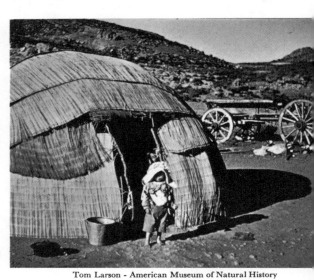

Tom Larson - American Museum of Natural History

A Hottentot child in front of his hut.

Two Zulu women proudly display their beadwork.

Courtesy of the South African Tourist Corporation

Wachagga women carry bananas to market.

Elvajean Hall

A Kikuyu market in Kenya.

The white residents of Johannesburg represent Africa's largest concentration of people of European descent.

246

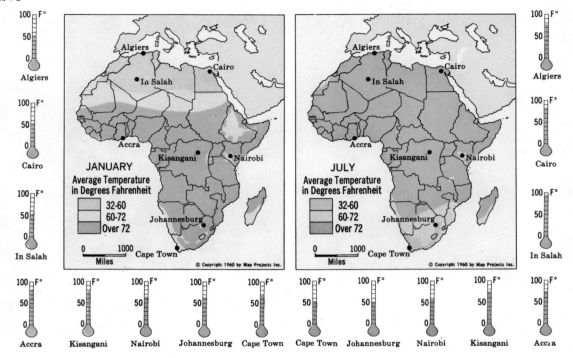

These maps show the average temperature and rainfall of Africa. The symbols around the edge are keyed to important African cities. You will see that the temperature of a place does not necessarily correspond to its distance from the equator. You will also notice that south of the equator the seasons are reversed. Midsummer there is in January, and midwinter comes in July.

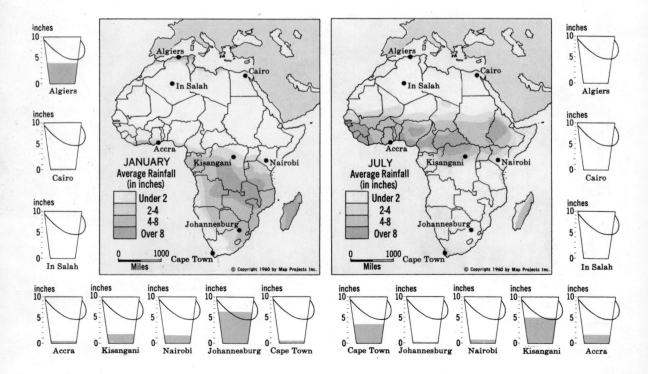

CLIMATE AND PRODUCTS

Three-quarters of Africa — about 9 million square miles — lies within the Tropics. Except in a few mountainous parts the climate of this huge area varies from warm to hot, and the only real seasons are the wet and dry seasons.

Looking at the maps on the opposite page we see that the main climate zones correspond to a considerable degree to what has already been said about the different areas of vegetation. Along the Equator, the centre of the tropical forests, the weather is always hot and the rainfall heavy. Temperatures range from 70° to 90°F and there is rain daily, even in the driest periods. As the land rises towards the east, both temperature and rainfall become less. In July the average temperature in Addis Ababa, 8,000 feet above sea level, is 17°F lower than it is at Freetown, which is at about the same latitude but in the lowlands of the West Coast. The highest mountains, like Kilimanjaro, are snow-capped all the year round. Rainfall gradually decreases as we move from the tropical forests to the savanna of the north or south, where there are definite dry and wet seasons of varying lengths, the dry season lengthening as the desert is approached. Cool weather alternates with warm. In the dry season, because of the high temperatures, the savannas dry up. Some trees lose their leaves, and the ground becomes too dry for arable farming.

The highest temperatures in Africa are not found on the Equator but in the great deserts. The highest temperature ever recorded in the world was 136°F in the Libyan Sahara. (This, of course, was the *shade* temperature. In the sun the temperature would have been very much higher. And in the desert there is virtually no shade.) It is said that the surface of the ground is sometimes as hot as 170°F. Such temperatures are hot enough to cause the rocks of the desert to crack. On the other hand, the temperature may fall as much as 60°F at night, and in the northern regions frost is quite common in the winter months. The desert climate is very dry, and so there is little vegetation. In some places there is practically no rainfall, and what little there is comes as swift violent storms that can cause local floods. Conditions in the southern deserts, though similar to those in the Sahara, are less extreme.

The northern and southern coastal districts of Africa have a Mediterranean

Unloading a cargo of sugar cane and grain from a Nile sailing vessel.

Joe Barnell - Shostal

Buyers and sellers bargain for red peppers at the open-air market in Dakar, Senegal.

type of climate, with hot, dry summers and cool, rainy winters. Because of this rainfall, most crops are raised in the winter. Summer crops depend entirely on irrigation.

Over 90 per cent of the people of Africa live off the land and its products. Most of them farm, tilling their small plots of land in the traditional manner. Some keep cattle, and a few of the most primitive tribes depend for their food on game and wild plants.

Those who farm in Africa have many problems. The most important are those

A lone herdsman grazes his cattle on the fertile plains at the foot of Mt Meru in Tanzania.

Gordon Douglas - FPG

Africans thresh and winnow grain near Lesotho's High Maluti Mountains.

created by the unreliable supply of water. In the broad savanna lands, where so many people live, the rainfall varies widely from place to place and from year to year. Sometimes the rainfall is not enough to keep the crops alive, and thousands of people go hungry. In other years the rain comes too early or too late. When it does come, it comes in abrupt, heavy downpours, either causing flooding or soil erosion.

The heat is another serious problem. In much of Europe, Asia, and North America 25 inches of rain a year will support farming. But the moisture in the soil is dried up very quickly in hot climates. So a much heavier rainfall or a system of regular irrigation is necessary if farming is to succeed.

The common method of farming on the savanna is to clear a small piece of land by burning off the wild growth. The soil is then broken up and the ash worked in as a fertiliser. Crops are grown on it for a few years, after which the farmer abandons it, moving on to another patch. The abandoned field is soon covered by natural growth which binds the soil and gradually restores its fertility. However, if all the nutrients have been worked out of the soil, nothing will grow, and it quickly turns to desert. There is very little agricultural machinery in Africa. While tractors and similar implements greatly raise production, in many places oxen are a far more valuable asset, for not only do they help with the work, but they create manure for the land as well.

Most Africans live mainly on cereals

Tribesmen from regions south of the Sahara come to the cotton market at Fort Lamy, Chad Republic.

and starches. They do not get enough meat to eat, which means they suffer from lack of protein. Many tribes depend on wild game for their meat supply. Over large areas of Africa it is impossible to raise livestock because of the tsetse fly, which transmits a deadly disease called *nagana* in animals, and 'sleeping sickness' in human beings. Even those tribes which have large herds of cattle do not get enough meat, because they regard their cattle as wealth and will not kill them. Little fish is eaten in Africa except in the immediate neighbourhood of lakes or rivers. Fish spoils quickly in hot climates.

Until new crops were introduced by Europeans, the Africans grew only millet (a kind of coarse cereal) and some rice. Groundnuts, cassava, maize, tobacco, potatoes, coconuts, cocoa beans, and bananas were introduced from America. Citrus fruits came from Portugal. Wheat and barley also came from Europe. The date palm was introduced by the Arabs, who also brought the clove trees to Zanzibar in the nineteenth century.

In the coastal areas bordering the Mediterranean, the fertile valleys are good for farming. Cereals such as wheat and barley, and fruits like figs, grapes,

Fronds of the date palm are a familiar North African sight. The tree usually signals an oasis.

A Liberian slices into the tough bark of a rubber tree, preparing to tap the valuable liquid latex.

Stephanie Dinkins - House of Photography

Native cattle grazing on the high pastures of the Jos Plateau in Nigeria.

W. R. Donagho - Shostal

Workers with machetes cut sisal leaves and pile them on flat-beds for transport to the coast.

and olives, grow very well in this area.

Nearer to the Sahara farms give way to the tents of the nomads, who drive their flocks of sheep from pasture to pasture, from waterhole to waterhole. Crops can only be grown at oases.

On the open savanna, millet and maize are grown, as well as tobacco and cotton. Rice grows near rivers. In the drier areas some of the tribes breed horses and cattle. Large-scale spraying with D.D.T. is beginning to eliminate the tsetse fly, thus making millions of acres of land available for stock-breeding.

In the healthy uplands of Kenya there are many coffee plantations and here, and in other parts of East Africa, cattle breeding is an important pursuit. The main crops of West Africa are palm-oil, groundnuts, and cocoa beans.

The continent has also great stores of mineral wealth, most of which are still unexploited. South Africa is famous for its diamonds and gold, and there are immense copper mines in Zambia and also the Democratic Republic of the Congo (Katanga). Africa has also important deposits of tin, iron, chromium, manganese, cobalt, uranium, and bauxite. South Africa and Nigeria are the only countries with large coal deposits, but oil and natural gas have been found in the Sahara and Libya.

British Information Service

A native farmer in Sierra Leone prepares to harvest the last of the year's cacao crop.

THE EXPLORATION OF AFRICA

We owe our knowledge of Africa to the efforts and courage of many men — sailors and soldiers, adventurers, traders, and missionaries — of whom these are the most important:

GIL EANNES (Portuguese) in 1434 sailed past Cape Bojador on the north-west coast of Africa, and showed the way to later navigators. Previously it had been thought the sea beyond Cape Bojador was filled with monsters, and that in any case strong currents would drive ships back.

NUNO TRISTÃO (Portuguese) discovered the mouth of the Senegal River in 1445, and brought back news of green and fertile country beyond the desert.

BARTHOLOMEU DIAZ (Portuguese) in 1487 was driven by strong winds round the Cape of Good Hope, and passed Algoa Bay beyond Port Elizabeth.

VASCO DA GAMA (Portuguese) sailed round the Cape of Good Hope and along the east coast of Africa and reached India in 1498.

JAMES BRUCE (Scottish) travelled through Ethiopia in 1770—2, tracing the course of the Blue Nile.

MUNGO PARK (Scottish) travelled up the Gambia River in 1795, and then crossed the savanna to reach the Niger. On his second trip in 1805 he explored over 1,000 miles of the Niger before being killed in an attack by natives at the Bussa Rapids.

HUGH CLAPPERTON (English) crossed the desert from Tripoli to Lake Chad in 1821 and explored the centre of the Sudan. In 1825 he started north from the Guinea coast, and after two years' travelling through the jungle, reached the Niger at Bussa. He died at Sokoto.

RICHARD LANDER (English) descended the Niger from Bussa all the way in 1830—1, proving it did not flow either into the Nile or the Congo, as many had thought.

RENÉ CAILLIÉ (French) crossed the Sahara disguised as an Arab, in 1827, reaching Timbuktu.

HEINRICH BARTH (German) made a map of the Sudan and part of the Sahara between 1850 and 1855. He was the sole survivor of a British expedition, and he carried on single-handed for months.

KRAPF AND REBMANN (German missionaries) discovered Mount Kenya and Mount Kilimanjaro in East Africa in 1848—9.

DAVID LIVINGSTONE (Scottish missionary) spent most of his life in Africa. Between 1849 and his death in 1873 he explored the Kalahari Desert, the Zambezi River, Lake Nyasa, the

AFRICA
EXPLORATION

- .... Diogo Cão (Port.)—1482
- .... Bartholomeu Dias (Port.)—1488
- – – – Vasco da Gama (Port.)—1498
- ————— James Bruce (Scotch)—1770-72
- ————— Mungo Park (Scotch)—1795-96; 1805
- – · – · Capt. Hugh Clapperton (Br.)—1821; 1825-27
- – ·· – Richard Lander (Br.)—1830-31
- – – – René Caillie (Fr.)—1827-28
- .... Heinrich Barth (Ger.)—1850-55
- ————— David Livingstone (Br.)—1849-1873
- ————— Henry M. Stanley (Br.-Amer.)—1871; 1874-77

© Copyright 1960 by Map Projects Inc.

CITIES OLD AND NEW

Stephanie Dinkins - House of Photography

The mud-walled city of Kano, in northern Nigeria, has been an important trade centre for 1,000 years.

Shiré River, and the upper course of the Congo. He discovered the Victoria Falls in 1855.

HENRY M. STANLEY (English — American) made a famous trip to rescue Livingstone in 1871. In 1874—7 Stanley followed the Congo down to its mouth, opening up the region for other travellers.

PIERRE SAVORGNAN DE BRAZZA (French) explored the area round the Lower Congo, 1875—80.

The cities of Africa span thousands of years of history: the first cities were those of ancient Egypt — Alexandria, Thebes, Memphis. Then came seafarers from Phoenicia, Greece, and Rome, crossing the Mediterranean to found such North African outposts as Carthage and Tingis (which is now called Tangier). For centuries North Africa was a Roman Province.

Even hundreds of years after the Arabs conquered North Africa the only cities were those on the coast and a few almost legendary towns that served as trading posts in the western Sahara. Of these Timbuktu and Kano (Nigeria), whose 1,000-year-old walls still stand, are two of the best known.

But today Africa can boast dozens of major cities. Some are not as large or as thickly populated as those of Europe and America, but they are often just as busy and just as modern. Some of the most

Dakar, capital of the Senegalese Republic, has many modern districts. It is a major African port.

Charles May - Photo Researchers

H. Wilhelmy

The world's largest mosque is in Cairo. This city has long been a centre of Islam.

exciting new architecture in the world is to be found in the newly independent states of Africa, where old cities are being expanded. These cities present a striking contrast between the old and the new Africa. Each one has its modern quarter. Fine office buildings, luxurious hotels, smart shops, and blocks of flats line the broad streets. There are fine restaurants and cafés, and modern hospitals and government buildings.

But only a mile or two away many Africans live as they have lived for hundreds of years. In the cities of North Africa, the *casbah,* or native quarter, is still a crowded place of narrow, winding streets and heavily shuttered houses. Merchants still sell their goods from open stalls in the market-place or *bazaar.*

Not all of the new Africa is modern office buildings and luxurious hotels. There is much poverty and misery. Natives coming from tribal reserves often find it difficult to adjust to life in industrialised cities, and many of them must live in slums in the hearts of big cities, or in shanty towns on the outskirts.

Cars and modern buildings in the centre of Addis Ababa, capital of Ethiopia.

Agence Rapho

Raymond Bricon

Much of North Africa's trade is carried on in open-air market places like this one in Marrakesh, Morocco.

The modern city of Salisbury, capital and largest city of Rhodesia, is located in the savanna.

Hans von Meiss - Photo Researchers

Courtesy of the South African Tourist Corporation

The city of Cape Town, South Africa, is spread out at the foot of dramatic, flat-topped Table Mountain.

Veiled women in the narrow streets of Tangier only 40 miles from Gibraltar.

Charles Trieschmann - Camera Clix

Herbert Lanks - Monkmeyer

A colourful and bustling street scene in Kinshasa, capital of the Democratic Republic of the Congo.

Goods waiting for export on the docks of 2,300-year-old Alexandria, the chief port of Egypt.

Charles Trieschmann - Camera Clix

Arched gateways and medieval battlements guard the ancient entrances to Tunis's Moslem quarter.

Johannesburg, Africa's third largest city, is surrounded by the huge mounds of debris from its gold mines.

COMMUNICATIONS

There are striking contrasts in the way people travel about in Africa. Communications are either of the most modern or most primitive kinds. Vast areas of Africa are crossed by neither roads nor railways, so travellers in areas where there are no rivers must either walk or go by air.

Fast efficient transport is difficult to run economically in Africa, for three reasons. One is the great distances involved, another is the problem of building roads or railways across deserts or through dense jungles. The third is the shortage of skilled labour and materials.

The chief railway lines are in South Africa, North Africa, and Egypt. But perhaps the most important ones are the smaller railways that link the navigable stretches of Africa's rivers. The rivers are Africa's greatest highways, both for goods and passengers. But most of the big rivers are broken by waterfalls or rapids, so railways have had to be built to bypass them.

Sturdy river steamers ply the Nile, the Niger, the Congo, and other waterways. There are a few cabins, and most of the passengers usually camp out on the upper deck.

Many hundreds of miles of roads are now being constructed in Africa, but most of them are far from being adequate modern highways. Very few are surfaced, and in wet weather many are impassable. Far from being arterial roads, most of them merely lead to the nearest river port or railway station. Cars are rare, and what traffic there is mostly consists of buses and lorries. Under these circumstances air travel naturally assumes great

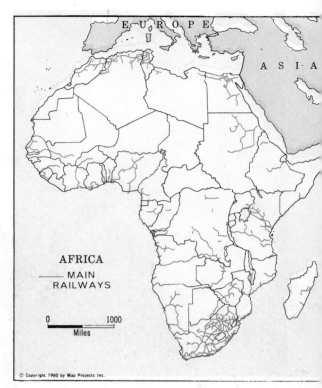

AFRICA
— MAIN RAILWAYS

0 — 1000
Miles

© Copyright 1960 by Map Projects Inc.

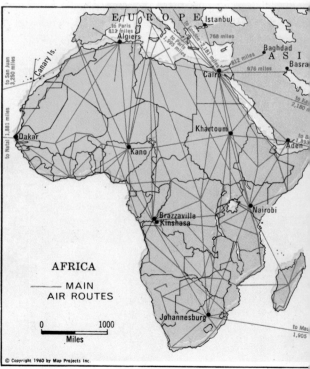

AFRICA
— MAIN AIR ROUTES

0 — 1000
Miles

© Copyright 1960 by Map Projects Inc.

importance. It has succeeded, not merely in saving some people's time, but in opening up many remote areas. But the

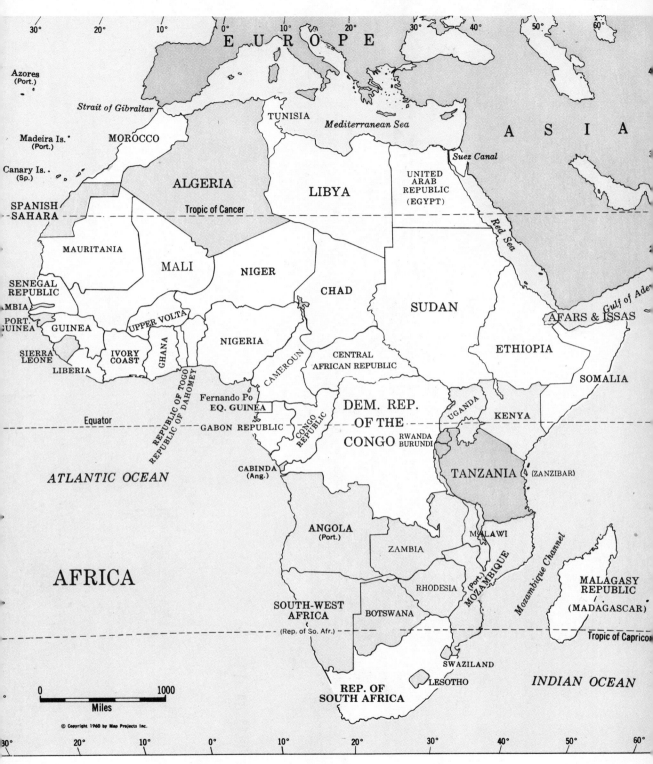

AFRICA

aeroplane has its limitations. It is very expensive to operate, so that the only goods that can make use of it are those that are light, compact, and valuable, and, as for passengers, few people can afford to pay the fare.

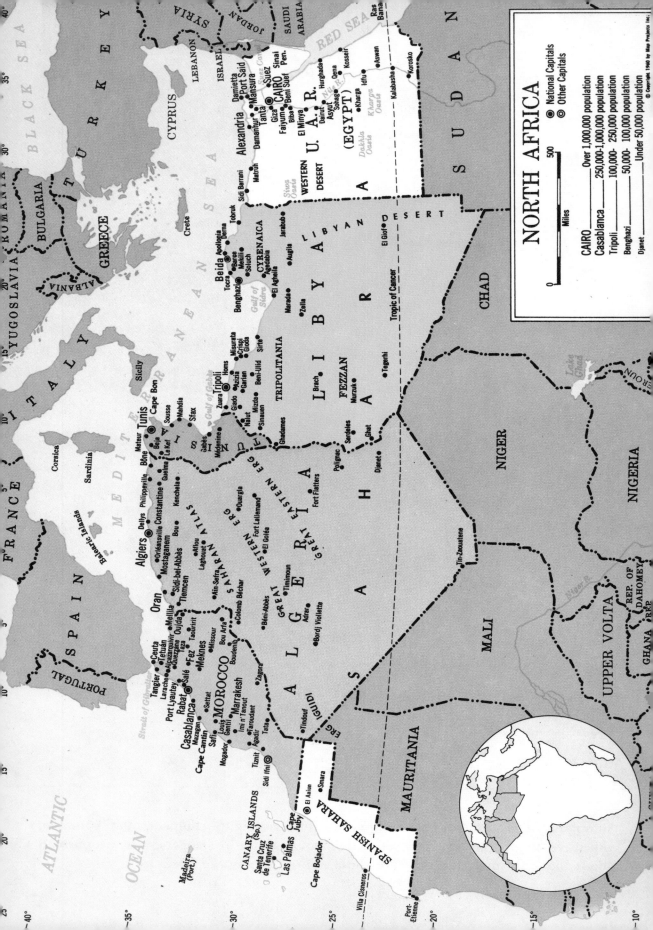

NORTH AFRICA

●	National Capitals
◎	Other Capitals

CAIRO	Over 1,000,000 population
Casablanca	250,000–1,000,000 population
Tripoli	100,000–250,000 population
Benghazi	50,000–100,000 population
Djanet	Under 50,000 population

Miles

0   500

Copyright 1960 by Map Projects Inc.

BLACK SEA

TURKEY   SYRIA   JORDAN   SAUDI ARABIA

RED SEA   Ras Banana

ROMANIA   BULGARIA   GREECE   ALBANIA   YUGOSLAVIA

LEBANON   CYPRUS   ISRAEL

Suez Canal

Damietta   Port Said   Suez   Sinai Pen.
Mansura   CAIRO
Tanta   Giza   Faiyum   Beni Suef
Alexandria   Damanhur   Biba
  El Minya
  Asyut   Kosseir
  Dairut   Hurghada
  Sohage   Qena
  Idfu   Aswan
  Kharga   Korosko
  Kalabasha

U. A. R.

WESTERN DESERT   (EGYPT)

Matruh   Siwa Oasis

Dakhla Oasis   Kharga Oasis

Sidi Barrani

SUDAN

MEDITERRANEAN SEA

Crete

Tobruk   Derna
Apollonia   Barce   Mekili
Beida   Tocra
Benghazi   Soluch   El Agheila
  Agedabia
  Maraba   Augila
  Zella   Jarabub

CYRENAICA

Gulf of Sidra

Jalo

Marada

El Giof   DESERT

LIBYAN DESERT

L I B Y A

Tropic of Cancer

CHAD

ITALY   Sicily   Sardinia   Corsica

FRANCE   Balearic Islands

SPAIN   PORTUGAL

Strait of Gibraltar

Gulf of Gabes

Misurata   Crispi
Homs   Gioda
Tripoli   Sirte
Zuara   Zizia   Beni-Ulid
  Giado   Garian
  Mizda
  Nalut   Sinauen
  Ghadames

TRIPOLITANIA

Brach   FEZZAN
Murzuk   Tegerhi

Sebha

Sarteles   Ghat

Djanet

S A H A R A

Tin-Zaouatene

NIGER

NIGERIA

Tunis   Cape Bon
Mateur   Sousse
Beja   Le Kef   Sfax
Bône   Philippeville   Mahdia
Guelma   Constantine
Kenchela
Dellys   Algiers
Orléansville   Bou
Mostaganem   Ouargla
Oran   Laghouat   Fort Lallemand
Sidi-bel-Abbès   El Goléa
Tlemcen   Aïn-Sefra
Timimoun
  Adrar
Béni-Abbès
Colomb Béchar   Fort Flatters
  Bordj Viollette
Polignac

Gabès   Médenine

T U N I S I A

WESTERN ERG   GREAT EASTERN ERG

SAHARAN ATLAS

GREAT WESTERN ERG

A L G E R I A

Ceuta   Melilla
Tangier   Tetuán
Larache   Alcazarquivir   Ouezzane
Port Lyautey   Taza
Rabat   Fez   Taourirt
Salé   Meknes
Casablanca   Missour
Mazagan   Settat   Bou Arfa
Cape Cantin   Louis Gentil   Boudenib
Safi   Marrakesh   Imi-n-Tanout
Mogador   Taroudant
Cape Ghir   Agadir
  Tiznit   Zagora
  Tata
Sidi Ifni

M O R O C C O

ERG IGUIDI

ERG CHECH

MALI

MAURITANIA

UPPER VOLTA

REP. OF DAHOMEY
GHANA REP.

Smara
El Aiun

SPANISH SAHARA

Cape Juby

CANARY ISLANDS

Madeira (Port.)

Santa Cruz de Tenerife   Las Palmas

Cape Bojador

Villa Cisneros

Port-Etienne

ATLANTIC OCEAN

Lake Chad

Niger R.

Nile R.

CAMEROUN

An ancient Berber fortress-village nestling in a valley in the Atlas Mountains.

NORTH AFRICA

North Africa is rather like an island. It is separated from other lands by the Atlantic and the Mediterranean, and from the rest of Africa by the Sahara Desert. The Arabs call it by the name *Djezira-el-Magreb,* or the Western Isle.

North Africa has a long and fascinating history. The oldest inhabitants were the Berbers, hence the term 'Barbary'. But many other people have since intruded into the Berbers' country: Phoenicians, Greeks, Romans, Vandals, and finally Arabs. And although it later came under the rule of the Turks, French, and Spaniards, North Africa has remained mainly Arabic in language, in religion, and in culture to this day.

Excluding Egypt, North Africa is composed of five countries: Morocco, Spanish Sahara, Tunisia, Algeria, and Libya. The first three are narrow strips of land fringing the coast, the two last extend from the coast deep into the desert.

Egypt will be considered separately because it belongs geographically to the basin of the Nile.

Much of North Africa consists of plateaus and mountains ranges. Some of the mountains are covered with snow in winter. Where winter rainfall is abundant, the farms and vineyards yield good crops and the mountains are forested; but, as one moves southward from the coast, the basins between the mountains become drier; forests give way to wiry grasses or scrubs. Finally the desert takes over completely, relieved only by the occasional oases.

The Kingdom of Morocco, with an area of 170,000 square miles, is approximately four-fifths of the size of France. Almost all of its population of about 14.1 million are Moslems. The capital is Rabat, but the main commercial town is Casablanca. The more colourful ancient cities are Marrakesh and Fez.

North Africa is rich in historic remains. This is the famous Roman theatre at Leptis Magna.

When Morocco gained independence in 1956, Spain gave up her protectorate of Spanish Morocco. Ifni gained independence in 1968. The only possessions that Spain still has within the Morroccan borders are a number of towns on the Mediterranean coast which include Ceuta and Mililla.

In the casbahs (the native quarters) of the large towns, and throughout the old walled cities of Morocco, the women are always veiled and the men wear flowing robes and cloaks, and always keep their heads covered. The shops and market-places have exotic foods, rich silks, jewels, swords, and beautiful leather work. Five times a day the muezzin — the priests of Allah — call the Faithful to prayer from the minarets over the mosques.

The national dish of Morocco is *couscous*, which is made from semolina. It plays much the same part in a North African meal as rice does in an Indian one. Just as rice is eaten with all sorts of curries, so *couscous* is eaten with all sorts of meat and vegetables and even with peeled grapes.

The fertile fields of Morocco yield a harvest of wheat, barley, and vegetables. There are many vineyards in Morocco, and some wine is made, though only for Europeans, as all intoxicating drinks are forbidden to Moslems. More olives are being grown, and other crops include figs, almonds, and citrus fruits.

Where the land is drier, arable farming gives place to stock-breeding. Cattle are kept, as well as sheep and goats, and horses and camels. Raw wool forms an important export, as do cork and timber from Morocco's forests — especially from the moist slopes of the Atlas mountains. There is good fishing off the coast. Sardine-fishing, combined with canning factories, is quite an important industry.

The mineral resources of Morocco are of great note, and many railways have been built to help their development. Morocco has some manganese and a certain amount of iron ore, lead, coal, and oil. However, much the most important mineral consists of the great deposits of phosphates from which fertilisers are made. Morocco is the world's largest exporter of phosphates which make up nearly a quarter of her total exports.

Since Ifni's independence, Spanish West Africa has consisted only of the Spanish Sahara, which is larger than the United Kingdom, and lies south-west of Morocco. It is a desolate and practically useless area on the shoulder of the continent, but with unexploited phosphate deposits. Fishing along the coast provides almost the only livelihood.

Considerably larger than Libya, Algeria is the biggest North African country and the most important after Egypt. Nevertheless of its 878,000 square miles, more than nine-tenths lying south of the Atlas mountains are desert.

Consequently the bulk of Algeria's 12.1 million people live in the small remaining tenth, in the north. This area, the Fell, is fertile farming land. The coastal plains, valleys, and terraced lower slopes of the hills grow enormous crops of wheat and barley. The vineyards yield abundant quantities of wine. Olives, tobacco, fruit, vegetables, and dates are also grown in

The Sidi Kacem refinery in Morocco refines oil from the important new fields in the Sahara.

Roland Paskoff - Photo Researchers

A Moroccan girl with a baby on her back harvests wheat with a sickle, the method of Biblical times.

John Peter Taylor - Rapho

large quantities. The plateaus that stretch southwards to the desert are drier and less fertile, and chiefly provide grazing land for sheep and goats.

Algeria's principal natural resources are oil, iron, natural gas, and phosphates. These resources are largely unexploited: though 3 million tons of iron ore are exported every year, mostly to Britain, large deposits remain unworked. The oilfields of the Sahara are of great importance to Algeria's economy. However there is — as yet — little industry, and, though these minerals are important exports, they do not provide employment for many people.

The Republic of Tunisia, lying to the north-east of Algeria, is the smallest of the North African states, with an area of 48,300 square miles. Most of the population of just over 4 million are Moslems. Almost all of them earn their living either by farming the rich coastal plains, or through the mining of Tunisia's natural resources.

Charles May - Photo Researchers

An open square in Fez, Morocco, holds scores of huge wooden vats where leather goods are dyed.

About half the cultivated land produces cereals — especially wheat and barley, with some oats. The chief agricultural exports are olive oil, wine, and dates.

Camels are more than 'ships of the desert.' A Libyan farmer yokes one to his primitive plough to farm his land.

Tom Hollyman - Photo Researchers

An Algerian orange grove. Fruit is an important Algerian export.

Tunisia's mineral output is important — exports include phosphates, iron ore, lead, and zinc.

Tunisia was well-known to the ancient world. The ruins of Carthage are near the present capital, Tunis.

Libya is a very big country, having an area of nearly 680,000 square miles. Yet the population is only a little over 1½ million. Of these over a third live in the chief towns, and of the remainder many are Bedouin nomads driving their sheep and goats from oasis to oasis.

Libya is divided into three distinct regions: the two most important, Tripolitania and Cyrenaica, and the Fezzan. Tripolitania lies in the west. Its capital, Tripoli, is a clean and modern town, looking on to the Mediterranean.

Cyrenaica is the name of the eastern part of Libya. Its capital is Benghazi. Benghazi and Tripoli are the joint capitals of Libya, and almost a third of the total population live there. It is planned to build a new capital at Beida.

Ghadames is the most important town of the Fezzan, the desert area in the south. Part of the town is built underground to escape the gruelling heat of the desert.

Although Libya has always been regarded as one of the most beautiful countries in Africa — with many famous Greek, Roman, and Byzantine remains — until recently it was also one of the poorest. This was largely due to Libya's dependence on agriculture, but also to the damage caused during the Second World War.

However, the discovery of oil and natural gas in great abundance in 1958 has altered the situation and will enable vast improvements to be made. Already the Libyan government is making great efforts to increase the production of cereals, olives, dates, citrus fruit, vegetables, and forest products. The communications system and the capacity of the ports — particularly Benghazi — are being rapidly expanded, and the new town built at Beida.

Courtesy of TWA - Trans World Airlines

The three great Pyramids near Cairo rise from the desert sands. The green areas are fields irrigated by the Nile.

EGYPT, LAND OF THE NILE

The greatest oasis in the Sahara, one that is 700 miles long, is the valley of the Nile. Flowing through the length of Egypt, or the United Arab Republic, it is the lifeline of the nation. Its waters, flowing from sources deep in the rain-forests of Central Africa and the mountains of Ethiopia, are the life-blood of Egypt.

Except along the Mediterranean coast it scarcely ever rains in Egypt. At Cairo about an inch of rain falls in a year. Over nine-tenths of the country is desert. All farming depends on the Nile, but in the past the Nile has been a most wasteful river. Every August and September for thousands of years the Nile overflowed its banks, irrigating the parched soil. Yet so large was the volume of the flood-water that much of it was wasted, and when the waters drained off they carried away much of the topsoil. Finally when the floods were fully drained away, the land was short of water again.

Irrigation and water storage are thus of the utmost importance. Many canals have been dug to lead the flood-waters into basins, which are flat fields enclosed by low embankments. Various water-

Charles Trieschmann - Camera Clix

The Archimedean screw, a spiral lifting device, raises water from irrigation canals to the fields.

Ed Drews - Photo Researchers

An Egyptian woman helps her husband harvest vegetables. The Nile is behind them.

lifting devices are used to raise the waters of the Nile up to the higher fields. About 100 years ago the government began to build dams along the river at strategic points. These dams succeeded in increasing the size of the harvest, but they did nothing to store water for use during the long dry period. The Aswan Dam was the first to create a reservoir to hold back a body of water which could be used throughout the year. Now a new High Dam has been built at Aswan which is changing the pattern of the flow of the Nile — and of the life of Egypt — for ever. The reservoir created by this dam now extends 124 miles into the Sudan, and it will be of basic importance both for irrigation and the production of electricity to support the growing demands of Egyptian industry.

Although towns such as Cairo are modernised, many of the people in the provinces of Egypt still live in very primitive conditions. However, the Egyptian government is making great efforts to bring modern education, medical care, and farming methods to the backward areas of Egypt. The chief crops are

Shallow-draft dahabiyas ply the Nile, their lateen-rigged sails set to catch the slightest breeze.

Ewing Krainin - Alpha

Hieroglyphics on the mighty Karnak Temple pillars tell the ancient stories of the Pharaohs.

Courtesy of TWA - Trans World Airlines

Raymond Bricon

Against the backdrop of a colourful desert sunset, Bedouins lead their camels to the night's camp.

cotton and rice in Lower Egypt, that is to say, round the delta of the Nile, and sugar-cane in Upper Egypt. Miscellaneous food crops are grown on the small plots belonging to the peasants.

The Faiyum is a basin in the western desert of Egypt. It lies below sea-level and as it is connected to the Nile by a channel it has become a major oasis. In this region the peasants grow all kinds of citrus and other fruits, together with grapes and olives.

The population of Egypt, now over 30.9 million, is growing so fast that the increased crops produced by the control

An isolated village sits in the gravel desert that surrounds the Egyptian city of Thebes.

Paul F. Milhollan

of the waters of the Nile are still not enough to support the country. Egypt is therefore turning to industry. Many looms have been started for the weaving of Egyptian cotton. Other industries include metal-working, sugar-refining, and the manufacture of glass, leather goods, and fertilisers.

The chief port of the country is Alexandria, on the Nile delta, a port whose history goes back 2,300 years. The delta itself is an immense triangle of sand, through which flow the seven branches of the river.

The pyramids of Egypt rank among the wonders of the world. They were built as tombs for the ancient Pharaohs;

one of them, the great pyramid of Cheops, is built of 2½ million separate blocks of stone, and is estimated to weigh nearly 5 million tons. The Egyptians of today, however, are more concerned with building factories, and ports for the future.

Before the construction of the Suez Canal there was no direct link between the Mediterranean and the Red Sea.

The work was started in 1859, but progressed slowly, and it was not till 1869 that the canal was finally opened. In the following year 500 vessels went through. By 1913, yearly transits had increased to over 5,000, and by 1955 to nearly three times that number, while in that year the goods carried for the first time exceeded 100 million tons.

Since its construction the canal has been progressively increased in width and depth. It can now take ships drawing thirty-seven feet and the minimum width of the central channel is 200 feet. Of the total length of 101 miles, fifty-six consist of lakes. The remainder was dug out by hand above water level and by mechanical dredgers below. The difference in water level at the two ends does not exceed four feet, so no locks have had to be provided. Measured by the volume of traffic, the Suez Canal was the world's greatest man-made waterway until fighting between the Arabs and Israel caused it to be closed in 1967.

Giant sand dunes cover the 'Great Erg' region of the Sahara. Dunes are sculptured by the wind.

Bernheim-Conant AMNH - FLO

At a more flourishing Saharan oasis than the one above, springs yield enough water for irrigation canals.

THE DESERT LANDS

Sahara is an Arabic word meaning 'emptiness'. No better word could be chosen, for the Sahara Desert is 3½ million square miles of 'emptiness'. This immense area of sand and rock stretches from the Atlantic Ocean to the Red Sea and cuts off the northern part of Africa from the bulk of the continent.

The word desert always brings a vision of sand, but in fact only a small part of the Sahara consists of sand dunes. Like all dunes, they are constantly shifting under the action of the wind. This section, called the Great Erg, is the most feared of all. Most of the Sahara is made up of rocky plateaus and vast flat plains of loose stones and pebbles.

In the middle of the Sahara are huge mountain chains, chief amongst which are the Ahaggar Mountains occupying an area comparable to that of the Alps, but their peaks do not rise much higher than 8,000 feet. They were created by volcanic eruptions millions of years ago. Many of the peaks are extinct volcanoes.

Dwellers of this date-palm oasis raise precious water from their well with a primitive sweep.

Raymond Bricon

A camel train winds across the trackless Sahara. Caravan guides can memorise the routes.

Raymond Bricon

A caravan pitches its tents near a 'ksar' — an oasis village once fortified against Tuareg marauders.

Scientists at one time thought that the Sahara was the bed of an ancient ocean that had dried up. But nowadays they believe it was formed by the weathering of the mountains. The sharp change between the heat of the day and the cold of the night, added to the action of the constant winds and occasional violent rain-storms or sand-storms, tend to crack and break up rocks into smaller and smaller pieces, which are finally reduced to grains of sand. This process is still going on. Many thousands of years from now, the present-day mountains in the Sahara will, in turn, have been reduced to sand. During the weathering processes the salts contained in the rocks are not washed away, and salty areas and crusts are formed.

The 'emptiness' of the Sahara must not be taken too literally, for the desert is not utterly bare. Much of the rocky part is thinly covered by a scraggy growth of coarse grass or stunted bushes. In certain cases the underground water is near enough to the surface for many desert plants to sink their long roots into it. These are the oases of the Sahara. In some, there is enough water for wells

to be dug, and even for land to be cultivated. There are in fact oases of all degrees, from tiny clumps of bushes and a trickle of water to those whose many

Raymond Bricon

Tea-drinking is a ritual among the Tuareg.

Women of the Tuareg tribe spend much of their spare time dressing each other's hair.

Raymond Bricon

Joe Barnell - Shostal

An Egyptian tractor crew works beside a native-built irrigation canal in Egypt's Liberation Province, a major land-reform and reclamation project.

springs give rise to towns with populations of several thousand. A typical oasis grows dates, citrus fruits, and vegetables.

Sometimes, instead of digging downward to make a well, people dig horizontally into the side of a hill to make what is called a *foggara*. If the channel strikes water under the hill, it will flow outward into the oasis without having to be pumped.

Travellers across the desert move from oasis to oasis. Fifty years ago the Sahara could only be crossed by camel, 'the ship of the desert'. Camels have adapted themselves by nature to cope with the problems of the desert. The nourishment and liquid stored in the fatty tissues of their bodies, particularly in their humps, enables them to go without food or water for several days. Therefore, for crossing the great areas of shifting sand dunes, the camel has no rival.

There may be over a hundred camels in an Arab caravan, whose leaders are

The export of sheep and goats is a big trade in Tunisia. The quality is very high.

Camera Press Ltd

White buildings cover the steep hills rising from the busy harbour of Algiers, Algeria's capital.

expert navigators, who know every land-mark on their route.

Nowadays it is also possible, though difficult and sometimes dangerous, to cross the Sahara in a car. Drivers must notify the authorities of their departure and their route. If they do not reach their destination within twenty-four hours of the expected time, a rescue team is sent to search for them. The major oases in the roads are from 200—300 miles apart, and breakdowns can be fatal. Anyone stranded in the Sahara without water in summer is unlikely to live much more than a day.

The inhabitants of the desert, nearly all of whom are Moslems, are of mixed Berber and Arab stock. They fall into two main types: those who live perma-nently at the oases, and those who wander across the Sahara, from one well or oasis to another. Of the desert nomads the Tuareg are of Berber origin, while the Bedouin are Arabs.

In the south-eastern part of the Sahara live the Tibbus, a word which means 'the rock people', for their home is in the rocky Tibesti Mountains near the Sudan. They are of partly Negro stock.

The most interesting of the peoples of the Sahara are the Tuareg. Their origin is obscure, but they are thought by some to be descendants of Berbers who fled to the Sahara before the advance of the many waves of conquerors who poured into North Africa. They are still a proud and independent people. They are no-mads, wandering over the desert with their goats, sheep, and camels.

Whereas in the rest of the Arab world the women are veiled, amongst the Tuareg it is the faces of the women that are uncovered while those of the men are veiled. One explanation that has been offered is that the Tuareg wanted to distinguish themselves from other Arabs. More probably the veil is simply a good means of protection from the desert sun.

H. Mensching

Because of long dry periods, water is precious. Algerian slopes are carefully irrigated and contour ploughed.

FIVE AFRICAN STATES

The Sudan is the largest country in the whole of Africa, covering an area of nearly a million square miles. It is almost entirely an agricultural and pastoral country, with no very important mineral resources. There is considerable variation in the climatic conditions: desert and semi-desert in the north, humid in the south.

In the central and northern zones water-shortage is a great problem. The Sennar dam on the Blue Nile has made possible the irrigation of the fertile *djezireh* zone between the Blue and White Nile, and the spread of cotton plantations.

Another dam is projected on the Blue Nile at Roseires. The lake formed by the new Aswan dam just built in Egypt, which extends some 124 miles into the Sudan, should also help to irrigate this parched region.

Cotton accounts for at least half of the Sudan's total exports. The next most important being gum arabic — of which the Sudan produces the bulk of the world's supply.

The principal towns are Khartoum, the capital, which has, together with Khartoum North, a population of over

Stephanie Dinkins - FLO

The opening of Ghana's Parliament.

A. G. Hervey

Natural gas from Hassi R'Mel in the Sahara is exported to Britain. These flare-stacks are known locally as 'Les Torches'.

193,000; and Omdurman with 167,000. The old port of Fuakin has lost its importance to Port Sudan, which handles three-quarters of the country's overseas trade.

The Chad Republic can be divided into two parts: the desert in the north and the savanna regions in the south. There are no known mineral deposits and, since the deserts of the north are unproductive, the economy rests on the produce of the south. Cotton and groundnuts are grown as cash crops, but livestock makes up the most important source of wealth. About 500,000 out of the total population of 3.4 million are nomadic Arabs.

Niger is a huge, thinly populated country, mainly taken up by the Sahara desert. There has been an extensive search for minerals and deposits of iron ore and tin and uranium have been reported. The south is the most important region for agriculture: here the greater rainfall

Paul Hufner - Shostal

Modern buildings contrast with Cairo's slums.

(about 25 inches a year) and the Niger river enable the inhabitants to rear large flocks of sheep, goats, and cattle. The chief food crop is millet, and the groundnuts are grown for export.

The capital is Niamey, a route centre on the Niger. Most trade is with Nigeria, but there is an increasing amount with Dahomey.

Mali is a vast landlocked country sparsely populated. Large areas are desert or semi-desert, but some areas, particularly in the south in the Niger valley, are extremely fertile. Chief crops are rice, cotton, and groundnuts, but away from the flood plains the rearing of cattle, sheep, and goats is more important than agriculture. Of the towns, Bamako, the capital, is the most important, being on

Bob Crone - Annan Photo Features

Maintenance work in progress along the banks of the Suez Canal.

The new High Dam at Aswan is vital to Egypt's future.

the end of the railway to Dakar (Senegal), which is Mali's chief link with the outside world. Timbuktu has declined in importance as a caravan and route centre.

Mauritania forms the bridge between North and West Africa. Agriculturally it is a poor country, but there is a considerable cattle population, dates are grown, and the fishing industry is important and capable of considerable expansion. However, Mauritania's principal resources are the large deposits of high-grade iron ore at Fort Gouraud, accounting for 90 per cent of her exports, and the considerable deposits of copper near Akjoujt.

The chief towns are Port Etienne, a fishing centre and port expected to expand greatly with the growth of the mining industry; and Fort Gouraud round which the industry will be centred.

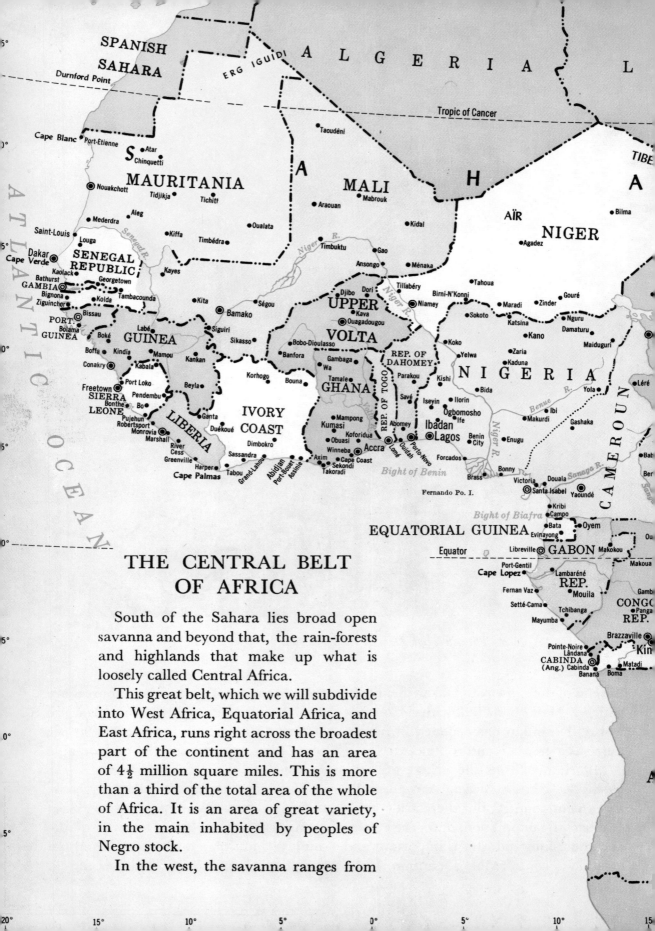

THE CENTRAL BELT OF AFRICA

South of the Sahara lies broad open savanna and beyond that, the rain-forests and highlands that make up what is loosely called Central Africa.

This great belt, which we will subdivide into West Africa, Equatorial Africa, and East Africa, runs right across the broadest part of the continent and has an area of 4½ million square miles. This is more than a third of the total area of the whole of Africa. It is an area of great variety, in the main inhabited by peoples of Negro stock.

In the west, the savanna ranges from

Charles Trieschmann - Camera Clix

The dense growth of head-high grasses with scattered bushes and trees is typical of savanna landscapes.

the semi-desert countries bordering the Sahara to the coastal forests. In some coastal areas impenetrable mangrove swamps extend for many miles. In the east the grasslands of the Sudan rise to the mountainous regions of Ethiopia and to the high plateau of East Africa, with its great peaks like Mount Kili-manjaro, Mount Kenya, and Ruwenzori, and the broad plains which are the home of big game.

Between these western and eastern regions lie the wet, humid jungles of the central equatorial plateau, and the immense basin of the Congo.

Central Africa is the land of tribal chiefs and witch-doctors, of the tsetse fly and the malaria-carrying mosquito. Yet, even here, modern cities are springing up alongside the jungle villages of mud and thatch. Though almost entirely undeveloped it is an area of great natural resources, and great potential wealth.

The Central African savanna consists of a belt of rolling uplands about 700 miles in breadth, covered with grassland scattered trees, and shrubs. Part of it is used for arable farming or stock-breeding. The plains in the east, covered with tall grasses, are the big game country.

A Nigerian sounds an enormous horn to announce the arrival of a plane at Kano airport.

Stephanie Dinkins - FLO

Cattle-breeding is carried on for the most part in the northern section of this belt, where the short grass makes good grazing land for the herds. Of the African tribes who go in for cattle-breeding the Masai of East Africa, a tall, proud tribe of renowned warriors, are the most famous. The Masai are almost untouched by civilisation, and refuse to grow crops or learn handicrafts. They eat no meat, but live on the milk and blood of their herds.

Cattle-breeding is often restricted by the tsetse fly. Thousands of head of cattle are killed by it. However, in recent years some progress has been made in clearing regions by chemical sprays, and by forbidding the movement of infected cattle into the newly cleared areas.

Hans von Meiss - Photo Researchers

A woman of the Samburu tribe and her child guarding native flocks on the Kenya plains.

Dense rain-forest borders the Ogooué River in Cameroun, scene of Dr Schweitzer's work.

B. E. Lindroos - Gilloon

WEST AFRICA

Perhaps the most interesting part of Africa today is West Africa. In the rush of progress the old and the new provide striking contrasts. Huts with corrugated iron roofs stand next to modern office buildings, and African taxi-drivers, dressed in picturesque native robes, steer their cabs through the traffic.

West Africa stretches from Cape Verde on the Atlantic to the mountains of Cameroun in the east, and from the edge of the Sahara in the north to the swampy coast of the Gulf of Guinea. Its chief rivers are the Niger, the Volta, and the Senegal.

By and large, West Africans are happy and friendly people. The men are tall and good-looking. The women dress in gaily coloured cotton clothes and in some areas have turbans that make them look

Local produce on sale in a new, covered, concrete market-place in Abidjan, Ivory Coast.

like princesses of the Arabian Nights.

There are few good natural harbours along the coast of West Africa. The coast is smooth and unindented and the water off-shore shallow. Consequently ocean-going vessels have to unload by lighter — the most famous example being the huge canoe-like boats used by the boatmen of Accra. The best ports on the west coast are Freetown (Sierra Leone), Lagos (Nigeria), and Takoradi (Ghana).

Senegal, formerly the oldest of the French African colonies, is distinguished in being the intellectual centre of French-speaking Africa. In the past its economy has been almost completely dependent on groundnuts, but efforts are being made to reduce the country's dependence on this crop: an oil refinery is planned, and fishing and the new phosphate industry are being developed. Other important industries are textiles and the manufacture of salt, by evaporation of sea water. Dakar, the capital, is the largest town and one of the chief ports of Africa. Its industries include the extraction and refining of groundnut oil and the manufacture of soap, cement, and textiles. There are railway workshops and ship-repairing yards. Dakar airport is the largest in

Dugout canoes serve as ferries across a crocodile-infested river in Nigeria.

Todd Webb - Photo Library

Surf-boats were necessary for loading and unloading cargo at Accra, Ghana, when the port was used.

West Africa. Over 10 per cent of Senegal's total population of 3½ million live in and around Dakar.

Gambia is a long, narrow strip of territory bordering the lower and middle reaches of the Gambia river for just over 200 miles inland. The width of Gambia is about twenty miles near the coast and about twelve miles further inland.

Gambia is one of the poorest countries in Africa; 95 per cent of her exports consist of groundnuts, and there seems little chance of extending agriculture, except for local consumption.

Guinea is a rapidly developing country with considerable agricultural resources and mineral deposits. Guinea is also one of the most dynamic and politically important states in the whole of Africa. Diamonds, and, most important, iron ore and bauxite, are being exploited, and there is a growing use of the country's hydro-electric potential.

Sierra Leone is one of the smallest

Citizens of Accra queue up for water when the dry season cuts the normal supply.

Huge 'dunce's-cap' thatched huts in a typical Liberian village.

Charles May - Shostal

Alfred Zulliger - Shostal

Capt. K. C. Torrens - Alpha

Fishermen's painted canoes are colourful sight on the beach in Ghana.

Charles May - Shostal

The modern Supreme Court buildings in Ghana are fine examples of modern architecture.

of West African states — its area is only 27,925 square miles. On the other hand its population is almost 2½ million (70 per square mile), which is dense by African standards.

Most of the population is engaged in subsistence farming, but Sierra Leone has traditionally exported palm kernels and oil, and is the leading world producer of piassava, used in the manufacture of brooms and hard brushes. However, Sierra Leone's principal export is diamonds, and she also has extensive deposits of very rich iron ore and, to a lesser

extent, deposits of chromite.

The capital is Freetown, which has one of the finest harbours in Africa, and which is very important not only to Sierra Leone but to the economy of the whole West Coast.

Liberia is the oldest independent state in West Africa, having been chosen in 1820 as a home for freed American slaves. The chief cash crop is rubber, though the coffee industry is being developed. However, minerals are of growing importance to the Liberian economy. Gold production is declining, but diamond output

Workmen in Senegal pile up a huge mound of peanuts for shipment. Peanuts are Senegal's chief crop.

Ewing Galloway

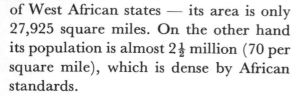

Richard Harrington - Annan Photo Features

A cacao grower inspects the pods on one of his trees to see whether they are ready to harvest.

Shostal

Two Sudanese scoop up cotton as a third bales it. The Gezira is a cotton-growing region of the Sudan.

increasing; most important of all there are rich deposits of iron ore north of the capital, Monrovia, and near the border with the Ivory Coast.

The Ivory Coast, with a population of more than 3.8 million, is one of the most thriving territories of West Africa, with an economy based upon an increasingly commercialised agriculture. Coffee and cocoa are easily the two most important exports, and other important export products are timber and bananas.

For many years the development of the territory was hindered by the very dense rain-forests of the southern third of the country, and the difficult coastline: cliffs along the western half of the coast, sand-bars and lagoons along the east. However, roads are now opening up the forests, and the Vridi Canal pierces the sand-bar opposite Abidjan, the chief port and capital.

Unlike many countries of West Africa, the Republic of Upper Volta is both agriculturally unproductive and without mineral resources. Large areas in the west are infertile, extensive areas in the east unhealthy. The remaining areas are

Logs of valuable tropical wood float in a Ghanaian harbour awaiting transport to lumber mills.

Modern machinery stockpiles iron ore on the loading docks of Liberia.

Capt. K. C. Torrens - Alpha

Stutts - Rapho Guillumette

An African clothed in ritual robes moves down a jungle path to a pagan shrine in Ife, Nigeria.

densely populated and poor. The only exports of any size are cattle and manpower, which go to Ghana and the Ivory Coast. A new dam project is transforming a barren plain near Zhorgo for rice and sugar growing. There are similar plans for other parts of the country.

Ghana is one of the richest countries in Central Africa, with large mineral resources. These include gold (before independence Ghana was known as the Gold Coast), diamonds, manganese, and bauxite. The chief export is cocoa, and a third of the world's supply comes from Ghana. A disease called 'swollen root' is a great menace to the industry, and at one time threatened to wipe it out. It has now been brought under control, but because of this threat, farmers are trying to diversify exports. A dam is being constructed across the Volta near Ajena which will be important for irrigation and as a source of hydro-electric power. This power will enable a bauxite-smelting industry to be set up nearby.

Accra is the capital (population 532,600) and formerly an important port, which is now outmoded. The chief ports today are Takoradi and Tema, a new site which

Brazzaville boasts a large, modern airport.

is of particular importance with the completion of the Volta project.

The Federation of Nigeria, with a population of more than 62 million, has the largest population and highest population density in Africa.

The Niger and its principal tributary, the Benue, divide the country into three

A steamer on the Congo chugs up-river between jungle-lined banks, pushing a barge ahead of it.

Wayne Fredericks - House of Photography

Modern buildings line the streets of Kinhasa capital city of the Democratic Republic of the Congo.

Martin Simpson - Annan Photo Features

A Congolese child helps with chores.

parts, roughly corresponding to the three political regions of the Federation — the Northern Region being slightly larger than the other two put together. In the north are the monotonous 'High Plains of Hausaland', in the south-west the lower

The tallest smoke-stack in Africa dominates this slag heap near Lubumbashi, in the Katanga region.

Charles Trieschmann - Camera Clix

plateau of the Yoruba country, while south-eastern Nigeria is a land of vales and escarpments.

Nigeria is primarily an agricultural country. Large quantities of oil-palm products come from the north-east and the southern rain-forest belt. Cocoa is grown for export in the south-west, centred on Ibadan; some plantation rubber is being produced near Benin; and the area around Kano, focus for caravan routes to the Sahara, is important for millet, groundnuts, and cotton.

Nigeria has deposits of coal, tin, and columbite. The coal is of great importance as no other large reserves are known in West Africa. Nigeria is the world's leading producer of columbite, used to make special steels for jet engines, etc.

Lagos is the Federal capital and leading port. Much export traffic, including coal, passes through Port Harcourt, and the largest city is Ibadan. Kano is a traditionally important market centre for trans-Saharan traffic.

Nigeria's chief exports are palm produce, groundnuts and oil, cocoa, cotton, and rubber.

Dahomey and Togo, lying between Nigeria and Ghana, are amongst the smallest and poorest territories in West

Young Africans in Kenya study modern science in the Royal Technical College, Nairobi.

British Information Service

This village is more typical of the Congo than modern cities like Kinshasa and Lubumbashi.

EQUATORIAL AFRICA

The dominant feature of Equatorial Africa is the rain-forest. Nourished by a warm climate and an abundant rainfall throughout the year, broad-leaved evergreen trees rise to amazing heights. This region is not entirely covered by forests. The height of the land varies greatly along the equatorial belt. There are mangrove swamps and mountains near the coast of Cameroun. And in the east of the Congo basin the land rises to high open forests, where dry and rainy seasons alternate, and the trees shed their leaves accordingly.

The heart of the rain-forest is the Democratic Republic of the Congo once known as the Belgian Congo. Over 16 million people, divided into more than 200 tribes, live in its 900,000 square miles. Most of them are concentrated in a few areas, where conditions are relatively healthy and most suitable for raising crops. The rainforest is the haunt of

Africa. Nevertheless, Dahomey, though largely dependent on French economic aid, is an important producer of oil-palm produce; and the wealth of Togo has been greatly increased recently by the discovery and exploitation of phosphates and bauxite near Lomé, the capital.

The capital of Dahomey is Porto Novo, but the largest town is Cotonou, the chief port and leading commercial centre of the country.

A group of men drive animals laden with sacks of grain down a flooded African road.

Ethiopian villagers check the condition of beeswax hardening in moulds. Beeswax is exported.

gorillas and chimpanzees. It is also the home of the Congo peacock and the rare okapi, a relative of the giraffe, but no bigger than a mule, which has become adapted to forest life.

Together with its tributaries, the Congo River dominates everything. It is the chief artery of communications and transport. River steamers ply the Congo and its tributaries. Some of them, specially fitted out, serve as shops for the smaller villages of the interior.

Like all the major African rivers, the Congo falls steeply towards the sea from a central plateau. Accordingly its navigable stretches are interrupted by waterfalls and rapids. All the heavy waterborne traffic has to be carried past these obstacles by a series of short, but extremely important, railways. For instance, just below Kinshasa, the capital of the Republic, the river passes through a series of violent rapids. So goods are unloaded and sent by rail to Matadi, the chief port, where they are reloaded. Another port, Ango-Ango, is used by tankers, and a pipeline connects it with Kinshasa, where fuel-oil is needed for the Congo riversteamers. Economically the most important area of the Democratic Republic of the Congo is Katanga, the southeastern area of the Congo Basin. Katanga is one of the greatest mineral-bearing areas in the world, particularly for copper. It is also rich in tin and zinc, has more cobalt than any area in the world, and is one of the chief sources of uranium. Other minerals include: manganese, tungsten, and coal. Kinshasa is a very modern city, and so too is Lubumbashi, the principal town of the Katanga region.

Rich farmlands lie part fallow, part cultivated beneath the ramparts of an Ethiopian mountain range.

Hans von Meiss - Photo Researchers

Washday is a busy time at this public laundry in Mombasa. Use of the tubs is free to the public.

The Cameroun Republic falls into two very different regions; tropical rain forests in the south, dry savanna in the north.

In the tropical north there is a large agricultural population. The chief crops are millet, groundnuts, and cotton, while cattle rearing is also very important.

In the equatorial south coffee, cocoa, bananas, tobacco, palm kernels, and wild rubber are produced.

It is though that there are large deposits of bauxite in Cameroun, and the aluminium industry is already well established, using imported aluminium and the hydro-electric power generated by the ultra-modern dam at Edea.

The most important outlet of Cameroun is Douala, on the Sanaga estuary.

To the north and west of the Congo basin is a cluster of independent states formed from what was formerly French Equatorial Africa. These are Gabon, the Congo Republic, and the Central African Republic. They are all economically poor and undeveloped countries. Of the

Nairobi, the capital of Kenya, is a fine city with a magnificent climate. It is famous as the 'safari capital' of Africa.

Safari Productions - Photo Researchers

Thousands of animals gather at a waterhole in the Serengeti Plains, famous game region.

three Gabon is the most advanced, though even here most of the leading agricultural products are 'wild' rather than cultivated. Most agriculture is subsistence level. Lack of transport is a great handicap, especially for the Central African Re-

An isolated native village set down in Kenya's acacia-dotted savanna lands.

public where millet, maize, cotton, sisal, and tobacco are grown on the savanna lands. This region is capable of great development as a cattle-breeding area.

The Congo Republic has small quantities of copper, diamonds, gold, and zinc, and enormous deposits of potash salts. Manganese, uranium concentrates and natural gas are exported from Gabon.

The only industries of any note are plywood and petrol products from Gabon.

Brazzaville in the Congo Republic, on the opposite bank of the river Congo to Kinshasa, is the most important town, and the rail link with Pointe-Noire is important for the mining and agriculture of both the Congo and Gabon.

Rwanda and Burundi have dense populations and a healthy climate. Cattle-rearing and farming are carried on. Coffee is important, but Rwanda's chief asset is manpower, which goes to Katanga.

THE EASTERN HIGHLANDS

As we move eastward the savanna ends abruptly at a mountain barrier that forms the highlands of Ethiopia, a rugged land with a history that goes back thousands of years. Legend has it that Ethiopa was once ruled by the Queen of Sheba.

Ethiopia's volcanic mountains rise to 15,000 feet. On the higher levels cattle, sheep, and goats are kept, while, on the lower slopes, a variety of crops is grown, including grain, sugar-cane, cotton, coffee, dates, figs, and citrus fruits. The produce of the drier plains consists of gum arabic, beeswax, and of frankincense and myrrh.

Still further east, the land drops swiftly to the Red Sea and the Indian Ocean. Most of the coastal lands are desert. South of Ethiopia, the East African

Safari Productions - Photo Researchers

A Moslem in Tanzania weaves a straw sleeping mat. Mats like these are popular with tourists.

Plateau rises sharply from the coast. It is separated from the Central African Plateau by the Great African Rift Valley, which contains a string of long, narrow, deep lakes. The plateau is a region of high plains and mountains that used to be

Moshi Mosque in Tanzania is a religious centre for Moslems. In the background is Mt Kilimanjaro.

Hans von Meiss - Photo Researchers

Hans von Meiss - Photo Researchers

A family in a Uganda village spreads out coffee to dry before shipping it to market.

Hans von Meiss - Photo Researchers

Tea is a major product of Uganda. Trees are planted to provide shade for the tea shrubs.

known as British East Africa. Now the various territories are independent members of the Commonwealth.

Much of this region, especially Kenya, is 5,000 feet or more above sea-level, which makes for a comfortable climate, even though Kenya's highlands run right across the Equator. Temperatures range from about 80°F during the day to as little as 35°F at night. Three-quarters of Kenya gets less than 30 inches of rain a year, and most of the central and northern areas between the coastal plain and the highlands are arid.

Kenya's chief commercial crops are coffee, tea, sisal, wattle extract, pyrethum, and cotton, the most productive areas being north and west of Nairobi.

Instead of nets, these fishermen in Uganda use a circle of woven papyrus.

Safari Productions - Photo Researchers

Arab sailors tend their dhow on the waterfront of the ancient seaport of Zanzibar.

Clove trees blossom on a plantation in Zanzibar. Cloves are the island's chief crop.

Other crops, including fruit and vegetables, and even wheat and barley, are grown, especially round Nairobi.

Nairobi is the chief town, with a population of more than 479,000. Its importance has increased greatly with the opening up of the Kenya Highlands, especially the rich coffee and sisal areas tapped by the Fort Hall railway. Nairobi also has a very important international airport. Mombasa is the only port of Kenya, and the new modern harbour at Kilindini probably makes it the best harbour on the whole east coast of Africa. It handles a considerable amount of the traffic of Uganda and north-east Tanzania as well as that of Kenya.

Industry is increasing; at present it is mainly food processing. Sodium carbonate and a small quantity of gold are also produced. Minerals are numerous but in small quantities.

Nairobi is the great centre for safari. There are six national parks and six game reserves in Kenya. One of them, the Tsavo reserve, is 8,000 square miles in area and is kept specially for elephants. South of Nairobi, on the other side of the Tanzania frontier, is another area rich in animal life — the famous Serengeti plains.

Tanzania (Tanganyika) is larger than Kenya and Uganda put together. Much of it is dry. Large areas are covered by scrub and grassland. Farming is poor, except in the regions surrounding Mount Kilimanjaro, which is reasonably well

Arab influence in Zanzibar is shown here by the style of the shopping arcade and the heavily veiled Moslem woman.

The narrow, winding streets and Arab-style houses of Zanzibar resemble those of North Africa.

watered. The rain falls on the sides of the mountain and feeds the streams and lakes of the surrounding country, providing enough water for farming. The main

Drilling for oil at Afam, Nigeria.

crop is sisal, which thrives on poor, dry soil. Coffee, cotton, and oil seeds are also grown successfully. Livestock is very important — there are more cattle in Tanzania than in any other country of the Commonwealth.

Tanzania has recently become an important producer of minerals, especially diamonds, lead, and gold. Tanzania is now one of the world's leading diamond producers. Other minerals exported include salt, mica, tin, and small quantities of silver and copper. Large coal deposits also exist.

Dar es Salaam is the capital and chief port of Tanzania.

Uganda, a relatively small country with no outlet to the sea, is an intermediate territory between the northern savanna and Equatorial Africa. In the north, the swamps merge with those of the Sudan. In the south-west, it borders the Congo rain-forest. Uganda is fertile and prosperous. The main crop is cotton, but tobacco, tea, coffee, and sugar are also grown. Copper is its chief mineral export.

Lake Victoria is a huge, shallow body of water lying between Kenya, Uganda, and Tanzania. It occupies a depression in the plateau and is the largest lake in Africa. Of the other lakes which lie in a chain along the Great Rift Valley the most important are Lake Rudolf, Lake Albert, Lake Edward, Lake Kivu, Lake Tanganyika, and Lake Nyasa. Of these, Lake Tanganyika and Lake Nyasa are much the biggest.

Although Lake Victoria is the second largest body of fresh water in the world, its greatest depth is only 250 feet. Its waters are infested with crocodiles, hippopotamus, and a mollusc which

Ploughing in Ethiopia. Oxen are a valuable asset to African farmers.

harbours the pernicious flat-worm bil-harzia. The lake is important as the source of the White Nile. The dam at Owen Falls helps to control the flow of water in the Nile, as well as providing Uganda with electricity. Eventually this dam may help to provide cheap hydro-electric power for a large area of the Congo Basin as well.

Fish from Uganda's 13,695 square miles of lake water are an important source of food.

About 22½ miles off the coast lies the island of Zanzibar, the other part of Tanzania. Formerly a British protectorate it has elected to join Tanganyika, independent within the British Commonwealth.

Zanzibar used to be a busy centre for Arab slave-traders. Now Zanzibar, together with its sister island of Pemba, exports a large part of the world's total supply of cloves and copra.

Broad-sailed Arab dhows are a common sight in Zanzibar harbour. Arab seamen sail their dhows to India and back, using the monsoons (the north-east monsoon and the south-west monsoon), which blow continually for a whole season. The single journey takes about a fortnight.

Pyrethrum oil extractors in Tanzania.

The rocky coastline and jutting headlands of Pringle Bay, South Africa.

SOUTHERN AFRICA

The relatively narrow southern part of the continent differs greatly from the northern and central sections. As we have already seen, the belt of savanna is not so broad as the northern savanna. It forms an intermediate area between the Congo rain-forest and the deserts of south-west Africa and Botswana, which are small compared to the Sahara.

At the southern tip of the continent we are no longer in the tropics. The Republic of South Africa lies almost entirely south of the Tropic of Capricorn. Here, as in South America, the seasons are reversed compared with those in Europe, and Christmas, for example, falls in the middle of summer.

The healthy climate of this area soon attracted white settlers, and colonies were founded long ago by the Portuguese, the Dutch, and the British.

This southern part of the continent is a region of considerable variety. Zambia and Rhodesia are great mining countries. South Africa has rich arable and grazing land wherever there is a supply of water. On the coast are industrial towns and seaside resorts.

Horse and rider pause to view the majesty of 630-foot Maletsunyane Falls, in Lesotho, South Africa.

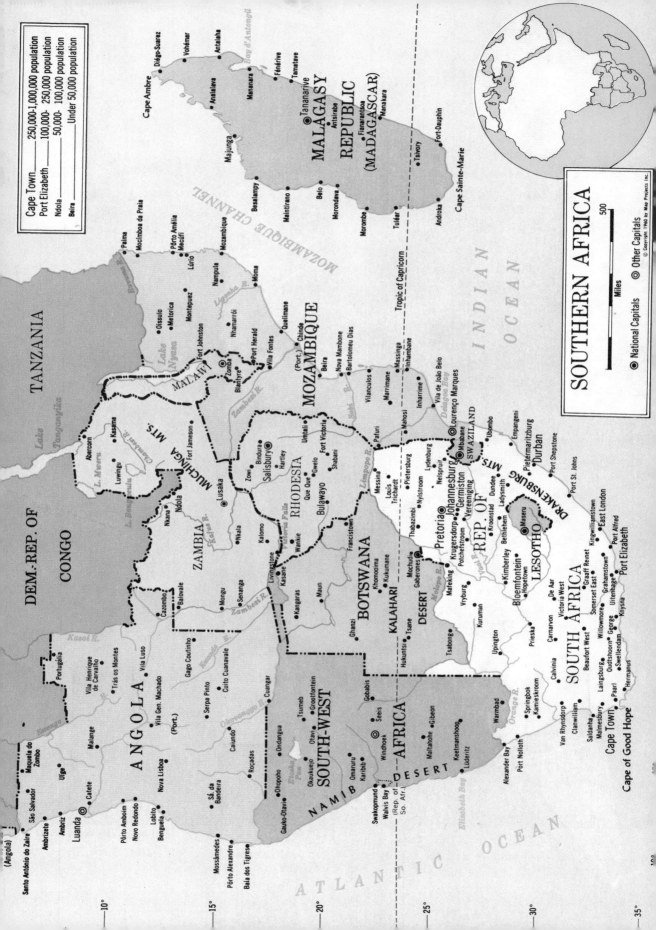

SOUTHERN AFRICA

Cape Town	250,000–1,000,000 population
Port Elizabeth	100,000– 250,000 population
Ndola	50,000– 100,000 population
Beira	Under 50,000 population

Miles

● National Capitals   ◎ Other Capitals

© Copyright 1960 by Map Projects Inc.

TANZANIA

DEM. REP. OF CONGO

(Angola)

ANGOLA

ZAMBIA

MALAWI

MOZAMBIQUE

MALAGASY REPUBLIC (MADAGASCAR)

RHODESIA

SOUTH-WEST AFRICA

BOTSWANA

KALAHARI DESERT

NAMIB DESERT

SWAZILAND

REP. OF SOUTH AFRICA

LESOTHO

DRAKENSBURG MTS.

MUCHINGA MTS.

MOZAMBIQUE CHANNEL

INDIAN OCEAN

ATLANTIC OCEAN

Tropic of Capricorn

Cape of Good Hope

THE MALAGASY REPUBLIC (MADAGASCAR)

Madagascar (the Malagasy Republic) is one of the world's largest islands. It is nearly 1,000 miles long, and has an area of 228,000 square miles, which is nearly four times the size of England and Wales. It lies some 250 miles off the nearest point of the east coast of Africa, from which it is separated by the Mozambique Channel. The eastern half of the island consists of a high mountainous region 3,000 to 5,000 feet above sea-level.

The people of Madagascar, the Malagasy, originally came from South-East Asia, and Africa. The Asiatic and Negro groups intermarried and today the inhabitants are, for the most part, a mixture of the two races. The language spoken is much like that of the early settlers of the Pacific islands. The capital of the island is Tananarive, in the central

Sheridan H. Garth

The streets of the Malagasy Republic are full of busy traffic — some of it odd-looking to European eyes.

Pierre Massin - House of Photography

At the cattle-farm centre of Ponte de Fiana, Madagascar's humped cattle are bred for hides.

Pierre Massin - House of Photography

In the central mountains of Madagascar, Tananarive, the capital city, clings to the sloping hillside.

highlands, about 100 miles from the coast.

Rice, maize, and other crops are grown for food. The chief export crops are coffee, vanilla, and sugar-cane. The cattle of the island are the zebus, which are humped and bony creatures reared more for their hides than for either milk or meat. The animals and vegetation of Madagascar are distinct from those of the African mainland. Madagascar has sometimes been called the Red Isle, because of the red soil that covers the greater part of the island.

Martin Simpson - Annan Photo Features

South Africa exports large quantities of fruit. This pineapple field is in Natal Province.

SOUTH AFRICA, A SPACIOUS LAND

The Republic of South Africa covers more than 472,000 square miles, an area slightly larger than France, Spain, Portugal, and the Low Countries put together. It is the most powerful state of Southern Africa, if not of the whole continent.

The population is about 20 million, of whom about 13.6 million are Bantu. About 2 million, called the Cape Coloureds, are of mixed blood, and half a million are Asiatic, leaving less than one-fifth of the population of pure white descent. The Asiatic section of the population are mainly Indians living in Natal. Of the four provinces, the people of the Cape and Natal are predominantly of British descent, while the peope of the Orange Free State and the Transvaal are predominantly Afrikaners, people of Dutch descent.

Gordon Douglas - Photo Library

The landscape of Transvaal — flowering trees, rocky crags, level grasslands.

The 'Union of South Africa', as it used to be called until May 1961, was formed after the Boer War, fought at the turn of the century, by joining together what had previously been separate Dutch and British colonies. Transvaal and the Orange Free State had been Dutch, and Natal and Cape Colony had been British. After the defeat of the Boers these colonies were united. At the

Martin Simpson - Annan Photo Features

A Zulu youth wanders the grass-covered hillsides of Natal Province with his donkeys.

Wayne Fredericks - House of Photography

Zulu ricksha 'boys' dress in colourful tribal costumes to attract customers in Durban.

same time the Union was made self-governing. The colonials of Dutch extraction are called Afrikaners, and the language they speak is called Afrikaans.

It is derived from Dutch, and has been influenced by other European languages.

South Africa consists of a high central plateau, bounded by mountains in the east and dry lands towards the west. Hills and valleys alternate, coming down in great 'steps' towards the coast.

Most of the country gets little rainfall, though when the rain does come it is often so heavy that it washes away the soil. The few rivers are generally either flooded or dry. In some areas dams have been built to create reservoirs for irrigation; elsewhere there are deep wells.

The Cape and Natal form the coastal regions of South Africa. They are the most fertile regions, and their scenery is the most picturesque. The coastal provinces were the first areas to be settled

Gordon Douglas - Photo Library

Fishing, picnicking, and painting are popular activities at the South African resort of Knysna.

Rupert Leach - Shostal

More than half a million people live in Durban, South Africa's chief port.

Martin S. Klein

Thousands enjoy sand, sun, and surf on Durban's beaches. Summer there is December to February.

by Europeans. The Portuguese landed there as long ago as 1482. When it was realised that whoever controlled the Cape of Good Hope was master of the sea route to India, both the Dutch and the English began to colonise the Cape. The only African tribes there at that time were primitive Bushmen and Hottentots.

In the interior of Cape Province river valleys curve through mountains carpeted, in spring, with wild flowers. Orchards and vineyards climb the slopes of the valleys.

On the coast, modern towns have sprung up behind broad, curving beaches. The capital of the province is Cape Town, which sits at the foot of the flat-topped Table Mountain.

Wheat is the chief crop in the Cape, but fruit, especially oranges and apples, is grown everywhere. And Cape vineyards make excellent wine, much of which is exported.

Natal is often called the garden province of South Africa. It receives a considerable quantity of rainfall, and grows citrus fruits, bananas, pineapples, and papaws. But the chief crop is sugar-cane.

The most important town in Natal is Durban, which is South Africa's chief port. Exports from Durban include large quantities of coal, as well as gold and other minerals from the interior of the country. Durban is also South Africa's most popular holiday resort.

An Indian woman of Natal poses with her children. Most Natal Indians are shopkeepers or gardeners.

John and Bini Moss - Photo Researchers

Rolling fields of the Transkei are used for grain crops and cattle breeding.

African women working in the fields of a South African soya bean plantation.

Behind the mountains that separate the east coast of South Africa from the central plateau, is the *veld* — rolling grassland something like the savanna — lying largely in the Transvaal and the Orange Free State. These two former colonies, now provinces, were created by what is known as the Great Trek, which is one of the milestones of South African history. It began in 1836, when the pressure of British colonists in the coastal regions began forcing the Dutch farmers (the Boers) into the interior. The word Boer, at one time widely used for all Afrikaners, really means farmer.

The Boers hitched sixteen oxen to their huge covered wagons, and set out across the grassy plains. They faced thirst and starvation, attacks by hostile Zulus and other warrior tribes. They were tired and sick, but they plodded on. They crossed the Orange River and founded the Orange Free State; they crossed the Vaal and founded the Transvaal.

Depending on the altitude and the amount of rainfall, the veld is now used for arable farming or for grazing cattle.

A typical farm in the Orange Free State is a very lonely place. Immense herds of Merino sheep, famous for their silky wool, graze on the veld. In the lower veld of the Transvaal grazing gives way to arable farming.

John and Bini Moss - Photo Researchers

Maize, called mealies locally, is a staple of the African diet.

H. E. Street - Shostal

Cattle graze on the treeless plains of the High Veld, over 6,000 feet up.

Government buildings in Pretoria, South Africa's capital, frame the statue of Boer hero Louis Botha.

Ndebele tribesmen, who live in villages near Pretoria, are famed for their magnificent decorative work.

H. E. Street - Shostal

Town Hall Square provides a fine open space in the centre of Johannesburg's business quarter.

The chief crops are maize, wheat, and citrus fruit. About a third of the Transvaal is covered by the treeless, grassy, High Veld. But most of it is Bushveld, with scattered shrubs dotting the flat lands that lie between range after range of low hills. The farms of the Transvaal produce cotton, tobacco, and groundnuts. Orchards and cattle ranches also add to the produce of the region; wool hides, and skins are important exports.

The Transvaal is the centre of the mining industry of South Africa. Besides the world-famous Johannesburg gold mines, there are coal, diamonds, asbestos, platinum, chromium, manganese, and copper. Iron-ore from the important deposits north-west of Pretoria is fed into the enormous blast furnaces and steel mills at Pretoria, and near Vereeniging on the Vaal. West of Port Elizabeth, the first important natural gas field is going into production.

Pretoria, the capital of the Transvaal, is the seat of government. The legislature is in Cape Town. The most important city of South Africa is Johannesburg.

The Kruger National Park is the most famous of all the African game reserves. About half the size of Switzerland, it is the greatest sanctuary of wild life in the world, where one can see lions, leopards, elephants, giraffes, zebras, crocodiles, baboons, and many other animals.

M. M. Schechter

A lazy lioness rests by the roadside in the Kruger National Park. Visitors must stay in their cars.

M. M. Schechter

A sable antelope forages at sunset on the open plains of the Kruger National Park.

THE MINES OF SOUTH AFRICA

South Africa is a store-house of mineral wealth. The gold produced amounts to nearly half of all the gold mined in the world. Its diamond mines yield fabulous jewels.

The discovery of gold in the Transvaal was the making of Johannesburg, the third largest town of Africa. Only founded in 1886, its population has already grown to over a million. About two-fifths are white. These include the mineowners, and form virtually all the financial, commercial, and professional community. The African majority are mainly mine workers and domestic servants.

Johannesburg stands on the Witwatersrand, a plateau 6,000 feet above sea-level, beneath which the vein of gold-bearing ore stretches for 100 miles. Mineshafts and tunnels run thousands of feet deep beneath the town. On its outskirts are great slag-heaps of waste material from the mining operations. Johannesburg is the biggest of the towns of Southern Africa that have arisen with European colonisation. It comprises, on the one hand, a thriving, busy modern town such as might easily be standing in Europe or America, and, on the other, the African 'locations' on the very outskirts of the city where the living conditions provide a marked contrast with the whites' suburbs.

In addition to the African labourers living on the numerous locations, hundreds of thousands of mine workers live in compounds built by the mine owners outside Johannesburg. These workers are Bantus, many of whom have come from neighbouring countries. Recently whole 'new towns' have been built for the coloured employees of the mines and factories.

Long before gold was found, diamonds were being mined in South Africa. The

Johannesburg's fabulous gold mines, with their huge dumps of debris, create a striking backdrop for the city.

This unexciting rock is rich gold ore.

great centre was the mining town of Kimberley. The mine nearby is called the Big Hole. It is three-quarters of a mile wide and nearly a third of a mile deep — one of the largest man-made holes on earth. Millions of pounds worth of diamonds have been mined from it. Diamonds are measured in carats. A carat is two-tenths of a gramme. The value of a diamond depends on its weight, its colour (a bluish-white being the best), and on the skill with which it has been cut. The biggest diamond ever found was the Cullinan, which came, not from the Big Hole, but from a mine near Pretoria. It was the size of a man's fist. There are also diamond fields near the mouth of the Orange River. In this area anyone may spot a diamond lying

A compound: built to house Africans hired to labour in the Johannesburg gold mines.

South Africa are very limited in their usefulness. One such area, known as the Upper Karroo, occupies much of northern Cape Province and western Orange Free State. It stands on the plateau at a height of 3,000 to 4,000 feet. Rainfall is uncertain, coming in short violent showers, and makes agriculture very difficult. Where there is a farm, a wind pump may be seen bringing water to the surface.

Vegetation consists mostly of stunted shrubs, but the plants provide food for large flocks of Merino sheep and goats. Wool is one of the country's chief exports. The same area is famous for its Karakul sheep. These animals are bred for the beautiful tightly-curled skins of the young lambs, known as 'Persian Lamb'.

in the sandy desert or on the beaches. But the area is closely guarded, and even visitors are searched when they leave the area.

The dry lands in the western half of

Further south and at lower levels, like steps down from the high plateau to the coast, are the Great Karroo and the Little Karroo. In these areas, too, sheep farming is the chief occupation.

Mine workers forget daily toil in the excitement of tribal dances. Teams compete before packed stands.

Constance Stuart - Black Star

A fortune in gems is held in these hands. But synthetic diamond manufacture may cut their value.

Elizabeth Morton - American Museum of Natural History

Water slowly fills one of the first great diamond mines to be worked at Kimberley.

B. E. Lindroos - Gilloon

The Kariba dam on the Zambezi river under construction.

The completed Kariba dam in Rhodesia. Lake Kariba is the world's largest man-made lake.

THE RHODESIAS

The mining area of South Africa extends northwards into Rhodesia and Zambia (formerly Southern Rhodesia and Northern Rhodesia) and Malawi. The name Rhodesia was taken from Cecil Rhodes, the British millionaire and adventurer, who was a major figure in the development of British Africa.

Much of Zambia and Rhodesia is a great expanse of savanna. On the grassy plateau of Rhodesia a great deal of cattle-ranching is done. The most important crops are maize and tobacco. The coalfields at Wankie produced 2 million tons a year, but this is not nearly enough to meet the needs of an area that is rapidly becoming industrialised. In Salisbury, the capital, and Bulawayo, the chief railway centre, there are textile mills and machine-tool plants. The mines

This is typical housing for Africans in Angola.

Hans von Meiss - Photo Researchers

A huge steam shovel looks like a toy as it digs ore from an open-cast copper mine in Zambia.

of the Copper Belt of Zambia (Northern Rhodesia) produce even more metal than the neighbouring Katanga region in the Congo.

The border between the Rhodesias is formed largely by the Zambezi River. The town of Livingstone, named after the famous explorer, is right on the border, at Victoria Falls. In the narrow Kariba Gorge in Rhodesia, a great dam has been built across the Zambezi, and the power station there is already supplying the area with electricity. The reservoir will store water for the irrigation of millions of acres of this still largely undeveloped territory.

Malawi is a long strip of territory running along the western shore of Lake Nyasa. Formerly a British Protectorate, most of the people of newly independent Malawi are Negroes. Malawi has great possibilities as a farming country. Tea and tobacco are raised in the highlands, and cotton on the Lower Shire Valley.

COLONIES AND NATIVE RESERVES

To the east and west of Zambia, Rhodesia and Malawi are the two great Portuguese territories of Africa: on the east, Mozambique, on the west, Angola. Both are almost completely undeveloped.

Angola has a population of 5 million

Martin S. Klein

Lourenço Marques is a leading African port.

Gordon Douglas - FPG

Negroes labour in the vineyard tending grapevines. South Africa produces excellent red and white wines.

Groups of fenced huts make up the village of Kanye, Botswana, on the edge of the Kalahari Desert.

M. M. Schechter

Sixt Bartholdi

A common sight on the South African veld are the windmills which pump water for livestock and farming.

in an area of 481,000 square miles. In the savanna, cattle-breeding is carried on and a variety of crops are grown, including coffee and groundnuts, sugar-cane, and maize. A vein of gold has recently been discovered in north central Angola.

Mozambique has a population of over 6.5 million in an area of just under 300,000 square miles. The chief crops here are sugar-cane, cotton, sisal, and coconut products — copra, from which coconut oil is produced and fibre for rope-making, etc. The most flourishing parts of the country are the capital, Lourenço Marques, and Beira, which are two of the chief ports of Africa. From them many of the exports of Zambia, Rhodesia, and South Africa are shipped.

South-West Africa, with a population

Courtesy of the South African Tourist Corporation

African women pound cassava roots in huge tubs to make a pasty meal which is their main food.

South African tribesmen are proud of their long-horned cattle, which they regard as a sign of wealth.

of about 610,000, is a dry plateau falling abruptly to the sea. Much of it is desert, for part of the Kalahari Desert extends into it. It is a United Nations trust territory administered by South Africa. Scattered on the desolate countryside are ranches on which cattle, sheep, and goats are bred. A few metals (tin, lead, copper, and zinc) are worked in the northern area of the country, and there are important coastal diamond fields.

In this part of Africa three areas were, in the past, set aside as native reserves. Much the largest of these is Botswana, which lies between Rhodesia, South-West Africa, and South Africa. In this

In Botswana, African families wait patiently in long lines for X-ray examinations.

large area, more than twice the size of the United Kingdom, there are only about 543,000 people, nearly all of them Bantu tribesmen. The southern part of Botswana is occupied by the Kalahari Desert, whose few inhabitants are Bushmen, one of the world's oldest races.

The northern part of Botwsana consists of swamps. Large nickel ore deposits have been found here.

The two other areas are enclaves, that is, they lie like islands surrounded by a foreign country. Lesotho lies within the frontiers of the Republic of South Africa, and Swaziland between South Africa and Mozambique. Until recently both of them were administered by Britain. However, both countries are now independent. They are more thickly populated than Botswana, but the land is poor. The tribes live in *kraals,* or villages, and follow the traditional ways of tribal

Youngsters gather around the pump in a Botswana village. Behind them is a clinic.

life. They rear cattle and live near their herds in small round huts. In spite of the freedom they enjoy and the generally bad living conditions on the Rand, many of the younger men in the reserves drift towards the mining areas of South Africa or seek work in the towns.

The scenery of South Africa combines rugged mountains and fertile valleys.

Forests cover the lower slopes of the Rocky Mountains. Still higher are barren or snow-covered peaks. This mountain wall stretches from the south-western United States northward across Canada into Alaska.

THIS IS NORTH AMERICA

North America is the northern half of the New World. It consists of Canada, the United States, and Mexico. In the course of this century, the United States has become one of the two greatest powers in the world. Canada too has made enormous strides, and her status today is utterly different from what it was in 1900, when she was still a British Crown Colony. Compared with the countries of Europe, both these states are continental in their dimensions, Canada alone being as large as the whole of Europe. If we are accustomed to compact states that can be crossed from end to end in a matter of hours, it is difficult even to imagine the vast spaciousness of the countries that make up the land mass of North America.

Compared to the complicated outline of Europe, the map of North America shows us a solid block, extending from the icy Arctic Ocean to the warm seas of the Tropics. An appreciable amount of Alaska and Northern Canada lies within the Arctic Circle.

New York and Los Angeles, on opposite sides of the continent, are 2,500 miles apart, whereas the distance from the west coast of Ireland to St John's, Newfoundland, is less than 2,000 miles. As for North America's natural resources, they too are on the same scale. Technologically, Americans are in the first rank. Financially, the United States is the richest country in the world. With such assets, it is only natural that the United States should be a leading world power.

NORTH AMERICA

Scale 1:30,000,000

0   100 200 300 400 500 Miles

NEW YORK	Cities over	1,000,000 population
Milwaukee	Cities of 250,000 –	1,000,000 population
Galveston	Cities under	250,000 population
⊛ Capitals of Countries		

Depths in feet: Heights in feet:

over 650	0–650		Below sea level	0–650	650–1650	1650–4900	over 4900

Arid regions⋯ Tundra▨ Swamp, marsh▦   Railways━ Canals▬ Head of navigation⊕ Falls⤲

PHYSICAL FEATURES

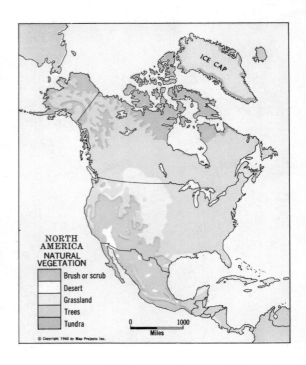

NORTH
AMERICA
NATURAL
VEGETATION
- Brush or scrub
- Desert
- Grassland
- Trees
- Tundra

© Copyright 1960 by Map Projects Inc.

0   1000
Miles

The mountains and plains of North America are in keeping with the rest, simple and vast. The detail, of course, varies greatly. The Atlantic coast, for instance, changes from the rocky cliffs of Maine to the gently shelving sandy beaches of Florida. Sometimes there are great estuaries like those which serve the ports of New York and Philadelphia, or, greatest of all, that of the St Lawrence in Canada. Inland from a broad coastal plain the mountains begin. The Appalachians consist of a number of parallel ranges extending from the Gulf of St Lawrence in the north to western Alabama in the south. The highest peak, in North Carolina, is less than 7,000 feet in height. They were high enough, in early colonial days, to halt penetration into the country. The presence of coal and oil has, in Pennsylvania, transformed them into an industrial zone.

On the western side, stretching from Alaska to New Mexico, are the vast ranges of the Rocky Mountains, whose snowy peaks remind us of the Alps. This great mountain system consists, for the most part, of two great chains, one running down the Pacific coast, the other more or less parallel to it some hundreds of miles inland, between which there are many plateaus and river valleys. With all their rainfall, snow, and glaciers, these mountains offer an immense reserve of water-power, which can be converted into electricity. More important still is the vast mineral wealth lying beneath.

Between the Rockies and the Appalachians the whole centre of the country consists of huge plains drained by the great river system of the Mississippi and its affluents.

Northern North America is covered by thousands of square miles of marshy Arctic tundra.

Rutherford Platt

USDA

Farm buildings, fields, and highways on the level prairies of the North American Mid-West form neat chequered patterns when seen from the air.

The forested slopes of Vermont's Green Mountains shelter this tiny village. The white spire of the village church is a familiar landmark.

This is the California coast. For more than 1,000 miles the waters of the blue Pacific Ocean crash on the western shoreline of the U.S.A.

Winston Pote - Shostal

Courtesy of TWA - Trans World Airlines

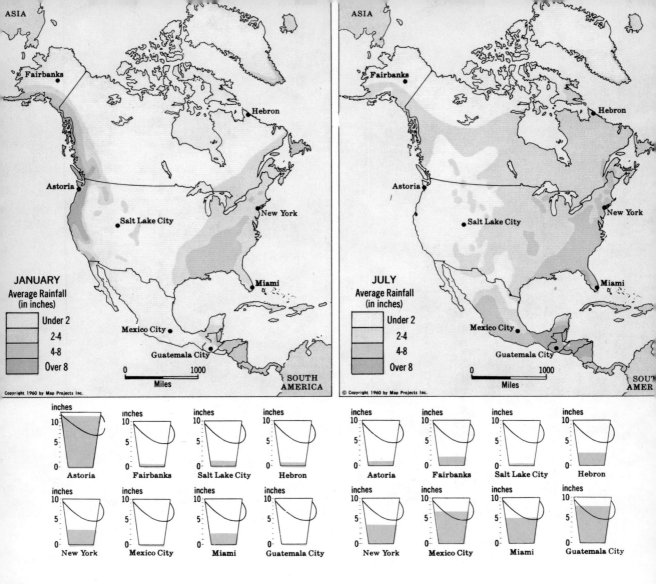

JANUARY
Average Rainfall
(in inches)
Under 2
2-4
4-8
Over 8

JULY
Average Rainfall
(in inches)
Under 2
2-4
4-8
Over 8

CLIMATE

The two temperature charts show which areas of North America are the warmest and the coldest. The southern-most band, going right across the continent, is the hottest, being the closest to the Equator. Further north the differences between the temperatures of January and July are greater. In the middle zone, temperatures are similar to those in Central Europe, with four clear-cut seasons and with abrupt periods of heat and cold. In the south, the winters are short, and the temperature in January generally mild. To the north, the winters are long and cold, and spring and autumn are very short.

It is, above all, in Canada that the winters are the longest and the coldest, with snow lying for many months. Summer is short. In the west the climate is somewhat exceptional owing to the presence of the Rocky Mountains. The mountains in the north are covered with snow. The days may be warm, but the nights

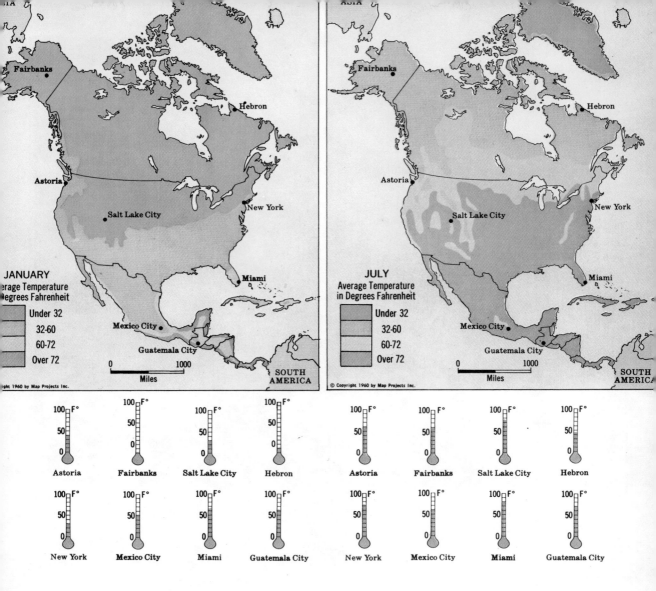

JANUARY
Average Temperature
in Degrees Fahrenheit

Under 32
32-60
60-72
Over 72

0   1000
Miles

SOUTH
AMERICA

© Copyright 1960 by Map Projects Inc.

JULY
Average Temperature
in Degrees Fahrenheit

Under 32
32-60
60-72
Over 72

0   1000
Miles

SOUTH
AMERICA

© Copyright 1960 by Map Projects Inc.

Astoria   Fairbanks   Salt Lake City   Hebron

New York   Mexico City   Miami   Guatemala City

Astoria   Fairbanks   Salt Lake City   Hebron

New York   Mexico City   Miami   Guatemala City

are always cold. The mountains in the south have a temperate climate, mild enough to have favoured the Aztec civilisation of Mexico. Moreover, sea breezes bring warmth to the land, so that in winter there is a relatively mild belt stretching all along the coast almost to Alaska, in which the average temperature is above freezing point.

The amount and distribution of rainfall also affects the climate. A glance at the appropriate map will show that the Pacific coast of Alaska, Canada, and the United States has abundant rainfall, again due to the presence of the Rockies.

On the eastern side of the Rocky Mountains is a vast dry area extending from Canada to Mexico. It is far from any sea, so has little opportunity of capturing moisture from the air. Further east, in the south-eastern United States, we find a climate increasing in humidity, for this area comes within reach of air masses from the Atlantic and the Gulf of Mexico. The north-eastern States also receive ample rainfall.

Canadian Govt Travel Bureau Photo

Niagara Falls, Ontario. Today the great power of the Niagara River has been harnessed, by a dam built above the falls, for hydro-electric purposes.

This is desert country in the south-western United States. Navajo Indians graze their flocks of sheep and goats on these dry pastures.

The Bahamas are popular with tourists from all over the world — but particularly with those from the United States.

Royal Lowy - American Indian Archives

Bahamas Tourist Board

THE PEOPLES OF NORTH AMERICA

North America has a population of 300 million which, on the average, amounts to about twenty-eight per square mile. Thus, compared to Europe, which has 224 per square mile or Asia, with 163 per square mile, it is a thinly populated continent.

Of course, the population is not spread evenly over all the land area. It is concentrated in towns, and thinly spread in the rural areas. The towns themselves are sometimes far apart, sometimes close together, and in some parts of the continent there is not so much as a village

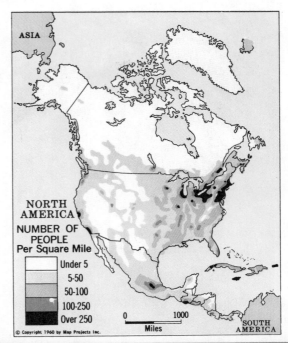

NORTH AMERICA
NUMBER OF PEOPLE
Per Square Mile

- Under 5
- 5-50
- 50-100
- 100-250
- Over 250

0   1000
Miles

ASIA

SOUTH AMERICA

© Copyright 1960 by Map Projects Inc.

Van Bucher - Photo Researchers

Manhattan Island, in New York City, is North America's most densely populated area. People from every part of the world have come here to live.

These Sioux Indians represent the 350,000 Indians that live in the United States today. Many more Indians live in Canada, Mexico, Central America, and the Caribbean islands, as well as in South America.

for many miles. The population is also very varied, being composed of many different races, Eskimos, American ('Red') Indians, white immigrants from Europe, and Negro descendants of slaves imported from Africa.

The first inhabitants were American Indians, believed to have come from Asia across the Bering Straits. This happened so long ago that scholars have not been

able to fix the date, even roughly. When the first European explorers discovered the New World, there were some 5 million Indians in North America. The bulk of them lived on the high plateaus of Mexico and Central America. There were less than a million, scattered in different tribes, in what is now the United States and Canada.

Perhaps the largest of the waves of

Four-fifths of Mexico's people are at least part Indian. Over a quarter are pure Indian.

Over nine-tenths of Haiti's people are Negroes. The official language of Haiti is French.

immigrants from Europe came from Ireland as a result of the Irish Potato Famine of 1846. A great many others, particularly from Germany and Scandinavia, came during the American Civil War, and in the seventies, when the great American wheat-lands were opened up.

Besides the immigrants we have been speaking of, who were all Europeans, others of a different sort had been entering the country. In the Southern states, and in the West Indies, Negroes from Africa had been brought over as slaves. They were particularly useful on the large plantations of tobacco and cotton. As a result, today one-tenth of the population of the United States is Negro. At the beginning of the century yet another racial influx began with the immigration of Chinese and Japanese into the States along the Pacific Coast. Besides these distinctive races, there are, amongst the European immigrants and their descendants, national groups like

Courtesy of the Puerto Rico News Service

Over 650 people per square mile crowd Puerto Rico. Yet more than half of the people are farmers.

the Irish and the Poles, who retain their individual character. Nevertheless, the American way of life does a great deal to bind all these various elements into a united whole.

Guatemala has Central America's largest population. Many are descendants of the ancient Mayas.

Courtesy of the Pan American Coffee Bureau

NORTH AMERICA

ARCTIC OCEAN

U. S. S. R.

BERING SEA

Bering Strait

Wrangel I.

Prince Patrick I.

Sverdrup Is.

Ellesmere I.

GREENLAND (Denmark)

ICELAND

Denmark Strait

BEAUFORT SEA

Banks I.

Melville I.

Devon I.

BAFFIN BAY

DAVIS STRAIT

Arctic Circle

ALASKA

Bristol Bay

Kodiak I.

Alexander Archipelago

YUKON

Victoria Island

Prince of Wales I.

NORTHWEST TERRITORIES

Foxe Basin

Baffin Island

Hudson Strait

Great Bear Lake

Great Slave Lake

HUDSON BAY

LABRADOR

NEWFOUNDLAND

Queen Charlotte Islands

BRITISH COLUMBIA

ALBERTA

SASKATCHEWAN

MANITOBA

Lake Winnipeg

ONTARIO

James Bay

QUEBEC

NEWFOUNDLAND

C. Breton I.

Vancouver Island

C A N A D A

Prince Edward Island

NEW BRUNS.

NOVA SCOTIA

MAINE

PACIFIC OCEAN

WASHINGTON

OREGON

IDAHO

MONTANA

NORTH DAKOTA

SOUTH DAKOTA

WYOMING

MINNESOTA

L. Superior

MICHIGAN

L. Huron

WISC.

L. Michigan

NEVADA

UTAH

COLORADO

NEBRASKA

IOWA

ILLINOIS

IND.

OHIO

PENNA.

NEW YORK

N.H.

VT.

MASS.

CT. R.I.

N.J.

MD. DEL.

CALIFORNIA

UNITED STATES

KANSAS

MISSOURI

KENTUCKY

W. VA.

VIRGINIA

ATLANTIC OCEAN

ARIZONA

NEW MEXICO

OKLAHOMA

ARK.

TENNESSEE

NORTH CAROLINA

SOUTH CAROLINA

MISS.

ALABAMA

GEORGIA

TEXAS

LOUISIANA

FLORIDA

Bahama Islands (Br.)

Tropic of Cancer

120°

Gulf of California

GULF OF MEXICO

Straits of Florida

Yucatán Channel

CUBA

HAITI

PUERTO RICO (U.S.A.)

DOMINICAN REPUBLIC

10°

MEXICO

Gulf of Campeche

JAMAICA

CARIBBEAN SEA

BRITISH HONDURAS

HONDURAS

GUATEMALA

EL SALVADOR

NICARAGUA

Canal Zone (U.S.A.)

VENEZUELA

COSTA RICA

PANAMA

80°

COLOMBIA

HAWAII

Kauai

Niihau

Oahu

Molokai

Lanai

Maui

Kahoolawe

Hawaii

PACIFIC OCEAN

0   50   100
Miles

160°   158°   156°

0   500   1000
Miles

© Copyright 1960 by Map Projects Inc.

COMMUNICATIONS

The three maps on this page give a picture of the lines of communication in North America. In the thickly settled areas in the East there is a dense network of roads, railways, and air services. With large populations working in towns, transport is necessary to take them to and from their jobs, to carry the goods they manufacture, and keep them supplied with raw materials.

In the relatively empty areas of Canada, Mexico, and Central America, neither passengers nor freight are sufficient to make building many railways worthwhile, particularly when the country is too difficult for easy railway construction.

In North America there are 4 million miles of main roads and 102 million motor vehicles. Special 'super highways' have been built to accommodate these enormous numbers. But even so the problem of traffic control is still unsolved. In the

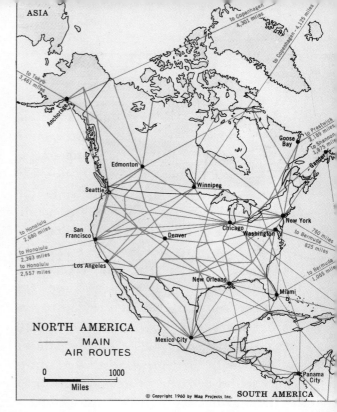

United States alone, 42 million truck-loads of goods per year are carried by rail. Internal air services cover 8000 million miles a year, carrying over 45 million passengers.

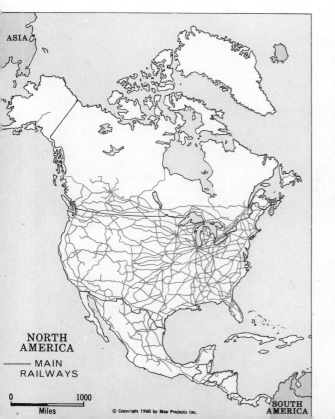

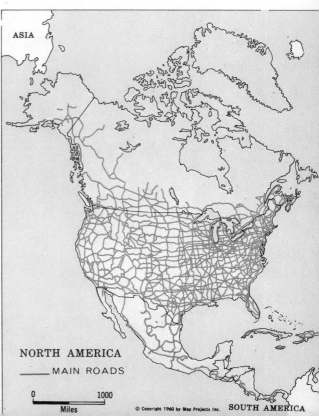

LEADING TOWNS AND CITIES

If North America has huge mountain ranges and vast plains it has also a large number of great cities, including one of the greatest in the world. Of the 128 cities in the world whose metropolitan areas have populations exceeding a million, North America possesses 35.

These towns have grown up within the last hundred years, keeping pace with the development of industry and the construction of railways. Previously the large towns had all been on the coast or on the rivers, but, with the coming of railways, they grew wherever mines were found or industry developed.

The towns have grown most thickly in the north-east of the United States, between Boston and Baltimore — an area which includes New York and Philadelphia. Another area is on the

Courtesy of TWA - Trans World Airlines

The capital of the United States is Washington, D.C., a city site chosen by George Washington.

Great Lakes (Chicago, Detroit, etc.), and yet another stretches from Pittsburgh, down the Ohio River basin, and on to St Louis on the Mississippi. In Canada the thickest area is from Quebec on the St Lawrence to Toronto on Lake Ontario. All these areas together occupy only a small but important portion of North America, which is very often referred to

Across the historic Common is the city of Boston, site of many Revolutionary War landmarks.

Ewing Galloway

Chicago, industrial and communications centre of the Mid-West, is located on Lake Michigan. It is famed for its meat-packing industry.

as the 'American Manufacturing Belt'.

The American Manufacturing Belt is the greatest industrial workshop of the United States and Canada. It contains more than 400 manufacturing towns. Fifty of these are along the Atlantic

Across the Hudson River are the famous skyscrapers of Manhattan Island, the centre of New York. In 1626 the island was purchased from the Indians for twenty-four dollars-worth of trinkets by the West India Company. North America's largest city, New York is visited by millions of tourists each year.

Courtesy of American Airlines

Philadelphia is a city rich in history. Its Independence Hall, where the Declaration of Independence was signed, houses the Liberty Bell.

seaboard of the southern Great Lakes. Well over 200 of them are on navigable rivers. Some are on canals. All but seventy

of them can be reached by water, and those owe their growth to the presence of railways.

New York is the greatest urban centre in the world. Together with its suburbs it now has a population of over 16 million. It is also the greatest port in the country, and, as a financial centre, its wealth and its influence are formidable. Yet it is not the capital of the United States, nor even the capital of New York State, that role being assigned to the relatively small town of Albany.

The capital of the United States is Washington. When the country gained its independence, there was some jealousy between the various States as to which capital should be chosen as the seat of government. To avoid friction, it was finally decided to set aside a separate

Detroit, Michigan, is a great industrial city famous for its manufacture of motor vehicles.

Photographic Survey Corp. - Annan Photo Features

Courtesy of TWA - Trans World Airlines

The Golden Gate Bridge spans San Francisco Bay. San Francisco has a fine natural harbour.

district on which a national capital should be built. This is called the District of Columbia, and the capital is officially called Washington D.C. — the initials being rather important since there are several Washingtons in the country. Washington lies on the banks of the Potomac. Its most famous buildings are the Capitol, seat of Congress, and the White House, the President's residence.

In Montreal, Canada's largest city, both the French and the English languages are used.

Quebec Province - Photo Driscoll

C. Perry Weimer - House of Photography

Havana is Cuba's capital and the largest city in the Caribbean. The Spanish-Colonial city has a magnificent climate and fine ocean beaches.

Probably the oldest North American city, Mexico City is the capital of Mexico and one of the world's largest towns. Its wide avenues pass Aztec ruins, old Spanish churches, and ultra-modern buildings.

Josef Muench

G. H. Jarrett - FPG

This bridge over the St Lawrence Seaway connects two friendly neighbours — Canada and the United States.

CANADA

Canada has a slightly larger area than the United States, and only two countries are larger: the U.S.S.R. and China. Canada spreads over nearly half of North America, yet it has only one-fifteenth of the population. Vast areas in the north are uninhabited.

Ottawa, with 494,500 inhabitants, is the capital of Canada, but Montreal, with a population of 2,437,000 is the largest city and the economic centre of the country. It lies on the St Lawrence, and is the country's chief port. Toronto, with a slightly smaller population, is another great commercial and banking centre. It also has a textile industry.

On three sides, Canada is bordered by the sea: by the Atlantic, the Pacific, and the Arctic Ocean. On the south she has a frontier some 3,000 miles long with the United States. And it shows how close these two countries are that this frontier should be totally undefended.

Cod drying in the sun is still a common sight in the Atlantic Provinces of Canada. But today great quantities of fish are quick-frozen, tinned, and shipped to all parts of the world.

INDUSTRIES OF CANADA

Fishing was one of Canada's first industries. Fishermen from Europe are believed to have caught large quantities of fish off the coast of Newfoundland before any explorer sighted the mainland of North America. That is not altogether surprising since the shallow waters they fished in, called the Grand Banks, were both stormy and foggy. The Grand Banks still form an important fishing ground. From New Brunswick to the tip of Labrador is an indented coastline totalling some 5,000 miles, with many shel-

tered harbours and with great schools of cod, herring, halibut, mackerel, and haddock, making this coast one of the world's great fishing grounds.

Canada's Pacific coast is also famous for its fisheries. Deep fjords and a shallow ledge, fifty to 100 miles off-shore, are excellent feeding ground for fish, and British Columbia today ranks close to the Atlantic Provinces in the value of its hauls.

The salmon is the king of fish on the Pacific Coast. The sock-eye salmon is particularly valued by the tinning industry, though other kinds of salmon are often larger.

There are few countries in the world which possess so great a wealth in the form of forests as Canada.

The saw-mills are at work incessantly. British Columbia stands first in the lumber trade, Quebec and Ontario coming second and third. Between them, these three Provinces account for four-fifths of Canada's timber.

Much of the Pacific area is covered by forests, producing softwoods (firs, pines, etc.) and, in particular, the giant Douglas fir, which provides some of the finest timber of North America. Although in rather northerly latitudes the area has, as we have seen, a mild climate, owing to the temperate moist winds from the Pacific, the rainfall is heavy. All these factors favour the rapid growth of trees.

Much of the wood, particularly from

W. D. McKinney - FPG

Salmon have made the north Pacific coast one of the North America's most important fishing regions.

This mine at Beaverlodge, Saskatchewan, is producing one of Canada's important mineral resources — uranium.

George Hunter - Shostal

Petroleum has fast become a leading mineral resource of Canada.

eastern Canada, is turned into pulp, which is the chief raw material for paper-making. Canada's first pulp-mill was built less than 100 years ago, but the industry has grown rapidly. Today more than 100 pulp and paper-mills are at work.

This has become an important industry, and its rapid development is due, not only to the abundant supply of wood, but also to the ready supply of water-power which keeps the mills running.

Furs were one of Canada's earliest products. Trappers explored much of the Canadian wilderness. A few trappers are still working the snow-blanketed northern forests, but today most of Canada's fur comes from fur farms. Fur farming started on Prince Edward Island in the Gulf of St Lawrence: fox, mink, chinchilla, and marten being reared in captivity. It was so successful that the example was soon followed in other Provinces. Nearly 10 million pounds sterling worth of furs come from Canada each year.

If trapping brought a handful of Canadians into the wild country of the north, gold brought thousands. It has been found right across the country, from Newfoundland in the east, to the Yukon far in the north-west. Many of the early camps were so inaccessible that they could only be reached by boat or by long difficult treks overland. When the gold was exhausted the camps were abandoned. If a strike turned out to be really big, the rough camp was replaced by a proper town. Much the same thing is happening today.

Canada is the third biggest producer of gold in the world behind South Africa and the U.S.S.R. Most of it is mined in an area sometimes called 'The Valley of Gold' which stretches from central Ontario eastward into Quebec. Despite the large quantity mined, it is believed that reserves have barely been touched.

Prospectors hunting for gold sometimes find other minerals. Occasionally deposits of great value are found in this way, or even quite by accident. About seventy-five years ago, rocks were being blasted near Sudbury in Ontario, where a railway was being built. In the process, huge deposits of copper and nickel were revealed. The mines are still working today. In fact, three-fifths of the world's supply of nickel comes from there, and the reserves will last for 100 years.

At Sudbury, copper and platinum are

mined, along with nickel. With every pound of nickel, two pounds of copper are extracted; about two-fifths of the world's supply of platinum also comes from Sudbury.

The world's growing industries need more and more raw materials, and a constant search for minerals is today being carried out in northern Canada. Modern prospectors, however, are not the lonely adventurers of the past. They are trained geologists, and their surveys are done by air. Aircraft have done more than anything else to open up northern Canada. They can carry geologists and their equipment to the most isolated places, keep them supplied in all weathers, and furnish air photographs which speed up the work of survey enormously.

An important part of their work is the search for pitchblende. It is from pitchblende that radium and uranium are extracted. It was first discovered at the

Joe Barnell - Shostal

The Yellow Knife Mine, on the Great Slave Lake, produces a large share of Canada's gold.

Steep Rock Mine, north-west of Lake Superior, is one of Canada's richest sources of iron ore.

G. H. Jarrett - FPG

Tom Hollyman - Researchers

A farmer in Alberta harvests wheat, the leading crop of Alberta, Saskatchewan, and Manitoba.

eastern end of Great Bear Lake, far to the north. A mining town, Port Radium, has grown up on the site, which is only twenty-eight miles from the Arctic Circle.

Further discoveries of pitchblende have recently been made, and another town, this one called Uranium City, has grown up on the northern shore of Lake Athabaska, in Central Canada. Uranium City has grown from a wilderness to a town of several thousand within the space of a few years.

No mineral is more important than iron however. An enormous deposit of iron-ore is now being mined from Lac Jeannine to the lonely Ungava area, on the border of Quebec and Labrador.

How to get this 'far away' iron-ore to the steel-mills was quite a problem. Eventually a railway was built 360 miles in length from the mines to Sept Isles, a port at the mouth of the St Lawrence, where the ore is loaded on to ships.

Canada has enormous supplies of coal. Unfortunately it is situated in the wrong places. The industries that need it are in the St Lawrence lowlands and round the Great Lakes, but three-fifths of the coal comes from Alberta and British Columbia on the other side of the country. Most of the rest comes from the Atlantic Provinces. As a result, the industrial areas import a good deal of coal from the United States. Canada is rich in oil and natural gas. A few years ago a gigantic field of oil was found near Edmonton, in Alberta, and oil now ranks first in value among Canada's mineral resources.

In this plant at Sarnia, Ontario, synthetic rubber is manufactured from available raw materials.

Malak - Annan Photo Features

These Hereford cattle are part of a vast herd on a ranch in Alberta.

Clemson - Annan Photo Features

Courtesy of Aluminium Limited, Montreal

This aluminium plant at Kitimat is the largest in the world.

AGRICULTURE

Farming has a very important place in Canada's economy, although far more people are now employed in the manufacturing industries. There are two great agricultural areas. In the east, there are the lowlands round the St Lawrence and the Great Lakes. Further west are the prairies of Manitoba, Saskatchewan, and Alberta. Both these areas are in the south. Further north, the summer is too short for crops to grow and ripen. Thus only a very small part of the land is suitable for farming.

The lowlands of the Great Lakes and St Lawrence are sometimes called Canada's Heartland. It is less than a tenth of the country. Yet it houses more than two-thirds of the population and contains four-fifths of the country's factories. It produces half of Canada's agricultural produce. In this it is helped by the fact that the ground is not hilly and thus is easily ploughed, and also by the summers being warmer than in any other region. Moreover the St Lawrence Seaway has opened the whole area to the Atlantic and thus to the countries overseas. The Canadian Heartland is really the Canadian part of a farming area that includes the north-eastern part of the United States. It is sometimes known as the 'hay and dairy region'. Much of the land on the Canadian side is stony. It none the less makes excellent pastures and is ideal for growing hay and oats, as winter fodder.

The other area is part of the great stretch of plains that reach from the Gulf of Mexico to the Arctic Ocean. The Canadian portion consists of Manitoba, Saskatchewan, and Alberta, which are known as the Prairie Provinces.

Here are the log-sorting ponds and the great saw mills of Victoria, British Columbia. Wood is also used in the pulp and paper industries.

The country here has been farmed ever since the first settlers arrived. The soil is rich, but the winters long, making the growing season short. Drought is often experienced. Under these conditions only a few cereals can be grown.

First among them is spring wheat. It is grown on more than three-quarters of the area. It is the farmer's favourite crop, for it demands little rain, and ripens rapidly. Moreover this Canadian 'hard' wheat has a ready market in Europe for bread and biscuit making.

Some parts of the Prairie Provinces are too dry even for wheat. Here are the ranches. Canada's ranches are enormous and the herds on them often consist of several thousand head of cattle.

Special crops grow in some areas. In the Annapolis-Cornwallis Valley for instance, in Nova Scotia, apples are grown that are known the world over. Grapes and peaches of the finest quality come from the Niagara Peninsula in Ontario. Potatoes are grown in New Brunswick and Prince Edward Island.

The rugged land of British Columbia is for the most part unsuited for anything but forestry. In a few districts however, fruit and vegetables and bulbs are grown, and dairy-farming flourishes round the larger towns. Most of the farming is done near the mouth of the Fraser River and in the southern part of Vancouver Island. These areas get abundant rainfall, and the growing season is longer.

Canada is rapidly becoming one of the great industrial nations of the world. Her industry is centred on the Great Lakes and St Lawrence lowland. Raw materials from every quarter converge here to supply the factories.

Mineral ore, wood-pulp, furs and timber come from the mines and forests of Ontario and Quebec. From the Prairie Provinces come wheat, meat, and oil. And from the Atlantic Provinces come coal, wood, and food products.

Much of the energy consumed in the factories is derived from water-power. It is converted into electricity, of which Canada uses an enormous quantity. In particular, a great quantity of power is provided by the Niagara Falls.

Canada's industrial plain extends from Windsor (just opposite Detroit), between Lake Erie and Lake Huron, to Quebec. It includes Toronto and Montreal. This area is served by a network of roads and railways, which make transport easy, as well as the great St Lawrence Seaway.

Logs come tumbling down swift Canadian streams on their way to the sawmills. About 46 per cent of the land is forested.

First among the industries come wood-pulp and paper-making. Few areas in the world are better suited for it. Forests lie on the one side, and the great markets of the United States on the other. And water-power is available in abundance.

Water-power is also used in the rapidly growing aluminium industry in both the St Lawrence River valley and in British Columbia. The manufacture of plastics, textiles, and chemicals, all require great quantities of water and electricity.

The production of iron and steel has for long taken a leading place in Canadian industry. Hamilton in Ontario, is sometimes called the Pittsburgh of Canada, Pittsburgh being the greatest American iron and steel centre.

Canada is a great commercial nation, and imports and exports play a great part in her trade. Before the last war, the United Kingdom was the greatest buyer of Canadian goods, but that place has now been taken by the United States.

The paper industry depends on timber resources.

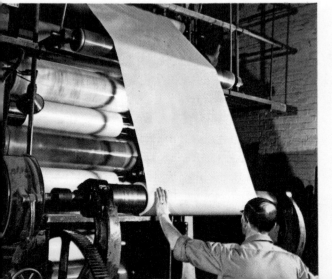

UNITED STATES

NEW YORK	Over 1,000,000 population
Toledo	250,000–1,000,000 population
Pasadena	100,000–250,000 population
Decatur	50,000–100,000 population
Temple	Under 50,000 population

© Copyright 1960 by Map Projects Inc.

0 — 300
Miles

◉ National Capital
◎ State Capitals

Under the shadow of the majestic Rocky Mountains, a herd of fine beef cattle grazes in a high meadow in Wyoming. Note the winding pattern of the stream that carries away water from melting snow.

THE U.S.A.

With a favourable climate, a fertile soil, and vast mineral and fuel resources, the 202 million people of the United States have for long enjoyed a very high standard of living. The country has only 6 per cent of the world's land area and less than 7 per cent of the world's population. Yet the people of the United States consume nearly half of all that the world produces.

Cy La Tour - Photo Library

The United States consumes 140 million tons of iron ore each year to produce steel.

THE NORTH-EAST

Industry is largely concentrated in the north-eastern States of the U.S.A. The output of the factories varies from heavy locomotives to precision instruments, from the finest silk to the roughest canvas, from paper and pens to aircraft and nuclear-driven submarines. In fact, in this area literally everything that can be made is made.

The Port of New York Authority

New York's crowded harbour serves the world's busiest port. It handles 400 ships a day.

Of the manufacturing towns in this area, New York and Pittsburgh have already been mentioned. Philadelphia is the fourth largest town in the country. Its industry includes the manufacture of carpets and rugs, and a wide range of textiles and clothing. Baltimore is one of the most important Atlantic ports.

Its population of nearly 2 million is engaged in a number of industries, including canning and preserving.

Boston with a total urban population

Pittsburgh, at the junction of the Allegheny and Monongahela rivers, is North America's greatest steel centre.

USDA

Forests of the North-East and Canada provide the raw material for this paper mill in Maine.

Colourful fishing boats crowd the docks at New Bedford, Mass., once the world's greatest whaling port.

Unusually fertile soils plus careful farming methods have made south-eastern Pennsylvania one of the United States' most prosperous agricultural regions. Farmers have tilled this soil for 250 years.

of 3.2 million is a historic town with a high standing in the world of culture. Its industries include printing and publishing, sugar refining, and clothing manufacture.

Fishing has always been an important industry in the north-east. Towns like Boston and Portland began as little fishing villages.

With modern times, fishing has changed. Sail has given way to steam or to the diesel engine. Nets that were once hauled in by hand are now hauled in by winches. The typical modern fishing vessel is the steam or motor trawler, which drags her nets along the bottom of the sea.

To assist navigation, vessels are fitted with echo-sounders. This instrument, the forerunner of radar, transmits sound waves which bounce off the bottom of the sea and return. The instrument gives the depth of the water by measuring the time the echo has taken. The same method is also used to locate shoals of fish.

Much of New England's soil is rough and stony. Compared with the rest of America the growing season is short. Accordingly, many farmers go in for dairy-farming. Thus green meadows, hayfields, hayricks, and cow-sheds contribute much to the New England landscape.

Further south, farming is more mixed. On a long, narrow strip of land, running down the Atlantic Coast from Long Island to Maryland, huge fields of vegetables dot the landscape. The soil here is light and easy to cultivate. There is plenty of rain and the growing season lasts a good six months. This 'truck farming' is like market gardening on a much larger scale.

THE MIDDLE WEST

No other farming area of the world equals the Middle West either in production or in the prosperity of its farmers. The Middle West is an enormous area, and the farms themselves are big and highly mechanised. They produce nine-tenths of the soya beans grown in the country, three-fifths of the wheat, four-fifths of the maize, three-fifths of all livestock, and seven-eighths of the pigs.

Maize is grown in the southern part, often called the 'corn belt', which includes western Ohio, Indiana, Illinois, Iowa, Missouri, Nebraska, and Kansas. Maize is the 'pioneer' American crop. American farmers learnt its cultivation from the Indians. As the pioneers moved westward, they took their maize-growing with them. In the Middle West they found an ideal climate for it. Maize likes the heat both by day and night; it also likes rain. In hot, rainy weather, the plant will sometimes grow an inch or more in a day. Most farmers feed their maize to pigs and cattle, as that is a more profitable way of using it. Though maize is the largest individual crop, it is grown on less than half the land. On the remainder a variety of crops are grown, including soya beans, oats, wheat, and hay.

In the northern part, the long, cold winters, and cool, moist summers are

This Mid-Western scene shows how contour farming follows the contours of the land, to avoid soil erosion.

USDA

A. M. Wettach - Shostal

Well-managed dairy farms like this make Wisconsin's farmers prosperous.

unfavourable for the growing of maize, but are ideal for dairy-farming.

The western parts of the Middle West are drier. From the Dakotas southward is wheat country. The farms here are positively enormous, and one can drive for miles and see nothing but endless fields of wheat, waving in the breeze.

The Middle West has everything necessary to make it into a great manufacturing area. There are abundant deposits of coal, natural gas and oil, iron ore, timber, and all kinds of raw materials. There is a large labour force: Chicago,

In Illinois broad fields of maize provide farmers with their most valuable cash crop.

Max Duk - Black Star

Courtesy of General Mills Co., Inc.

Grain is stored in huge elevators at flour mills in Minneapolis, Minnesota.

Ewing Galloway

The steel industry's demand for iron ore created this large mine in Minnesota's Mesabi range.

with a population of over 6.7 million, being the region's biggest city.

For a long time the processing of foodstuffs ranked first amongst Mid-Western industries. But recently metal production and the manufacture of ma-chinery and motor-cars have taken the leading place.

Once, practically all slaughtering and

Detroit's vehicle factories operate night and day. The motor industry is the largest steel user in the U.S.A.

Ewing Galloway

Mild winters and abundant sunshine and rainfall make Florida a great citrus-growing state.

meat-packing was done on the farms where the livestock was reared. Now, with fast transport and refrigeration available, animals are taken to great packing stations in the larger towns.

Many tons of wheat are delivered by rail to the mills in Minneapolis, Kansas City, St Louis, and Wichita. Buffalo, on Lake Erie, is another great milling centre. It is cheaper to transport goods by water

Tobacco is dried before being further processed.
USDA

than by rail, so every year huge grain ships deliver their cargoes of wheat to the Buffalo mills.

Cheap water-borne transport also favours the growth of an important iron and steel industry along the shores of the Lower Great Lakes. Ships have been specially designed to carry iron ore from the mines of Minnesota, Wisconsin, and northern Michigan to the blast furnaces and steel mills of towns such as Gary, which lies on Lake Michigan, a little to the south-east of Chicago. Coal and limestone (also essential for the production of iron and steel) come from mines and quarries in the neighbourhood. Sea-borne ships can sail 2,347 miles from the Gulf of St Lawrence on the Atlantic to the extreme western end of Lake Superior, using the St Lawrence Seaway. Shiploads of iron ore can therefore come direct from the rich deposits newly opened up in Labrador, or from any part of the world.

More than half the motor vehicles manufactured in the United States are made in the Middle West, and the great centre of this industry is Detroit.

THE SOUTH

The South is, for the most part, a land of hot summers, and mild winters. Rainfall is abundant.

For a long time this vast agricultural area specialised in three main crops: cotton, tobacco, and maize. Cotton and tobacco were grown for the market, maize for subsistence and animal-feed.

These crops did the soil a lot of harm. All three are grown in rows, and the land between the rows has to be hoed. As a result, there is not enough vegetation left to protect the soil during heavy rains. The rains in the South are very heavy indeed. During summer thunderstorms, the rain streams off the land carrying good soil with it. In some places great gullies have been formed, and the land has had to be abandoned.

Big changes are taking place, for farmers are now making a great effort to conserve and improve their soil. Fertilisers are being widely used, and fields are being ploughed *along* rather than *across* the contours so that they hold back the rain. This is called contour farming.

USDA

Mechanical cotton-pickers are replacing hand labour in the cotton fields of the South.

New crops are being produced, including groundnuts and soya beans. But the greatest change in Southern farming has been the development of cattle-breeding. Discarded cotton lands have become ranches which, in some cases, are larger even than those of the West. The mild Southern winter makes it possible for cattle to graze all the year round. Today,

Texas, long famous for cowpunchers and cattle, still leads the United States in livestock production.

Bob Taylor - FPG

Josef Muench

Closeness to raw materials, abundant and cheap fuel supplies, and a good location on the Gulf Coast . . . all these combine to make Houston, Texas, a centre of the chemical industry.

the South is becoming cowboy country.

The South, though essentially an agricultural region, is becoming increasingly industrialised. Sulphur and salt are found in great domes along the coast of the Gulf of Mexico, in Louisiana and Texas. All the United States' sulphur comes from this source, which amounts to nearly 70 per cent of the world's total production. Sulphur and salt form the basis for a growing chemical industry.

Phosphates, too, are of great importance, and Florida and Tennessee supply most of the nation's needs.

Bauxite is found in many areas of the South, but 90 per cent of the amount

Sulphur from nearby Gulf Coast mines is loaded on to a ship in Galveston harbour.

Frank E. Meitz - Shostal

Oil-fields, like these, produce crude oil which must then be processed at a refinery.

Fred Bond - FPG

United States Information Service

The Telstar communications satellite enables television to span the world. Cape Kennedy, Florida, is the centre of United States' space research.

B. A. Lang, Sr. - Shostal

Refining petroleum is one of the leading industries in the South. Huge oil-refineries dotting the landscape are a common sight.

Granite quarries like this are abundant in Georgia.

Herbert Lanks - Black Star

extracted comes from central Arkansas.

There are also great deposits of iron ore, but these have only been exploited in a few places — such as Birmingham, Alabama. One bed of ore near Birmingham stretches for over twenty-five miles. With such masses of iron ore close at hand, Birmingham has naturally become an important producer of iron and steel.

The South has supplies of every source of energy: coal, oil, natural gas, and water-power. It is impossible even to estimate the quantity of oil that lies beneath the swamps and plains of the South, and Southern coal-fields provide two-fifths of the total production of the United States, and the Southern Appalachians is one of the areas of the United States in which water-power has been most exploited.

More than half the land in the South is covered with forests. Two-fifths of the country's timber, more than half the wood-pulp, and one-third of the paper made comes from this region.

WESTERN UNITED STATES

0 100 200 300
Miles

◎ State Capitals

LOS ANGELES ——— Over 1,000,000 population
Portland ———— 250,000-1,000,000 population
Phoenix ———— 100,000- 250,000 population
Bakersfield ———— 50,000- 100,000 population
Roswell ———————— Under 50,000 population

© Copyright 1960 by Map Projects Inc.

Ripening oranges cover the neatly spaced trees of this California orange grove.

In the spring, sheep are driven high into Western mountains to seek fresh, green pastures.

Courtesy of the Boeing Airplane Company

Huge aircraft factories in California and Washington produce modern jet aeroplanes.

THE WEST

D. Horter - FPG

In the Pacific North-West, salmon rank first in value among the fish resources.

There are few places in the world where the land is put to such a variety of uses as the West. The determining factor is generally rainfall which is sufficient for arable farming in only a few places in the West.

There are vast areas of desert. But there are some places where enough rain falls to allow scrub to grow and thus make ranching possible. In some areas the vegetation is so thin that it takes 120 acres to support a single head of cattle. Thus ranches tend to be enormous, some being of over half a million acres.

Cattle branding is a busy time on Western ranches. Brands help to distinguish cattle from different herds.

USDA

The driest land is used for sheep, for they can browse on leaves, weeds, and woody plants which cattle will not eat, and can be moved into the mountains in summer time.

In contrast to the great Western ranch, is the small irrigated farm producing fine crops of vegetables, and melons.

The three coastal States of the West: California, Oregon, and Washington, are thriving agriculturally. But there is a great difference in the kind of crops produced in central and southern California and in the northern farmlands.

Today four-fifths of California's farmlands are used for grazing or to grow cereals. However, the crops of the remaining fifth are the most valuable: cotton, vegetables, fruit, especially grapes, and dairy-farming.

California is now second only to Texas as a cotton-producing state, and grows half the country's fruit and vegetables.

The more northern states of Oregon and Washington have a coastal belt with a maritime climate — mild winter, relatively cool summers, and abundant rainfall. It is ideal country for dairy-

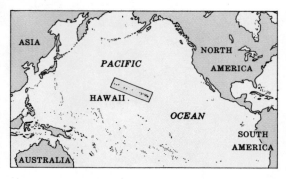

farming, and, indeed, over four-fifths of the land is used for grazing or to grow hay or other fodder crops. Both Washington and Oregon are also important fruit-growing states, the former being the leading state for apples and hops.

In the western mountain states the most important industry is mining. More than half the labour force is employed in it. When mining began here over 100 years ago the miners were only interested in gold and silver, and had little use for the copper, lead, and zinc they found with the precious metals. But today they are more important in the western states than gold and silver.

The population of the West Coast is growing fast. By 1970 California had become the most populous state.

It is easy to see why Lumahai Beach, on the island of Kauai, Hawaii, is popular for holidays.

Ray Atkeson

ALASKA

The chief industrial area is around Los Angeles. Only New York, Chicago, Detroit, and Philadelphia have a larger industrial population than Los Angeles. Seventy years ago it was a country town. Then oil was discovered and the cinema industry began to grow up — centred on the suburb of Hollywood.

However, it was during the Second World War that Los Angeles became a really great manufacturing town. The building of aircraft became the chief industry, but there were many others, including motor-car assembly, tyre manufacture, food stuffs, and machinery. Now nearly 7 million people live in Los Angeles.

Another great industrial area on the West Coast is San Francisco Bay. A fine harbour and a well-equipped port have attracted many industries. Food-processing and oil refining have long been carried out there, and now electronics is becoming an important industry.

The third industrial area is in the north-west. Seattle and Tacoma are both inland ports engaged in the lumber trade. Shipbuilding, too, is carried on in Seattle, which is the largest town in Washington.

Portland, Oregon, is also an inland port. Its manufactures include wood-products, foundry and machine-shop products, and tinned foods.

Alaska was bought by the United States from Russia in 1867. The price was 7 million dollars, about a penny an acre, but even at that modest price, many people thought the Russians had got the best of the bargain.

Today we know better. Each year the minerals produced in Alaska are worth about three times the purchase price and the fish caught in Alaskan waters is more than four times more valuable than the minerals. Many countries have bought shares in Alaska's oil reserves.

There are also the enormous reserves of timber that have hardly been touched.

Alaska is a country whose importance has grown with the advance of aviation. More people own and fly aircraft than in any other state. Alaska is by far the largest state in the Union, but it has very few roads and still fewer railways. Such towns as there are, are far apart. Accordingly those who have to travel are practically forced to fly.

Where prospectors once panned for gold, today large dredges scoop up gold-bearing gravel from the Yukon River basin near Fairbanks.

Charles C. Ray - Shostal

Snow-capped Mount Popocatepetl rises nearly 18,000 feet above sea level. It is Mexico's second-highest mountain. Once an active volcano, it still at times emits vast clouds of smoke.

MEXICO, LAND OF CONTRASTS

Mexico has, within its frontiers, examples of almost all types of physical feature. At least two-thirds of the country is mountainous, and the slopes are so steep that people when they travel do not think of east and west, or north and south, but only of up or down.

The remaining third of Mexico is low. There are narrow valleys, broad basins, swampy coasts, and an extensive limestone plain with underground rivers.

In the south, the climate is damp, and part of this region consists of tropical rain-forests. In the north, on the other hand, there are deserts.

The immense interior tableland rises to over 8,000 feet, but in the lowlands, however, the heat is intense.

Parts of the land are practically uninhabited. On the central plateaus it is quite otherwise. Mexico City is an over-populated area. It is the fourth largest city in North America, after New York, Los Angeles and Chicago.

In 1519, the first European landed on the coast of Mexico. He was the Spaniard

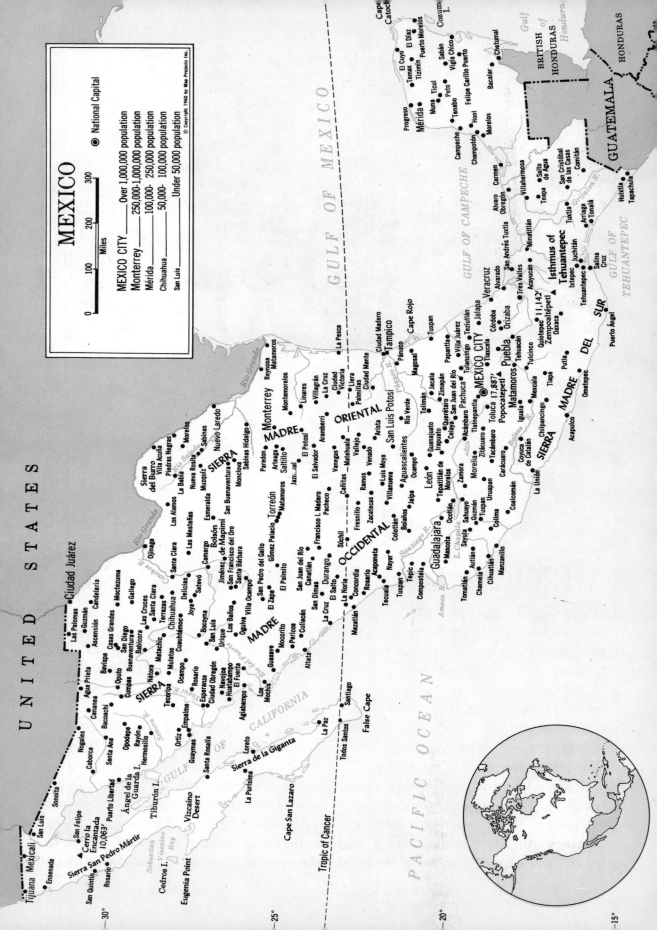

This ancient pyramid is one of many found in the Central Valley of Mexico, where a large part of Mexico's population lives today.

Hernando Cortes. Cortes fought his way to the capital of the ruling Indians, the Aztecs. Before the Aztecs, Mexico had been ruled by the Toltecs, and before them, by the Mayas, whose remains go back to the fourth century. Both the Mayas and the Toltecs were highly civilised, but the Aztecs, who overran the country in the twelfth century, were a brutal, warlike people, most of whose civilisation was acquired from their defeated enemies.

The Aztec capital was far from being an Indian village. On the contrary, it was a genuine town with beautiful palaces, splendid temples, and many enormous pyramids. The Aztecs knew how to weave, and they were good craftsmen in gold, silver and copper.

The beautiful things they made and their fine towns are, however, only one side of the picture. On the other, are the altars of their gods, drenched with the blood of human sacrifices. In the years before the Spanish arrived, 20,000 victims a year, some of them children, were sacrificed to win the favour of the rain god alone. The priesthood was enormous. Cortes found that over 5,000 priests were attached to the great temple of Mexico City.

Aztec, Toltec, and Maya remains can still be seen in Mexico today. The fine pyramids are as highly considered as those of Egypt. Many of the people in Mexico today are directly descended from those ancient tribes.

In 1525, the great silver vein of Guanajuato was discovered, and for 400 years the mine poured out an endless stream of silver, amounting to between one- and two-fifths of the entire supply of the world. Hundreds of millions of pounds' worth of silver has come from Guanajuato. Today Mexico still produces nearly a quarter of the world's silver

Much of the world's supply of silver comes from mines like this one in the Mexican highlands.

Mexican oil is refined at modern plants like this one at Salamanca, over a mile above sea level.

supply. Minerals in great variety are found in Mexico. Besides gold and silver, there is copper, iron, lead, zinc, mercury, graphite, manganese, coal, oil, and many others. Oil was first discovered in 1901 near Tampico, and a few years later one of the greatest 'gushers' ever known was struck. It produced over 60,000 barrels of oil a day. It flowed so fast from the well that earth reservoirs had to be hurriedly built to hold it back. Today Mexico has several huge oil refineries, but still has to export crude oil and import refined products — principally petrol, of course.

Mexico has excellent prospects for becoming an industrial country. Hitherto most manufacturing has been done by craftsmen at home or in very small workshops. Leather goods, basketwork, pottery, silver work — all done by hand — still constitute an important part of industry. But changes are taking place.

Cotton mills have been constructed in

the textile centres of Puebla and Orizaba, south-east of Mexico City. Monterrey, the established iron and steel centre of the country, has recently added new blast furnaces. Many United States manufacturers have set up branch establishments in Mexico, particularly in Mexico City These factories are producing machinery, drugs, radios, chemicals and a wide range of other products.

Mexico still imports many manufactured goods, but she is rapidly becoming more self-supporting. Nearly three-quarters of her imports come from the United States, which in turn takes well over half of Mexico's exports.

The bulk of the Mexican population is not urban, but lives in villages little different from those of the Indians before them. In Indian times all the land belonged to the tribe. When the Spaniards conquered Mexico the King of Spain divided the country among the *Con-quistadores* — and in this way a few thousand Spaniards soon owned practically all the farmland of Mexico.

These large estates became known as *haciendas,* that being the Spanish term for a large farm worked by tenants or labourers instead of by the owner.

Most of the villages used to be part of haciendas. But a few years ago the Mexican government began to buy large haciendas, and allotted the land to the men who had been working it, so that they could farm it for themselves.

The diet of the peasants is more or less summed up by the two words *tortillas* and *frijoles,* the first being maize pancakes, the second broad beans. Much the biggest part is played by maize, which was grown long before the Spaniards arrived in the country, and still takes up half of Mexico's arable land.

Though taking second place, broad beans are none the less important. They

Herbert Lanks - Gendreau

An adobe brick-maker plies his ancient craft at Valle de Guadalupe in central Mexico.

William Neil Smith

A Tarahumara Indian girl grinds maize into flour with her metate *and rubbing stone.*

Herbert Lanks - Gendreau

Traditional ways of life change slowly in Mexican villages like this one.

contain a lot of protein, and can thus take the place of meat, which most peasants are too poor to buy except on rare occasions.

Arable farming land is limited by the fact that much of the country is too high and too rough for ploughing. In fact arable land amounts to no more than one-twentieth of the total area of the whole country.

Cattle are reared in the dry country in the north. The ranches are big, some of them enormous. They are so dry that many of the cattle are taken to other parts of Mexico to be fattened before slaughtering. The leanest cattle of all are sold as they are, merely for their hides and for the making of tallow.

As in the United States, green patches occur here and there in the vast stretches of desert. They are particularly visible from the air. These patches indicate areas where irrigation is possible, and the government undertakes irrigation projects wherever they are feasible.

Mexico's largest irrigation project is in the Laguna district near the town of Torreon. More than half the arable land here is used for growing cotton, which

Mexican women do their washing at the communal laundry, while a farmer hoes his maize in the background. Corn is Mexico's chief food crop.

Ray Manley - Shostal

This irrigation project at Culiacán, in western Mexico, provides water for a booming farming region.

has now become one of the country's leading exports.

On the cool, high central plateaus, wheat and maize are grown. The slopes of the mountains produce coffee, while the hot coastal plain produces bananas, sugar-cane, and coconuts. At each height a different crop is grown, since the height determines the temperature.

From the Yucatan Peninsula come two important products. One is raised on plantations in the drier north, while the other is gathered in the tropical rain forest in the south. The plantation crop is a species of agave which produces a fibre called henequen, used in the manufacture of twine. Mexico produces half of the world's henequen, but now faces competition with sisal, grown chiefly in East Africa. The other product of Yucatan is *chicle* which is the milky juice of a tree called *sapodilla*. Chicle is used to make chewing gum.

MEXICO CITY

Mexico City is the capital of a Federal Republic which became an independent state about 150 years ago, before which it had been for 300 years under Spanish rule. In 1900 the population was just under 300,000. By 1969 it had grown to over 5.5 million. The city possesses a great cathedral built on the site of a former Aztec temple. The national palace is built on the site where the palaces of Cortes and, before him, that of Montezuma once stood.

Indian fishermen of Lake Patzcuaro are famous for their butterfly-shaped nets.

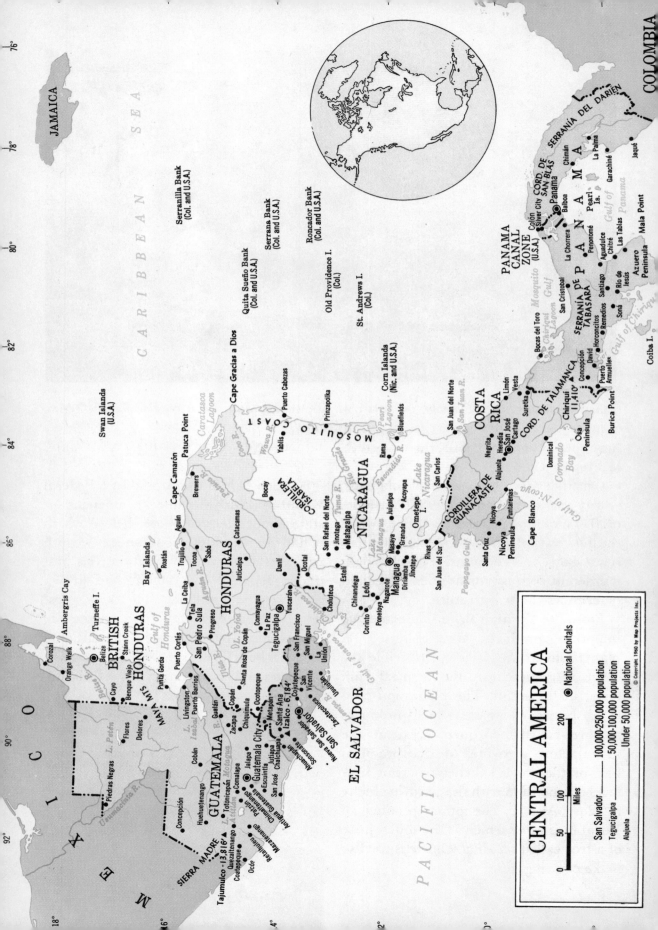

Ruins of the ancient Maya civilisation are found in both Mexico and Guatemala.

CENTRAL AMERICA

Central America is a narrow bridge of land joining North America to South America. Though over 500 miles in width at its broadest point, it is relatively narrow compared with the enormous masses of land which it joins. It consists of British Honduras, Guatemala, Honduras, Salvador, Nicaragua, Costa Rica, and Panama. All are independent states, except British Honduras, which is a British Crown Colony. In 1821 Central America joined Mexico in becoming independent. For a while all except Panama became part of Mexico. However, by 1842 the map of Central America was as we see it today.

The history of British Honduras is somewhat different from that of the others. Almost continuously, since the seventeenth century, British settlers, orig-

Lake Atitlan, completely surrounded by volcanoes, is in the highlands of Guatemala.

These women are taking great loads of flowers to a village market in Honduras.

Courtesy of the Pan American Coffee Bureau

Careful picking of only the ripe berries makes Central American coffee especially valuable.

inally composed of buccaneers, had established themselves on the shores of the Gulf of Honduras. Nominally under the Spanish king, they were in fact largely independent, and were constantly attacking their neighbours. It was only in the nineteenth century, however, that Great Britain formally laid claim to the colony, and it was not till 1862 that her

Bananas make up more than three-fifths of the value of Panama's exports.

Courtesy of the United Fruit Company

sovereignty was completely recognised.

The population of Central America is largely Indian in descent. Guatemala is the most Indian of the states. There, three-fifths of the population are descended from the Mayas.

Some of the people of Central America have maintained their ancient traditions. They live in small villages, and each village has its own manners and customs, and even its own style of clothing.

In these tropical countries, the plains are so hot that no one lives there if they can avoid it. Nearly all the big towns and most of the roads, railways, airports, and even farms are found high above sea-level. In some of the countries only a quarter of the population lives on the plains. In the highlands, coffee is the chief crop. It was first planted in Costa Rica more than 150 years ago. Today it is grown in all the Central American countries. Most of it is grown between 2,000 and 4,500 feet above sea-level.

Great care is lavished on the coffee shrub. Sometimes trees are planted under the shade of taller trees, as shade-ripened coffee has a peculiarly delicate flavour.

Care is also needed for the harvesting, as only the ripe, dark red berries are picked. The coffee pickers return to the same tree again and again, each time picking only the ripe berries. The work is slow and laborious, but the coffee has a very fine reputation.

The soil is rich and deep, and contains volcanic ash, which is particularly favourable for coffee growing. The climate too, is perfect. The hills on which coffee is planted are high enough to give a moderate temperature, without the danger of frost. Moreover, fifty to sixty inches of rain fall in the year, and there

John Strohm

An odd mixture of Christian and Pagan ritual at Chichicastenango, Guatemala.

Courtesy of the United Fruit Company

is always a dry season for harvesting.

The coastal plains are devoted to the growing of bananas — the hot, wet climate is ideal for their cultivation. Banana growing is a big undertaking. First the forest has to be cleared and the roots of the trees pulled up out of the soil. Then engineers have to construct

Spraying operations are carried on regularly to prevent the spread of banana diseases.

a system of drains to prevent the low land being flooded. Rails have to be laid throughout the plantation and down to the sea ports. Towns also have to be built, for some plantations employ thousands.

Indians gather around a pottery seller in a Guatemalan market village.

Herbert Lanks - Shosta

This ship is sailing through the Gaillard Cut, one of the highest points on the Panama Canal.

THE PANAMA CANAL

The idea of a canal across the Isthmus of Panama to link the Atlantic and Pacific was first projected by the Spaniards in the sixteenth century.

The importance of a canal linking the Atlantic and Pacific Oceans is that it reduces the voyage of a ship sailing, for example, from New York to San Francisco, by more than half. In 1879 a French Panama Canal Company was formed, with Ferdinand de Lesseps (of Suez Canal fame) as president. Work was actually started, but the company got into greater and greater difficulties, and

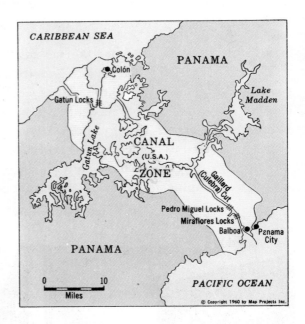

The Miraflores Locks lower ships from the Gaillard Cut to the Pacific Ocean.

the United States took over the task. The canal took thirteen years to build, and cost 367 million dollars.

The construction of the Panama Canal was one of the greatest engineering enterprises of modern times. It was much more difficult than the Suez Canal, owing to the relatively high land.

It takes a ship about eight hours to pass through the Canal. In 1968 there were 13,199 transits of ocean-going merchant vessels through the Canal, and the tolls paid totalled nearly 84 million dollars.

St Lucia is a beautiful tropical island in the Caribbean, and a member of the British Commonwealth. Its fertile valleys and narrow coastal plains are mainly used in growing sugar-cane, the island's chief product.

THE WEST INDIES

The east coast of Central America is washed by the Caribbean Sea. This sea is girdled by a line of islands running in a great curve to near the eastern end of the coast of Venezuela. They are called the West Indies, a reminder that Columbus was looking for a westward route to India when he discovered America. These islands are the tops of mountain ranges rising above the sea. Cuba, the biggest, is larger than Portugal; Jamaica is about twice the size of Lancashire. Many are much smaller, and there are thousands of tiny islands, too small for anyone to live on. But more than fifty of them are populated.

In the north the West Indies run in two main lines. The Bahamas form the outer line. Within them are the larger islands of the Greater Antilles: Cuba, Hispaniola, Puerto Rico, and Jamaica. East of Puerto Rico, the Virgin Islands begin the long chain of the Lesser Antilles. Finally there is another group of islands off the coast of Venezuela, the largest being Curaçao.

Cuba is a communist country with close ties with the U.S.S.R. Puerto Rico is closely linked with the United States. Hispaniola is shared by Haiti and the Dominican Republic; Martinique and Guadeloupe are French; Jamaica, Barbados and Trinidad and Tobago are in the Commonwealth, and most of the other islands are associated with Britain.

Asphalt is the principal export of Trinidad.

The West Indies have a maritime climate, and the moist Trade Winds blow in from the Atlantic. Accordingly, the windward slopes of the mountains have plenty of wet weather, while the lee slopes are often quite dry. San Juan, for instance, on the northern coast of Puerto Rico, receives over 60 inches of rain in a year, while Ponce on the southern coast, receives only 36. Some of the highest islands receive a very heavy rainfall indeed. One weather reporting station on the windward side of the Blue Mountains in Jamaica records an annual rainfall of 222 inches. At the same time in Kingston, on the other side of the mountains, only thirty miles away, the average rainfall is 29 inches

On the windward or weather side of the islands, the sea is inclined to be rough, which made them dangerous for shipping in the old days of sail. There were safer anchorages on the lee side. That is why almost all the big towns are found on the western or southern coasts.

The mild tropical climate favours the growth of a great variety of crops. Much the most important is the sugar-cane. Planting the cane is done in the early spring, but it does not have to be repeated

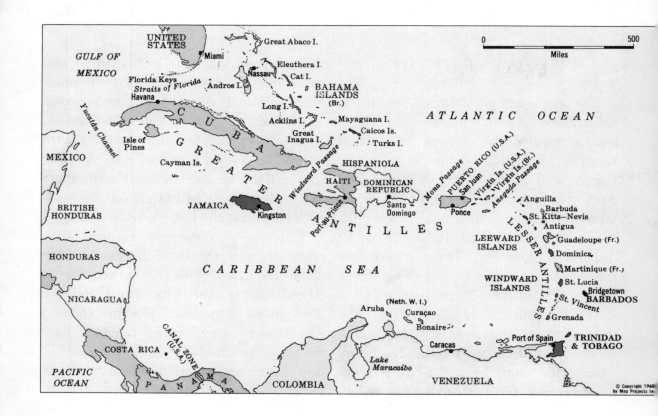

Courtesy of the Puerto Rico News Service

Huge fields of sugar-cane occupy Puerto Rico's fertile valleys.

each year, for new plants grow from the stalks of the old ones. In some places planting machines are used, but in most cases the work, both of planting and tending the sugar-cane, is done by hand. For tending the plants in summer and autumn little labour is needed, and seasonal unemployment is the great curse of the sugar-growing industry. But from the harvest onwards, from December to June, every available hand is hard at work. The cane is cut by hand, then driven to the mill in ox-wagons, lorries, or railway trucks. At the mill, it is cut into pieces, crushed by huge rollers, and then, finally, the juice is boiled until hard crystals of sugar are formed.

Although sugar-cane is by far the most important crop of the lowlands, many other crops are grown: pineapples, grape-fruit, bananas, etc., most of which are exported to North America or Europe.

As a rule, in the mountains the slopes are too steep and the soil too thin for farming. Here and there however, particularly in Western Cuba, Haiti, Puerto Rico, and Eastern Jamaica, special high-land crops — such as coffee and tobacco — are grown. The mountains are thinly populated, and the other crops are grown merely for subsistence. Sweet potatoes are important to the people's diet.

Cuba is famous for the cigar-tobacco in which the island specialises.

THE ISLANDS

Jamaica has a total population approaching 2 million, of whom 377,000 live in the capital, Kingston. The country is very mountainous: the highest peak, in the Bue Mountains, being 7,388 feet. For a long time sugar-growing and rum-making were almost Jamaica's only industries. In the nineteenth century fruit growing, particularly bananas, took the lead, but in recent years bananas have suffered heavily from banana disease. Sugar-growing has again taken the leading place in agriculture, but coffee is also of prime importance, and the tourist trade is now another source of revenue.

The production of bauxite has increased enormously in recent years, and Jamaica is now the world's leading exporter of this mineral.

Trinidad, less than half the size of Jamaica, has a population approaching a million, the greater part of which is of African descent. About a fifth of the population is of East Indian origin, while the remainder are of English, French, Spanish, and Portuguese descent. The capital is Port of Spain, with a population of 94,000, which is well situated in the lee of the north-west corner of the island. Trinidad is much less mountainous than Jamaica, its heights barely reaching 3,000 feet. As a result rather more than half the island is capable of being cultivated. The exports are sugar, rum, cocoa, grapefruit, and coconuts. Besides these, Trinidad has rich oil wells and deposits of asphalt, the exports of which now exceed all other products.

Trinidad was joined politically with Tobago, a smaller island to the north-east, in 1889. Together they became an independent member state of the Commonwealth in 1962.

Barbados. This island, the most easterly of the West Indies has a population of over 250,000, about 12,000 of whom live in the capital, Bridgetown. Except for one part, the island is of coral formation, and it is

Many Puerto Rican farmers use tiny hillside patches like this one to produce tobacco.

Courtesy of the Puerto Rico News Service

Much of the hard work of cutting sugar-cane is still done by hand in Cuba.

Courtesy of the United Fruit Company

These women, in the highlands of Grenada, are preparing coffee berries for drying. The berries must be carefully dried to ensure a good flavour.

almost entirely surrounded by coral reefs, which make the coast dangerous. The island has only one harbour. It is relatively flat and for the most part covered with a thin layer of very fertile soil, composed largely of volcanic ash blown from the Soufrière, the volcano of St Vincent 100 miles away. Barbados was the first British colony to have sugar plantations.

The Windward Islands. This term was once used for all the islands to windward of the Carribean Sea, but it is now used for a group of British islands, Grenada, St Vincent, St Lucia, and Dominica, with a group of small islands known as the Grenadines between Grenada and St Vincent. All are of volcanic origin.

The Leeward Islands. These are another small group of British islands, lying to the north.

The Bahamas are the last group of British islands in the West Indies. They consist of a chain of coral islands whose total area adds up to only a little less than that of Jamaica. Their total population is a little over 165,500 of which over 50,000 live in the capital, Nassau. The Bahamas live chiefly on the tourist trade, particularly from the United States. Collecting sponges, once a thriving industry, has not yet recovered from a disease which did a great deal of damage in 1939.

BERMUDA

The Bermudas are a group of about 150 islands, which however are generally called by the singular name Bermuda. Bermuda does not actually belong to the West Indies for it lies some 800 miles to the northward.

All the islands are connected by bridges or causeways. The entire length of the chain is twenty-two miles and the total area is twenty-two square miles. The population is 50,000, about one third of whom are white. Only about a quarter of the total area is suitable land for farming, but it is fully used for market gardening and bulb growing. The climate is pleasant and very healthy. Winter temperatures vary from around 60° to 70°F.

Passengers wait for a bus in Haiti, part of the Caribbean island of Hispaniola.

The Andes are new mountains, still sharp and very high. The chain runs all the way down the west coast.

THIS IS SOUTH AMERICA

South America is almost completely surrounded by water. Only the Isthmus of Panama, linking it to North America, prevents it being an island. It is almost 7 million square miles in area, about one-eighth of the total land surface of the world, yet its total population is no more than about 170 million, or less than one-twentieth of the total world population. It is not always realised that South America lies not south, but south-east of North America. The meridian of New York passes through only the westernmost countries of South America.

The eleven republics of South America are Argentina, Bolivia, Brazil, Chile, Colombia, Ecuador, Paraguay, Peru, Uruguay, Guyana and Venezuela. There are also two colonies: French Guiana, and Surinam or Dutch Guiana.

A great mountain system, the Andes, extends along the entire western edge of the continent.

The Andes constitute the longest continuous mountain system in the world, extending for 4,400 miles from the Caribbean Sea in the north to Tierra del Fuego in the south. They are the highest mountains in the world except for the Himalayas. Several of the peaks are over 21,000 feet high, and the highest, Mount Aconcagua, reaches a height of 22,835 feet. At their widest point, in Bolivia, the Andes are 400 miles wide; but in most places the width is no more than 150 miles. In the northern part the mountains divide into two ranges with deep valleys between, and there are wide plateaus, sometimes 10,000 feet high.

The other two mountainous areas are the Pacaraima and Guiana Highlands in the north, and the Brazilian Plateau and Coast Ranges in the eastern bulge of the continent, especially inland from Rio de Janeiro. A few of them rise as high as 9,000 feet, but they have no sharp

SOUTH AMERICA

Scale 1:30,000,000

0   100   200   300   400   500 Miles

SÃO PAULO   *Cities over   1,000,000 population*
Barranquilla *Cities of 250,000 — 1,000,000 population*
Puerto Montt *Cities under   250,000 population*
              ⊙ *Capitals of Countries*

Depths in feet: Heights in feet:

| Below sea level | 0-650 | 650-1650 | 1650-4900 | over 4900 |

650   0-650

⸻ Railways   ----- Canals ↧ Head of navigation ✕ Falls
⸱⸱⸱ Salt lake   Swamp, marsh

Chile's Atacama Desert is one of the driest places on earth. Much of it was once the bottom of a lake.

crested peaks like those of the Andes.

The Guiana Highlands extend from Venezuela into Guyana, Surinam, and northern Brazil. They are almost unoccupied as they are very rugged and inaccessible. The Brazilian Highlands, commencing 400 miles south of the Amazon River, cover a much larger area. They are highest along the coast at the Tropic of Capricorn. There the coast is rugged with natural harbours. This eastern portion has rich soil and a good deal of forest. It is the most populated part of Brazil. The western portion is savanna grassland — the Mato Grosso.

The west coast of South America is forbidding, being mostly composed of gaunt rocky cliffs, rising straight up from the sea. A belt of barren desert runs along the coast for 1,000 miles from southern Ecuador to northern Chile. The coastline is so straight that harbours are few except in the north and south.

East of the Andes, in the south, is a high plateau called Patagonia, which stretches all the way to the east coast. Several rivers run through it. In many of the valleys there are lakes formed by the glaciers of the Ice Age. Except round rivers and lakes, Patagonia is barren.

South America has three great rivers, the Orinoco, the Amazon, and the Parana-Paraguay system. The Orinoco rises in the Southern Guiana Highlands, flows in a great semi-circle north-west, north, and east, emptying into the Atlantic through a wide delta south of Trinidad. Some of its tributaries rise in the Andes. It is 1,800 miles long and is navigable for more than half its length.

The Amazon is the second longest river in the world, draining with its tributaries at least half the continent. Its hot, steamy plain varies in width from twenty to 800 miles.

The Amazon and its tributaries have

well over 5,600 miles of water navigable by shallow-draft boats, and ocean-going ships can steam up as far as Manaus, nearly 1,000 miles from the coast. Vessels drawing 14 feet can go up-river as far as Iquitos, in Peru, over 2,300 miles from the coast. The Amazon brings down so much water to the sea that the latter is fresh for forty miles around the mouth, and it carries so much alluvium that the Atlantic is muddy for 200 miles.

The Parana and Paraguay rivers drain the southern part of the Brazilian Highlands and the Central Andes. Their basins form South America's third great plain. The northern part of the Parana-Paraguay plain is an almost empty area of wooded grassland called the Gran Chaco. It is an almost flat plain, sloping gradually from the foot of the Andes to the Paraguay River. In the south is a vast fertile plain called the Humid Pampas.

The Parana River empties into a gigantic estuary called the Rio de la Plata, or River Plate, which is 170 miles long

Tristan da Cunha, the loneliest island in the world, is situated in the South Atlantic about mid-way between South America and Africa.

and 140 miles broad at the mouth.

South America, particularly the great area drained by the Amazon and its tributaries, is one of the last 'frontiers' of the world. Sparsely populated and underdeveloped, its potential as a source of raw materials and food is prodigious.

The winding Amazon River flows over 2,000 miles through lowlands covered with dense rain-forest.

388

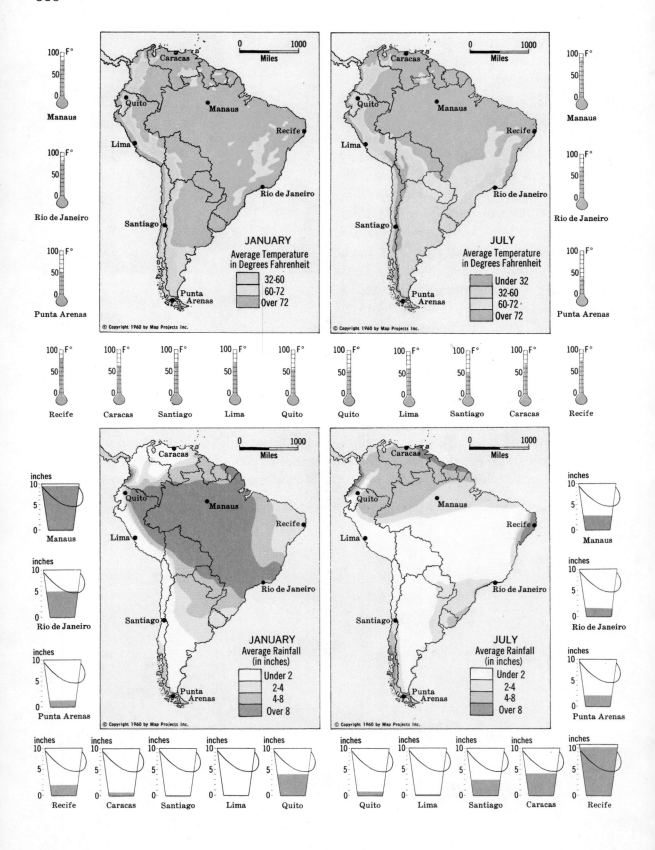

Manaus

100 F°
50
0

Rio de Janeiro

100 F°
50
0

Punta Arenas

100 F°
50
0

JANUARY
Average Temperature
in Degrees Fahrenheit

32-60
60-72
Over 72

© Copyright 1960 by Map Projects Inc.

JULY
Average Temperature
in Degrees Fahrenheit

Under 32
32-60
60-72
Over 72

© Copyright 1960 by Map Projects Inc.

Manaus

100 F°
50
0

Rio de Janeiro

100 F°
50
0

Punta Arenas

100 F°
50
0

100 F° 100 F° 100 F° 100 F° 100 F°
50   50   50   50   50
0   0   0   0   0
Recife Caracas Santiago Lima   Quito

100 F° 100 F° 100 F° 100 F° 100 F°
50   50   50   50   50
0   0   0   0   0
Quito   Lima   Santiago Caracas Recife

JANUARY
Average Rainfall
(in inches)

Under 2
2-4
4-8
Over 8

© Copyright 1960 by Map Projects Inc.

JULY
Average Rainfall
(in inches)

Under 2
2-4
4-8
Over 8

© Copyright 1960 by Map Projects Inc.

inches
10
5
0
Manaus

inches
10
5
0
Rio de Janeiro

inches
10
5
0
Punta Arenas

inches
10
5
0
Manaus

inches
10
5
0
Rio de Janeiro

inches
10
5
0
Punta Arenas

inches   inches   inches   inches   inches
10   10   10   10   10
5   5   5   5   5
0   0   0   0   0
Recife   Caracas Santiago Lima   Quito

inches   inches   inches   inches   inches
10   10   10   10   10
5   5   5   5   5
0   0   0   0   0
Quito   Lima   Santiago Caracas Recife

CLIMATE AND VEGETATION

Most of South America lies south of the Equator, which means that the seasons are reversed compared with Europe. All of South America lies within the tropics except Uruguay, most of Argentina, Chile, a small portion of southern Brazil, and half of Paraguay.

In the equatorial region, the average temperature is over 70°F, but such a temperature, constantly maintained, and with a high degree of humidity, is difficult for northerners to bear. In the mountains the climate is much less extreme. At Quito, for instance, which is right on the Equator but at an altitude of nearly 10,000 feet, the average temperature is only 55° F., winter and summer alike. One of the worst climates is at Manaus, on the Amazon, where the average temperature is just over 80° F. all the year, and it rains for 240 days in the year. In other regions rain is seasonal, falling mostly in summer and irregularly at other times. Indeed, in north-east Brazil and on the north coast of Venezuela, droughts occur. On the Pacific side, the coasts of Peru and northern Chile are cold and cloudy, being swept by the Peruvian current of cold water from the south.

Plant life in South America is divided into several broad zones, corresponding to the climate and land forms. In the hot rainy areas of the Amazon basin is the tropical rain-forest. The trees here are tall and straight. They are always green, and they grow so close together that their tops interlace to form a dense canopy. The forest floor gets too little light for undergrowth to grow, but along the

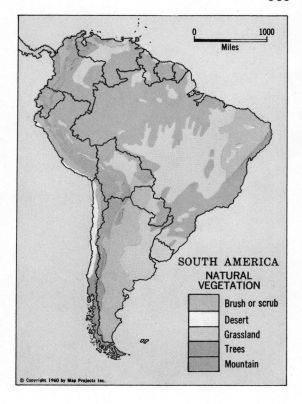

SOUTH AMERICA
NATURAL
VEGETATION

Brush or scrub
Desert
Grassland
Trees
Mountain

© Copyright 1960 by Map Projects Inc.

streams where the light gets through, the undergrowth is so thick that a man can hardly make his way through it.

North and south of the tropical rain-forest, where the weather is hot but the rainfall irregular, plants must be able to live through a dry season. This region is the savanna where vegetation consists of tall grasses with scattered bushes and shrubs or, occasionally, where the land is moister, open woodland. Grasses may grow to heights of twelve feet. Along the streams grow taller trees. In the dry season, many trees and shrubs lose their leaves and the grass becomes dry and brown.

The Andes form a very complex zone. In the north, the vegetation is similar to that of the lowlands nearby, that is to say, rain-forests in the wet areas, and savanna in the dry areas. Further south, where it is cooler and drier, conifers

Tom Hollyman - Photo Researchers

Some passes in Bolivia's towering mountains are higher than the peaks of the Rocky Mountains — 13,000 feet.

(pines, firs, etc.) and deciduous trees (those which shed their leaves) replace the broad-leaved evergreens of the rain-forest.

Above the tree-line, the slopes and plateaus are covered with short grass and shrubs. The vegetation becomes sparser as it approaches the snow-line. Above the snow-line there are no plants at all.

South of the Tropic of Capricorn the continent becomes drier. Much of the land is covered with a similar sort of

Lake Titicaca is over 12,000 feet up. The Aymara Indians make their rafts of woven reeds.

Courtesy of PANAGRA

A general view of Stanley, the capital of the Falkland Islands, a lonely British outpost off the extreme tip of South America.

grass to the prairies of North America. In the cold, dry region of Patagonia, the grass gives way to desert. The cool, rainy region in the south-west is covered with a dense forest of mixed conifers and deciduous trees.

The beaded hat and coin-spangled belt are special fiesta decorations of the Araucanians of Chile.

This young Aymara boy wears the typical hat and cape worn by Bolivians in the region of Lake Titicaca.

THE PEOPLES OF SOUTH AMERICA

South America has a population of about 170 million, which works out, on the average, at 20 per square mile. That is a very scanty population compared to that of Europe, which has 210 per square mile. As in other parts of the world, it is very unequally distributed.

It is thought that the first people to come to South America came from Asia. They may well have come from Siberia over the Bering Strait into Alaska, and gradually moved down through North and finally into South America. Columbus called them Indians because, when he landed on one of the Bahamas, he thought he had reached India. When Magellan, sailing far to the south, found the passage through to the Pacific which bears his name, the search for the route to India stopped and the conquest of South America began in earnest. It was the Spaniards who started. They landed on the north coast, and worked their way

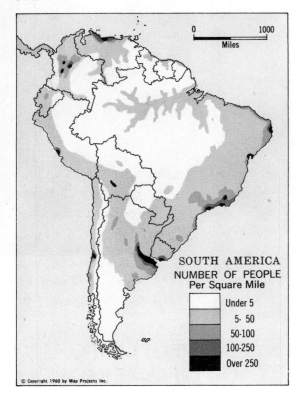

SOUTH AMERICA
NUMBER OF PEOPLE
Per Square Mile

	Under 5
	5- 50
	50-100
	100-250
	Over 250

© Copyright 1960 by Map Projects Inc.

them were by this time firmly established on the continent.

However, the American War of Independence and then the French Revolution stirred up ideas of freedom amongst the people of South America. One by one they rose against their rulers and after a succession of wars, the map looked much as it does today.

When the first white explorers arrived, Indians were scattered widely over the continent. Three-quarters of them were in the northern Andes near the west coast. Farming was much easier there than in the tropical lowlands, where the soil was generally poor and crops were ravaged by insects.

These Indians included two very advanced civilisations. The largest was the Inca Empire which included the Quechuas and Aymaras of Ecuador, Bolivia, and Peru, and a few Araucanians in northern Chile. A smaller group consisted of the Chibchas of Colombia.

The first white explorers were men from Spain and Portugal, where there was very little prejudice about marrying people of another race. Many of them married Indian women. Their children were called *mestizo,* which meant of mixed blood. Today by far the largest part of the

far into the interior. They overran Peru, Ecuador, Colombia, and much of Chile. Driving still further south, they established colonies by the Rio de la Plata and later in Paraguay.

While the Spaniards advanced from the north-west, the Portuguese took possession of the east coast. Within a short time they had occupied the whole Brazilian coast. Spain and Portugal between

This young boy is one of the many Negro people who work on coffee plantations in Brazil.

An Arawak Indian mother travels with her three children in a flat-bottomed wooden canoe.

population of South America is Indian or part Indian. In Colombia, Venezuela, and Chile two-thirds of the people are mestizos. In Paraguay almost the entire population is mestizo. There is no country where there are not some mestizos.

Some Indians however did not mix with whites. In Ecuador, Bolivia, and Peru more than half the people are of pure Indian stock. But these pure Indians live almost entirely in the mountains.

When the Portuguese began settling

Fujihira - Monkmeyer

A Quechua of Ecuador plays a wooden flute. Most of the Inca peoples were Quechuas.

The Latacunga market in Ecuador is in an ancient Inca town, once destroyed by an earthquake.

Ewing Krainin - Alpha

The adventurous, hard-riding cowboys of South America are called gauchos.

on the east coast of Brazil, they found only a few Indians, and these were not willing to work on the plantations. Accordingly, the Portuguese brought African slaves. Of the population of Brazil today more than 5 million have Negroid blood. Most of them live either on the east coast or in the west central part of Brazil near the goldfields. Along the remainder of the coast and along some of the rivers the people are mixed Portuguese, Indians, and Negroes.

This little Colombian girl, dressed in her Sunday best, is on her way home from church.

There were no settlers on the land south of the Rio de la Plata until the nineteenth century. When European settlers did come, the Indians had already been driven out. As a result the people of Argentina are almost entirely white.

In this great mixture of peoples there are a few groups whose way of life has hardly changed. Such are the Bush Negroes of the Guiana jungles. They are descended from runaway slaves of the seventeenth century. In Guyana there are large numbers of East Indians who were brought over at the same time as those who went to Trinidad. They are Hindus and have retained Asian customs.

Some colonies of European emigrants have clung jealously to their identity and refused to intermingle with others, and there are Indians at the southern tip of the continent who live exactly as their ancestors did in the Stone Age.

Only a third of the population lives in towns. Those who do, live very much like the townsfolk of Europe or North America, except that the slums are worse and more sharply in contrast to the handsome modern buildings of the better-class quarters.

Bogota, Colombia, is built so high in the Andes that it is most easily reached by aeroplane.

São Paulo : the commercial and financial centre of Brazil.

THE TOWNS OF SOUTH AMERICA

The towns of South America, though not so old as those of Europe and Asia, have far more history than the towns of North America. A number of them, like Quito, Bogota, and Cuzco were Indian capitals long before the Spaniards arrived. Many others were founded in the sixteenth and seventeenth centuries by the Spanish and Portuguese conquistadors.

In the warmer regions, the Spanish preferred to build their towns high up, where the climate was more agreeable. Such places were, however, generally less accessible, and the majority of towns were built in valleys, where they could be reached by boat and where there was land on which to grow crops for the population. Today the largest towns are those that can be reached by water.

Some towns were built for mine workers, others as residential towns for wealthy landowners. Manufactures started late in South America, and factories tended to spring up where there was already a population to man them. Few specifically industrial towns have been built.

Though many of the old towns have beautiful buildings, South America is better known for its advanced modern architecture and town planning. Brasilia, for example, the capital of Brazil, is the most modern city in the world.

Towns have grown rapidly in recent years with the development of industry

Z. F. A.

The Plaza de Mayo in Buenos Aires, the capital and chief sea-port of Argentina.

and the provision of better communications; and to them comes a steady stream of people from the villages, anxious to escape the montony and privations of life on the land.

Buenos Aires, the capital of the Argentine, with a population of 7 million, is the largest city in South America.

São Paulo is a thriving manufacturing city, the fastest growing and largest city in Brazil.

Dana Brown - FPG

It is a great industrial town and a flourishing port, being the outlet for the massive export of Argentine beef and grain. With its surroundings it houses one-fifth of the population of the country.

São Paulo is Brazil's largest town and one of the fastest-growing cities in the world. It is also the centre of the country's richest agricultural area, which is also the great coffee-growin garea. It possesses a wide range of industries. It is built on high ground, some forty miles from its port, Santos.

Rio de Janeiro, a town of 3.8 million inhabitants, was the capital of Brazil until 1960, when this function was taken over by the newly built capital, Brasilia, in the centre of the country. Founded by the Portuguese in 1567, it stands on a deep landlocked bay. Though it has some industry, its chief concern is shipping. Its beautiful setting and fine beaches make it a popular holiday resort.

Allan - Pan American World Airways

The cone-shaped peak of Sugar Loaf Mountain guards the entrance to Rio de Janeiro's harbour.

Montevideo, the capital of Uruguay, is the centre of a flourishing agricultural region and is also an important port. It has a pleasant climate and serves as a resort for the wealthy classes of both Brazil and Argentina.

La Paz, in the Andes, is the highest capital in the world, sited nearly 12,000 feet above sea-level. It is built at the bottom of a deep gorge which provides shelter from the cold winds of the bleak plateau, or Altiplano. Remote as it is, La Paz is nevertheless the industrial centre of Bolivia. It was founded in 1548.

Quito, the capital of Ecuador, is another mountain town. It is built on the

Lima is the capital and cultural centre of Peru. The cathedral on the Plaza de Armas dates back to the sixteenth century. Lima's San Marcos University, founded in 1551, is one of the oldest in the Americas.

Courtesy of PANAGRA

Montevideo, Uruguay, is so pleasant that tourists come to it from Brazil and Argentina.

side of a dead volcano. Its temperature is unusually steady, the monthly average never changing by more than seven-tenths of a degree.

Santiago, capital of Chile, stands on a broad plain at the foot of the Andes. Founded in 1541, it has been repeatedly destroyed by either Indian attacks, earthquakes or floods, but it has now grown to be the fourth largest city, with 2.4 million inhabitants, in South America. Nearly a quarter of the population of Chile lives in or around Santiago, which enjoys a pleasant climate, and is the commercial and industrial centre of the country.

Lima, the capital of Peru, was founded by Pizarro, the Spanish conquistador, in 1535. For more than 300 years it was the largest and the wealthiest city of South America. Its university, founded in 1551, is the oldest on the continent.

Bogota, the capital of Colombia, has little industry but is a famous cultural centre. It was founded by the Spaniards in 1538, the town being built on the site of a former Indian capital. There are several universities, the oldest dating from 1572, with students from many countries.

Caracas, the capital of Venezuela, stands six miles from the coast of the Caribbean at an altitude of 3,000 feet.

The Spanish founded La Paz in a deep canyon sunk in a wind-swept plateau. It is 12,000 feet up in the mountains.

Joe Barnell - Shostal

Most of the old buildings in Santiago, Chile, have been destroyed by earthquakes. It is now a modern city.

Owing to its elevation, it has a pleasant climate. Founded in 1567, it has been largely rebuilt in recent years and is famous for its modern architecture. It is the centre of a flourishing agricultural region, and is developing industrially.

Much of Caracas has been rebuilt recently. Prosperity from oil has made this possible.

Hamilton Wright Organization, Inc.

0   1000

Miles

© Copyright 1960 by Map Projects Inc.

Equator

Cape São Roque

Tropic of Capricorn

30°

PACIFIC

OCEAN

ATLANTIC OCEAN

COMMUNICATIONS

South America depends heavily on sea transport.

Aircraft are being used more and more, and for passengers and postal services they provide a very efficient form of transport, but not for heavy, or bulky, goods-

In mountainous regions the cost of building railways is so great that freight charges are very high. In Venezuela, for instance, 217 bridges had to be built, and eighty-six tunnels cut, to construct a railway only 200 miles long.

Proper roads, practicable in all weathers, are gradually being constructed. Where such roads exist, a lorry can carry goods at one-twentieth of the cost of mule transport. But roads, too, are expensive to build, particularly those built inland from the west coast. In the whole length of Chile, which stretches for 2,740 miles, there are only half a dozen roads over the mountains.

Naturally flat countries like Argentina

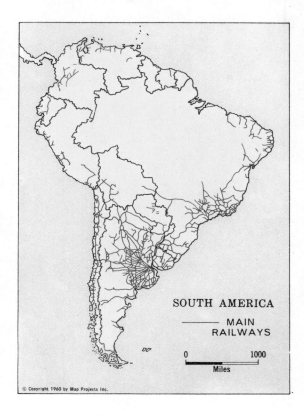

SOUTH AMERICA

———— MAIN
RAILWAYS

0   1000

Miles

© Copyright 1960 by Map Projects Inc.

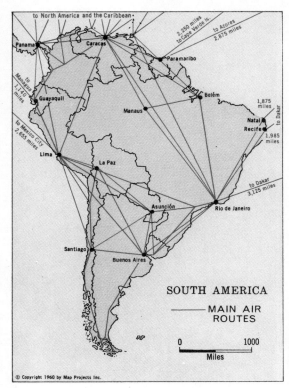

SOUTH AMERICA

———— MAIN AIR
ROUTES

0   1000

Miles

© Copyright 1960 by Map Projects Inc.

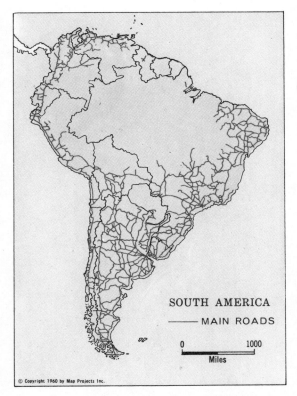

SOUTH AMERICA

———— MAIN ROADS

0   1000

Miles

© Copyright 1960 by Map Projects Inc.

and Uruguay have long stretches of railway lines. The Argentine pampas have a network of lines converging on the main ports, but very few good roads, because the dusty soil blows about in the dry season and turns into a sea of mud as soon as it rains. Uruguay has good roads and railways, for it has supplies of gravel.

In the north and north-east, rivers form the chief means of transport. The Guianas have hardly any railways or good all-weather roads. Most rivers, however, are only navigable for a limited distance, in fact up to the first waterfall or rapids. One river is so narrow that ships are unable to turn in it, and, having reached their destination, have then to be towed stern-first downstream. Brazil has no roads or railways at all except in the coastal belt. Elsewhere all transport is by water. The Amazon is navigable by large ships for nearly 1,000 miles from the sea, and for over 1,300 miles further for vessels drawing no more than 14 feet.

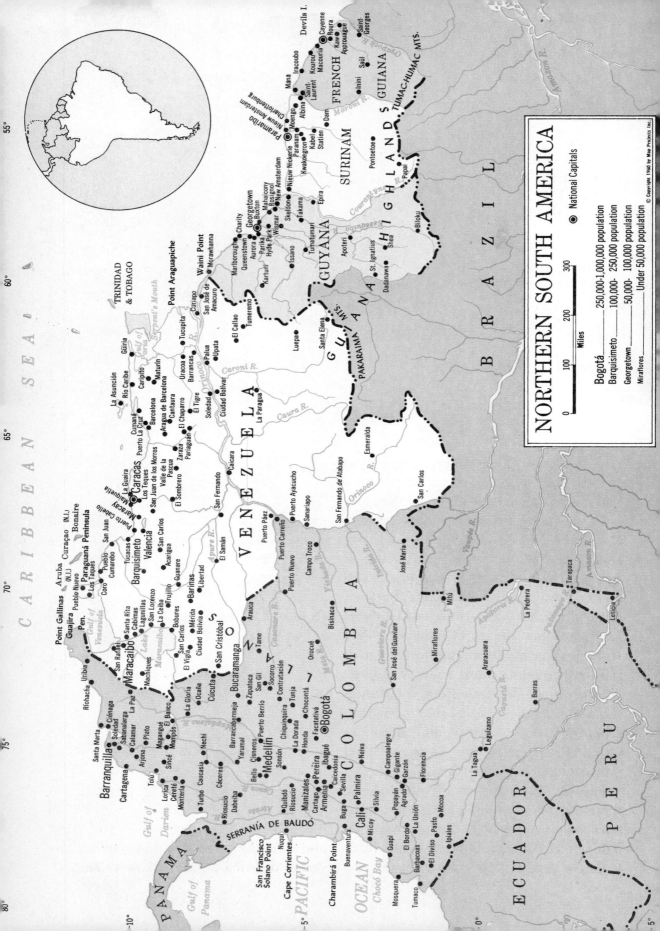

NORTHERN SOUTH AMERICA

⊙ National Capitals

Bogotá	250,000-1,000,000 population
Barquisimeto	100,000- 250,000 population
Georgetown	50,000- 100,000 population
Miraflores	Under 50,000 population

Miles
0   100   200   300

© Copyright 1960 by Map Projects Inc.

CARIBBEAN SEA

TRINIDAD & TOBAGO

Serpent's Mouth

Gulf of Paria

PACIFIC OCEAN

Gulf of Panama

Gulf of Darién

Gulf of Venezuela

Lake Maracaibo

PANAMA

VENEZUELA

COLOMBIA

GUYANA

SURINAM

FRENCH GUIANA

BRAZIL

PERU

ECUADOR

GUIANA HIGHLANDS

TUMAC-HUMAC MTS.

Oyapock R.

Amazon R.

SERRANÍA DE BAUDÓ

PAKARAIMA MTS.

GUIANA MTS.

Orinoco R.

Caroni R.

Caura R.

Apure R.

Meta R.

Guaviare R.

Vichada R.

Caquetá R.

Putumayo R.

Napo R.

Aruba (N.I.)

Curaçao (N.I.)

Bonaire

Paraguaná Peninsula

Guajira Pen.

Cities and places:
Devils I., Cayenne, Noura, Kaw, Saint-Georges, Approuague, Saül, Inini, Macouria, Kourou, Kourou, Saint-Laurent, Albina, Moengo, Paramaribo, Nieuw Amsterdam, Charlottenburg, Mana, Iracoubo, Dam, Moron R., Papai, Repai, Station, Kabel, Paranam, Kwakoegron, Pontoetoe, Biloku, Shea, St. Ignatius, Dadanawa, Apoteri, Issano, Kartuni, Tumatumari, Takama, Skeldon, Epira, Wismar, Hyde Park, Parika, Buxton, Georgetown, Rosignol, New Amsterdam, Mahaicony, Charity, Aurora, Queenstown, Marlborough, Morawhanna, Waini Point, Point Araguapiche, Curiapo, San José de Amacuro, Tumeremo, El Callao, Santa Elena, Luepa, Esmeralda, San Carlos, San Fernando de Atabapo, Sanariapo, Puerto Ayacucho, José María, Mitú, La Pedrera, Tarapacá, Leticia, Barras, Araracuara, Miraflores, Leguízamo, La Tagua, Puerto Carreño, Puerto Nuevo, Campo Troco, Bisinaca, San José del Guaviare, Orocué, Arauca, Tame, Campoalegre, Gigante, Garzón, Florencia, Mocoa, Ipiales, Barbacoas, El Diviso, Pasto, El Bordo, Popayán, La Unión, Silvia, Agrado, Neiva, Guapi, Micay, Cali, Palmira, Buga, Armenia, Sevilla, Caicedonia, Bagué, Facatativá, Bogotá, Tunja, Chiquinquirá, La Dorada, Honda, Chocontá, Contratación, Zapatoca, San Gil, Socorro, Bucaramanga, Ocaña, Cúcuta, San Cristóbal, Ciudad Bolivia, El Vigía, San Carlos, Mérida, Trujillo, Bobures, La Ceiba, Barinas, Guanare, Acarigua, San Carlos, Valencia, Barquisimeto, El Tocuyo, Libertad, El Samán, San Fernando, Caicara, Ciudad Bolívar, Soledad, Cantaura, Araguá de Barcelona, El Tigre, El Chaparro, Barcelona, Maturín, Carúpano, Río Caribe, Cumaná, La Asunción, Güiria, Pariaguán, Zaraza, Valle de la Pascua, El Sombrero, San Juan de los Morros, Los Teques, Caracas, La Guaira, Maiquetía, Puerto Cabello, Tucacas, Coro, Pueblo Nuevo, Los Taques, San Juan, Santa Rita, Lagunillas, Cabimas, Maracaibo, Machiques, La Paz, San Rafael, Uribia, Riohacha, Santa Marta, Ciénaga, Soledad, Barranquilla, Sabanalarga, Cartagena, Calamar, Arjona, Tolú, Plato, Magangué, Mompós, Sincelejo, Lorica, Cereté, Montería, Turbo, Caucasia, Cáceres, Nechí, Yarumal, Barrancabermeja, Puerto Berrío, Cisneros, Medellín, Sonsón, Bello, Manizales, Pereira, Cartago, Pasto, Quibdó, Riosucio, Dabeiba, Istmina, Andagoya, Tumaco, Mosquera, Buenaventura, Charambirá Point, Cape Corrientes, San Francisco Solano Point, Chocó Bay, Nuquí, Point Gallinas, Pueblo Nuevo, Curiapita, Uracoa, Tucupita, Palua, Upata, La Paragua, Caripito, Barrancas, La Gloria, El Banco, Ocaña, Catalina, Tunja, Choachí, Buga

In villages like this, Surinam's 'Negroes' carry on the way of life of their African ancestors.

THE NORTH OF SOUTH AMERICA
THE GUIANAS: VENEZUELA: COLOMBIA

The Guianas are, as we have seen, a densely forested region. The Spanish and Portuguese conquerors disliked forests and made no serious attempt to settle there. When settlers came from Northern Europe, the Spanish and Portuguese did not take the trouble to drive them out.

In the seventeenth century Surinam (Dutch Guiana) belonged to the British, who, however, exchanged it for the Dutch colonies on the Hudson River, which, as a matter of fact, they had already taken over. The Dutch were convinced that Surinam was the more valuable.

French Guiana is the smallest of the three with an area of 35,000 square miles. Surinam covers 55,000 square miles and independent Guyana (formerly British Guiana) 83,000 square miles.

More than half the inhabitants of Surinam and Guyana are East Indians. Most of the remainder are Negroes with a certain number of mixed origin and a few American Indians such as Arawaks, Caribs, etc. The population of French Guiana is mostly Negro.

In the whole of Guiana, nine-tenths of the population live in one-hundredth part of the country, the mountains being too rugged for settlement. The population of French Guiana is only 44,000 and over half lives in Cayenne, which is the capital and the only town of any consequence. Surinam is much more densely populated with about 400,000 inhabitants. More than a third of them live in the capital, Paramaribo. The population of Guyana is nearly 700,000.

Fritz Henle - Photo Researchers

Canal barges take sugar-cane to the refinery in the marshy lowlands of Guyana.

Most people live and work on the sugar plantations on the coast in the neighbourhood of Georgetown, the capital, and the only other town of size, New Amsterdam.

By far the most valuable resource of Surinam is bauxite, and this mineral is produced in large quantities in Guyana; and Surinam is, in fact, second only to Jamaica among the world's leading bauxite producers. Mining for gold and diamonds is carried out in Guyana, and a little gold is found in French Guiana.

Plywood is made in Surinam. The Dutch government is now surveying the forests with a view to controlling and conserving the timber resources of the

country. Timber is a valuable product of Guyana, too. There are many lumber mills on the coast, which prepare it for shipping.

Both the largest exports from Guyana are raw sugar and its products, rum and molasses. The chief crop in Surinam is rice, but fruit and various other crops are grown along the coast. In French Guiana the people only grow enough for their own subsistence. The only food product exported is shrimps, which are sent to the U.S.

The early Spaniards, exploring the region round Lake Maracaibo, found Indian villages built on piles in the shallow water. It was this discovery which prompted the name of Little Venice or Venezuela. Colombia was named after Christopher Columbus. The people in these two countries live in the mountains. In Venezuela the greater part live in the Venezuelan Highlands, a continuation of the eastern chain of the Andes. The Guiana Highlands, on the other hand, which occupy the southern half of the country, are practically uninhabited. In Colombia most of the people live in narrow mountain valleys, and there is

The city of Medellin, in a high mountain valley, is the chief market manufacturing city of Colombia.

Charles Perry Weimer - House of Photography

Buxton Village in Guyana is a typical Asian Indian village. These women are Hindus.

This Hindu farmer in Surinam threshes his rice by letting cattle trample the grain from the chaff.

a large area practically uninhabited.

This is the great lowland of the Orinoco, south-east of the Andes, which constitutes two-thirds of the country.

The Venezuelan coastal range rises abruptly from the narrow coastal plain. The latter is very hot and dry, but the mountains are cool and have plenty of rain. Almost all the activity of the country is concentrated here. In one of the valleys of this range is Lake Valencia and the town of the same name. In another is Caracas, the capital of the country, standing about 3,000 feet above sea-level and with a climate of perpetual spring. It has a population of over a million, and is a magnificent city of wide avenues and modern buildings.

Bogota, the capital of Colombia, is also a mountain town, being in the eastern chain of the Andes. It is a very inaccessible capital, but flourishes as a home of art and learning.

Two-thirds of the people of Colombia work on the land. More than four-fifths of the country's exports are agricultural. In Venezuela, on the other hand, only half the people are on the land. Oil and other minerals make up more than 95 per cent of the exports, although the government has called for diversification.

Oil production is quite a recent development in Venezuela. It is extracted in the region round Lake Maracaibo.

Since Lake Maracaibo was too shallow for shipping, a refinery and a loading port capable of taking ocean-going ships was built on the western side of the Paraguana Peninsula. A pipe-line runs from the wells to the refinery. The lake has been dredged, however, and since 1956 ships have been able to get in to load oil, coffee, and other products.

The mountains north-east of the lake were, until recently, a dry, desolate, and almost uninhabited area. Now it has been

Freighters carry bauxite from Guyana and Surinam to aluminium refineries in North America.

provided with roads, and a huge oil refinery has been built there. In fact, a vast industrial centre is being planned which will bring prosperity to the region. Oil and natural gas have also been found on the Orinoco plains. The oil is piped to the coast for shipping, and the gas used to supply several towns.

Oil wells exist also in Colombia near the Venezuelan frontier and in the Magdalena valley. A pipe-line runs from the wells to the coast.

Until the second half of the nineteenth century no one except a few explorers had ever been into the heavily forested mountain area of south-east Venezuela, which is part of the Guiana Highlands. Then a rich vein of gold was discovered at El Callao, and it has been mined there ever since. A still more important development, however, is of more recent date.

Rich deposits of iron ore were discovered in the mountains, and two private companies are working mines near the Caroni River. A state-owned steel industry has also been established near Puerto Ordaz, and as a result the area

Jerry Cooke - Photo Researchers

This brightly lit Venezuelan oil refinery works a busy round-the-clock schedule.

is developing as the centre of a heavy industrial complex.

In Colombia a steel mill has recently been built north-east of Bogota, where nearly all the raw materials for steel manufacture are available. There are emerald mines in the same area near Bogota, but they only work intermittently. Another important mining region of Colombia is the thinly settled Atrato Valley in the north-west of the country, near the Panamanian frontier. Here gold and platinum are found. Colombia has long been one of the leading platinum producing countries, and now the Atrato Valley gold mines promise to be the richest in South America.

In Colombia, commerce and industry are chiefly concentrated in the isolated region of Antioquia in the central chain of the Andes. The towns of this region are built in the narrow valleys carved by the rivers. Travel is so difficult over the steep mountains that the region was formerly almost completely cut off from the rest of the country. The leading industry is weaving, which is centred on

Shallow Lake Maracaibo's great oil field is tapped by oil derricks standing far out from shore.

Fritz Henle - Photo Researchers

Fritz Henle - Photo Researchers

Iron ore from Cerro Bolivar is loaded aboard ocean-going freighters at Puerto Ordaz, on the Orinoco River. From here it is shipped to steel mills in Pennsylvania and Alabama.

the town of Medellin. About half the industrial workers are employed in textile mills. Other manufactures include drugs, chemicals, and electrical appliances.

The biggest agricultural area of Venezuela is the Valley of Valencia and its surrounding slopes. Here cotton is grown for the textile factories of Valencia and

The mine at Paz del Rio supplies iron ore for Colombia's newly developed steel industry.

Robert Leahey - Shostal

The trampling hoofs of horses thresh wheat spread in a circle of stones in the Venezuelan Andes.

Caracas; here food is grown for the towns; and from here comes dairy produce.

Coffee and cacao (cocoa beans) are grown on plantations. Colombian coffee is of outstanding quality, and is one of the country's most important exports. There are large coffee plantations along parts of the Magdalena Valley. Coffee-growing is all the more advantageous because it can be done on slopes unsuitable for most other uses.

Large numbers of cattle are raised in Venezuela and Colombia. Sometimes they graze in the hot lowlands, but they do better in the cooler climate of the mountain pastures. The plains of the Orinoco Valley are far from ideal cattle ranges. The grasses are low in food value; in the dry season, they are too hard to be eaten, and in the wet season, there are extensive floods.

COMMUNICATIONS

Communications have always been a big problem in Venezuela and Colombia. In Colombia especially, the high mountains divide the population into isolated groups, which are only now beginning to be able to make contact with each other.

In Venezuela the building of roads and railways was found to be so expensive that most goods were still being carried by pack-mules until a few years ago. One of the first roads practicable in all weathers was that built from La Guaira on the coast to Caracas in the mountains, six miles away. To cover this distance the road had to wind upwards for twenty-three miles to get over a mountain pass 3,400 feet high. Since then a much shorter road has been built, going through the mountains with the aid of bridges and tunnels instead of over them.

In the mountain district of Colombia, the river Magdalena has for long provided the main highway to the sea. In its long course, it passes through many of the most productive areas of the country, but it is not always a good highway. For one thing it is subject to drought in the dry season. For another thing, there are impassable areas, particularly at Honda. In such areas, goods are unshipped and carried overland between one navigable section of the river and the next. Despite these problems, the river is navigable for 900 miles, and steamers ascend to La Dorada, 592 miles from the mouth at Barranquilla. The port of Cartagena, which has the best harbour on the north coast of South America, is linked by canals with the Magdalena and also by an all-weather road with

Courtesy of the Pan American Coffee Bureau

When coffee berries turn cherry-red they are ready for picking. Coffee beans are their seeds.

the important town of Medellin.

Colombia was the first country of the Western Hemisphere to have a commercial air service, and it is still a leading country in the sphere of air travel.

Venezuela has preferred to concentrate on building arterial roads practicable in all weathers. It now has a considerable network of them, and road transport has developed enormously.

Colombian workers spread coffee beans in the sun to dry. Before roasting the beans are a pale colour.

Annan Photo Features

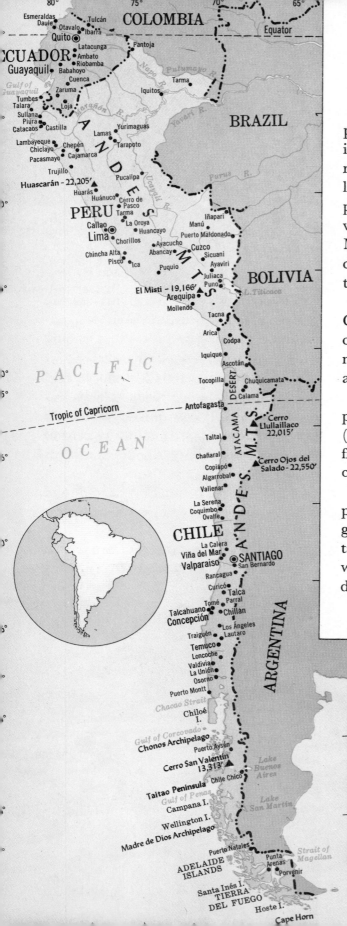

COLOMBIA

80° 75° 70° 65°

Equator

Esmeraldas
Daule
Otavalo · Tulcán
Ibarra
Quito ◉
ECUADOR Latacunga
Guayaquil · Ambato
Babahoyo · Riobamba
Cuenca
Zaruma
Loja
Tumbes
Talara
Sullana
Piura
Catacaos · Castilla
Lambayeque
Chiclayo · Chepén
Pacasmayo
Trujillo
Huascarán – 22,205'
Huarás
Huánuco
Cerro de Pasco
PERU Tarma · La Oroya
Callao · Huancayo
Lima ◉
Chorillos
Chincha Alta · Ayacucho
Pisco · Ica · Abancay
Puquio

Pantoja

Napo R.
Putumayo R.

BRAZIL

Tarma

Iquitos

Yurimaguas
Lamas
Tarapoto

Cajamarca

Pucallpa

Ucayali R.
Marañón R.
Yavari R.
Purus R.

Manú
Iñapari
Puerto Maldonado
Cuzco
Sicuani
Ayaviri
Juliaca
Puno

BOLIVIA

L. Titicaca

El Misti – 19,166'
Arequipa
Mollendo

Tacna

Arica

Codpa

Iquique

Ascotán

Tocopilla · Chuquicamata
Calama

DESERT

Antofagasta

Cerro Llullaillaco 22,015'

Taltal

Chañaral

Cerro Ojos del Salado – 22,550'

Copiapó
Algarrobal
Vallenar

La Serena
Coquimbo
Ovalle

CHILE

La Calera
Viña del Mar ◉ SANTIAGO
Valparaíso · San Bernardo
Rancagua
Curicó
Talca
Tomé · Parral
Talcahuano · Chillán
Concepción
Los Ángeles
Traiguén · Lautaro
Temuco
Loncoche
Valdivia
La Unión
Osorno
Puerto Montt

Chacao Strait

Chiloé I.

Gulf of Corcovado

Chonos Archipelago
Puerto Aysén

Cerro San Valentín 13,313'

Taitao Peninsula
Gulf of Penas
Campana I.

Wellington I.
Madre de Dios Archipelago

Puerto Natales

ADELAIDE ISLANDS

Santa Inés I.
TIERRA DEL FUEGO
Hoste I.

Cape Horn

ARGENTINA

ANDES M.T.S.
ATACAMA
ANDES MTS.

Tropic of Capricorn

PACIFIC

OCEAN

Gulf of Guayaquil

Lake Buenos Aires
Chile Chico
Lake San Martín

Punta Arenas
Porvenir
Strait of Magellan

THREE COUNTRIES OF THE ANDES

The countries of the Andes have small populations, but, as so much of their area is uninhabitable, the habitable parts are relatively crowded. Many of the 5.5 million people of Ecuador and the 12 million people of Peru live in tight clusters in the valleys between high mountain peaks. Most of the rest live on the parts of the coast that do not suffer from being either too wet or too dry.

Nine-tenths of the 9.7 million people of Chile live in the central third of the country. Nothing can be grown in the northern desert and the south is too wet and stormy.

In Ecuador and Peru, four-fifths of the people are pure Indians or mestizos (mixed race). Most of them are descended from the Indians who inhabited the country at the time of the Incas.

The Incas were skilful engineers. They paved their roads and built bridges across gorges. They dug out terraces on mountain slopes to prevent the soil being washed away. They made irrigation ditches for dry areas. They had no carts

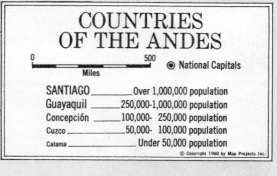

COUNTRIES OF THE ANDES

0 ——————— 500
Miles

◉ National Capitals

SANTIAGO _____ Over 1,000,000 population
Guayaquil _____ 250,000-1,000,000 population
Concepción _____ 100,000- 250,000 population
Cuzco _____ 50,000- 100,000 population
Calama _____ Under 50,000 population

© Copyright 1960 by Map Projects Inc.

The volcanoes in Ecuador tower over the valleys. Their peaks are always wreathed in clouds.

as they did not understand the use of a wheel, yet they were capable of moving ten-ton blocks of stone for long distances to use for building. These blocks are so closely fitted together that it is impossible to insert the blade of a knife between them. Buildings constructed with these fitted stones have withstood earthquakes that have caused modern buildings to crumble.

The Incas designed beautiful pottery and cloth, and made exquisite objects of gold and silver. Although they had no writing they managed to keep accounts using a system of knots. Their calculations followed a decimal system of their own invention, and they knew a great deal about the stars.

The Araucanian Indians who inhabited Chile were nomadic hunters and fishers, but they did a certain amount of farming as they moved from place to place. The northern Araucanians were conquered by the Incas, but the southern tribes, who lived in the forests, knew how to defend themselves so well among the trees that they were never conquered.

The hardiest and bravest Spanish soldiers were sent to conquer these Indians, and many of them married Araucanian women. It is from these mixed marriages that the mestizos, found today in central Chile, are descended. About two-thirds of the Chileans are mestizos.

The Indian farmers of Ecuador and Peru live mostly in high mountain valleys and are very poor.

So mountainous are these areas that it is practically impossible to send any

A winding stream cuts its way through the Andes in Peru, providing irrigation for valley farms.

In primitive parts of Peru, potatoes are planted much as they were in the days of the Incas.

produce away, so the peasants grow just what they need for their own use.

Crops change progressively with the altitude. No crop can stand the height so well as potatoes, which can be grown up to 14,000 feet. Below them barley is grown and, below the barley, wheat. Below 11,000 feet the peasants grow maize and lucerne, which is a clover-like plant grown for fodder. Cotton and sugar-cane are grown in the lower valleys.

Only the cattle are taken to market, for they can generally be driven there down the mountain tracks. They lose so much weight on the trip, however, that they have to be fattened again before being sold.

Many of the Indians are tenant farmers. These are descendants of the original population whom the Spaniards turned into slaves. They work under large landowners descended from the conquistadors. They have been emanci-pated from slavery but they are still very badly off.

Other Indians work their own land or they farm co-operatively in groups, much as they did during the Inca Empire. They know hardly anything of modern farming methods. In some cases, instead of ploughs drawn by oxen, they use small foot ploughs or even hoes. Corn is winnowed by tossing it up in the wind, or threshed under foot by animals on a threshing floor.

There are a few commercial farms in the mountains of Peru. The produce is not sent down to the coast, but sold to mining towns nearby.

Cattle can graze on areas too high even for potatoes. But some slopes, especially in Peru, are too high for cattle and are used for grazing sheep, alpacas, llamas, and vicunas. Shepherds keep flocks at heights sometimes of as much as 17,000 feet.

Macchu Picchu was a lost city, built before the time of the Incas. It has only recently been rediscovered.

A herd of llamas and sheep passes by ancient Incan irrigation terraces cut into the mountain slopes.

This open-cast copper mine at Chuquicamata, Chile, is one of the largest in the world.

On the coastal plain of Ecuador, the population is chiefly mestizo and Negro. On their small farms they grow bananas, coffee, and rice. Negroes were the first to grow bananas in this area. Now bananas are the country's biggest export crop. Shipping them is difficult and expensive, however, so that banana-growing is not very profitable. They are carried by mules or porters, loaded on to lorries, and driven to river-boats or barges. On the coast they have to be transferred from the one set of boats into banana boats lying at anchor, as in the ports the water is too shallow for them to come alongside.

The most fertile region in Ecuador is the plain north-east of Guayaquil. The climate is hot and moist, and the soil is rich. Coffee and rice are grown here. But fresh land is cleared for each crop, instead of fertilising the land and using it again and again. This wasteful method of using the soil is gradually spoiling much of the land and landscape of South America.

It is hard to believe that the strip of desert on the west coast of Peru could be any use for farming. Fine crops are grown there nevertheless. Along the coast are forty oases stretching like green stripes across the dry land. Streams flowing down the mountains cross the desert to the coast, and their water is used to irrigate the land. In this cool, dry, cloudy region, cotton, sugar-cane and rice are grown. And in the middle section there are also vineyards and vegetable farms to supply the towns.

The cool coastal climate along the Peruvian coast is caused by the cold ocean current (the Humboldt current) that sweeps up the shore from the south. This current is full of fish, which are eaten by the millions of sea birds which nest on the off-shore islands. The birds' droppings form guano, the valuable fertiliser, which is one of Peru's exports.

In a Peruvian mountain valley 15,000 feet up, this mine produces tin, gold, silver, lead and zinc.

Charles Perry Weimer - House of Photography

The landowners of central Chile are much closer to their land, and to their tenants, than most of the other South American landowners. They live on their haciendas instead of enjoying the comforts and pleasures of a town. Many of them have as much Indian blood in their veins as their tenants.

The owner raises cattle and grows fodder for it. And he also plants wheat. Chile and Argentina are the only countries in South America where more wheat is grown than maize. On small farms fruit and olives are often grown instead of grain. Chile does not grow enough food to feed her population, and has to import large amounts every year.

Grapes grow particularly well in the central valley. Almost every farm and hacienda has vineyards, some of them very large. The raisins and wine made from Chilean grapes are famous. They are sold to North America and Europe as well as to South American countries.

The hacienda system is changing in Chile. Many of the large estates are being divided and sold to small farmers. Some people have pushed southward to clear areas of the forest on which to make farms. They were led by small groups of Germans, who have opened up the country, building good roads and strong permanent homes. Enormous numbers of trees have to be cut down to make a farm. Most of the wood is used for fuel rather than lumber.

Four-fifths of the population of Ecuador live and work on the land. The country is not devoid of mineral wealth, however. There is gold near Esmeraldas, though the Spaniards did not find it. There is an oil field west of Guayaquil on the Santa Elena peninsula, and near the river Putumayo. Copper, iron, lead and coal are found in the mountains and the empty country to the east.

An oil refinery at Talara, Peru, processes oil from several fields in the north of Peru.

Charles Perry Weimer - House of Photography

Ores mined nearby are processed in these smelters at Cerro de Pasco. The work is done by skilled Indians.

The people of Peru are also chiefly occupied with agriculture, though somewhat less than her neighbour is.

Copper and iron ore are produced near the coast, but the chief mining towns of Peru are high in the mountains. In the seventeenth century an enormous deposit of silver ore was found near Cerro de Pasco. This silver mine was worked for hundreds of years. The silver was smelted and made into rough bars. These were carried down a mountain track from a height of nearly 15,000 feet to Lima, 200 miles away.

Eventually the deposit began to be exhausted. Mining had practically ceased when, in the early years of this century, a mining company took over the area hoping to find other minerals. An amazing railway was built up the mountains from Lima, going over innumerable bridges and along rocky ledges cut out of the mountainside, winding through spiral tunnels and zig-zagging up the slopes. It was a very expensive undertaking, but it has been proved worth while, for it has served a double purpose, taking equipment to the mines and bringing down the ores.

Many valuable minerals have been found in the mines round Cerro de Pasco. There are deposits of gold, lead, zinc, bismuth and vanadium and new veins of silver have been discovered. Copper takes the first place, however. It is the most important metal in Peru and one of the chief exports.

Coal, has been found near Cerro de Pasco and at Alta Chicama. This is an important discovery, because South America has so little. The supply is estimated to be considerable, and Peru is likely to become the leading producer in South America. There are oil wells on the coast and continental shelf in the extreme north. It is refined for export at Talara.

Most of the exports from Chile's fertile Middle Valley go through the port of Valparaiso.

Much of Chile's mineral wealth lies below the Atacama Desert. In colonial times this desert was used as a highway, but otherwise no one went near it.

The first minerals to be worked were silver and copper. But the prospectors who located these metals also found deposits of sodium nitrate in the dried up lake beds of the desert. For a time the demand for nitrates as fertilisers and for the manufacture of explosives created a nitrate boom which made Chile prosperous. However the nitrate boom came to an end when a way was found to extract nitrogen from the air. Now the Atacama supplies only one-tenth of the world's nitrates. Iodine is a by-product.

At present the largest mineral export of the country is copper. Chile has 40 per cent of the world supply. Most of it comes from three mines high in the Andes, two in the Atacama region and the third south of Santiago. Chile also has some coal, and iron ore has taken over from nitrates as the second largest export.

A nationally owned steel works has been built near Concepción. Sulphur too is found in the Andes, but it is too hard to bocome very profitable. The deposits are inside the craters of extremely high volcanoes. A little sulphur is extracted, but it is difficult for the mine workers to get into the craters, and the thin air makes work difficult. Accordingly Chile's exports of sulphur are small. Gold, silver, and other metals are also produced.

Turning now to manufactures, Ecuador has very little industry of any kind. Panama hats are made in several places, and cloth and leather goods are produced in the capital, Quito.

There is considerably more industry in Peru. The capital, Lima, has long been the centre of government, social life, and commerce, and lately it has also become an industrial centre. It has many small factories, engaged on such things as food-processing and weaving and the manufacture of soap, cigarettes, leather goods, and matches.

In Chile about 60 per cent of the total population live in towns, which are growing fast. Santiago, the capital, is a sprawling mass of new buildings and factories which dwarf the town.

Valparaiso, the port of Santiago, was built on the coast at the foot of a steep incline. As the city grew it crept up the slope. In the modern town there are many parts to which people travel not by bus but by lift. Two other towns which are rapidly becoming industralised are Concepción and Valdivia. The lure of the factory is bringing many people from the country into the town.

The industries of central Chile use raw materials from many parts of the country. Grapes come from local vineyards. Wool is brought down mountain tracks from the upper reaches of the Andes, and hides are similarly brought down to the tanneries. Corn is made into flour and beer. In Valdivia there are furniture factories using wood from local forests and a new steel industry has been started.

THE FAR SOUTH

Tierra del Fuego, which means the Land of Fire, is an island at the extreme tip of South America.

The extreme south is a region of snow-covered mountains and glaciers, of storms and pounding seas.

The town of Ushuaia, on Tierra del Fuego is the most southerly town in the world. A more important town is Punta Arenas, on the northern side of the Magellan Strait.

Punta Arenas is the only important centre in this region. It stands on the only part of Chile that lies east of the Andes. This region is sheltered from wind and rain by the mountains. To the north of the town is good sheep-rearing country, and as many as 3 million sheep are kept and reared there.

During the Second World War oil was discovered on Tierra del Fuego, and there are now a hundred wells in an area that was uninhabited a generation ago.

Ushuaia in Argentine Tierra del Fuego is the southernmost permanent town in the world.

Patrice Hartley - Rapho Guillumette

Cattle are brought to this part of the Argentine pampa to be fattened before they are sold.

THE SOUTHERN COUNTRIES — ARGENTINA

Next to Brazil, Argentina is the biggest country in South America. It has a million square miles and 23.6 million people, that is to say nearly a sixth of the total area of South America and a sixth of the total population. Unlike most South Americans, the Argentines are accus-

A group of Argentine gauchos prepares to cook the evening meal over a fire on the pampa.

tomed to prosperity. Most of the people can read and write. Only a quarter of them work on the land.

Over 90 per cent of the population is white. There are hardly any Negroes, and most of the mestizo population is along the borders of other countries.

The western frontier of Argentina is for the most part in the Andes. It is very dry in the north, but further south there are oases in the foothills near the Sierra de Cordoba.

Tucuman was once a fortress at the southern end of the great Inca road from Cuzco in the Andes. Later it became a centre at which travellers fitted themselves out for journeys to the east or the west. Now it is the centre of the Argentine sugar plantations. Protected by the mountains, the region enjoys a warm climate with abundant rain; it never freezes.

A little further on, the climate is either too dry or too cold.

South of Tucuman are the oases of the dry belt. At each river that comes down from the mountains, there is an irrigated strip of land. Many Italians live in the settlements round these oases. The largest are San Juan, Mendoza, and San Rafael. Their most lucrative crop is grapes.

An important oil field has been found in north-west Argentina, and uranium has been discovered in the Andean foothills. There are bauxite deposits at San Isidro.

The Entre Rios province, which lies between the Parana and Uruguay rivers, is rolling, green, well-wooded country. Where the Parana and Iquazú rivers drop over the edge of the Parana plateau there are magnificent waterfalls.

The northern part of Entre Rios is cattle country. The southern part is one of Argentina's biggest sheep and flax districts. Maté is cultivated in the far north. Maté is a shrub of the holly family, used for making a sort of tea very popular in Argentina, Uruguay, and Brazil. There are few people on the maté plantations for most of the year, but at harvest people pour in from as far as Brazil and Paraguay to pick the leaves.

The Gran Chaco is an enormous low-lying area shared by Argentina, Bolivia, and Paraguay. The Argentinian part is covered with scrub and grass. In the east the rivers overflow their banks in summer covering vast areas with water. The Pilcomayo River which forms part of the frontier between Argentina and Paraguay changes its course so often at the time of flood that the frontier is constantly shifting. Cotton is planted on some of the shifting floodlands after the water has drained off.

The scrub forests of the Chaco contain millions of quebracho trees, which yield tannin for tanning leather. Their wood, which is very hard, is used for railway sleepers. The mills which extract the tannin require a great deal of water and have to be built on rivers.

Eric Pavel - FLO

People come from far away to harvest maté leaves, from which a popular beverage is made.

Heavy quebracho logs are loaded on to carriers by primitive methods, then hauled by oxen.

Joe Barnell - Shostal

SOUTHERN SOUTH AMERICA

Cotton is also grown in this region, mostly by squatters, who clear the land or move in after the wood-cutters have cleared it.

The dry southern part of Argentina is called Patagonia. Only one per cent of the population live there. There are constant gales, which whip up waves on the lakes at the foot of the Andes. Spectacular mountains are covered with glaciers. Practically the only habitable places in Patagonia are the gorges that cross the dry plateau.

The sheep ranches are enormous. They cover thousands of square miles, and usually have their headquarters in a gorge where there is a supply of water. Sheep are also raised on Tierra del Fuego.

The pampas are the south-eastern part

These cattle are bred from prime English stock brought into Argentina in the nineteenth century.

of the great Argentine plains. The Dry Pampa where rainfall is scanty is to the west and south. The Humid Pampa is to the east. The Humid Pampa is a boundless plain, which was covered with tall, rustling grass when the early explorers

On a sheep ranch in dry, wind-swept Patagonia, water is pumped by a windmill.

Joe Barnell - Shostal

Teams of mules guided by their riders pull the ploughs on an Argentine sugar-cane plantation.

The Humid Pampa today is divided into four agricultural regions. In the east cattle are reared for beef, and sheep for wool and mutton. Butter too has become an important product. The western and southern parts are entirely devoted to wheat, lucerne, and cattle. This is the area that borders on the Dry Pampa. In the north the maize region round Rosario is thickly settled by Italians. All

came. The winters are mild and the summers are hot. The rainfall is plentiful. The growing season is longer in the north than in the south and west.

This entire area, except for a few hills, is covered with deep fertile soil. It is made of dust blown from the dry west and south and silt carried down by the rivers. The Argentinian cattle ranchers improved the quality of their beef by breeding from British cattle. These were not as hardy as the native breed, and special food had to be grown for them. Labour for arable farming came from Italy, Spain, and many other countries. Some of the tenants planted their own wheat, and eventually wheat became a very important crop.

It is difficult to maintain good roads on the Pampa. Where there is no grass, the fine soil blows away in the dry season and turns to deep mud as soon as it rains. But building railways, on such level ground, is a very simple matter. Railways fan out from all the Pampa ports into the agricultural areas, covering far more ground than the arterial roads.

Art D'Arazien - Shostal

Cattle ranges in Argentina's dry north-west depend on streams from the Andes for irrigation.

Newly sheared sheep are gathered near the headquarters of a Patagonian sheep ranch.

Gerard Oppenheimer - Alpha

Straggling cattle graze beside a stream on the vast stretches of Argentina's western pampas.

round Buenos Aires there is a region of vegetable and fruit farming. Some of the market gardens reach right into the edges of the city.

Buenos Aires attracted the early colonists because its harbour had deep enough water for their ships. With the development of the Humid Pampa, it has become the biggest town in Latin America. The port, however, is not deep enough for modern ships without constant dredging. In 1935 an entirely new port was built directly north of the old one.

Argentina heads the South American countries in the matter of trade. It lacks oil, coal, and steel. But it ships almost all the wheat, linseed, and maize, most of the meat, and more than half the wool, hides, and other grains that leave the continent. No other country in the world exports so much fresh meat.

URUGUAY

This, the smallest of the South American republics, has an area of only 72,000 square miles and a population of less than 3 million. But Uruguay makes full use of her land; no part of it is unoccupied. The capital is Montevideo, with a population of just over a million. The Uruguayans are mostly white, being of Spanish and Italian descent. There are a few whites from other European countries, and a certain number of Negroes. Near the frontiers are some mestizos.

The country of Uruguay is an intermediate region, sloping down from the Brazilian plateaus to the Humid Pampa of the Argentine. A strip of low land runs down the Atlantic coast and along the Rio de la Plata, but most of the

Julien Bryan - Photo Researchers

This Uruguayan market-gardener raises vegetables and potatoes for the city markets.

Art D'Arazien - Shostal

Hides are unloaded at a Buenos Aires tannery. The bales hold wool for textile factories.

country is hilly. There are no great plains like the pampas, but grassy slopes and wooded valleys. There are no extremes of temperature, and rainfall is adequate throughout the year.

British traders were the first to realise the value of the grassland of Argentina and Uruguay. In 1840 they introduced a good breed of sheep for wool, and within ten years there were about 2 million sheep being reared in Uruguay.

Until the middle of the nineteenth century the millions of cattle reared on

In Buenos Aires' harbour the mud must be dredged constantly and held back by walls.

Eric Pavel FLO

These Uruguayan gauchos herd horses. Much land in Uruguay is used for horse and cattle raising.

the unfenced pastures of Uruguay were used only for tallow, hides, and salt beef. Eventually meat-processing plants were built and, at the same time, barbed-wire fences were put up to separate cattle, so as to make scientific breeding possible. Refrigeration made it possible to ship meat to other countries. British breeds replaced the native Uruguayan cattle.

Today Uruguay has more livestock in proportion to its population than any other country in the world except New Zealand. About four-fifths of the land is used for grazing, the remaining fifth, in the south, being used for raising crops, including rice, sugarbeets, grapes and fruit trees.

The railways in the country were British built. There is a state-owned civil airline to the interior. Roads surfaced with gravel have recently been built and much of the country's transportation is now motorised.

Montevideo, besides being the seat of the government, is the commercial and industrial centre of the country. Its industry is of recent growth, but there are already many factories, most of which use local material. Electricity is derived from a power-dam on the Rio Negro and from a power-station in the town which uses imported coal. Montevideo is also the base of a fishing fleet and a popular holiday resort.

It is unusual for a country in which almost half the workers are on the land to be prosperous, but this is the case in Uruguay, where food is cheap and there is a welfare state rather like the one in Britain.

These sheep are in an open field, but Uruguay builds fenced runways for them in settled areas.

A new hydro-electric power-plant 150 miles from Montevideo supplies much of the city's power.

BRAZIL, THE GIANT OF SOUTH AMERICA

Brazil contains almost half the population of South America. The United States of Brazil is larger than the United States of America excluding Alaska. If we exclude Venezuela and the Guianas, Brazil is as large as all the other South American countries put together. It is composed of twenty-two States, a Federal District, and four Territories. Brazil is the only independent country of South America where the official language is not Spanish but Portuguese. The bulk of the inhabitants of Brazil are concentrated on or near the coast. Most of the north and west is very thinly populated.

Brazil has more land capable of being farmed than any other country of its size. It has the finest natural harbour in the world. It has the longest navigable river in the world. The resources of its forests are endless, and it is known to possess great stores of iron-ore and manganese.

That it has not attracted more settlers is largely because its wealth is very inconveniently placed for man to make use of.

The coast consists for the most part of steep cliffs. They are especially steep behind the two largest towns, São Paulo and Rio de Janeiro. Most of the rivers rise in the highlands behind the coast, but instead of running towards the sea they wander off for hundreds of miles, to join either the Parana River in the south or the Amazon in the north. They are therefore useless as a means of transport from the coast.

The Amazon, the longest navigable river in the world, wanders endlessly through the immense forests of the interior whose trees are of great value. It might provide a highway for this timber, but unfortunately the wealth of the forests is very scattered indeed, and there are too few people living there to collect it. Only when the Amazon region is much more developed will the river prove its true worth as an inland waterway.

Tropical Recife is a port named after the coral reef which shelters its spacious harbour.

Charles Perry Weimer - House of Photography

In Brazil's most southerly state, Rio Grande do Sul, most people live in valleys and lowlands.

THE AMAZON

The Amazon country of Brazil is a vast area of forests and rivers. Upstream, the Amazon plain is 800 miles wide. It narrows as it passes between the Brazilian and Guiana Highlands, then broadens again to occupy the greater part of the north coast of Brazil. In spite of the enormous amount of silt brought down each year, the river has never succeeded in forming a delta. That is because of a phenomenon known as a tidal bore, which is a wave of water five to twelve feet high, which advances upstream with a roar at a speed of from ten to fifteen miles an hour. Fourteen great rivers discharge into the Amazon, and a multitude of secondary rivers which in any other part of the world would themselves be called great rivers.

When the Amazon overflows its banks, as it does regularly, it floods an area twenty to sixty miles wide on either side. Some of the silt brought down by the Amazon is deposited on the flooded surface. This makes the soil very rich, but the land is flooded so often that farmers can make very little use of it.

Most people think that the climate of the tropical Amazon must be unbearably hot. Actually the temperature itself is not unduly high. But the air is laden with moisture, and even ordinary summer heat becomes very difficult to bear. There is no dry season here, only one that is less wet. Both in summer and winter there are sudden sharp showers, and then, with equal suddenness, the sky is clear and without clouds again.

The nights however, are almost always brilliant and clear.

There are thousands of different sorts of trees in the forest of the Amazon Basin, but they grow quite haphazardly. Rarely can one find a number of the same sort of trees growing together. The value of some of the trees is very high indeed. But, as has already been pointed out, they are so widely scattered that it is not profitable to attempt to exploit them on a large scale.

What the forest chiefly lacks is population. There are very few areas in the

The Amazon jungle, often so dense that travel through it is impossible, crowds to the edge of the river.

Charles Perry Weimer - House of Photography

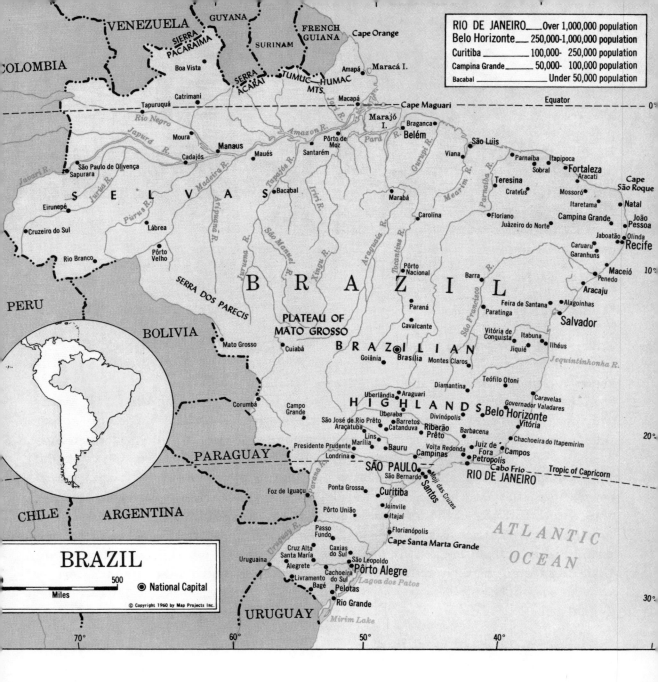

world of its size which are so thinly populated. Compare it, for example, with Alaska, which is considered a very thinly populated area, with one person to about every $2\frac{1}{2}$ square miles. In the Amazon basin there is one person to about every square mile. Half of these live near the coast, however, so that further up the river there must often

be no more than one person to every 2 or 3 square miles. Ever since the Amazon was explored attempts have been made to exploit its riches. But those who have tried have always encountered one great stumbling block: the absence of any people to do the work.

The isolated groups of Indians that live in the forest fear the white man

Indians of the Amazon Valley live as they have for hundreds of years, untouched by civilisation.

This huge opera house at Manaus was built during the prosperous days of the Amazon rubber boom.

and avoid him. Their fears are not altogether unfounded, for the early explorers brought disease, and sold the Indians into slavery.

Even today contact with civilisation often seems to wither the spirit of the Indians so that many tribes have died out. Diseases like measles and influenza, to which the Indians have no natural resistance, still take a heavy toll. The more remote tribes are fiercely independent, and are still untouched by civilisation. This cannot be regretted since it has proved so mixed a blessing to many Indian tribes.

Rubber gatherers in the Amazon jungle smoke the latex in huts until it can be formed into a ball.

AMAZON FORESTS

Rubber trees have the largest place in the story of the Amazon forests. When the world began to be in need of rubber, around the middle of the nineteenth century, Brazil possessed most of the rubber trees in the world. People rushed to buy land along the Amazon, then set out on a frantic search for hands to work for them. Indians from the eastern side of the Andes, where law did not run, were seized and enslaved. And workers came from the dry areas in the east at the rate of 20,000 a year.

Most of the towns along the Amazon were originally bases for the rubber traffic. The biggest boom towns were Belém and Manaus.

The Brazilian rubber boom came to an end when an Englishman smuggled some seeds out of the country, and rubber plantations were started in Malaya and Sumatra. The trees on the Asian plantations yielded three to six times as much rubber as those growing wild in the Amazon forests. And workers could gather three times as much when the trees were

all in one place. Within thirty years Malaya and Sumatra were producing most of the world's rubber, whereas business in Brazil had declined almost to nothing.

This country produces most of the Brazil nuts in the world. But the nuts are gathered from wild trees, not cultivated ones. There are farms which produce cotton, while the main food crops are manioc, maize, rice, and beans.

A new development is the growing of black pepper and jute by Japanese immigrants near Santarem. At a small factory, the jute is made into the bags in which coffee and sugar are shipped. And jute is also used for other purposes. One of the most important things about the jute plantations is that for the first time the rich Brazilian flood-plains are being put to regular use.

North-eastern Brazil falls into two distinct regions climatically. Along the coast is an area that has regular rainfall. The western part alternates between long droughts and disastrous floods, in ad-

dition to which the soil is too poor for anything to grow but stunted trees and brush.

Most of eastern Brazil is mountainous, though there are a few low-lying areas along the coast. The São Francisco River rises in the Brazilian highlands, in the state of Minas Gerais, flows northward for a considerable distance, then curves eastwards to discharge itself on the east coast. It is not much used as a waterway, nor does it do much in the way of irrigation, but its power-stations supply a large part of the country's electricity.

Freighters are able to travel far up the Amazon, even to the foothills of the Andes.

Harold Schultz - Birnback

Most homes in Manaus are small floating houses built on rafts. A dugout canoe serves as transportation.

AGRICULTURE AND INDUSTRY

The early colonists soon realised that sugar-cane would grow well in the northeast. They cleared the forests around Salvador and Recife, and brought in Negro slaves to work on the plantations. These spread rapidly until all suitable land had been used up.

At the same time Portugal offered enormous grants for cattle-breeding. Cattlemen became as rich as sugar planters.

The tobacco fields of Bahia state are mostly worked by descendants of freed Negro slaves. Every inch of land is used for production, but the farms are tiny and the farmers are poor. This is the only region, apart from one other in the south, in which fertilisers are used regularly. Much of the tobacco crop is made into cigars in small local factories.

Most of the land, however, in this part of Brazil is used for the grazing of cattle and goats. The cattle are put on the better land, while the goats succeed in finding food in the poor, dry areas. In these areas, the main product is goat skins. For cattle, on the other hand, trees have to be cleared and grass planted.

Efforts have been made to control floods and to conserve water for the dry periods. In the past they have usually failed, however, because of bad planning. Dykes built along rivers have crumbled under the pressure of a flood. Reservoirs have been built where there was no suitable land to irrigate.

Some useful produce grows wild in this area: cord is made from tree cotton, hammocks of caroé fibre. Carnauba wax, of which Brazil is the chief source, is used for polishes and cosmetics and the babaçu palm gives a valuable oil. Cacao beans are grown on large plantations along the coast near Bahia. Workers come from the interior for the harvest.

A number of new roads have been

One of the earliest settlements in Brazil was at Salvador, now capital and port of Bahia State.

built in the north-east, and the people are now, for the first time, beginning to depend on the exchange of goods instead of trying to be self-sufficient.

South-eastern Brazil consists of the states of São Paulo, Minas Gerais, Espirito Santo, Rio de Janeiro and Guanabara. Behind them in the interior, is the vast, sparsely inhabited area that forms the states of Mato Grosso and Goiás.

The state of Minas Gerais consists for the most part of large estates *(fazendas)* on which stock-breeding and dairy-farming are carried out.

The early settlements in Minas Gerais

People from all along the river come to sell their goods on market day in Belém.

were built along roads. Colonial roads were built over the mountains, going wherever the forest was thinnest. Later, railways were built and, for them, level ground was chosen when possible. People moved towards the railways, and many of the early settlements were abandoned. Now new arterial roads are replacing the railways.

Minas Gerais is rich in minerals. Iron and many other important metals are present, as well as precious stones. Gold and diamonds were discovered at the beginning of the eighteenth century.

The iron ore present is estimated to be nearly a quarter of the world's reserves, and it has become one of the country's leading exports. A new, large-scale steel plant at Volta Redonda produces pig iron and steel, but coal for smelting has to be imported from the United States.

Rio de Janeiro is a magnificent city, built on the shores of a perfect natural harbour. The town was originally built as a shipping port for the gold from Minas Gerais. With a high wall of rock behind it, it was well placed for defence against Indians and Spaniards. Today it is the commercial capital of the whole country.

The land of eastern Brazil is not all divided up into fazendas. In the Paraiba Valley which receives fertile deposits from occasional floods, modern farms have been started. In this area many farmers who had previously worked the old land-shifting cultivation method have now adopted more modern methods.

The State of São Paulo was first settled by adventurers who came seeking their fortunes. When the gold of Minas Gerais was found, people from all over Brazil poured into the east. The surface gold was eventually exhausted at a time when

Brasilia, the new capital of Brazil, features some of the most exciting architecture to be found anywhere in the world.

Brazilian Embassy

After the coffee beans are harvested, they must be spread in the sun to dry.

Paulo Afonso Falls is a tremendous cascade that drops 275 feet and supplies much of Brazil's power.

coffee became popular in England and North America. Accordingly, large numbers moved off to the land round São Paulo city to plant coffee trees. Before long Brazil was supplying three-quarters of the world's coffee. By 1920 the country's coffee production had risen enormously. In fact it had reached a point at which Brazil was growing twice as much as the needs of the whole world. And new trees were still being planted.

Coffee growers began to lose money, but then a new boom started with the urgent demand for cotton. Young coffee trees were hastily pulled up to make room for cotton. Many coffee growers switched over entirely to cotton, and new plantations were started by new growers.

During the last war cotton could not be sold to Japan or Europe, and many cotton planters switched once more, this time to oranges, since Brazil is second only to the U.S. in orange exports. Oranges may be destined to supplant cotton altogether. Already, so little cotton is being grown that local textile manufacturers are beginning to be afraid they will soon have to import it.

There are now many progressive mod-ern farms in the state of São Paulo. The government has encouraged immigrants from Japan and Europe, and people have also come from other parts of Brazil. The farms of the Parana settlers are on the São Paulo border. Although they are actually in the state of Paraná, the roads and railways connect with São Paulo, so they look on that as their centre.

These farms have been very successful. Exhausted land has been renewed. Virgin forest is being preserved. Mixed crops are grown, instead of single crops. Fertilisers and modern machinery are used. Where the land slopes, it is terraced so that the soil will not wash off. Roads and railways are carefully organised to connect the farmers with the markets at which they must sell their produce.

But the São Paulo coffee planters still work on the fazenda system. The tenant clears the forest and plants the coffee shrub for the owner. In return he may plant his own crops between the rows until the trees begin to bear, after about five years. Then he moves on. The owner harvests the coffee until the crop declines, then he too moves on and starts again,

Joe Barnell - Shostal

Southern Brazil grows large quantities of rice. Here, a machine does the hard work of threshing.

Joe Barnell - Shostal

On the open prairies of Brazil's far south are great livestock ranches similar to those of Argentina.

on fresh land. It is a wasteful procedure.

São Paulo is the richest state in Brazil. With a population of 16.3 million it produces nearly half the coffee, more than half the cotton, and a quarter of the sugar produced by the whole country. The city of São Paulo is the largest manufacturing town in Latin America. The hydro-electric power-stations of the state produce three-fifths of the country's power.

We find a very different picture when we turn from this productive area to the vast highland country of Mato Grosso and Goias. Though forming more than one-fifth of the area of Brazil, these two states have only about 3 per cent of the country's population. There are a few successful farms within reach of roads, but much of the area has reverted to cattle grazing, because farmers had no means of getting their produce to any potential market.

The mining region near Corumba produces iron and manganese, and has brought sufficient prosperity to the town for an airport to have been constructed.

CENTRAL BRAZIL

The physical centre of Brazil lies in that vast, almost empty area, and on this spot the new capital, Brasilia, has been built. Brasilia did not grow haphazardly like other towns, but was completely planned in advance.

It was designed to house half a million government workers and those who provide them with goods and services, and it was inaugurated in April 1960. In choosing this spot for the capital the government hoped that settlers would be attracted to clear the surrounding forests and grow food for the townsfolk.

This is not the first time such an attempt has been made to open up the interior of the country. The state of Minas Gerais built a similar new capital, Belo Horizonte, but after fifty years there are still hardly any farms round this beautiful town, and all the food still has to be brought in from other areas.

Southern Brazil consists of three states, Parana, Santa Catarina, and Rio Grande Do Sul. Plains follow the coast, except where it is flanked by the Great Escarpment. The first two states are plateaus with a few high mountains. Further to the south and west are lowlands bordering on northern Argentina and Uruguay.

The Parana Plateau is one of the largest lava plateaus in the world. Deep gorges have been cut by the rivers that cross it. At the heads of these gorges are spectacular waterfalls with a drop of several hundred feet.

Most of the area has plentiful rainfall throughout the year. In the north are thick forests of tropical trees. In the south trees become thinner and the land is covered with grass. The cool highlands are covered with dense pine forests. The minerals of this area are mainly copper and iron, but there are also some low-grade coal deposits.

The southern Brazilians are of European, but not Portuguese descent. They are of German, Swiss, Austrian, Italian,

Eric Pavel - FLO

Volta Redonda is a giant modern steel manufacturing centre near Rio de Janeiro.

and in Parana, of Polish and Russian origin. These settlers were not like most of the others in Brazil. They did not expect to make a quick and easy fortune, but settled down to establish permanent homes and villages.

The first settlements in the south sponsored by the Brazilian government were often badly placed so that the farmers could not reach any market.

The new wheat growing settlements in the state of Parana are better planned. Each settlement is located so as to have access to one of the old-established roads, and these settlements have prospered from the start.

The large estates survive chiefly in the open plains where gauchos roam with cattle and sheep, and in the Jacui River valley where people of Portuguese descent grow rice for large landowners. In the cattle country, the main products are hides, wool, and salt beef. The beef is processed in many large factories situated around in Pelotas.

In the forests of western Parana, maté (Paraguayan tea) is grown. Porto Alegre is an important road and rail centre and has numerous factories.

Coffee beans must be carefully roasted so as not to spoil their flavour and aroma.

Joe Barnell - Shostal

COUNTRIES OF THE INTERIOR — BOLIVIA

Bolivia is quite a large country having an area twice that of France. But most of its population of nearly 5 million live in an area only half that of Holland.

Although practically all of the country's income is derived from mining, only about 4 per cent of the people are miners. Most of the people live either in the mountains or on the Altiplano, a high, bleak plateau between the eastern and western ranges of the Andes. To prevent overpopulation the government is gradually moving families to the tropical areas.

is sufficient rain to grow crops without irrigation. The lake is very large, being 120 miles long, and in some places it is over a hundred fathoms deep. Here the Aymaras, an Indian people, grow potatoes and grain and keep herds of llamas.

The main farming regions of Bolivia are the warm, well-watered valleys of the eastern chain of the Andes. The people here are mostly mestizos or Europeans. Where the valleys are narrow, farms cling to the streams for miles. Various grains are grown, and fruit does well on the lower slopes. Farm produce is sold to the mining towns in the mountains. Sucre, the legal capital of Bolivia, is located in one of these basins. There are few setters in the Yungas, the rainy, forest-covered eastern slopes of the Andes. There is some gold mining, and a few planters grow cacao beans, sugar, and coca bushes, whose leaves contain the drug cocaine. Some wild rubber is gathered in the forests, and cattle are grazed on the wet savanna.

The south-eastern part of Bolivia is relatively dry. Its vegetation is stunted forest and grassland. Oil was discovered in

Ewing Krainin - Photo Researchers

Lake Titicaca is one of the few dependable sources of water for farming in the Bolivian highlands.

The Altiplano is over 12,000 feet above sea-level. La Paz, the seat of the Bolivian Government, is situated at the bottom of a gorge 1,400 feet deep in the Altiplano. In the area round Lake Titicaca, there

The faces of this Paraguayan farm couple examining the cotton crop show a lifetime of hard work.

Eric Pavel - FLO

INTERIOR SOUTH AMERICA

0	100	200

Miles

⊚ National Capitals

La Paz ———————— 250,000-1,000,000 population
Asunción ———————— 100,000- 250,000 population
Cochabamba ———————— 50,000- 100,000 population
Puerto Cooper ———————— Under 50,000 population

© Copyright 1960 by Map Projects Inc.

1920, and, with it, this isolated region became important.

Pipelines have been laid to refineries at Cochabamba and Sucre, and to Arica, the Chilean seaport. There is an arterial road between Santa Cruz, the chief town of the Chaco, and Cochabamba.

The mountains of Bolivia are rich

in metal. The copper mine at Corocoro has been worked since Inca times. It is one of the two sources of pure copper in the whole Western Hemisphere.

Another mining centre is Potosi, which stands nearly 14,000 feet above sea-level. The town was founded in 1547, two years after the first discovery of silver in the mountain which towers above it.

The mountain also contains tin, bismuth and tungsten. Temperatures are very low here, because of the altitude. The mines at Oruro and Uncia have now become more important. Though their ores are not as rich as those of Potosi, they are easier to work. Tin is the chief product of those mines, but other metals include lead, zinc, and gold. Important uranium deposits have been found south-east of La Paz.

One of the most serious problems with which Bolivia is faced is that the country depends on one product, tin, for 68 per cent of its income. If the price of tin falls, the result is very serious.

Steep slopes and rocky soils of the Bolivian Andes make farming difficult and crop yields low.

Tom Hollyman - Photo Researchers

Davis Pratt, - Rapho Guillumette

The imposing Presidential Palace in Asuncion overlooks the Paraguay River.

PARAGUAY

Paraguay is less than half the size of Bolivia. The eastern third of the country is a plateau, between 1,000 and 2,000 feet high. The rest is a level plain.

In the north the Paraguay River, flowing southwards from the frontier with Brazil, first crosses the country, and then, having joined the Pilcomayo near the capital, Asuncion, it forms for a while the frontier with Argentina. The river is bordered by great swamps. West of it is the Gran Chaco. East of it are forests of tall trees, some of them evergreens.

Paraguay could well become a rich agricultural country like Uruguay. The climate is moderate, and there is enough rain for farming. The soil is rich.

Most of the population live in the hills between the plateau and the east bank of the Paraguay River. In this area the land is high enough to escape flooding and the farmers are near the country's chief waterway. Asuncion, the capital,

Caracas, Venezuela, with its clean, modern buildings, shows what the future may bring.

stands at a spot where the high ground comes up to the river.

The country's chief commercial crop

This Bolivian miner of Potosi must wear heavy clothing against the cold of the 14,000-foot height.

is cotton. Other crops are maize, sweet potatoes, rice, sugar-cane, and manioc, a plant from which a type of flour is made.

Another product which is exported is quebracho, which grows along the western bank of the Paraguay River and which, as we have seen, is used in tanning. Maté is sometimes grown as a crop and sometimes gathered wild. The eastern forests yield valuable timber.

Another export is orange-flower, or petitgrain oil, which is used in perfumes. Paraguay produces seven-tenths of the world's supply of this oil.

Deposits of iron, copper, and manganese have been discovered, but so far they have been very little exploited.

Plentiful rain supports lush tropical vegetation on the high, volcanic Pacific island of Tahiti.

THIS IS OCEANIA

The Pacific Ocean covers about a third of the world's surface. It is larger than any other ocean and larger than all the continents put together.

At its widest, from Panama to the Malay peninsula, the distance across the Pacific is about 12,500 miles. This is half the distance round the earth.

In this vast expanse of water, the land area is relatively small. The only great land-mass is the island of Australia, and that is a little less than the size of Europe, and less than one-twentieth of the area of the Pacific.

Complex chains of underwater mountains stretch south-east from Asia. The tops of some of them form the islands of Indonesia, New Guinea, and the Solomons. The New Hebrides and New Caledonia are also part of these chains, which appear above sea-level again as New Zealand.

Further to the north and east are other mountains. Most of them are submerged beneath the surface of the Pacific, but here and there are a few peaks rising above sea-level. These peaks form small and widely scattered islands.

In so vast a region there is naturally a great variety of landscape. In Australia alone, the country varies from desert to tropical forest.

So great is the variety in the Pacific that geographers distinguish seven types of islands, each type having its own characteristic landscape, soil, climate, and vegetation.

Treeless atolls are low coral islands. They have poor soil and little drinking water. There are plenty of sea-birds and fish around them, yet the natives avoid them, preferring islands with trees. But the treeless atolls make good landing grounds for aircraft and some of them are used as military air bases. The Canton and Johnson Islands are both groups of treeless atolls.

Dry-forest atolls are also low coral islands. Because of their salty air and brackish water few plants grow on them; those that do are especially adapted to these conditions and generally form a dry scrub forest.

Few people live on the dry-forest atolls. As on the treeless atolls there is often a shortage of drinking water, and it is hard to grow crops in the salty soil. Most of the Marshall and Ellice Islands, and many of the Tuamotu and northern Cook Islands are dry-forest atolls.

Moist atolls are the beautiful coral islands so often shown in films. They receive plenty of rain, and trees grow abundantly. Coconut palms and bread-fruit trees are everywhere. Excellent crops can be grown, producing food in plenty. Typical of the moist atolls are the Gilbert and Tokelau Islands.

Coral is made by a very small organism called a coral polyp, which lives in warm sea water. Coral polyps are very simple animals of the same family as the jelly fish. They absorb the carbonate of lime that is dissolved in sea water and with it form stony walls round their bodies. When they die, the limestone walls (the coral) remain, and a new generation of corals builds on the skeletons of the old. In that way, in the course of time, great thicknesses of coral are formed.

Coral often forms on the tops of submerged mountains just beneath the

Scrub vegetation and bare, eroded hills are characteristic of the drier regions of Australia.

Scott Polkinghorne - Photo Researchers

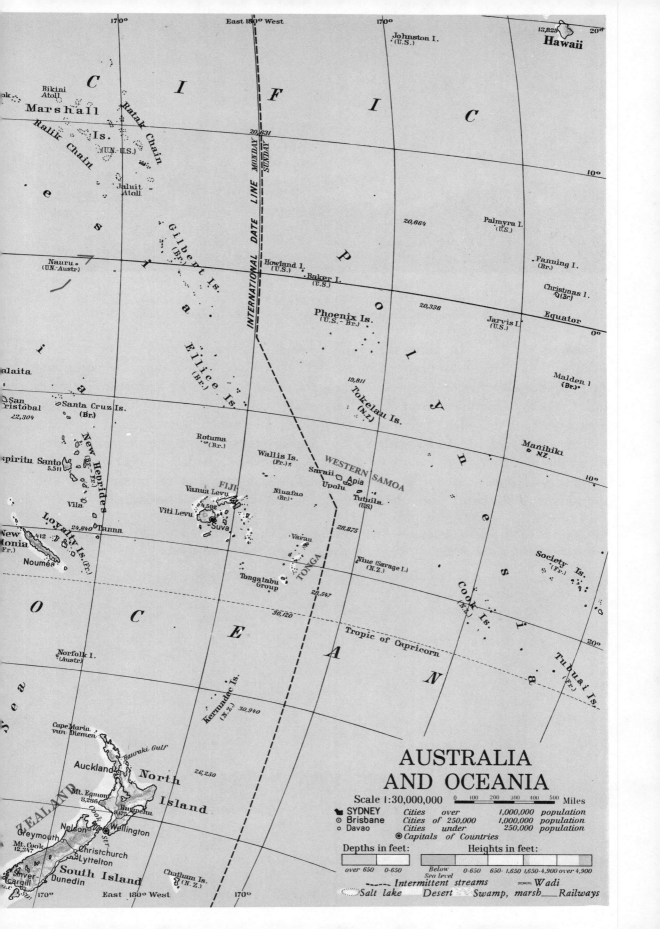

Hawaii Natural History Association

Streams of molten lava flow into the ocean as Hawaii's great volcano, Mauna Loa, erupts. The Pacific Ocean has long been a centre of volcanic activity, and many of the islands are of volcanic origin.

surface of the sea. In time the coral reaches the surface, and is battered by the waves. Gradually the coral is ground into 'sand', while the living coral keeps on growing round the edge. Eventually the typical coral reef is formed with sandy soil in the middle.

Raised coral islands are composed of layer upon layer of old coral. Some have been raised 200 feet and more above sea level. The coral of which they are composed forms limestone rocks. Limestone dissolves easily, so there are many caves and sinkholes. Because limestone soaks up water rapidly these islands are often quite dry. Some, like Nauru Island or Ocean Island, have rich deposits of phosphates, and phosphate mining is an industry.

This coral island is part of Australia's Great Barrier Reef. Stretching for 1,250 miles along Australia's north-eastern coast, the Great Barrier Reef is the world's largest single coral deposit.

Keith Gillett - Shosta

Frank Newton - FPG

Aerial view of an atoll showing the surrounding coral reef.

Unweathered volcanic islands have little vegetation. When rock is weathered it gradually breaks up, forming soil. These islands have little soil, except for what has accumulated in the bottoms of valleys, where the islanders grow their coconut palms and other crops. The Northern Marianas are examples of unweathered volcanic islands.

Weathered volcanic islands often rise hundreds of feet above sea-level. These islands have different soils and climates, providing a variety of plants. In them the natives can grow almost everything they need to live on. Only commercial minerals are lacking. The Hawaiian, Society, and Samoan Islands are good examples of weathered volcanic islands.

Continental islands contain rocks that were formed under conditions of great heat and pressure, which occur only on the continents or along their borders. These rocks are often very old, and because of their age the islands have an even greater variety of plants and soils than is possessed by the weathered volcanic islands.

These continental islands have therefore a great variety of landscape. They have high mountains, dense forests, and broad areas of swamp. On them human life has developed in many different ways. Continental islands have the great advantage of possessing mineral resources. Some of the most important ones in the Pacific are New Zealand, New Guinea, New Caledonia, Guadalcanal, New Britain, and New Ireland.

The spectacular fiords of New Zealand's South Island were formed by the action of glaciers.

Martin S. Klein

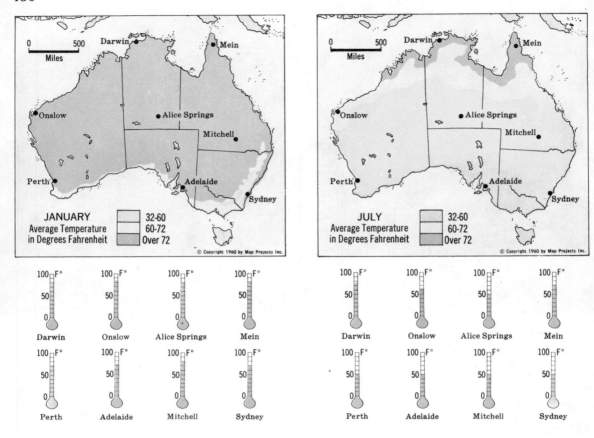

CLIMATE

The great variety of climate found in the Pacific depends primarily on the distance from the Equator, but it is also to some extent dependent on height above sea-level. Ocean currents also play their part.

The weather on islands on, or near, the Equator varies very little. Heavy and frequent rain is the rule, and there is very little difference in temperature between the warmest and coldest months.

The higher the island the more rainfall it gets. Air is forced to rise to pass over the mountains. It cools as it rises, and, since cold air cannot hold as much moisture as warm air, some of the moisture is released in the form of rain. Low-lying islands are relatively dry.

Great tropical storms, called typhoons, occur from time to time in the Pacific. They cause great damage. Trees are stripped of their branches and often uprooted; roofs are ripped off and whole buildings destroyed. Everyone has to stay under cover for protection. Even the largest ships have to heave-to to ride out the worst of these storms. When typhoons are particularly ferocious the wind may reach 150 miles an hour and can whip-up great tidal waves which sometimes sweep completely over any low-lying islands in their path.

The maps on these pages give some facts about the climate of Australia. As it is south of the Equator its seasons are the reverse of our own in the Northern

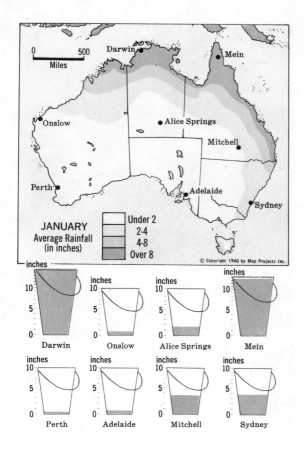

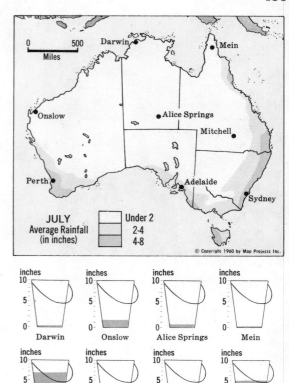

Hemisphere. In November, December, January, and February, when it is winter in the north, Australians are bathing and lying on the beaches. Their winter is from June to August.

Australia lies between the latitudes of 10° and 40° south. The tropical northern parts of the country are warm all the year round. The parts farther south are very nearly as hot in summer, but cooler in winter, though winters are generally mild throughout the country except on the high plateau and in the mountain regions.

Tropical Australia gets its rain from the summer monsoon. Rainfall is heavy near the coast, but diminishes rapidly in the more inland areas. During the cool season, which lasts from May to October, it is very dry.

The interior of the country is very dry, and so is much of Western Australia. Most of these areas consist of desert. The Great Sandy Desert and the Great Victoria Desert are amongst the largest deserts in the world.

South-western Australia and the coast of South Australia have mild rainy winters. The summers are hot and dry.

South-eastern Australia receives a fair amount of rain throughout the year. This has helped to make this part of the continent more densely settled than any other part. In south-eastern Australia the winters vary from cool to mild, and the summers are less hot than elsewhere.

Lying to the south is the island of Tasmania. Its climate is rather like that of New Zealand. It is far enough south to be immune from heat and drought.

Courtesy of Australian News and Information Bureau

The koala is a marsupial native to Australia. It lives on the eucalyptus leaves.

Alfred and Elma Milotte

The spiny ant-eater and the duck-billed platypus are unusual Australian mammals. Both lay eggs.

ANIMALS OF THE PACIFIC

In the remote past Australia and its islands were joined to Asia. But the land which linked them has been covered by the waters of the Pacific for hundreds of thousands of years. During this time, a great variety of plants and animals have developed in the Pacific area.

Many islands have native plants that are found in no other places in the word. Such plants are said to be *endemic*. In New Zealand, almost seven-tenths of the flowering plants are endemic. In New Caledonia, which boasts 2,500 species of flowering plants, four-fifths are found nowhere else in the world.

Islands that are isolated generally have only a few species of plants or animals, but those which are close to continents have many. The islands of Oceania have no native mammals at all apart from bats, and bats, of course, can travel great

Alfred and Elma Milotte

The bearlike Australian wombat is a marsupial like the kangaroo. It is 2 to 3 feet long, lives in a burrow, and feeds on plants and roots.

An emu inspects its eggs. This large flightless bird of Australia is related to the ostrich.

distances by flying. Cattle, deer, goats, pigs, rabbits, and rats are not native at all; all have been introduced by man.

Australia has been separated from other countries for so long that many of its animals are endemic. These animals have no close relatives anywhere else in the world.

Two-thirds of the native mammals of Australia are marsupials, which are animals that carry their young in pouches — like kangaroos and opossums. Australia's famous 'teddy bear', the Koala, is also a marsupial.

The only mammals to lay eggs come from Australia and its neighbouring islands; one of them is the duck-billed platypus found in Australia and Tasmania. The other is the echidna, or spiny ant-eater, found in Australia, Tasmania, and New Guinea.

Sharp teeth and a vicious temper gave the Tasmanian Devil its name. About the size of a badger, it sometimes kills sheep.

A baby wallaby peers out of its mother's pouch, where it nurses. The wallaby is a smaller relative of Australia's kangaroo.

Australian aborigines cook a simple meal of boiled fish. A boomerang lies on the ground nearby.

A group of New Guinea tribesmen, dressed for a ceremonial dance.

THE PEOPLES OF THE PACIFIC

The first white men who sailed across the Pacific mistakenly called the dark-skinned islanders Indians. That name did not last long. As more and more islands were discovered, the explorers found a great variety of native populations. In the western islands they had copper-coloured skin, straight black hair, and were expert boatmen. In the islands further to the east, the explorers found brown-skinned or black-skinned natives with curly or frizzy hair.

Who were these island people? Where had they come from? And how had they managed to sail thousands of miles across the ocean?

To understand their extraordinary voyages we must see them as the result of gradual progress. The island of Sumatra is, at its closest, about the same distance from the Malay peninsula as Calais is from Dover. It needed no great adventurous spirit or technical skill for

primitive people to cross the Malacca Straits. Once on the island of Sumatra, they could pass from island to island across still more narrow straits. In fact they could have travelled some 3,000 miles from the mainland of Asia without undertaking a single voyage of any great length. By that time they must have become skilful seafarers with some elementary understanding of navigation. It must also be realised that those who left an island did so as a rule under pressure from some stronger and more warlike tribe. The Kon Tiki expedition also proved that it was possible for some part of the population of the Pacific islands to have come from central South America on great balsa-wood rafts blown by the Trade Winds. This would account for some of the racial variation of the islands' inhabitants.

The islands of Indonesia have been occupied by man from the earliest times.

Further east, the smaller the islands became the more widely were they scattered. The Polynesian Islands, in the middle of the Pacific Ocean, were the last of these islands to be occupied.

This movement from island to island must have been spread over thousands of years. The people concerned must have come from different sources, for they seem to have differed greatly in appearance, language, and customs. As a result the people of the Pacific Islands fall into different groups. Scientists have divided them into four main groups, each of which is confined to one part of the island world.

The Australian aborigines ('original inhabitants') occupied this island continent long before its discovery by white

Indian women on Fiji wear their traditional saris. Indians have become farmers and merchants there.

men. Many aborigines have adopted civilisation — partially at least — but some have kept their primitive ways. These live in small groups, grow no crops and live by hunting and off wild-growing

Swimming is a popular sport in Australia, since most of the people live on or near the coasts. Here, Sunday bathers enjoy the surf at Bondi Beach in Sydney.

In sailing canoes like this one, the ancestors of the present islanders sailed all over the Pacific. The outrigger keeps the canoe from capisizing in heavy seas.

edible plants. Their chief weapon is the boomerang which, skilfully thrown, will come back to the thrower if it misses.

The aborigines are constantly on the move, always in search of food. They can move easily because they have no homes and very few possession of any sort.

The next group we come to are the people living in the islands of Melanesia. The people of the islands of Melanesia ('black islands') have dark skins and frizzy hair. These islands lie in several groups north-east of Australia. They are the Bismarck Archipelago, the Solomon Islands, the New Hebrides, the Fiji Islands, and New Caledonia. There are also a number of smaller islands. Melanesians use their canoes for both fishing and trading. They are firm believers in magic, and magicians are often the richest and the most important people amongst them.

The third Pacific Island group is called Micronesia, which means the 'small islands'. The islets of the Caroline,

Mariana, and Marshall groups form the bulk of Micronesia.

The Micronesians are skilful sailors. Their canoes are fitted with outriggers, which prevent them capsizing, so that they can be used for ocean voyages. Their triangular sails enable them to go about (to shift from one tack to another)

A Fijian builds a hut with a wooden frame and reed-matting walls.

very easily. The canoes of Micronesia are fastest of all the Pacific native craft.

Last of the island groups comes Polynesia, the word meaning 'many islands'. Polynesia covers an enormous area from Hawaii, in the north, to New Zealand in the south, and to Easter Island, which lies some 2,000 miles off the coast of Chile.

Of all the native people in the Pacific Islands, the Polynesians were from the first the most popular with the explorers. They are indeed a handsome and friendly people. They live by farming and fishing, but they do not have to work hard on their lovely islands, for food is plentiful.

In some places a mixture of races may be found. In New Guinea, for instance, though the bulk of the inhabitants are Melanesians, there are some Polynesian tribes. Other tribes are related to the Negritos of the Philippines and to kindred tribes in the Malay archipelago. Fijians are of mixed Polynesian and Melanesian stock.

New Zealand Maori children: descendants of fierce Polynesian warriors.

In more recent times many newcomers have arrived in the Pacific. In the Fiji Islands, for example, there are more Indians than native Fijians. Chinese traders have settled on many islands, and white people have come from nearly every country in Europe. The bulk of these live in Australia and New Zealand. The majority are of British origin, but Australia, which is in general still very thinly populated, is at present encouraging immigration from other countries.

A Polynesian family on Samoa watching dancers at a celebration. Polynesians are fond of singing and dancing, which they have developed to a fine art.

Sydney, Australia's largest city and leading port, has one of the world's finest natural harbours.

COUNTRIES AND CITIES OF THE PACIFIC

Many countries have had a hand in ruling the islands of the Pacific. Today most of them are controlled by the United States, Great Britain, and France, but some are administered by Australia and New Zealand, who also claim nearly half of Antarctica.

Australia and New Zealand are fully independent members of the British Commonwealth. Until this century the Australian continent was divided into five British colonies, with the island of Tasmania as a sixth. In January 1901, these six colonies were federated to become the six states of the Common-wealth of Australia. You may be surprised to hear of the *six* states of Australia when the map of Australia is divided into seven setions. This is because the largely uninhabited Northern Territory is not a state. It is governed by an administrative and legislative council and allowed to send one member to the House of Representatives. Although he could take part in debates, he has only had full voting rights since 1968.

Australians are predominantly towns-folk. Less than a third of the population live in the country. The towns, moreover, are growing all the time as people move

Courtesy of Australian News and Information Bureau

Melbourne is Australia's second largest city. As a port it serves a rich farming area.

away from the country or arrive as immigrants from Europe.

Mechanical farm equipment makes it possible for fewer people to grow Australia's crops. At the same time industry is continually growing, and industry is usually concentrated in large towns because there is a constant supply of labour and a market for the produce.

Half the people of Australia live in the six capitals of the states of the Commonwealth, and a third of the total

Canberra, Australia's capital since 1927, is a modern, well-planned city with fine houses and gardens.

Dick Hanley - Photo Researchers

Sydney has one of the world's finest natural harbours. Both Sydney and Melbourne have all the equipment of first-class commercial ports. Both of them have industries producing goods for local consumption. Their principal exports are wool, meat, hides, and wheat.

However, the capital of Australia is

Ralph Luce - Shostal

Suva, capital of the Fiji Islands, is a regular port of call for shipping lines and also a centre of island trading.

Courtesy of the New Zealand Travel Commission

Wellington, New Zealand, where British traditions are strong. Traffic keeps to the left as it does in the British Isles.

population live in the cities of Sydney and Melbourne alone.

Of the great cities of the Southern Hemisphere, Sydney and Melbourne in Australia rank fifth and sixth, after Buenos Aires, São Paulo, Santiago and Rio de Janeiro. They both have populations of more than 2 million.

neither the great city of Melbourne nor Sydney. The capital is Canberra, beautifully situated on high ground within a circle of wooded hills. When it was chosen in 1909 it was little more than a hamlet, but the population has risen to well over 90,000 and the town is still developing.

New Zealand has few large towns. Nevertheless the four largest of them, Wellington, Auckland, Christchurch, and Dunedin, contain more than a third of the population. Auckland is the largest and it is the country's leading seaport. The first Europeans to settle in the country founded Auckland in 1841. Well-

Martin S. Klein

Sheep graze on this wooded hillside overlooking Auckland, New Zealand's chief town and port.

ington, the capital, is the third largest town and it too is a seaport of some importance.

There are few real towns in the Pacific Islands, and not one of them could be called big. The largest is Suva, the capital of the Fiji Islands, which is on the island of Viti Levu, the largest of the group. It has a fine sheltered harbour, and most ships crossing the Pacific call there. Passenger ships call for fresh provisions and other supplies, while cargo ships load with sugar and copra. The population is only 54,000, but there is a medical school where native doctors are trained.

The only real town in the whole of Eastern Polynesia is Papeete on the French island of Tahiti, yet its population is only 22,000. Most of the larger business houses in Papeete are operated by Europeans, but there are many Chinese shopkeepers in the town. Nearly a fifth of the population is Chinese.

Tahiti's lush green mountains rise behind the harbour of Papeete, the capital of France's Pacific island territories. The exports are copra, vanilla, phosphates, and mother-of-pearl.

Heron Island, part of the Great Barrier Reef, is a popular Australian tourist resort.

Tasmania, Australia's island state, is separated from the mainland by the 150-mile-wide Bass Strait.

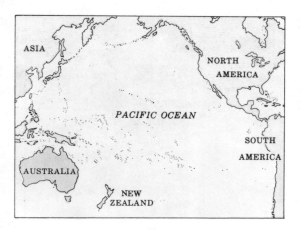

A desolate, dry plateau — about, 1,500,000 square miles — covers the western half of Australia.

AUSTRALIA, THE ISLAND CONTINENT

Until recently, Australia was one of the least known parts of the world. This is not altogether surprising considering its remoteness and the fact that it is little more than 350 years since Australia was discovered. The first European settlement in Australia was not made until 1788. Excluding the primitive aborigines, Australia is the most recently inhabited continent in the world. Physically, though, it may well be the oldest of all of the continents. Rocks have been discovered in the north-west of the island which are believed to have been above water for 1,600 million years. The aboriginal population, too, is an old one. Some of these Stone Age people are believed to have been living in Tasmania as long as 30,000 years ago.

Australia is the lowest of all the continents. The average elevation is less than 1,000 feet, and only one-seventeenth of the entire continent is over 2,000 feet. The highest peak, Mount Kosciusko, is only 7,328 feet above sea-level. The principal highland areas are the Great Dividing Range in the east and the vast plateau of Western Australia.

The first European settlements were made on the east coast. A few miles inland the Great Dividing Range raises its mountain barrier. It is not a high range, but it is not easily crossed, and it was not till 1813 that the first European settlers found their way to the other side.

George Leavens - Photo Researchers

Cattle and sheep graze on the well-watered uplands of New South Wales and Victoria.

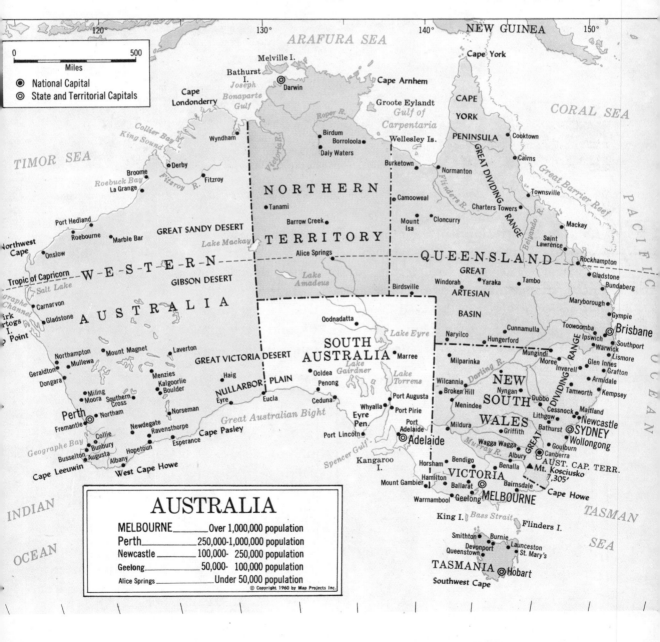

C. R Twidale

The Nullarbor Plain of South Australia is a 300-mile stretch of barren sand, rock, and sparse vegetation.

On the western slopes of the mountains the settlers found good country for growing wheat. The soil was fertile, and rainfall, though not abundant, was sufficient both for wheat and mixed farming. Further west the grassy plains of New South Wales seemed ideal for grazing sheep. To the north in tropical Queensland, the grazing proved suitable for cattle, despite the long winter drought.

As the settlers pushed on further to the west, the country became much drier. Beyond the Darling River, less than 500 miles from the coast, the grass became

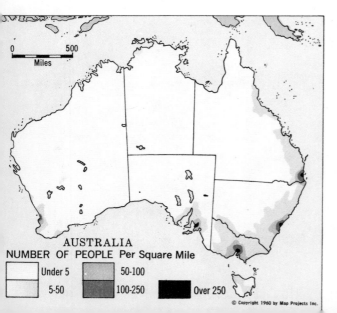

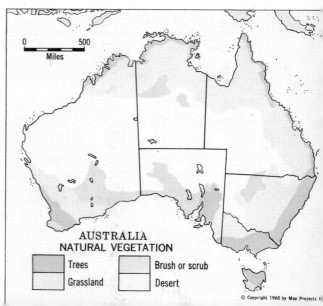

thinner and thinner, and soon the settlers were forced to face the disappointing fact that the interior of their land of promise was a desert.

The population map tells you the story as plainly as the map of natural vegetation. The interior of Australia, like the Sahara, is a vast area of emptiness. The bulk of the country's population lives in the south-eastern coastal region, where rainfall is adequate. Another populated district, though a much smaller one, is in the south-west, which has a Mediterranean-type climate.

Only one railway crosses Australia from east to west, and it avoids the interior of the country. A narrow gauge railway runs up to Alice Springs in the interior, but goes no further. From there on, to Port Darwin on the north coast, the journey has to be made by road.

Roads naturally concentrate round the chief towns. Most of these are seaports, however, and much of the traffic between them goes by sea.

In few countries of the world is air travel more important than in Australia. The population is only about $12\frac{1}{2}$ million, and the towns are far apart. The world-famous Flying Doctor Service brings medical attention to people living in the most remote areas.

The natural vegetation of Australia is strongly influenced by the prevailing temperature and rainfall. The most common tree is the evergreen eucalyptus. Of this tree there are over 400 species, ranging in size from the giants of the rainy south-eastern uplands, which rise to a height of 200 feet, to the dwarfed bushlike forms of the dry interior. Another common tree is the acacia. In the deserts there are bushes and tough, spiny grasses.

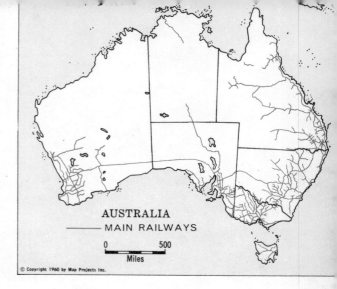

AUSTRALIA
MAIN RAILWAYS
0   500
Miles
© Copyright 1960 by Map Projects Inc.

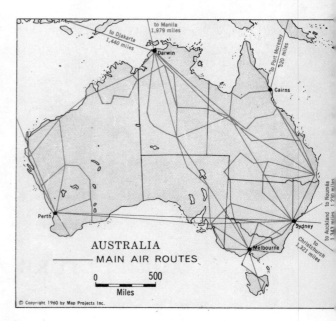

to Djakarta 1,440 miles   to Manila 1,979 miles   to Port Moresby 320 miles

Darwin

Cairns

Perth

Sydney

to Noumea 1,330 miles
to Auckland 1,343 miles
to Christchurch 1,321 miles

Melbourne

AUSTRALIA
MAIN AIR ROUTES
0   500
Miles
© Copyright 1960 by Map Projects Inc.

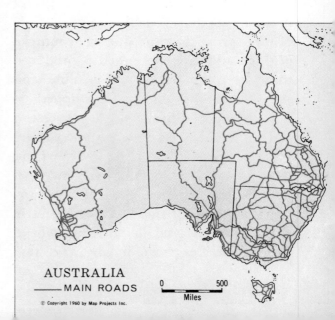

AUSTRALIA
MAIN ROADS
0   500
Miles
© Copyright 1960 by Map Projects Inc.

Sidney Press - Shostal

Ninety-five per cent of Australia's sugar cane is grown on the tropical coastal plain of Queensland.

AGRICULTURE AND RANCHING

We have seen that only a small part of Australia is suitable for farming, yet it is big enough to make Australia one of the great food-producing countries of the world. Far more food is produced than the Australians could possibly consume, and the surplus is shipped to England and other countries overseas.

The rolling plains of Australia are particularly suitable for growing wheat, which can withstand the heat and does not demand a great deal of moisture. Two-thirds of all the cultivated land in the country is used for growing wheat. Wheat can be grown in any area that receives a minimum of 12 inches of rain a year, though more is desirable. With that rainfall the yield is often only five or six bushels per acre, while with 20 inches of rain, thirty bushels may be harvested. With still more rain, the yield may be even higher. The average yield for the whole country is about 16 bushels per acre. This is slightly lower than the average in the United States and Canada, and Argentina, three of the other leading wheat producers.

The dry weather in summer is a great help to Australian farmers. The grain ripens well on the stalk, and the wheat can be harvested and threshed in one operation. Recently nearly 200 million bushels of wheat were harvested in a single season.

Some of the wheat farms are very large indeed, and farming is highly mechanised. With proper equipment, one or two men can manage hundreds of acres. Only about a third of the wheat produced is for home consumption, the remainder being exported.

The north-eastern State, Queensland, is largely within the tropics and tropical crops are grown. Sugar-cane was first planted there nearly 100 years ago. At first, workers were brought in from some of the Pacific islands, but later this was stopped. Nowadays all the heavy work of growing and harvesting sugar-cane is done by the Australians themselves. More sugar is grown than is needed for home consumption, and most of the surplus is shipped to New Zealand.

Australia has fine orchards and vineyards. Millions of bushels of apples are grown in Victoria, Western Australia, and Tasmania. A considerable amount is shipped to Europe, where they are marketed from March to June, at a time when no European apples are available, except those kept in cold storage. This reversal of the seasons in the two hemi-

Birnback

A Tasmanian apple orchard in bloom. Refrigerated ships enable Australia to export fruit to Europe.

Birnback

Hot, dry summers make the irrigated Murray River Valley a leading grape-growing district.

spheres helps the Australians to get good prices in Europe for their produce. In some years the vineyards produce nearly half a million tons of grapes. More than half are used for making wine, while most of the remainder are dried for sale as raisins, sultanas, or currants.

All this produce comes from slightly over a hundredth part of the total area of Australia.

We get a more typical picture of Australia, however, when we leave the arable and general farming of the coastal

Australia's wheat farmers use machinery for ploughing, planting, and harvesting.

Courtesy of Australian News and Information Bureau

Australian stockmen inspect a 'mob' of Merinos on a sheep station in New South Wales.

belt and turn westwards to the 'outback', the ranching country that extends far into the interior and reappears on the other side of the desert in Western Australia. The outback is the home of the great sheep ranches of Australia, known locally as stations. Some sheep stations on the drier pastures of the outback cover many thousands of acres.

Stations in the outback are often many miles apart, and the people who live on them keep in touch with their neighbours by radio. Lessons are broadcast for children who live hundreds of miles from the nearest school.

The first European settlers brought a few sheep with them when they arrived at Botany Bay, on the east coast of Australia. Nowadays, in a good year, the number of sheep in Australia exceeds 163 million. Three-quarters are Merinos, famous for their fine wool. The rest are crossbreds, reared for meat and wool.

Nearly half the sheep in Australia are reared in New South Wales. Most of the remainder are found on stations in south Queensland, Victoria, the coastal parts of South Australia, and Western Australia.

Shearing time is anxiously awaited by the sheep-breeders, for that is when the crop of wool can be estimated. Shearing is done at different times in different parts of Australia. It begins in April in Queensland, and by October has reached New South Wales. Shearing is very skilled work. The shearers travel across the country in groups called shearing gangs. The variations in the shearing periods give them time to move across the country from station to station and from state to state.

When the shearers arrive, the sheep are herded into narrow pens. They pass the shearers one by one and each is sheared in a matter of minutes. Each sheep yields

Dick Hanley - Photo Researchers

Australian sheep shearers use mechanical clippers to remove the heavy fleece.

about nine pounds of wool, and an expert shearer can clip 150 sheep a day. Australia is the leading wool-producing country in the world. Altogether Australia produces about 1,000 million pounds of wool each year which is more than a quarter of the world's total wool production.

In the vast, sparsely populated plain of the Northern Territory are some of the world's largest cattle ranches. One of them alone covers 12,686 square miles.

Getting cattle to market is a real problem in the Northern Territory. Many stations are hundreds of miles from a railway, to reach which the cattle have to be herded on long drives. These drives take weeks or even months, for the cattle can only travel ten or twelve miles a day or they will lose a lot of weight.

The Northern Territory is still what is known as pioneer country. Almost everything has still to be developed. But the rewards are great for those who know how to conquer the loneliness and rigours of pioneer life.

Cowboys drive a herd of beef cattle near Alice Spring, an oasis in dry Northern Territory.

Courtesy of Australian News and Information Bureau

Where forest cover has been removed, rainstorms leave deep gullies in the earth.

A windmill pumps water for irrigation in the dry outback near Alice Springs.

THE PROBLEMS OF THE LAND

So dry is the ranching country of Australia that at times the sheep and cattle are in acute need of water. During a dry year flocks and herds may have to be reduced by as much as a quarter, and even then millions may still die of thirst. At one time, long ago, Australia had a drought that lasted ten years, during which the flocks were reduced by half. When the drought finally came to an end, it took thirty years to rebuild the flocks to their original strength.

Looking at a map of Australia, one gets the impression there is far more water than there is. The rivers shown on the map are, in fact, often dry. In South Australia there are great lakes like Lake Eyre and Lake Torrens, but they are really only depressions which fill with water on rare occasions after it has rained, but which at other times are completely dry and covered with a glistening layer of salt. In Western Australia the big lakes, Lake Austin, Lake Macdonald, and Lake Mackay, are dry most of the year.

Fortunately some portions of Australia have large stores of underground water which can be reached by drilling deep wells, or 'bores' as they are called in Australia.

Thousands of bores have been drilled, too many perhaps, for in some parts of Australia so much underground water has been drawn off that the supply has diminished. More water must be found and more economical ways of using it be discovered if Australia is to continue to supply the world with large quantities of wool and meat.

Like farmers in many other parts of the world, Australians are learning by experience that they must take better care of their land. The wheat farmers, for instance, for many years ploughed up the soil west of the Great Dividing Range. Then came a time of drought. The covering of grass that once held the soil in place was gone and the soil began to blow away. Great clouds of dust swirled over the countryside. Once gone, this wind-blown soil could never be recovered. Australian farmers are at present at work devising new methods of tilling their land to prevent the same thing happening again.

Plants and animals, too, provide problems for the farmers. Great damage was caused at one time by the prickly pear, which is a kind of cactus. Settlers brought some prickly pears with them when they came to Australia more than a hundred years ago. By 1920 the plants had spread over 60 million acres of good grazing land. So thickly did they cover the ground that no grazing was possible. Finally in 1925 an insect called *Cactoblastis*, which kills prickly pears, was introduced from Argentina. Within a few years more than half the ruined land was again available for grazing.

The stock-breeders' worst enemy however, is the rabbit. There are millions of rabbits in Australia, and they eat the grass and brush on which the sheep graze. The rabbit was introduced by settlers, who brought it in just for the pleasure of hunting it. Since then the Australians have worked hard to get rid of their rabbits. As many as 25 million have been killed in a single year and thousands of miles of fences have been built to keep rabbits out of good pastures.

Artesian bores tap underground water supplies. Overuse makes many wells run dry each year.

New hope came a few years ago with the introduction of the rabbit disease, myxomatosis. In the first year it killed three-quarters of all the rabbits in Australia. Those that survied, however, built up a resistance to the disease, and it now looks as though Australians have not yet rid themselves of the rabbit pest.

Kangaroos are also something of a pest. They, too, feed on grass, and in their case, building fences will never keep them off grazing ground, for they can leap twenty feet into the air. Unfortunately a demand has grown up for kangaroo hides and meat and as a result they have been hunted so extensively that the species is now threatened with extinction.

A solitary acacia tree and barren red sand: a typical Australian desert scene.

A heavy dredge bringing up huge quantities of gold-bearing mud in New South Wales.

MINERAL RESOURCES

In 1849 men went from all over the world to the newly discovered gold fields of California. Two years later another gold rush started, this time on the other side of the Pacific, in Australia.

The first gold was discovered in New South Wales. Soon afterwards, still richer

A zinc refinery at Hobart, Tasmania.

deposits were discovered in Victoria. Within ten years the population of Australia had increased five-fold.

Gold is mined in every Australian state and territory. Gold worth hundreds of millions of pounds has been mined in Victoria alone. But today the great gold mining state is Western Australia, and the chief centre is Kalgoorlie in the Coolgardie gold-fields.

Australia is one of the leading countries in the production of lead and zinc, and the mines at Broken Hill in the dry western part of New South Wales are among the greatest in the world. After being worked for nearly eighty years the deposits are far from being exhausted. Recently large nickel deposits have been discovered in Western Australia.

Australian copper mines can produce enough to satisfy home consumption.

Small amounts of tin are also mined. But far more important than either of these two metals are the great deposits of coal and iron ore, for it is these that have formed the basis of Australia's development as a manufacturing country.

For many years Australia had to depend on imported manufactured goods. Because of the distance from Britain and the other manufacturing countries, the cost of those imports was very high. Now, with coal and iron of her own available, Australia is able to manufacture for herself.

The most important coal-fields are in eastern New South Wales which produces four-fifths of all the coal mined in the country.

The iron mines are centred at Iron Knob, which is a few miles inland from Spencer Gulf in South Australia. The ore is taken by rail to docks at Whyalla. From there it is shipped to the blast furnaces of Newcastle and Port Kembla.

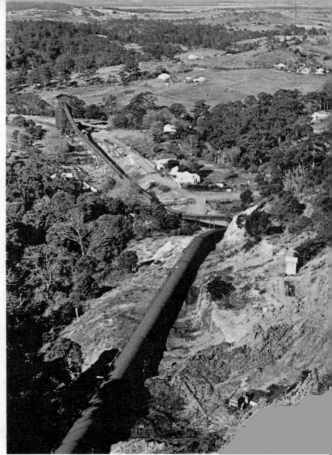

Fritz Goro - Monkmeyer

Coal is pulverised and pumped with water through this pipeline to the steelmaking centre of Port Kembla.

Iron ove is unloaded at Port Kembla's docks. Railway trucks carry the ore to the steel plants.

Birnback

A few years ago some new iron mines were opened in the neighbourhood of Yampi Sound on the north-west coast of Australia. Yampi Sound is 3,200 miles further by sea from Newcastle than is Whyalla. These new deposits assure Australia of a continuing supply of iron ore.

Coal is the chief, in fact almost the only, source of power. For in this country of limited rainfall there are few reliable sources of water-power, and oil and natural gas supplies are limited. If nuclear power is developed, it will have the benefit of the important uranium fields that have been discovered. Ore from these fields is refined at Port Pirie, in South Australia.

A steel plant at Port Kembla. Australia's steel industry employs about 25,000 men.

THE GROWTH OF AUSTRALIAN INDUSTRY

This factory produced the first cars to be made entirely in Australia.

The two World Wars greatly affected the development of industry in Australia. During the First World War, Australia was cut off from overseas supplies of manufactured goods. This gave a great incentive to the expansion of the iron and steel industry.

The situation in the Second World War was somewhat different, for this time the war had come to the Pacific. There was a time when Australia feared invasion, and the factories set to work urgently, manufacturing guns, ships, and aircraft. The electrical, chemical, and engineering industries grew rapidly. By

1945 Australia had really become an industrial country.

At present a third of all the Australian labour-force is employed in manufacturing industries. The value of the manufactured goods produced is actually greater than that of all the produce of the land and the mines put together, though agricultural produce makes up the bulk of exports.

The chief manufacturing states are New South Wales and Victoria, and industry has concentrated in the towns along the coast. Raw materials come by ship, or by rail from the outback. By ship again go the exported finished products. The towns provide manpower for the factories and in many cases a local market.

The most important Australian industries are meat-packing, fruit-processing, and flour-milling. Australian iron and steel are used to make farming implements and machinery, Australian copper for electrical equipment. In some

George Leavens - Photo Researchers

Australian farms supply food-processing plants like this one, where soup is made.

cases goods are assembled in Australia from parts manufactured in Britain or America, as with most Australian cars.

Australia's chief export is wool, most of which is shipped from Sydney: more than a million bales every year. Most of the other exports are the produce of the land (food, wine, etc.) or of the mines. Most manufactures are for home use.

Fat being removed from wool. When refined it makes lanolin, a valuable by-product.

Bill Brindle - Photo Researchers

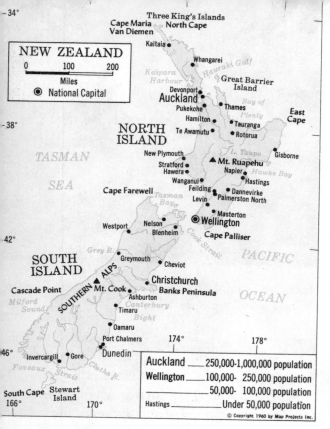

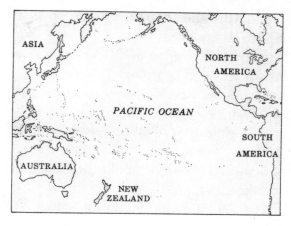

NEW ZELAND

The Dominion of New Zealand consists of two large islands and several small ones. Altogether they have an area of slightly more than 100,000 square miles, which is a little more than the area of Great Britain and Northern Ireland. But the population is only about 2½ million.

Australia and New Zealand are often coupled together, but in many ways they are utterly dissimilar. Australia is relatively flat, New Zealand mountainous; Australia is on the whole a dry country, New Zealand a very rainy one, which, when first discovered, was thickly forested. The aboriginal populations of the two countries are also very different — the Maoris of New Zealand having a much higher culture than the aborigines on the Australian continent.

On the whole, New Zealand has a cool, maritime climate. On the western side of the mountains, which receive warm, westerly winds, the climate is similar to that of the south coast of Ireland. On the other side of the mountains it is much drier. Snow and frost are rare on both islands, but the southern portion of South Island has cooler winters.

South Island has high, rugged mountains, running the whole length of the island and completely filling up the centre. The highest peak is Mount Cook,

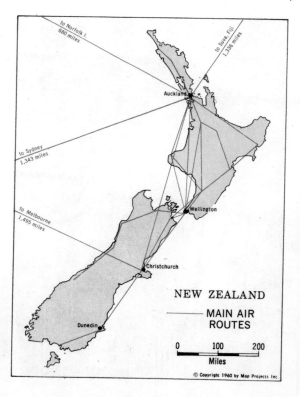

NEW ZEALAND

MAIN AIR ROUTES

0   100   200
Miles

Forest-clad mountains look down on Doubtful Sound in Fiord County, South Island, New Zealand.

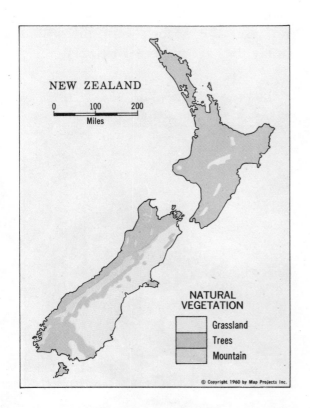

NEW ZEALAND

0   100   200
Miles

NATURAL
VEGETATION

☐ Grassland
☐ Trees
☐ Mountain

© Copyright 1960 by Map Projects Inc.

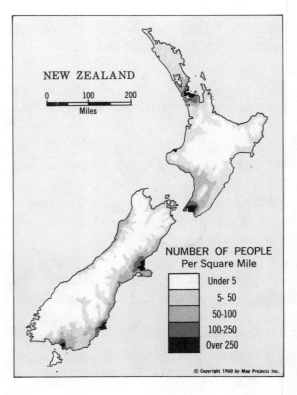

NEW ZEALAND

0   100   200
Miles

NUMBER OF PEOPLE
Per Square Mile

☐ Under 5
☐ 5- 50
☐ 50-100
☐ 100-250
☐ Over 250

© Copyright 1960 by Map Projects Inc.

which is over 12,000 feet above sea-level. Altogether South Island has seventeen peaks over 10,000 feet.

The south-western corner of South Island is called Fiord County, because of the many deep fiords that have been scoured out of the rocks by former glaciers. These beautiful fiords, together with the mountains, lakes, and wonderful snowy slopes for skiing, make South Island popular with tourists.

The mountains of North Island are not so high as those of South Island, but they are interesting for their active volcanoes and many hot springs.

For many ages New Zealand, like Australia, was cut off from any other land. However, unlike Australia, New Zealand is not rich in animal life. There are some species of plants and animal which are endemic, but most animals were introduced by Europeans. The most famous animals are the flightless birds, particularly the kiwi. Another, now extinct, was the moa, an ostrich-like bird which grew to a height of twelve feet.

New Zealand's only land mammal is the bat. Some of the animals introduced by the Europeans have become pests. Rabbits have caused much damage, and deer browse on pastures meant for sheep, and eat tree saplings.

Turning to plants, some interesting trees are the giant tree-fern and the rimu, totara, and kauri trees, which are valuable for their timber.

The first European to sight New Zealand was Abel Tasman, the greatest of the Dutch navigators, from whom Tasmania derives its name. He sailed along the coast of New Zealand in 1642, but it was almost 200 years before Europeans came to settle in any number in the country. The majority of these settlers came from Great Britain.

At first the native Maoris welcomed the settlers. Later they rose against them, and many years of fierce, though often extraordinarily chivalrous, fighting followed. Eventually the war came to an end, and the Maoris kept their land. Today they are respected citizens.

Volcanic peaks, some so high that they are snow-covered, surround Lake Wanaka on South Island.

Rupert Leach - FPG

A Maori mother bathes her son in one of the volcanic hot springs on North Island.

McKelzie - Shostal

A typical New Zealand farm, among rolling fields. Most New Zealand farms are family-owned.

THE PRODUCE OF THE LAND

New Zealand's abundant rainfall and mild all-year temperatures have produced some of the finest pasture in the world. On them graze pure-bred sheep and dairy cattle whose produce has made the country prosperous.

The farmlands of North Island are largely devoted to grazing. The dairy farms of North Island produce milk of the finest quality, while the province of Hawkes Bay is generally regarded as the finest sheep country in the world.

The quality of the grazing land of New Zealand is not due to natural conditions alone. The farmers themselves deserve much of the credit for it. They have planted the best grasses, fed the soil with fertilisers and lime, and taken constant care that no pasture should be over-grazed.

South Island has a larger area of farming country and here farming is more mixed. Wheat and fruit are grown and many vegetables, but the rearing of livestock is in no way neglected.

So mild is the climate that neither cattle nor sheep require shelter. They can be left to graze in the open all the year round.

Dairy herds are not of great size. Most dairy farmers have about fifty cows. There are nevertheless nearly 6 million head of cattle in the country.

The number of sheep is even greater, There are 50 million of them. They are not the Merinos reared on the dry Australian outback. The rich meadows of New Zealand make it more profitable to rear fat lambs — the Canterbury lamb we buy in our butcher's shops. Nevertheless, 10 per cent of the total wool production of the world comes from New Zealand.

With so much produce from the land,

Rupert Leach - FPG

New Zealand's mild, moist climate and rich grass-lands are ideal for raising high-quality sheep.

Katherine Tweed Robertson - Monkmeyer

Shocks of wheat dot the fields of New Zealand at harvest time.

it is only to be expected that many of the factories of New Zealand are engaged in processing food: meat, butter cheese,

Rupert Leach - FPG

Trained dogs are used on New Zealand's cattle and sheep ranches to help herd the animals.

processed milk, and other dairy products.

New Zealand is the world's greatest exporter of lamb and cheese, and it is second only to Denmark in the export of butter. The country rose to this position at the beginning of this century when refrigeration plants began to be installed in ships, making it possible to send food to every part of the world. Britain is New Zealand's most important customer.

In the export of wool, New Zealand ranks second only to Australia. Altogether, animal produce — meat, wool, hides, and dairy produce — make up more than 90 per cent of her exports. Auckland lies to the north of the rich Waikato dairy region, and in it some of the country's dairy produce is processed, making it one of the chief industrial towns. With the country's great forests, the lumber trade is naturally important, and timber exports are considerable.

OTHER INDUSTRIES

About one-fifth of the working population of New Zealand works in factories. They are not all engaged in food processing, but the other products are chiefly for home consumption. The manufacture of clothing and woollen cloth and the milling of flour have long been important industries. Newer industries are the assembly of motor-cars from parts made in other countries (usually in Europe and the United States), printing, paper-making, and the manufacture of chemicals and fertilisers.

The country's mineral resources are varied but not large. There are deposits of coal and gold on both North and

Water from melting glaciers drives the Roxbrough hydro-electric power station on South Island.

South Island, and on the latter, iron is mined. Other mineral products include mercury, manganese, tin, platinum, silver, tungsten, and oil. A steel plant on South Island uses local ore and coal. The chief mineral export is gold.

New Zealand's coal would soon be exhausted by industrial and domestic use if water-power was not freely used. The many mountain streams, fed by a large and regular rainfall, mean that building hydro-electric power-stations is easy, and electricity is plentiful and cheap. Natural gas from the North Island is piped to Auckland and Wellington for domestic use.

It is only logical to assume that, as the population of New Zealand increases, so too will the number and size of the manufacturing industries.

Government re-forestation schemes are doing much to stop soil erosion, and maintain the supply of timber.

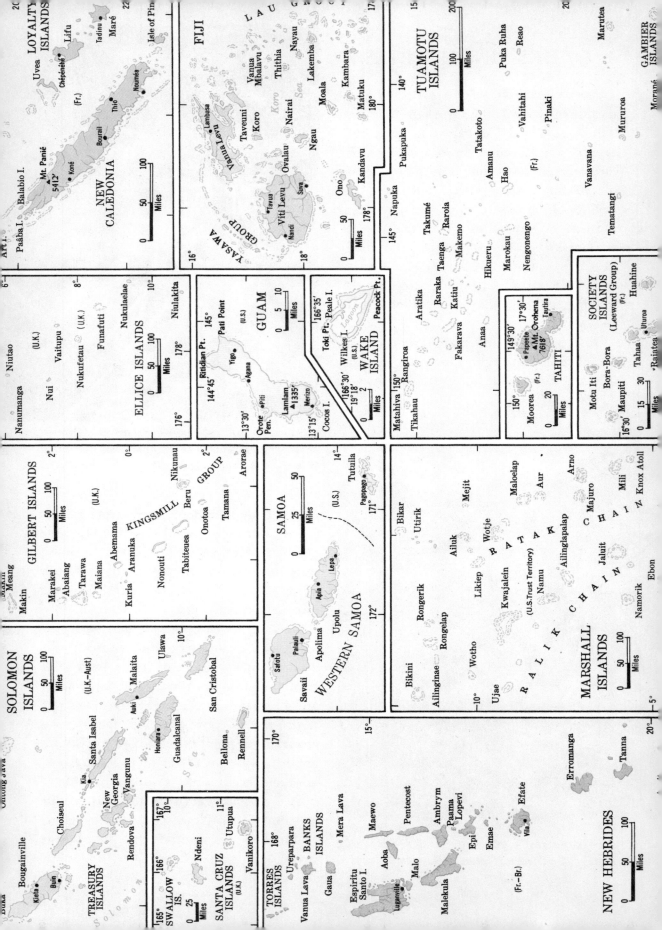

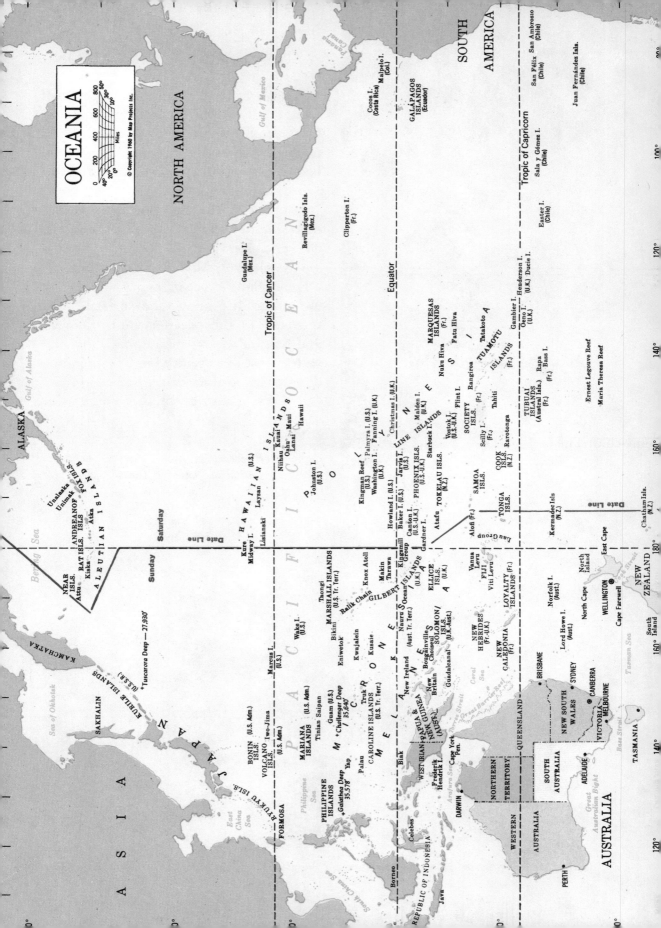

OCEANIA

Miles
0 200 400 600 800
© Copyright 1960 by Map Projects Inc.

NORTH AMERICA

SOUTH AMERICA

ASIA

ALASKA

AUSTRALIA

NEW ZEALAND

PACIFIC OCEAN

ISLANDS

MELANESIA

MICRONESIA

POLYNESIA

Tropic of Cancer

Equator

Tropic of Capricorn

Date Line

Date Line

Saturday

Sunday

THE PACIFIC ISLANDS

A vast area of water, tiny specks of land: that is the picture presented by Oceania. Scattered so widely, the islands naturally show us a great variety of landscape, people, vegetation, and, of course, animals.

Looking at the map you will see that most of the islands appear in clusters. These clusters usually occur where the sea is relatively shallow. From that relatively shallow ocean floor the peaks of mountains rise above the surface — for the floor of the ocean is quite uneven, and has folded into mountains, hills, and valleys, just like the dry land. Some of the depressions are very deep, and they are called troughs or deeps. Any area over

Craggy rock formations reveal the volcanic origin of Moorea, one of the Society Islands.

Rugged mountains and palm-clad shores are a frequent sight on volcanic islands like Huahine.

Katherine Tweed Robertson - Monkmeyer

Coconut palms shade the thatch-roofed huts of Nandi, a typical Fijian village.

3,000 fathoms (18,000 ft.) in depth is called a deep. The deepest of all is a strip just to the east of the Philippine Islands, in which a depth of 6½ miles has been recorded. In other words it is a mile deeper than Mount Everest, the world's highest mountain, is high.

Some of the islands rise high out of the Pacific. In Western New Guinea, for instance, there are peaks that tower more

Herbert Knapp

Samoan boys learn how to handle outrigger canoes at a very early age.

Frank Newton - FPG

This aerial view shows clearly the coral reefs surrounding a typical South Pacific atoll.

than 15,000 feet above sea-level. These peaks are topped by perpetual ice and snow, despite the fact that New Guinea lies just south of the Equator. Of course few islands are high enough to be snow-capped, though there are many fine moutains with craggy peaks. At the other extreme, some islands are so low on the horizon that, as you approach them, the coconut trees seem to be growing out of the sea. These are the coral islands or atolls.

Herbert Knapp

Sleek, swift canoes like this one are both a necessity and a source of pleasure to Polynesian islanders.

LIFE ON THE ISLANDS

On the whole the life of the coral islanders is simple. Their wants are few.

From the air, the atolls look like tiny beads of coral strung round a reef-enclosed lagoon. The quiet water of the lagoon provides a safe harbour for the islanders' outrigger canoes, and a good supply of fish.

At night the islanders wade out into the still water of the lagoon, some carrying torches. Fish are attracted by the torch light, and as soon as they appear, a net is thrown across the water and men, women and children all help to drag it in.

The islanders farm as well as fish, though the soil of the atolls is poor, and only a few plants will grow. The most important is the coconut. The flesh of the coconut contains an oil and is highly nourishing; so is the milk. On some waterless atolls coconut milk is the islanders' only drink.

The coconut palm plays a very big part in the life of these people. Not only does it supply them with food and drink

These natives of Maupiti, in the Society Islands, are netting fish in the shallow lagoon.

Ralph Luce - Shostal

The stone traps in this lagoon are 200 years old. Fish are driven into the traps and then netted.

This Samoan father is teaching his young son how to spear fish with the traditional wooden spear.

Fish are wrapped in leaves, cooked over white-hot stones, and then eaten with the fingers.

488

Herbert Knapp

After the coconuts are picked, they are cracked open. The meat is then prised from the shell and spread out to dry in the sun. Dried coconut meat, called copra, is a valuable export.

but the hollow shell becomes a flask, a cup, or the material for carved ornaments. The fibre of the husk is spun into cord. The trunk of the tree is used as building material and for making furniture, while the broad leaves can be used as thatch or for making baskets. The coconut palm is indeed almost a universal provider.

It also provides copra, which is an important article of commerce. Copra is the dried flesh of the coconut, from which the oil is pressed to make margarine, salad oil, fine soaps, and cosmetics.

Preparing copra for shipping is one of the most important occupations on the atolls. The coconuts are opened and the flesh is scraped out of the shell and spread out to dry in the sun. This sun-

dried copra is clean, and thus more valuable than the darker, smoke-dried copra of the high, rainy islands.

Here and there among the coconut palms are banana and breadfruit trees, or a small patch of taro — a plant with a starchy root that forms an important

This island boy has climbed the trunk of a coconut palm and is now selecting nuts to pick.

Herbert Knapp

Ralph Luce - Shostal

Watermelons, grown on the low coral island of Maupiti, find a ready market in nearby Tahiti.

Ralph Luce - Shostal

The taro grows best if it is planted in fertile, swampy soil.

part of the diet of the coral islanders.

A few pigs and chickens wander in and out of the palm-thatched huts. Fish from the lagoon, and bonito and tunny fish caught in the open sea, provide most of the proteins that the islanders ever get.

Even the appearance of modern developments like the aeroplane and the radio have not profoundly changed this simple way of life.

Herbert Knapp

The island boys soon learn how to split open a coconut with one stroke of their knives.

Herbert Knapp

Selected stalks of taro are replanted in the plantations, to ensure a good crop in future.

THE RESOURCES
OF THE
PACIFIC ISLANDS

When European traders began coming to the islands, they found the people still living in the Stone Age. When the traders displayed their wares, the islanders were anxious to acquire them but the problem was: what could they give in exchange? It was the traders who found the answer: they discovered gold, nickel, bauxite, and chromium. Sometimes the native islanders were engaged to work in the mines, but more often foreign labour was brought in from China, Java, or Japan. For one thing, the rough life and hard work of mining did not appeal to the islanders. In general the islanders gained very little from these mining operations.

Some of the most important of the

Herbert Knapp

Along with copra, bananas are a major Samoan export. They grow well on many Pacific islands.

Richard Harrington - Annan Photo Features

This train carries workers to the fields of a large sugar plantation on Viti Levu, Fiji.

mining operations were those on the 'guano islands'. Guano, as we saw when we were dealing with Peru, is a valuable fertiliser, consisting of phosphates formed of birds' droppings. The life of the guano diggers was hard and lonely. The best deposits were found on barren, treeless rocks where there was no protection from the sun. Almost all supplies came by ship and the food was often poor. The men often became sick and many died. As soon as the deposits were worked out, the islands were abandoned to the sea birds, who had been, of course, responsible for the deposits in the first place.

Two islands are especially important sources of phosphates. They are Ocean Island and Nauru, where there are some of the world's richest phosphate deposits, vital to the farmers of Australia, New Zealand, and Japan.

Far more important than mining, however, are the plantations. Coffee, cocoabeans, citrus fruits, bananas, pineapples, and cotton are all produced.

The Fiji, Hawaiian, and Mariana islands have enormous sugar plantations. The introduction of sugar-cane has brought great changes to these islands. Thousands of Asians were brought in to work on the plantations, and, even where the plantations have been abandoned, many of them have remained and now live side by side with the islanders.

More sugar than copra is produced in Oceania. But the production is concen-

Elvajean Hall

Fijian copra is boxed at a company plantation and then shipped overseas from the port of Suva.

trated in a few places, while the coconut is important almost everywhere. In some places the coconut palm, too, is grown on plantations. Sometimes these are small and privately owned. But on the Solomon and Fiji islands, and in New Guinea, copra is produced on a large scale, the plantations being owned by companies. Regardless of how it is produced, copra is a very important product to nearly all the people of Oceania.

A schooner unloads cattle at Tahiti. These boats carry most of the islands' freight.

Ralph Luce - Shostal

Courtesy of Australian News and Information Bureau

Cheap electricity derived from water-power is attracting new industries to Tasmania.

THE FUTURE OF OCEANIA

Elvajean Hall

Children in Fiji learn to read in an outdoor classroom. Today all Fijian children go to school.

What does the future hold for Australia and New Zealand and the thousands of Pacific islands? On many parts of the Pacific many places have already acquired a new importance. Islands that a few years ago were so isolated that they hardly ever saw a visitor, are now provided with landing strips and refuelling bases for aircraft. The air services of the Pacific are destined to become more and more important with the development of communications between North America, Australia, and Asia.

Australia and the 'continental' islands

contain some very ancient crystalline rocks in which mineral deposits are occasionally found. Sedimentary rocks (those formed by the building up of sediment deposited on the sea bottom) are also found in this region, and sometimes contain oil, so that besides the valuable minerals that have for years been mined in the Pacific, there are now a few oilfields being exploited both in New Guinea and Australia.

More minerals are almost certain to be discovered in the continental islands, and for them the future is particularly promising. Also, the people of this area have hardly begun to exploit their resources of fish. Echo-sounding equipment will help fishermen to detect large shoals, and improved methods of preparing tropical fish for marketing will certainly be developed. Quick-freezing, packing, and

George Leavens - Photo Researchers

The workers at this New Guinea plywood factory fly back to their village in the evening.

A new house being built on one of the Society Islands. Concrete is gradually replacing bamboo and thatch.

Ralph Luce - Shostal

floating tinning factories will do a lot to develop the industry.

Australia and New Zealand have from the first looked to Great Britain for their market. As the standard of living improves in South-East Asia and elsewhere, they will no doubt find many fresh markets near at hand. In fact Japan is Australia's biggest customer.

In the past Australia and New Zealand have been too distant from the great centres of population to attract many tourists. Yet they have many attractions: Australia's Great Barrier Reef, the fiords, snow-capped peaks, and lovely mountain lakes of New Zealand, and the coral beaches of the Pacific islands. In the future the development of fast, cheap, air travel will bring Oceania more within reach of holidaymakers.

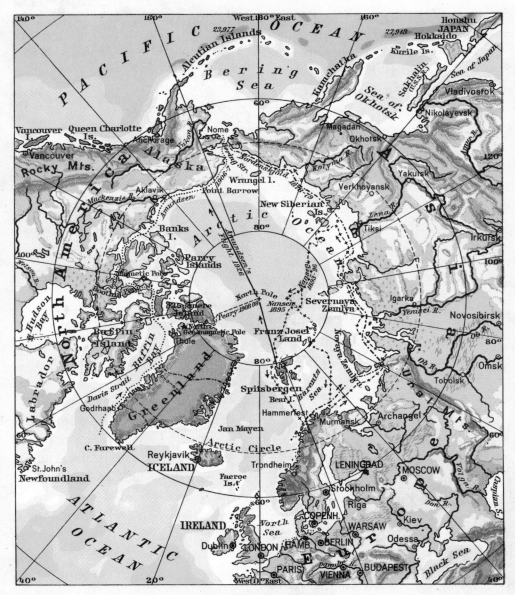

ARCTIC REGIONS

Scale 1:60,000,000

0   500   1000 Miles

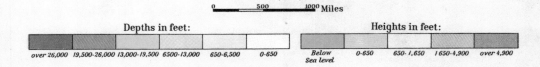

Depths in feet:

| over 26,000 | 19,500-26,000 | 13,000-19,500 | 6500-13,000 | 650-6,500 | 0-650 |

Heights in feet:

| Below Sea level | 0-650 | 650-1,650 | 1650-4,900 | over 4,900 |

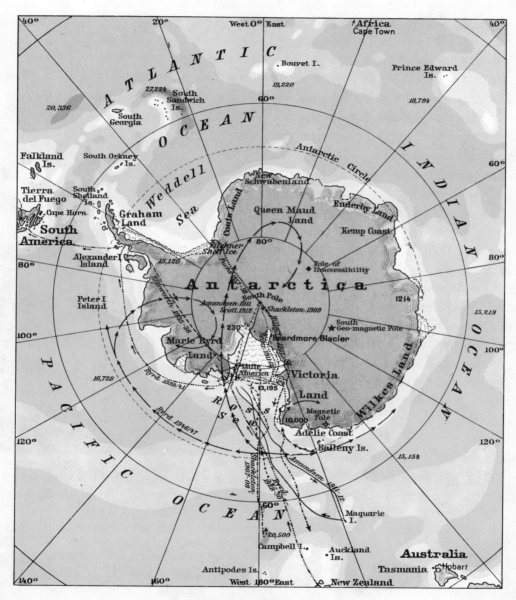

ANTARCTICA

Scale 1:60,000,000

0   500   1000 Miles

Depths in feet:

over 26,000	19,500–26,000	13,000–19,500	6,500–13,000	650–6,500	0–650

Heights in feet:

Below Sea level	0–650	650–1,650	1 650–4,900	over 4,900

THE POLAR REGIONS

An imaginary line called the Arctic Circle is drawn on the globe in latitude 66° 30' north. Within that circle lies the Arctic, one of the two polar regions. In the southern hemisphere, a similar line is drawn in latitude 66° 30' south. You may wonder why the lines should be drawn in those particular latitudes. The answer is that within those circles the sun never sets on midsummer's day, this being the phenomenon often called the midnight sun. Similarly, within those circles, the sun never rises in the middle of winter. The deeper you go into the polar regions, the longer is the period of continual daylight in summer and continual darkness in winter.

The chief characteristic of the polar regions is of course the extreme cold. The average temperature is below freezing point all the year round, so that ice and snow never melt. At the South Pole, a temperature of 101°F below zero has been recorded.

To such an extent do ice and snow dominate the landscape of the two polar regions that we often fail to realise how very different they really are. The Arctic is a 'hollow', a deep ocean basin. The Antarctic is a great mass of high land, which is in fact a continent, called Antarctica. Larger than Europe, this continent covers an area of more than 5 million square miles. Its average height

Joe Barnell - Shostal

The midnight sun lights up the sky over Narvik fjord, Norway, north of the Arctic Circle.

Vast snow-covered plateaus and towering mountains characterise Antarctica's frozen landscape.

Elmo Jones

This huge iceberg was once part of a glacier. The hole in it was carved by an underground river in the glacier.

of over 5,000 feet is higher than that of any other continent. The Arctic Ocean is about as deep as the Antarctic continent is high.

The land surrounding the Arctic Ocean has been inhabited — even if very thinly — for at least 1,000 years by sturdy Eskimos who live by hunting and fishing. No human being has ever made a home in Antarctica.

A herd of walruses sun themselves on the rocky Alaskan coast. These warm-blooded animals spend most of their lives in the water. Eskimos hunt them for their meat, blubber, hides, and valuable ivory tusks.

ANIMAL LIFE

The Arctic is rich in animal life. There are great herds of reindeer in northern Europe and Asia, while the caribou, the North American reindeer, roams the Arctic plains of that continent. A peculiar animal found in North America and in Greenland is the musk ox. Standing five or six feet high at the

Penguins live in colonies in the Antarctic. Their wings have turned into flippers, and they are powerful swimmers.

shoulder, in some ways it is half-way between an ox and a sheep. It has a long shaggy coat, reaching almost to the ground, which enables it to withstand the coldest Arctic winter.

Wolves and foxes sometimes follow reindeer, caribou, or musk ox, attacking stragglers from the herd.

But the best known of all the Arctic animals is the polar bear, which feeds on all sorts of marine animals from fish to seals and walruses.

Both birds and insects are found in great numbers on the land within the Arctic Circle. Millions of birds fly north each year to nest there during the summer months, and there is plenty of food for all as swarms of mosquitoes and flies hatch in the pools of stagnant water that collect on the Arctic plain in summer.

The Antarctic is a complete contrast to this. A tiny wingless mosquito is the only land animal, and it is only found in a few sheltered areas of Antarctica.

There are no land mammals at all, and the continent itself has no birds. The famous Antarctic penguins live on the pack ice around the edges of the continent, near the only source of food — the sea. Penguins are sea birds. They have adapted themselves so that their wings have become large flippers. They are superb swimmers and divers, but are, of course, completely flightless, and rather awkward on land.

The Arctic and Antarctic differ also in their plants. In the Antarctic, only a few mosses and lichens and hardy grasses grow on the rocky, ice-free slopes that catch the sun. Most of Antarctica is buried beneath a mantle of snow and ice, often more than 10,000 feet thick.

Summer months in the Arctic are less cold than in the Antarctic, though temperatures are not high enough for trees to grow. This treeless region in the

A polar bear cub prowls over an Arctic ice floe searching for food.

Arctic is called the tundra. But in summer, the tundra bursts into bloom. Travellers are often amazed to find beautiful meadows of rich mosses and flowering lichens within the Arctic Circle. The tundra is fine summer grazing land for reindeer, caribou, and the musk ox. Even in winter these animals can paw through the snow to find food on the tundra. This area is also the home of Arctic hares and lemmings.

The caribou, wild cousin of the European reindeer, ranges the North American tundra in search of lichens and grass. The caribou is a principal source of food for the Indians and Eskimos of the far north.

William W. Bacon - Rapho Guillumette

When a whale is killed, whole families of Eskimos with their dog teams go to bring the meat home.

LIFE IN THE ARCTIC

Nowhere in the inhabited world is life so hard as in the Arctic. The only people who have succeeded in making a permanent home there are the Eskimos. People of other races come on to the tundra in summer, driving their herds of reindeer. But when the winter closes in they move back to the more friendly forests further south.

The Eskimos live all along the extreme north of north-eastern Siberia, North America, and Greenland. Their total number has been estimated at 50,000.

Gambell, on St Lawrence Island off the Alaskan coast, is a typical modern Eskimo village.

Russ Kinne - Photo Researchers

Ages ago the Eskimos learned how to live in the Arctic. Since it was impossible to grow crops in the frozen soil of the tundra, they became skilled hunters and fishermen. Seals were their chief quarry, providing almost all their food. Seal skins were made into clothing, tools and implements from the bones, and seal oil could be used for fuel and light.

The threat of starvation was always present in the Arctic. By experience the Eskimos learned that if they killed too many seals in one place their source of food would be gone. Therefore they moved frequently to new hunting grounds.

They travelled on dog sleighs over the frozen surface of the sea, or the snow-covered tundra. The most well-known Eskimo boat is the one-man kayak, but for travelling in summer and for whale hunting the Eskimos preferred the larger umiak.

Today only in a few isolated places do Eskimos still live like their ancestors. For most Eskimos the old ways of life are changing rapidly. Contact with Americans and Europeans is causing these changes.

Fur traders started some of the changes in the Eskimos' way of life. To help them kill more seals, fur traders gave the Eskimos rifles, which were, naturally, much more effective than the traditional harpoon and bow-and-arrow.

Using their new rifles the Eskimos, at first, easily secured great supplies of seal meat and furs. But they killed too many seals. Soon no seals were to be found in the old, familiar hunting places. And with the seals gone, the Eskimos had nothing to trade and nothing to eat. In

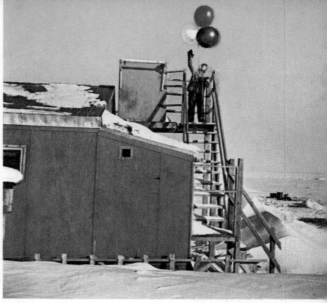

Releasing weather balloons at Thule, Greenland, one of the world's most northerly weather stations.

some parts of the Arctic, whole villages of Eskimos starved.

Some Eskimos have completely changed their way of life. They have given up all of the ways of their ancestors. The children go to school. Some Eskimos have become radio operators and pilots; others teachers and skilled mechanics. Probably no people on earth have changed their

Brightly patterned sweaters made by Eskimos in Greenland.

As penguins play in the foreground, a ship passes through a fog bank beneath towering Antarctic ice peaks.

way of life so rapidly as the Eskimos.

In Greenland, which is administered as a county by Denmark, many Eskimos have left their igloos and kayaks. They fish from motor-boats and have moved into fishing villages of wooden houses on the coast. The south-western coast is the most settled. The interior is a vast ice plateau surrounded by peaks and glaciers. In the north-east there is a vast Arctic desert with very little but ice. Even in the brief summer, temperatures very rarely rise above freezing point.

If we ignore the desolate icebound South Shetland Islands, Antarctica is a very isolated continent. The tip of South America, the nearest of the other continents, is about 1,000 miles away.

This great continent was almost unknown until modern times, much of it is still unexplored. That is not surprising for it is no easy task to approach the continent by ship. Sometimes great belts of pack-ice extend for hundreds of miles beyond the coast, and even the open seas

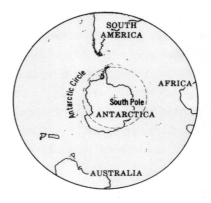

themselves are dangerous. Rough and stormy, they are also beset by drifting ice and giant icebergs. The coast of Antarctica itself is flanked by towering cliffs of ice, fifty to 200 feet high. Therefore it is hardly surprising that most of the exploration of Antarctica had to wait until suitable aircraft were developed, which could land men and equipment direct on to the continent.

Thrust up beneath the Antarctic ice-cap are some of the world's great mountain ranges. In Graham Land are peaks that rise more than 10,000 feet, while near the Ross Ice Shelf, the mountains can tower 15,000 feet above sea-level.

Eastern Antarctica is a high plateau. Geologists say that its composition is much like that of the African plateau. Since the latter is rich in minerals, they are inclined to think that great mineral wealth may well lie beneath the Antarctic ice-cap.

However this is not easy to substantiate, for it is extremely difficult to study rocks buried beneath thousands of feet of ice. But in a few places there are rocks that outcrop the ice, and these have been found to contain coal, copper, nickel, and some other minerals.

However, no large or particularly valuable deposits have been discovered and even if they were, the problems of mining under polar conditions would be great. Moreover, the transport of even the most valuable minerals to any market would probably be far more costly than they were worth. Therefore, Antarctica is unlikely to become a great mining centre in the foreseeable future.

The first men to be drawn towards the Antarctic were those who went for whaling. Whaling ships were sailing in the Antarctic as long ago as 1820. In those days whales were attacked with harpoons, hand-thrown from the ship's boats. Nowadays, whaling has been mechanised. Harpoons are fired from harpoon-guns mounted on the whaler itself. The whalers are accompanied by giant factory ships. As soon as two or three whales are caught, they are towed to a factory-ship where they are hoisted on board and dealt with. Almost every part of the whale's carcass has some value. The most important product is whale oil, which is extracted chiefly from the blubber, the layer of fat under the skin. Some of the flesh goes into cold storage to be used as whale meat, while the bones are crushed up into bonemeal, a valuable fertiliser.

So efficient did modern whaling methods become that it looked at one time as though whales would be completely exterminated. In order to prevent this strict regulations were drawn up to

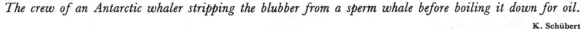

The crew of an Antarctic whaler stripping the blubber from a sperm whale before boiling it down for oil.

K. Schübert

National Academy of Sciences - IGY Photo

This observation tower at 'Little America' is part of an Antarctic weather station.

in reaching the Pole was a Norwegian Roald Amundsen, who reached it by a swift dash on skis, hoisting his country's flag over the Pole on 14 December, 1911. Meanwhile on 6 April, 1909, an American, Robert E. Peary, had reached the North Pole.

In recent years many scientists have gone to the Antarctic, building scientific stations, both on the continent and the surrounding islands. One of their aims is to discover the influence of this great frozen continent on the weather in other parts of the world, an influence which is believed to be considerable. Other scientists have been measuring the depth of the ice-cap, studying rock formation, and measuring the flow of off-shore ocean currents.

Surveying has also been proceeding, the work being greatly helped by aerial photography. This work has been done by many nations, scientific stations having been established by the United States and the U.S.S.R., Britain, and many others.

restrict whale-fishing. It is confined to certain months of the year; no young whale may be killed; and there is a limit to the total number that may be captured.

It was not until this century that explorers set out to cross Antarctica to reach the South Pole. There were several attempts, but the first man to succeed

An aeroplane is unloaded for use in Operation Deep-freeze, an Antarctic exploration project.

Dick Dempewolff - Monkmeyer

This titanium mine in Greenland exploits one of the barely touched mineral resources of the polar lands.

THE FUTURE OF THE POLAR REGIONS

So far man has done nothing to change the natural landscape of either the Arctic or the Antarctic. It is hard to believe that he will ever be able to do so. Even where quite large communities have been established, they are dug into the snow and virtually invisible from the surface. Small populations will no doubt go on living in the Arctic, but it is difficult to see how a population could maintain itself in Antarctica. The number of scientific teams working in the Antarctic and which are maintained from outside, will probably increase, and important work is likely to be done there (making Antarctica the only continent to be used solely as a laboratory). However, it is hoped by many people that eventually the separate national research teams will give up their competing claims and merge together in a common effort directed by the United Nations, or some other international authority.

The outlook in the Arctic is different. Valuable minerals like uranium have already been discovered within the Arctic Circle. The day will come when these minerals are wanted, as the more accessible sources become used up. In the future small mining communities may well be established, scattered across the Arctic. As things are at present, the provision of heat and power for the men working in them would be a very serious problem, but before long nuclear reactors will be more generally available, and they will provide the ideal solution.

NOTE In this Atlas we have tried to present a fair and balanced picture of the world, its countries, and its peoples. We have not stressed the divisions that occur, because the future well-being of the peoples of the world depends on what unites, not on what divides them.

All people, whatever their race, colour, religion, or political beliefs, have one thing in common: they are all citizens of one world. The well-being of one is the well-being of all.

FACTS AND FIGURES

EUROPE

PRINCIPAL COUNTRIES: AREA, POPULATION

COUNTRY	AREA IN SQ. MILES	POPULATION
Sweden	173,430	7,766,424
Norway	125,100	3,802,204
Denmark	16,576	4,849,191
Finland	130,100	4,701,000
Iceland	39,750	199,920
Great Britain and N. Ireland	94,250	55,283,000
Ireland (Eire)	26,600	2,912,000
Belgium	11,799	9,605,601
Netherlands	13,025	12,661,095
Luxembourg	998	335,234
France	212,660	50,600,000
West Germany	95,300	60,000,000
East Germany	41,700	17,090,000
Austria	32,500	7,349,000
Switzerland	15,944	6,147,000
Spain	194,945	32,411,407
Portugal	35,400	9,335,400
Italy	116,270	54,463,000
Greece	51,182	8,610,000
Poland	120,759	32,060,000
Czechoslovakia	49,370	14,271,547
Hungary	35,912	10,236,000
Yugoslavia	98,900	20,154,000
Albania	11,800	2,000,000
Romania	91,700	19,540,000
Bulgaria	42,796	8,309,000
Turkey (in Europe)	23,500	2,655,768
Soviet Union	8,599,600	237,000,000

Budapest (Hungary)	1,990,000
Athens (Greece)	1,852,709
Hamburg (W. Germany)	1,832,560
Istanbul (Turkey)	1,743,000
Barcelona (Spain)	1,697,102
Vienna (Austria)	1,688,000
Milan (Italy)	1,670,000
Kiev (U.S.S.R.)	1,476,000
Bucharest (Romania)	1,414,643
Copenhagen (Denmark)	1,377,605
Lisbon (Portugal)	1,334,775
Warsaw (Poland)	1,276,000
Stockholm (Sweden)	1,262,000
Munich (W. Germany)	1,244,237
Naples (Italy)	1,228,000
Baku (U.S.S.R.)	1,224,000
Gorki (U.S.S.R.)	1,139,000
Brussels (Belgium)	1,079,181
Birmingham (Britain)	1,075,000
Berlin, East (E. Germany)	1,074,000
Prague (Czechoslovakia)	1,030,000
Marseilles (France)	964,412
Glasgow (Britain)	961,000
Sofia (Bulgaria)	859,000
Amsterdam (Netherlands)	857,635
Belgrade (Yugoslavia)	843,209
Kazan (U.S.S.R.)	837,000
Helsinki (Finland)	679,000
Dublin (Eire)	620,554
Oslo (Norway)	484,275
Zürich (Switzerland)	432,500
Belfast (N. Ireland)	398,405

*These are the figures for the conurbation, not for the city alone.

PRINCIPAL TOWNS

TOWN	POPULATION*
Paris (France)	8,196,746
London (Britain)	7,763,820
Moscow (U.S.S.R.)	6,590,000
Leningrad (U.S.S.R.)	3,752,000
Madrid (Spain)	2,866,728
Rome (Italy)	2,630,535
Berlin, West (W. Germany)	2,163,306

HIGHEST MOUNTAINS

MOUNTAIN	HEIGHT IN FEET
Mount Communism (U.S.S.R.)	24,590
Lenin (U.S.S.R.)	23,380
Elbruz (U.S.S.R.)	18,540
Klyuchevskaya (U.S.S.R.)	15,912
Mont Blanc (France)	15,780
Monte Rosa (Italy)	15,217
Weisshorn (Switzerland)	14,800

Matterhorn (Switzerland — Italy)	14,780
Gross Glockner (Austria)	12,450
Mulhacen (Spain)	11,421
Aneto (Spain)	11,168
Olympus (Greece)	9,750

GREAT RIVERS

RIVER	LENGTH IN MILES
Lena (U.S.S.R.)	2,800
Amur (U.S.S.R.)	2,700
Yenisei (U.S.S.R.)	2,430
Ob (U.S.S.R.)	2,260
Volga (U.S.S.R.)	2,250
Danube (Western and Eastern Europe)	1,770
Ural (U.S.S.R.)	1,530
Dnieper (U.S.S.R.)	1,420
Rhine (Switzerland — France— Germany — Holland)	850
Elbe, (Western and Eastern Europe)	720
Loire (France)	628
Ebro (Spain)	575
Rhône (France)	505
Seine (France)	482
Po (Italy)	420

INLAND SEAS AND LAKES

SEA OR LAKE	AREA IN SQUARE MILES
Caspian Sea (U.S.S.R.)	169,380
Aral Sea (U.S.S.R.)	25,400
Baikal (U.S.S.R.)	12,670
Ladoga (U.S.S.R,)	7,100
Balkhash (U.S.S.R.)	6,900
Onega (U.S.S.R.)	3,800
Wener (Sweden)	2,480
Peipus (U.S.S.R.)	1,400
Geneva (France — Switzerland)	225
Constance (Switzerland, Austria, Germany)	208

ASIA

PRINCIPAL COUNTRIES: AREA POPULATION

COUNTRY	AREA IN SQ. MILES	POPULATION
Turkey (in Asia)	295,000	30,660,000
Lebanon	4,000	2,179,000
Israel	8,000	2,737,900
Jordan	37,000	2,105,000
Yemen	75,000	5,000,000
Iraq	171,600	8,634,000
Syria	71,229	5,634,000
Saudi Arabia	770,000	7,100,000
Bahrein	230	182,203
Kuwait	5,990	468,389
Muscat and Oman	82,000	750,000
Southern Yemen (Aden)	108,000	1,500,000
Iran	630,000	25,781,000
Afghanistan	250,000	16,111,000
India	1,259,000	523,893,000
Pakistan	365,529	109,520,000
Ceylon	25,300	11,700,000
Nepal	54,000	9,500,000
Bhutan	18,000	800,000
Burma	262,000	26,390,000
Thailand	198,456	33,693,000
Khmer Rep. (Cambodia)	67,000	6,500,000
Laos	91,450	2,825,000
North Vietnam	63,000	20,700,000
South Vietnam	66,281	17,100,000
China	3,760,000	730,000,000
Mongolia	1,750,000	1,120,000
Taiwan (Nationalist China)	13,885	13,297,000
Hong Kong	398	3,927,000
North Korea	47,000	13,000,000
South Korea	37,000	31,207,000
Japan	142,000	101,000,000
Philippines	114,834	34,660,000
Indonesia	575,890	118,000,000
Malaysia	127,281	8,676,658

PRINCIPAL TOWNS

TOWN	POPULATION*
Tokyo (Japan)	11,005,000

Shanghai (China)	10,700,000
Peking (China)	10,000,000
Bombay (India)	4,903,000
Calcutta (India)	4,765,000
Tientsin (China)	4,000,000
Hong Kong (Br. Crown Colony)	3,927,000
Lu-ta (China)	3,600,000
Osaka (Japan)	3,133,000
Canton (China)	3,000,000
Jakarta (Indonesia)	2,906,000
Delhi (India)	2,874,000
Teheran (Iran)	2,803,130
Karachi (Pakistan)	2,721,000
Bangkok (Thailand)	2,318,000
Wuhan (China)	2,146,000
Chungking (China)	2,121,000
Singapore (S.E. Asia)	1,956,000
Nagoya (Japan)	1,954,000
Yokohama (Japan)	1,954,000
Madras (India)	1,927,000
Baghdad (Iraq)	1,745,000
Lahore (Pakistan)	1,674,000
Harbin (China)	1,600,000
Sian (China)	1,500,000
Saigon-Cholon (South Vietnam)	1,485,000
Pusan (South Korea)	1,429,726
Nanking (China)	1,419,000
Manila (Philippines)	1,402,000
Kyoto (Japan)	1,379,000
Hyderabad (India)	1,328,000
Kobe (Japan)	1,288,000
Taipei (Taiwan)	1,221,112
Surabaya (Indonesia)	1,008,000
Bandung (Indonesia)	973,000
Pyongyang (North Korea)	940,000
Hanoi (North Vietnam)	850,000
Quezon (Philippines)	502,000
Cabul (Afghanistan)	456,000
Tel Aviv-Jaffa (Israel)	388,000
Jerusalem (Israel)	332,300
Amman (Jordan)	330,220
Kuala Lumpur (Malaysia)	316,000
Mecca (Saudi Arabia)	250,000
Katmandu (Nepal)	195,000
Ulan-Bator (Mongolia)	195,000
Vientiane (Laos)	162,000
Lhasa (Tibet)	40,000

*These are the figures for the conurbation, not for the city alone.

HIGHEST MOUNTAINS

MOUNTAIN	HEIGHT IN FEET
Everest (Nepal — Tibet)	29,028
K2-Godwin Austen (India)	28,250
Kanchenjunga (Nepal — Sikkim)	28,150
Makalu (Nepal — Tibet)	27,790
Cho Oyu (Nepal — Tibet)	26,867
Ararat (Turkey)	16,945
Kinabalu (Borneo)	13,455
Fujiyama (Japan)	12,395

GREAT LAKES

LAKE	AREA IN SQ. MILES
Urmia (Iran)	2,300
Koko Nor (China)	2,300
Hamun-i-Helmand (Afganistan-Iran)	2,000
Van (Turkey)	2,000
Tungtin (China)	1,450
Tonlé Sap (Cambodia)	770 (max)

LONGEST RIVERS

RIVER	LENGTH IN MILES
Yangtze Kiang (China)	3,400
Hwang Ho (China)	2,900
Mekong (China — Thailand)	2,600
Indus (India)	1,900
Brahmaputra (India)	1,800
Amur (China — Burma)	1,770
Salween (China — Burma)	1,750
Euphrates (Turkey — Syria — Iraq)	1,700
Ganges (India)	1,560
Irrawaddy (Burma)	1,300
Tigris (Turkey — Iraq)	1,150

AFRICA

PRINCIPAL COUNTRIES: AREA, POPULATION

COUNTRY	AREA IN SQ. MILES	POPULATION
Morocco	171,388	14,100,000
Algeria	878,160	12,102,000
Tunisia	48,332	4,460,000
Libya	679,203	1,564,000
Egypt	386,110	30,907,000
Sudan	967,500	14,979,000
Chad	485,750	3,400,000
Niger	449,400	3,330,000
Mali	448,200	4,700,000
Mauritania	449,800	1,200,000
Senegal	75,750	3,500,000
Gambia	4,000	315,486
Guinea	94,927	3,500,000
Sierra Leone	27,925	2,475,000
Liberia	43,000	1,290,000
Ivory Coast	124,510	3,840,000
Upper Volta	113,100	5,278,000
Ghana	91,842	8,400,000
Nigeria	356,669	62,600,000
Togo and Dahomey	21,500	3,900,000
Democratic Republic of the Congo	905,380	16,000,000
Cameroun	183,570	5,350,000
Gabon	103,089	480,000
Congo Republic	132,100	900,000
Central African Republic	238,220	1,466,000
Rwanda	10,166	3,300,000
Burundi	10,747	3,000,000
Ethiopia	395,000	23,900,000
Somalia	246,200	2,745,000
Kenya	224,960	9,948,000
Uganda	93,891	7,750,000
Tanzania	362,180	12,926,000
Malagasy	229,975	6,776,000
Republic of South Africa	472,685	20,000,000
Zambia	290,323	4,144,000
Angola	481,300	5,000,000
Rhodesia	150,333	4,740,000
Malawi	46,066	4,285,000

PRINCIPAL TOWNS

TOWN	POPULATION*
Cairo (Egypt)	4,220,000
Alexandria (Egypt)	1,801,000
Johannesburg (South Africa)	1,300,000
Casablanca (Morocco)	1,177,000
Algiers (Algeria)	943,000
Cape Town (South Africa)	807,000
Tunis (Tunisia)	764,000
Lagos (Nigeria)	665,000
Durban (South Africa)	662,847
Ibadan (Nigeria)	627,000
Addis Ababa (Ethiopia)	560,000
Kinshasa (Dem. Rep. of Congo)	508,000
Nairobi (Kenya)	479,000
Dakar (Senegal)	474,000
Pretoria (South Africa)	423,000
Salisbury (Rhodesia)	330,000
Oran (Algeria)	328,000
Port Said (Egypt)	283,000
Marrakesh (Morocco)	264,000

*These are the figures for the conurbation, not for the city alone.

HIGHEST MOUNTAINS

MOUNTAIN	HEIGHT IN FEET
Kilimanjaro (Tanzania)	19,565
Kenya (Kenya)	17,040
Ruwenzori (Dem. Rep. of Congo)	16,795
Ras Dashan (Ethiopia)	15,160
Elgon (Kenya)	14,178
Bale (Ethiopia)	14,131
Guna (Ethiopia)	13,881
Gughe (Ethiopia)	13,780
Toubkal (Morocco)	13,665
Talo (Ethiopia)	13,451
Cameroun (Cameroun)	13,350

LARGEST LAKES

LAKES	AREA IN SQ. MILES
Victoria (Central Africa)	26,828
Tanganyika (Central Africa)	12,700
Nyasa (Central Africa)	11,000
Chad (Central Africa)	8,000
Rudolf (Central Africa)	3,500
Albert (Central Africa)	2,064
Tana (Central Africa)	1,400
Leopold II (Central Africa)	900

GREAT RIVERS

RIVER	LENGTH IN MILES
Nile (Northern and Central Africa)	4,150
Congo (Central Africa)	2,900
Niger (Central Africa)	2,600
Zambezi (Southern Africa)	1,600
Ubangi-Uélé (Central Africa)	1,400
Orange (Southern Africa)	1,300
Kasai (Central Africa)	1,100
Limpopo (Southern Africa)	1,000
Okovanggo (Southern Africa)	1,000

NORTH AMERICA

PRINCIPAL COUNTRIES: AREA, POPULATION

COUNTRY	AREA IN SQ. MILES	POPULATION
Canada	3,851,113	20,857,000
U.S.A.	3,557,098	201,166,000
Mexico	760,373	47,267,000
Nicaragua	57,145	1,842,000
Cuba	44,206	8,073,000
Honduras	43,227	2,413,000
Guatemala	42,042	4,864,000
Panama	28,571	1,372,000
Costa Rica	19,695	1,640,000
Dominican Republic	19,303	4,029,000
Haiti	10,714	4,674,000
British Honduras	8,867	114,255
El Salvador	8,259	3,266,000

PRINCIPAL TOWNS

TOWN	POPULATION*
New York (U.S.A.)	11,400,000
Los Angeles (U.S.A.)	6,789,000
Chicago (U.S.A.)	6,732,000
Mexico City (Mexico)	5,584,000
Philadelphia (U.S.A.)	4,690,000
Detroit (U.S.A.)	4,060,000
Boston (U.S.A.)	3,201,000
San Francisco (U.S.A.)	2,958,000
Washington D.C. (U.S.A.)	2,615,000
Montreal (Canada)	2,436,817
Pittsburg (U.S.A.)	2,376,000
St Louis (U.S.A.)	2,284,000
Toronto (Canada)	2,158,496
Cleveland (U.S.A.)	2,004,000
Baltimore (U.S.A.)	1,980,000
Houston (U.S.A.)	1,740,000
Havana (Cuba)	1,544,000
Milwaukee (U.S.A.)	1,331,000

*These are the figures for the conurbation, not for the city alone.

HIGHEST MOUNTAINS

MOUNTAIN	HEIGHT IN FEET
Mount McKinley (Alaska)	20,320
Logan (Canada)	19,850
Orizaba (Mexico)	18,700
St Elias (Alaska — Canada)	18,008
Popocatepetl (Mexico)	17,887
Ixtacihautl (Mexico)	17,342
Foraker (Alaska)	17,280
Lucania (Canada)	17,150
Steele (Canada)	16,439
Bona (Alaska)	16,420
Sanford (Alaska)	16,208
Blackburn (Alaska)	16,140
Wood (Canada)	15,880
Whitney (California)	14,495

LARGEST LAKES

LAKE	AREA IN SQUARE MILES
Superior (Canada — U.S.A.)	31,820
Huron (Canada — U.S.A.)	23,010
Michigan (U.S.A.)	22,400
Great Bear (Canada)	12,000
Great Slave (Canada)	11,170
Erie (Canada — U.S.A.)	9,940
Winnipeg (Canada)	8,555
Ontario (Canada — U.S.A.)	7,540
Nicaragua (Nicaragua)	3,100
Athabaska (Canada)	3,066
Winnipegosis (Canada)	2,086
Manitoba (Canada)	1,817

GREAT RIVERS

RIVER	LENGTH IN MILES
Missouri (U.S.A.)	2,714
Mackenzie (Canada)	2,514
Mississippi (U.S.A.)	2,350
St Lawrence (Canada — U.S.A.)	2,350
Yukon (Canada — U.S.A.)	1,979
Rio Grande (U.S.A. — Mexico)	1,800
Arkansas (U.S.A.)	1,450
Colorado (U.S.A. — Mexico)	1,400
Ohio (U.S.A.)	1,306
Red (U.S.A.)	1,300
Saskatchewan (Canada)	1,205
Columbia (U.S.A.)	1,200
Peace (Canada)	1,054
Snake (U.S.A.)	1,038

SOUTH AMERICA

PRINCIPAL COUNTRIES: AREA, POPULATION

COUNTRY	AREA IN SQ. MILES	POPULATION
Guyana	83,000	710,000
Guiana, French	34,800	44,330
Surinam	55,100	400,000
Venezuela	352,100	9,686,000
Colombia	439,600	19,800,000
Ecuador	106,200	5,580,000
Peru	496,200	12,000,000
Chile	286,400	9,750,000
Argentina	1,084,100	23,600,000
Uruguay	72,200	2,780,000
Brazil	3,287,700	88,200,000
Bolivia	421,400	4,900,000
Paraguay	157,000	2,243,000

PRINCIPAL TOWNS

TOWN	POPULATION*
Buenos Aires (Argentina)	7,000,000
São Paulo (Brazil)	5,325,351
Rio de Janeiro (Brazil)	3,800,000
Santiago (Chile)	2,451,000
Bogota (Colombia)	2,148,000
Lima (Peru)	1,834,000
Caracas (Venezuela)	1,764,000
Montevideo (Uruguay)	1,200,000
Belo Horizonte (Brazil)	1,092,000
Recife (Brazil)	1,056,000
Medellin (Colombia)	921,000
Porto Alegre (Brazil)	889,000
Salvador (Brazil)	863,000
Rosario (Argentina)	672,000
Guayaquil (Ecuador)	652,000
Maracaibo (Venezuela)	559,000
La Paz (Bolivia)	482.637

*These are the figures for the conurbation, not for the city alone.

HIGHEST MOUNTAINS

MOUNTAIN	HEIGHT IN FEET
Aconcagua (Argentina)	23,835
Ojos del Salado (Argentina — Chile)	22,550
Tupungato (Argentina — Chile)	22,312
Huascarán (Peru)	22,205
Tocorpuri (Chile — Bolivia)	22,182
Llullaillaco (Argentina — Chile)	22,146
Mercedario (Argentina)	21,878
Yerupaja (Peru)	21,760
Incahuasi (Argentina — Chile)	21,720
Tres Cruces (Argentina — Chile)	21,720
Illampú (Bolivia)	21,490
Sajama (Bolivia)	21,390
Illimani (Bolivia)	21,185
Antofalla (Argentina)	21,129
Chimborazo (Ecuador)	20,577

LARGEST LAKES

LAKE	AREA IN SQUARE MILES
Maracaibo (Venezuela)	6,300
Titicaca (Bolivia — Peru)	3,200
Poopó (Bolivia)	970
Buenos Aires (Argentina)	865
Argentino (Argentina)	546
Mar Chiquita (Argentina)	450
Viedma (Argentina)	420
Colhué Huapi (Argentina)	310
Llanquihue (Chile)	240
Nahuel Huapí (Argentina)	210

GREAT RIVERS

RIVER	LENGTH IN MILES
Amazon (Andes — Brazil)	3,900
Madeira (Brazil)	2,100
Parana (Brazil — Paraguay — Argentina)	2,050
São Francisco (Brazil)	1,800
Orinoco (Venezuela)	1,700
Tocantins (Brazil)	1,640
Araguaia (Brazil)	1,630
Pilcomayo (Bolivia — Paraguay)	1,550
Negro (Brazil)	1,400
Paraguay (Brazil — Paraguay)	1,300
Juruá (Brazil)	1,250
Tapajóz (Brazil)	1,250
Xingú (Brazil)	1,230
Magdalena (Colombia)	1,000
Uruguay (Brazil — Uruguay)	1,000

OCEANIA

PRINCIPAL COUNTRIES: AREA, POPULATION

COUNTRY	AREA IN SQ. MILES	POPULATION
Australia	2,971,081	12,173,000
New Guinea	304,200	2,778,000
New Zealand	103,740	2,781,000
Polynesia		
Cook Is.	89	20,000
Ellice Is.	9	7,000
Marquesas Is.	492	5,147
Samoa	1,211	134,000
Society Is.	650	48,900
Tokelau Is.	6	2,000
Tonga Is.	270	81,000
Tuamotu	330	6,664
Micronesia		
Caroline Is.	461	40,800
Gilbert Is.	100	46,453
Mariana Is.	370	10,986
Marshall Is.	70	18,998
Nauru	8	6,056
Melanesia		
Bismarck Archipelago	19,200	163,300
Fiji Is.	7,036	476,727
New Caledonia	8,560	99,902
New Hebrides	5,700	80,000
Solomon Is.	16,000	193,800

PRINCIPAL TOWNS

TOWN	POPULATION*
Sydney (Australia)	2,445,000
Melbourne (Australia)	2,229,000
Adelaide (Australia)	727,000
Brisbane (Australia)	719,000
Auckland (New Zealand)	548,000
Perth (Australia)	500,000
Christchurch (New Zealand)	247,000
Newcastle (Australia)	234,000
Wellington (New Zealand)	168,000
Great Wollongong (Australia)	163,000
Hobart (Tasmania)	119,000
Hutt (New Zealand)	115,000
Dunedin (New Zealand)	109,000
Geelong (Australia)	105,000
Canberra (Australia)	86,000
Hamilton (New Zealand)	68,000
Launceston (Tasmania)	60,450
Suva (Fiji)	54,157
Nouméa (New Caledonia)	40,880
Papeete (Tahiti)	22,278

*These are the figures for the conurbation, not for the city alone.

HIGHEST MOUNTAINS

MOUNTAIN	HEIGHT IN FEET
Carstenz (New Guinea)	16,400
Idenburg (New Guinea)	15,750
Wilhelmina (New Guinea)	15,584
Wilhelm (New Guinea)	15,400
Victoria (New Guinea)	13,240
Albert Edward (New Guinea)	13,000
Cook (New Zealand)	12,349
Balbi (Bougainville, Solomon Is.)	10,170
Ruapehu (New Zealand)	9,175
Egmont (New Zealand)	8,286
Orohena (Tahiti)	7,618
Ulawan (New Britain, Bismarck Arch.)	7,546
Kosciusko (Australia)	7,328
Panié (New Caledonia)	5,412

LARGEST LAKES

LAKE	AREA IN SQUARE MILES
Eyre (Australia)	3,600
Torrens (Australia)	2,230
Gairdner (Australia)	1,500
Taupo (New Zealand)	232
Te Anau (New Zealand)	132
Wakatipu (New Zealand)	112

GREAT RIVERS

RIVER	LENGTH IN MILES
Murray (Australia)	1,600
Darling (Australia)	1,190
Murrumbidgee (Australia)	1,050
Sepik (New Guinea)	700
Fly (New Guinea)	650
Macquarie (Australia)	590
Flinders (Australia)	520
Mamberamo (New Guinea)	500
Condamine (Australia)	495

THE WORLD IN MAPS

This section of twenty-four pages depicts the World,
its physical and political organisation, the distribution of its people, its treasures,
and the condition of its communications and climate.

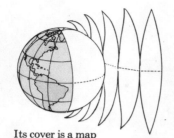

A globe is a model
of the earth   Its cover is a map

These gores will cover a globe of the size shown above

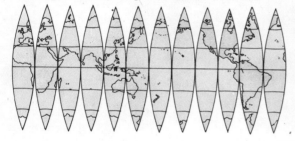

Here the Americas are moved to the left
to allow for a more compact form

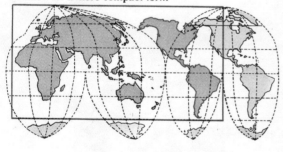

The red line indicates the limits of the maps on pages
514—515 and 520—521

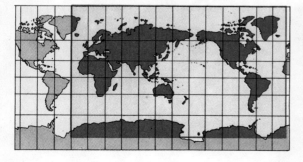

HOW THESE MAPS WERE DEVISED

The first thing to know about maps is that they are all distorted or twisted out of shape. Maps of the whole world are the most distorted of all, because the earth is round and maps are flat. To stretch the surface of a globe out on to a flat surface is bound to change the shape of the country represented on it.

The ordinary classroom globe is covered with a map which has first been printed on paper and then cut into 'gores'. Gores fit on to the spherical surface because, though flat, they are narrow enough to involve very little curvature when they are stuck in place.

A set of unmounted globe gores does not make a satisfactory map of the world because it is cut in too many places.

To show the shape of land more accurately, we 'gather' some of the gores in groups so that the distortion comes in the sea area. This is the projection used in this section, except for the physical map of the world on pages 522 and 523. Here it was desired to show the oceans as well as the continents as accurately as possible, and for that purpose another system was used, called the Miller Cylindrical Projection shown in the bottom diagram on this page.

On the next two pages are four global views of the earth, which will help you to keep the true proportions in mind.

NORTHERN HEMISPHERE

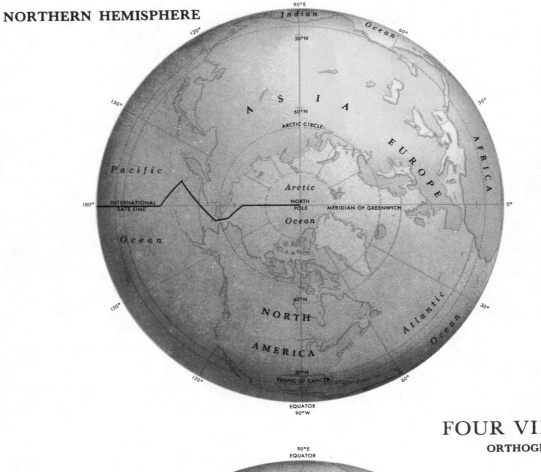

FOUR VIEWS

ORTHOGRAPHIC

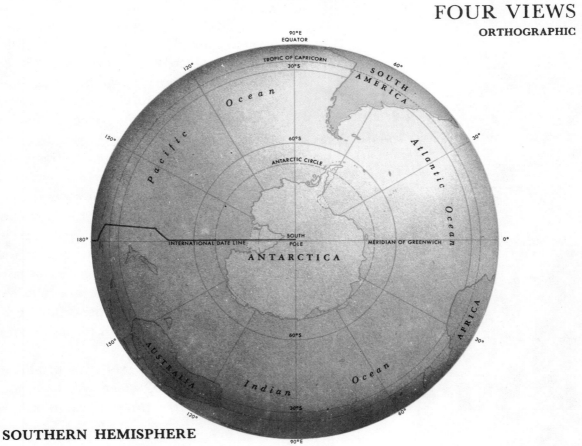

SOUTHERN HEMISPHERE

WESTERN HEMISPHERE

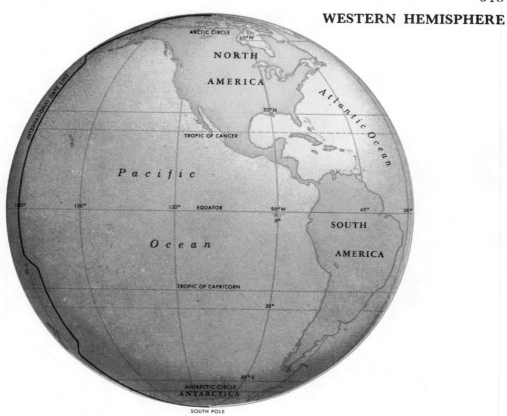

OF THE WORLD

PROJECTION

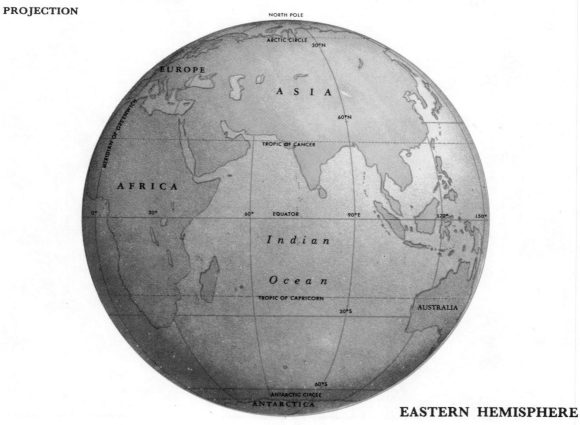

EASTERN HEMISPHERE

NORTH POLE

Arctic Ocean

QUEEN ELIZABETH ISLANDS

Ellesmere

GREENLAND

Beaufort Sea

Baffin Bay

ARCTIC CIRCLE

Wrangel

Bering Str.

Yukon

Mt. McKinley
20,270'

Mackenzie

Davis Strait

ICELAND

60°

EAST GREENLAND CURRENT

OYASHIO CURRENT

Bering Sea

Laurentian Upland

LABRADOR CURRENT

NEWFOUNDLAND

Aleutian Is.

Columbia

Rocky Mts.

Lake Winnipeg

Great Lakes

St. Lawrence

Hudson Bay

GULF STREAM

Great Plains

Missouri

Mississippi

Appalachians

MONDAY SUNDAY

CALIFORNIA CURRENT

Colorado

Ohio

GULF STREAM

30°

INTERNATIONAL DATE LINE

HAWAIIAN IS.

Rio Grande

Mexican Plateau

Gulf of Mexico

TROPIC OF CANCER

Atlantic

WEST INDIES

Pacific

Caribbean Sea

NORTH EQUATORIAL CURRENT

NESIA

Ocean

EQUATORIAL COUNTERCURRENT

Isthmus of Panama

Galápagos Is.

Llanos

Orinoco

EQUATOR 0°

ANESIA

SOUTH EQUATORIAL CURRENT

Amazon

Selvas

Madeira

Andes Mts.

POLYNESIA

PERU CURRENT

Mato Grosso

Paraná

Ocean

Easter I.

Paraguay

BRAZIL CURRENT

TROPIC OF CAPRICORN

Aconcagua
22,835'

30°

NEW ZEALAND

Pampas

Rio de la Plata

Magellan

Falkland Is.

South Georgia

Strait of

Tierra del Fuego

Cape Horn

60°

THE WORLD
Physical

Scale at the Equator 1:115,000,000

About 1,800 miles to the inch

MILLER CYLINDRICAL PROJECTION

WEST WIND DRIFT

ANTARCTIC CIRCLE

Graham Land

Bellingshausen Sea

Weddell Sea

Ross Sea

ANTARCTICA

Shelf Ice

Ross Shelf Ice

180°   150°   120°   90°   60°   30°

RAINFALL

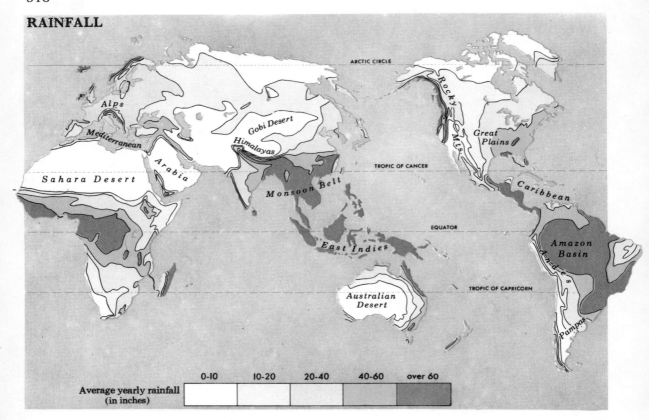

ARCTIC CIRCLE

Alps

Mediterranean

Sahara Desert

Arabia

Gobi Desert

Himalayas

Monsoon Belt

TROPIC OF CANCER

Rocky Mts.

Great Plains

Caribbean

EQUATOR

East Indies

Amazon Basin

Andes

Australian Desert

TROPIC OF CAPRICORN

Pampas

| 0-10 | 10-20 | 20-40 | 40-60 | over 60 |

Average yearly rainfall
(in inches)

TEMPERATURE

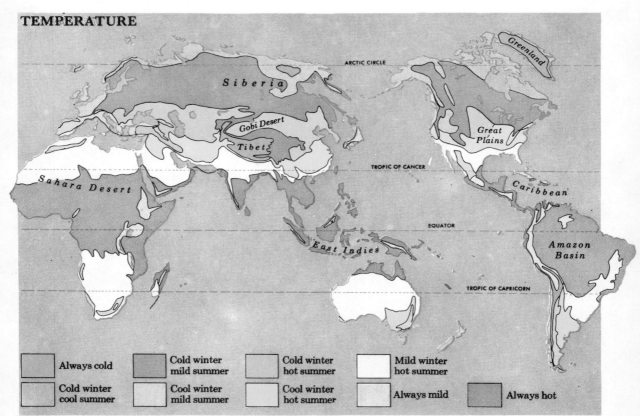

ARCTIC CIRCLE

Greenland

Siberia

Gobi Desert

Tibet

Great Plains

TROPIC OF CANCER

Sahara Desert

Caribbean

EQUATOR

East Indies

Amazon Basin

TROPIC OF CAPRICORN

| Always cold | Cold winter mild summer | Cold winter hot summer | Mild winter hot summer |
| Cold winter cool summer | Cool winter mild summer | Cool winter hot summer | Always mild | Always hot |

Water POWER SOURCES

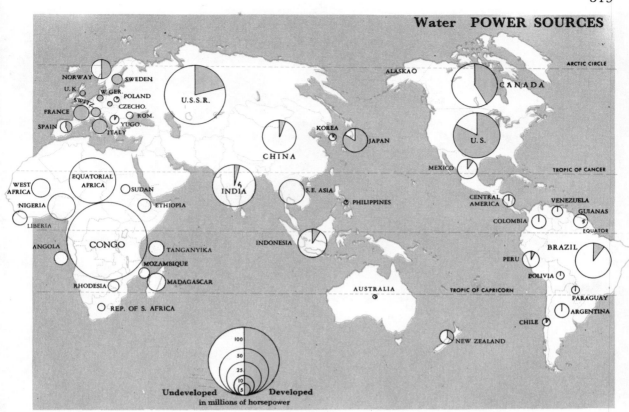

NORWAY SWEDEN
U.K.
W. GER. POLAND
SWITZ. CZECHO.
FRANCE ROM.
YUGO.
SPAIN ITALY

U.S.S.R.

ALASKA

CANADA

ARCTIC CIRCLE

KOREA
CHINA
JAPAN

U.S.

MEXICO

TROPIC OF CANCER

WEST AFRICA
EQUATORIAL AFRICA
SUDAN
ETHIOPIA

NIGERIA
LIBERIA

INDIA
S.E. ASIA
PHILIPPINES

CENTRAL AMERICA
VENEZUELA
GUIANAS
COLOMBIA
EQUATOR

ANGOLA
CONGO
TANGANYIKA
MOZAMBIQUE
MADAGASCAR
RHODESIA
REP. OF S. AFRICA

INDONESIA

PERU
BOLIVIA
BRAZIL

PARAGUAY
CHILE
ARGENTINA

AUSTRALIA

TROPIC OF CAPRICORN

NEW ZEALAND

100
50
25
10
5

Undeveloped   Developed
in millions of horsepower

Minerals POWER SOURCES

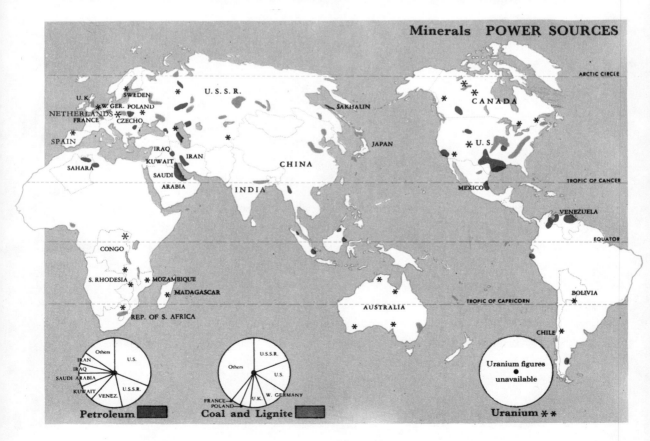

U.K.
SWEDEN
U.S.S.R.
NETHERLANDS
W. GER. POLAND
FRANCE CZECHO.
SPAIN

SAKHALIN

CANADA

ARCTIC CIRCLE

JAPAN

U.S.

IRAQ
KUWAIT IRAN
SAUDI ARABIA

CHINA

INDIA

MEXICO

TROPIC OF CANCER

SAHARA

VENEZUELA

EQUATOR

CONGO

S. RHODESIA
MOZAMBIQUE
MADAGASCAR
REP. OF S. AFRICA

AUSTRALIA

BOLIVIA

TROPIC OF CAPRICORN

CHILE

Others
U.S.
IRAN
IRAQ
SAUDI ARABIA
KUWAIT VENEZ.
U.S.S.R.

Petroleum

U.S.S.R.
Others
U.S.
W. GERMANY
FRANCE
POLAND
U.K.

Coal and Lignite

Uranium figures
unavailable

Uranium ✳✳

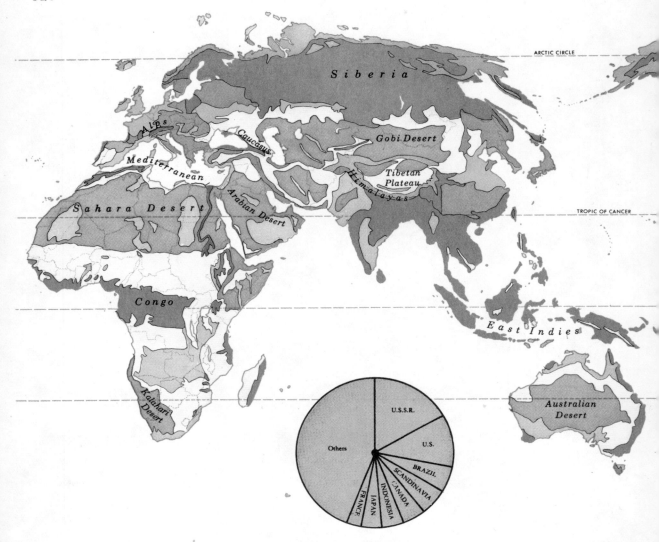

Labels on map: Siberia, Alps, Caucasus, Gobi Desert, Mediterranean, Himalayas, Tibetan Plateau, Sahara Desert, Arabian Desert, Congo, East Indies, Kalahari Desert, Australian Desert

Pie chart labels: U.S.S.R., U.S., BRAZIL, SCANDINAVIA, CANADA, INDONESIA, JAPAN, FRANCE, Others

Timber Production

This map of natural vegetation tells an interesting story. Vegetation depends on physical conditions; so the plants that grow in a particular area tell us much about rainfall, temperature, the nature of the soil, etc. Vegetation falls into three main types: forests, grasslands, and deserts. The number of individual species within these groups is unbelievably large.

Over large areas of the world, vegetation is determined largely by temperature and moisture.

There are exceptions, however. Plants may be found growing in conditions that would appear to favour another type of vegetation. Desert plants, for example, thrive in many places that have enough rainfall to support a grassland vegetation. The explanation in most cases is that the soil is very porous, and quickly dries out, even after heavy rainfall.

At one time, a quarter of the earth's surface was covered by forests, now it is less than one sixth. Great harm has been done by the reckless exploitation of forests. In many cases, where the forests

VEGETATION

Natural vegetation, unmodified by man

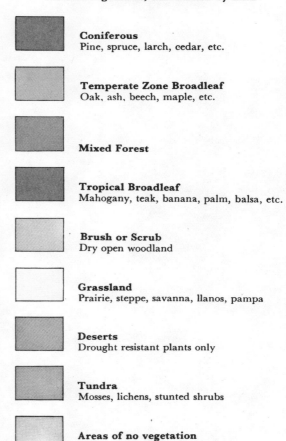

Coniferous
Pine, spruce, larch, cedar, etc.

Temperate Zone Broadleaf
Oak, ash, beech, maple, etc.

Mixed Forest

Tropical Broadleaf
Mahogany, teak, banana, palm, balsa, etc.

Brush or Scrub
Dry open woodland

Grassland
Prairie, steppe, savanna, llanos, pampa

Deserts
Drought resistant plants only

Tundra
Mosses, lichens, stunted shrubs

Areas of no vegetation
Ice caps, rock desert

have gone, the soil is incapable of supporting anything but the scantiest desert vegetation.

Forests are generally limited to places where summer temperatures average at least 50°F (10°C). The amount of rainfall required depends upon the temperature: where it is cool, the moisture does not evaporate quickly and 15 inches of rain a year are enough. In warmer places much more is needed, tropical forests requiring as much as 90 to 150 inches of rain yearly.

Grass requires considerably less rain. In fact grassland is typical of semi-arid conditions.

Originally grassland extended over a third of the earth's surface. As the soil formed on grassland is usually good, most prairies have been ploughed up for the growing of other crops.

This section of twenty-four pages depicts the world, its physical and political organisation, the distribution of its people, its treasures, and the condition of its communications and climate.

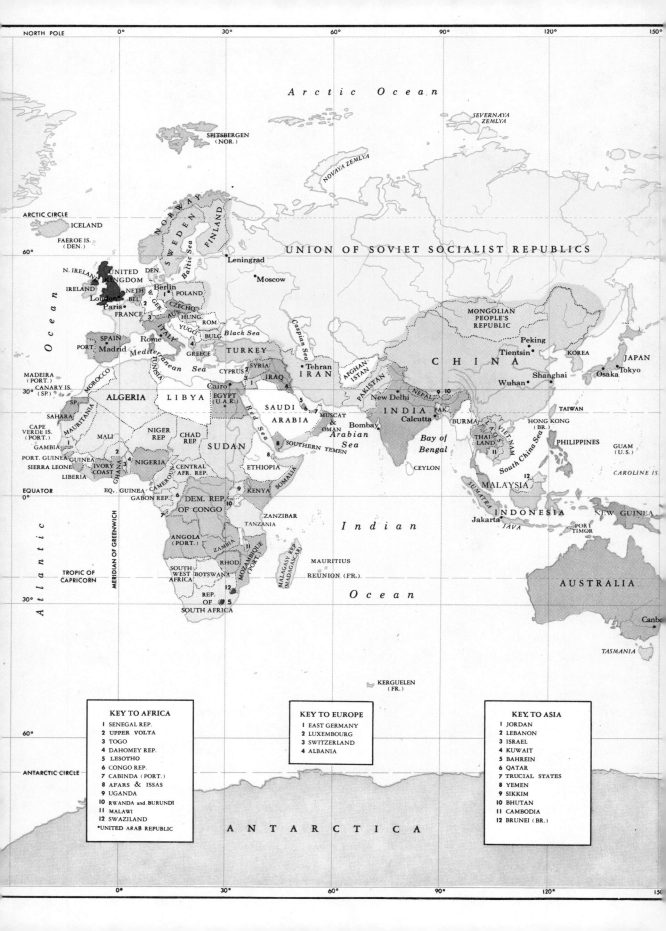

NORTH POLE   0°   30°   60°   90°   120°   150°

Arctic Ocean

SPITSBERGEN
(NOR.)

NOVAYA ZEMLYA

SEVERNAYA
ZEMLYA

ARCTIC CIRCLE   ICELAND

FAEROE IS.
(DEN.)

60°

UNION OF SOVIET SOCIALIST REPUBLICS

Baltic Sea   •Leningrad

N. IRELAND   UNITED   DEN.
KINGDOM
IRELAND   NETH.   •Moscow
London•   BEL.   W. GER.   Berlin
Paris•   1 POLAND
FRANCE   2   3   CZECHO
AUS.   HUNG.
ITALY   ROM.
YUGO.   BULG.   *Black Sea*
SPAIN   4   GREECE   TURKEY   *Caspian Sea*   MONGOLIAN
PEOPLE'S
REPUBLIC
PORT.   Madrid•   Rome•
Mediterranean Sea   TUNISIA   •Tehran   •Peking
MADEIRA   MOROCCO   CYPRUS 2   SYRIA   AFGHAN-   CHINA   Tientsin•   KOREA
(PORT.)   1   IRAQ   IRAN   ISTAN   •Shanghai   JAPAN
CANARY IS.   Cairo   3   PAKISTAN   Wuhan•   Osaka•   Tokyo
30°   (SP.)   EGYPT   NEPAL 9 10
ALGERIA   LIBYA   (U.A.R.)   5   New Delhi•   PAK.   TAIWAN
SP.   SAUDI   6 7 MUSCAT   INDIA   Calcutta   HONG KONG
SAHARA   ARABIA   &   Bombay•   BURMA   7   (BR.)
CAPE   MAURITANIA   OMAN   *Arabian*   VIETNAM
VERDE IS.   MALI   NIGER   CHAD   *Sea*   Bay of   THAI-   PHILIPPINES   GUAM
(PORT.)   REP   REP   8   SOUTHERN   Bengal   LAND   (U.S.)
GAMBIA   SUDAN   YEMEN   CEYLON   11   CAROLINE IS.
PORT. GUINEA   GUINEA   8   *South China Sea*
SIERRA LEONE   2   NIGERIA   ETHIOPIA   12
LIBERIA   IVORY   3   CENTRAL   MALAYSIA
COAST   4   CAMEROUN   AFR. REP.   9   KENYA   SUMATRA   INDONESIA   NEW GUINEA
EQUATOR   EQ. GUINEA   SOMALIA   Jakarta•   PORT.
0°   GABON REP.   6   DEM. REP.   10   JAVA   TIMOR
7   OF CONGO   ZANZIBAR
ANGOLA   TANZANIA   *Indian*
(PORT.)   ZAMBIA   11
TROPIC OF   MALAGASY REP.   *Ocean*   AUSTRALIA
CAPRICORN   SOUTH-   RHOD.   MOZAMBIQUE   (MADAGASCAR)
WEST   BOTSWANA   (PORT.)   MAURITIUS
AFRICA   12   REUNION (FR.)
30°   REP.   5
OF   Canbe•
SOUTH AFRICA

Atlantic Ocean

MERIDIAN OF GREENWICH

TASMANIA

KERGUELEN
(FR.)

60°

ANTARCTIC CIRCLE

ANTARCTICA

0°   30°   60°   90°   120°   150

KEY TO AFRICA	KEY TO EUROPE	KEY TO ASIA
1 SENEGAL REP.	1 EAST GERMANY	1 JORDAN
2 UPPER VOLTA	2 LUXEMBOURG	2 LEBANON
3 TOGO	3 SWITZERLAND	3 ISRAEL
4 DAHOMEY REP.	4 ALBANIA	4 KUWAIT
5 LESOTHO		5 BAHREIN
6 CONGO REP.		6 QATAR
7 CABINDA (PORT.)		7 TRUCIAL STATES
8 AFARS & ISSAS		8 YEMEN
9 UGANDA		9 SIKKIM
10 RWANDA and BURUNDI		10 BHUTAN
11 MALAWI		11 CAMBODIA
12 SWAZILAND		12 BRUNEI (BR.)
*UNITED ARAB REPUBLIC		

Arctic Ocean

QUEEN ELIZABETH ISLANDS

GREENLAND
(DEN.)

BANKS

VICTORIA

BAFFIN

ARCTIC CIRCLE

ICELAND

WRANGEL

ALASKA

Bering Sea

60°

Hudson Bay

C A N A D A

Davis Strait

NEWFOUNDLAND

ALEUTIAN IS.

HAWAIIAN IS.

Chicago   Detroit

New York

U N I T E D

Philadelphia

Washington

S T A T E S

Los Angeles

AZORES
(PORT.)

Atlantic

30°

MEXICO

Gulf of
Mexico

BERMUDA
(BR.)

TROPIC OF CANCER

CUBA

BAHAMA IS.
(BR.)

WAKE
(U.S.)

Pacific

Mexico City

BR.
HOND.

GUATEMALA

HAITI

DOM. REP.

PUERTO
RICO (U.S.)

VIRGIN IS. (U.S.-BR.)

GUADELOUPE (FR.)

MARTINIQUE (FR.)

CAPE VERDE IS.
(PORT.)

MARSHALL IS.
(U.S. TRUST.)

HOND. Caribbean Sea

NICARAGUA

EL SALVADOR

COSTA
RICA

PANAMA

VENEZUELA

GUYANA

SURINAM (NETH.)

FR. GUIANA

COLOMBIA

EQUATOR

0°

SOLOMON IS.
(BR.)

GALAPAGOS IS.
(ECUADOR)

ECUADOR

B R A Z I L

Ocean

NEW
HEBRIDES
(BR.-FR.)

SAMOA

FRENCH OCEANIA

PERU

FIJI IS.

TAHITI

Brasilia

Rio de
Janeiro

TROPIC OF CAPRICORN

NEW
CALEDONIA
(FR.)

TONGA

BOLIVIA

PARAGUAY

São Paulo

EASTER I.
(CHILE)

30°

CHILE

ARGENTINA

URUGUAY

Buenos Aires

Wellington
NEW ZEALAND

FALKLAND IS.
(BR.)

60°

THE WORLD
Political

Scale at the Equator 1:115,000,000
About 1800 miles to the inch

MILLER CYLINDRICAL PROJECTION

ANTARCTIC CIRCLE

Bellingshausen Sea

Weddell Sea

Ross Sea

Ross Shelf Ice

A N T A R C T I C A

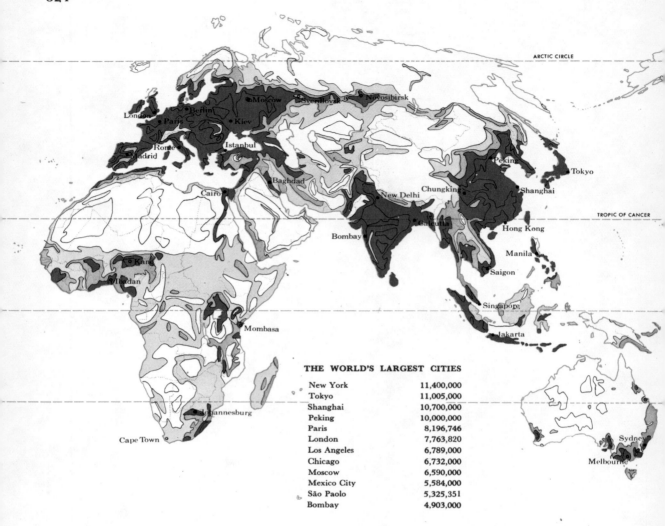

THE WORLD'S LARGEST CITIES	
New York	11,400,000
Tokyo	11,005,000
Shanghai	10,700,000
Peking	10,000,000
Paris	8,196,746
London	7,763,820
Los Angeles	6,789,000
Chicago	6,732,000
Moscow	6,590,000
Mexico City	5,584,000
São Paolo	5,325,351
Bombay	4,903,000

Over three thousand million people live in the world today and the population is increasing by more than a million a week. At that rate, by the end of the century, the world's population will number over 6,000 million, that is to say, more than twice what it is today.

This map shows that the greater part of the world is almost uninhabited. Other vast areas are thinly populated, while in some places great numbers of people are crowded together in small areas.

More than half the world's population is found in the Far East. Yet this portion of the earth represents only one-tenth of the habitable world. Another fifth of the world's population lives in Europe, which is less than one-twentieth of the habitable world. Antarctica is at the other extreme, with an area over than 5 million square miles and no permanent inhabitants.

The map shows four principal centres of population. The first is the Far East, the second India and Pakistan, the third Europe, and the fourth the industrial area of North America.

POPULATION

PERSONS PER SQUARE MILE

Uninhabited	0-5	5-25	25-50	50-100	100-250	over 250

THE 30 MOST POPULOUS COUNTRIES

1 China — 730,000,000
2 India — 523,893,000
3 U.S.S.R. — 237,000,000
4 U.S.A. — 201,166,000
5 Indonesia — 118,000,000
6 Pakistan — 109,520,000
7 Japan — 101,000,000
8 Germany (E & W) — 77,090,000
9 Brazil — 88,200,000
10 Nigeria — 62,600,000
11 United Kingdom — 55,283,000
12 Italy — 54,463,000
13 France — 50,600,000
14 Korea (N & S) — 44,207,000
15 Vietnam (N & S) — 37,800,000
16 Philippines — 34,660,000
17 Mexico — 47,267,000
18 Thailand — 33,693,000
19 Spain — 32,411,000
20 Poland — 32,060,000
21 Egypt — 30,907,000
22 Turkey — 33,539,000
23 Burma — 26,390,000
24 Iran — 25,781,000
25 Ethiopia — 23,900,000
26 Argentina — 23,600,000
27 Canada — 20,857,000
28 Yugoslavia — 20,154,000
29 Republic of South Africa — 20,000,000
30 Colombia — 19,800,000

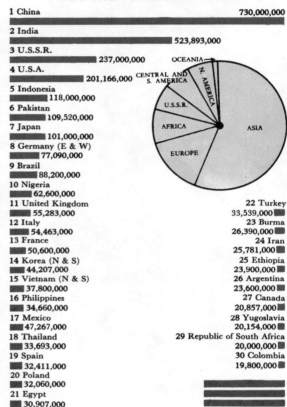

In Asia, the most thickly populated areas are the valleys and fertile plains, where there is good soil and water for irrigation. Asians concentrate in these areas because they live by agriculture. Industry may be growing rapidly, but the bulk of the people are still concentrated in good farming country.

In Europe and North America, the concentration of population follows a different pattern. In these continents the greatest number of people are concentrated in the areas where industry flourishes, and in ports and trading centres.

There seems little chance of solving the problem of overcrowding by sending large numbers of people to the less crowded areas of the earth.

People always move towards areas of greatest opportunity, and those are the more populated areas. Thus crowded areas become more crowded and under-populated areas even emptier.

Heat and drought combine to make a desert. About one-sixth of the earth's surface is desert.

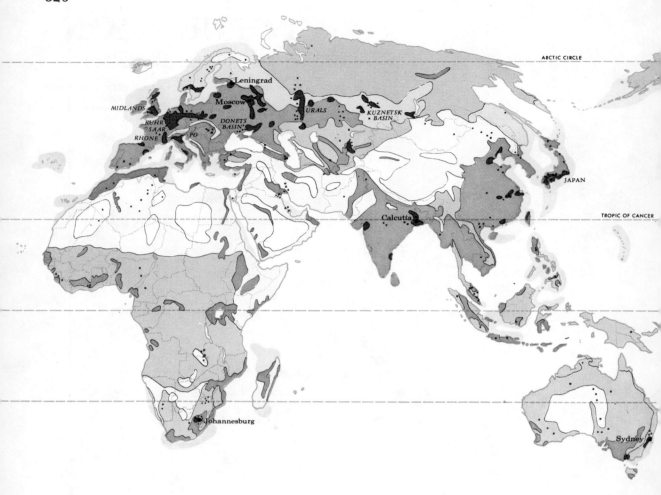

People earn their living in very different ways. The map above shows you how the chief human occupations are distributed over the earth.

Few people live by hunting and fishing. Food procured in this way does not keep long, and has to be eaten quickly. The supply of food is uncertain for these people and they are liable to periods of famine.

Nomadic herding is another primitive method of making a living. These people are nomads because they have to keep their flocks and herds moving in search of fresh pastures. It takes a large area of land to support a single animal so that those who follow this way of life are few.

Livestock bred on farms — usually cattle, sheep, horses, or goats — graze prepared pastures frequently supplemented by special fodder crops.

A small area of arable land can support many people. In the rice-fields of India, China, and Japan, which are intensively cultivated, a square mile can support over a thousand people. In this case the average holding is very small and most of the crop is consumed locally. In contrast just one of the huge wheat farms

HUMAN OCCUPATIONS

Ways of earning a living

Little or no economic activity
Ice caps, true deserts, high mountains

Nomadic herding
Chiefly in semi-desert areas

Hunting and Fishing
Primitive agriculture and sub-arctic
nomadic herding

Forestry
Timber, pulpwood for paper and
industrial uses

Stock breeding
Controlled, excluding dairy cattle

Agriculture
All types except primitive

Manufacturing and commerce

Commercial fishing

Mining

of the Canadian prairies, the American Middle West, or the pampas of the Argentine, may produce enough grain to feed several thousand people.

Forestry, like modern farming and ranching, is often a complex business demanding skill. Great care is taken in cutting and replanting to ensure continual forest growth and production.

Mining is one of the industries on which the machine age particularly depends. Minerals are often discovered in isolated places, and it is there that the mining community must develop. But the products of the mines soon find their way to the great centres of population, where they are converted into manufactured goods. Fishing on an industrial scale can involve travelling hundreds of miles from the home ports to the fishing grounds. Today, quick-freezing and canning make fresh fish available to people living far inland.

Industry and commerce are of great and growing importance. Millions who once worked on the land are now working in mills, factories, and offices. The greater part of such work is done in large towns.

AGRICULTURAL PRODUCTS Wheat Barley

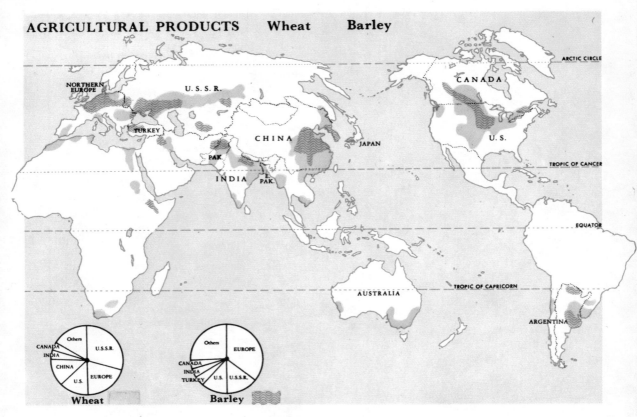

AGRICULTURAL PRODUCTS Maize Millet

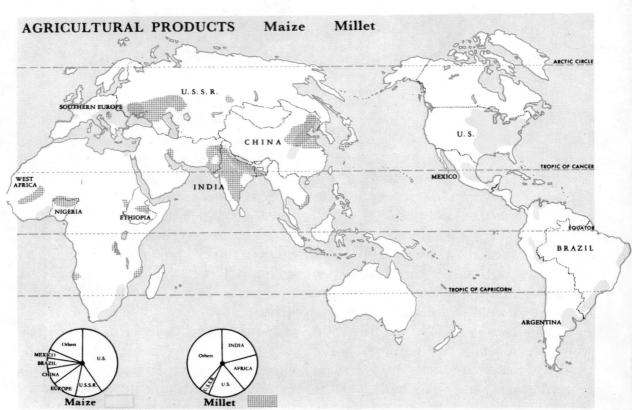

Oats   Rye   Rice   **AGRICULTURAL PRODUCTS**

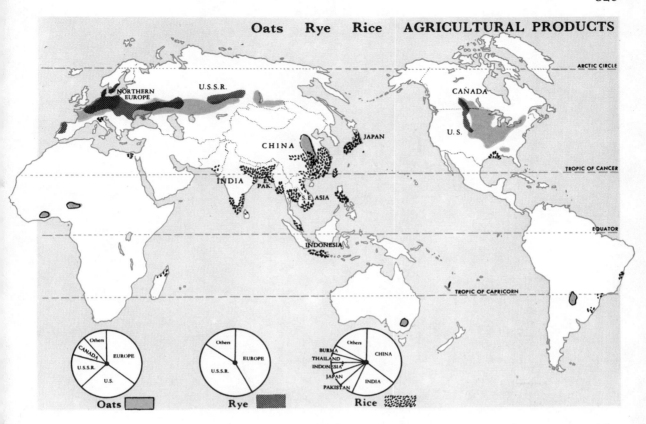

Sugar   Tea   Coffee   **AGRICULTURAL PRODUCTS**

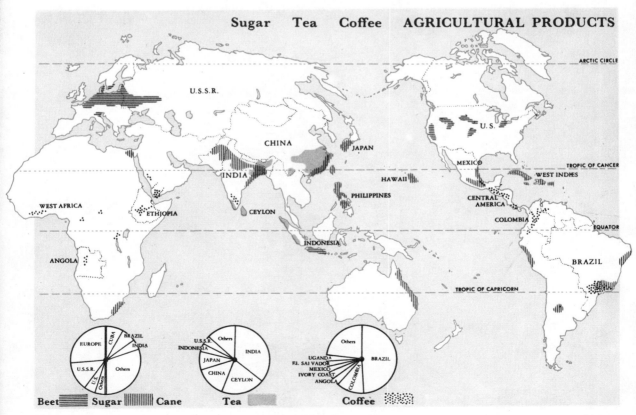

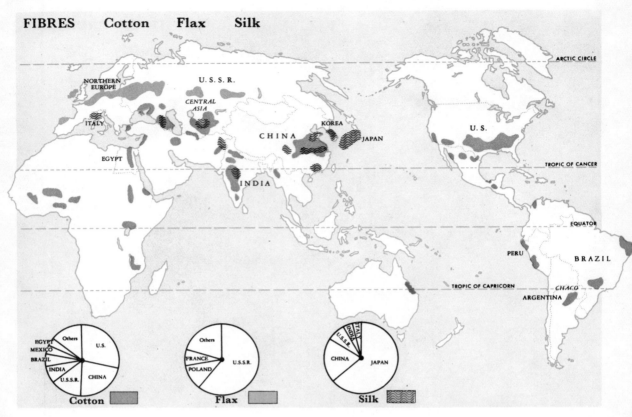

FIBRES   Cotton   Flax   Silk

Cotton

Flax

Silk

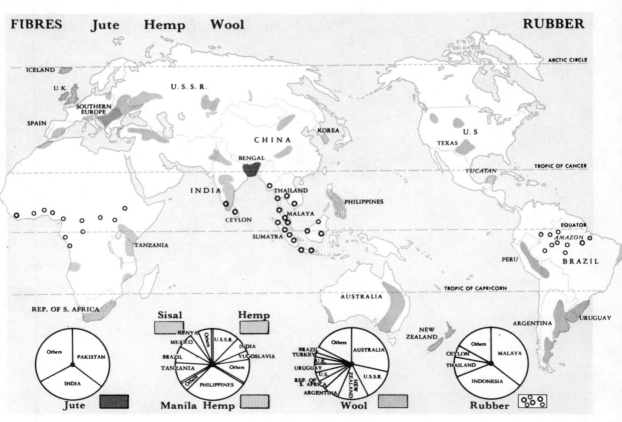

FIBRES   Jute   Hemp   Wool

RUBBER

Jute

Sisal   **Hemp**

Manila Hemp

Wool

Rubber

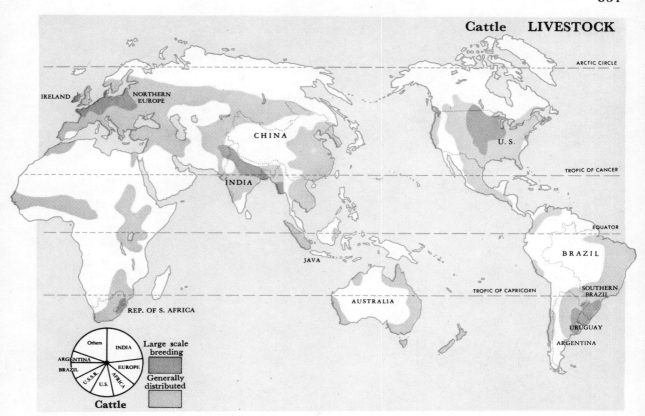

Cattle   LIVESTOCK

ARCTIC CIRCLE

IRELAND

NORTHERN EUROPE

CHINA

INDIA

U.S.

TROPIC OF CANCER

JAVA

EQUATOR

BRAZIL

AUSTRALIA

SOUTHERN BRAZIL

TROPIC OF CAPRICORN

URUGUAY

ARGENTINA

REP. OF S. AFRICA

Pie chart: Others, INDIA, ARGENTINA, EUROPE, BRAZIL, U.S.S.R., U.S., AFRICA

Large scale breeding

Generally distributed

Cattle

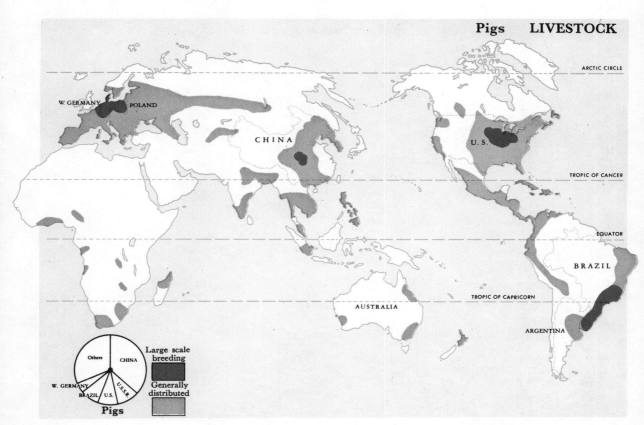

Pigs   LIVESTOCK

ARCTIC CIRCLE

W. GERMANY   POLAND

CHINA

U.S.

TROPIC OF CANCER

EQUATOR

BRAZIL

AUSTRALIA

TROPIC OF CAPRICORN

ARGENTINA

Pie chart: Others, CHINA, W. GERMANY, U.S.S.R., BRAZIL, U.S.

Large scale breeding

Generally distributed

Pigs

INDUSTRIAL MINERALS Iron Tungsten Molybdenum Vanadium

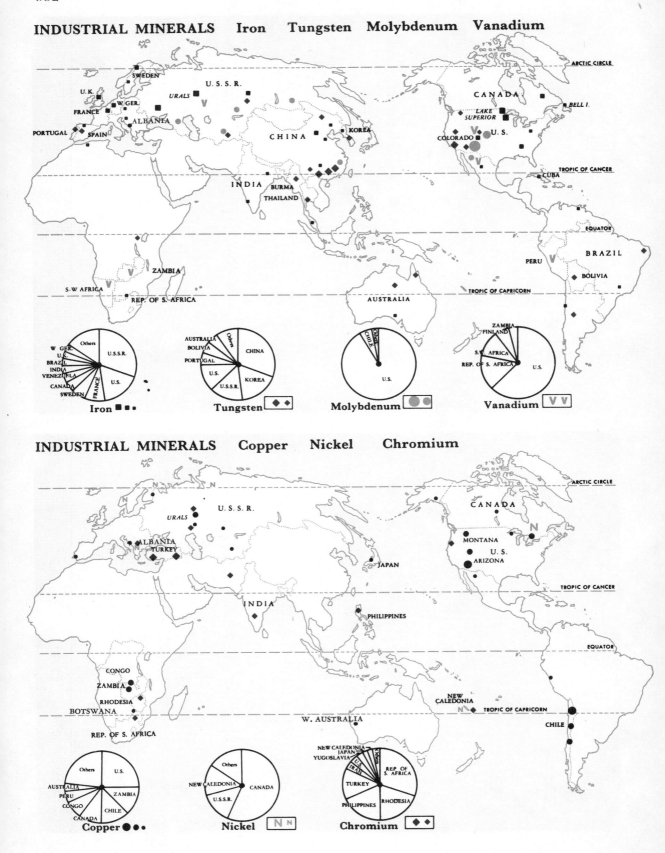

Iron ■ ■ •

Tungsten ◆ ◆

Molybdenum ● ●

Vanadium V V

INDUSTRIAL MINERALS Copper Nickel Chromium

Copper ● ● •

Nickel N N

Chromium ◆ ◆

Tin   Lead   INDUSTRIAL MINERALS

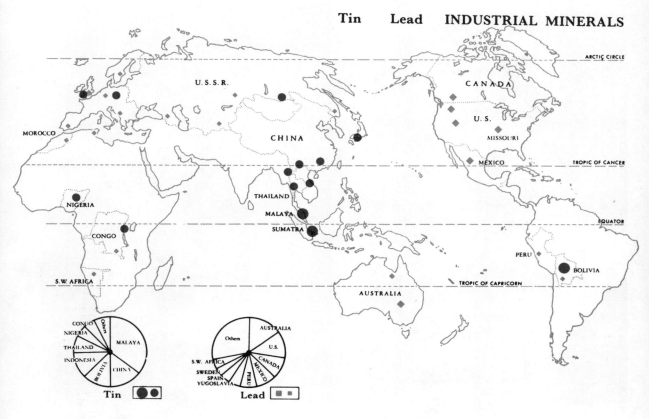

Zinc   Bauxite   INDUSTRIAL MINERALS

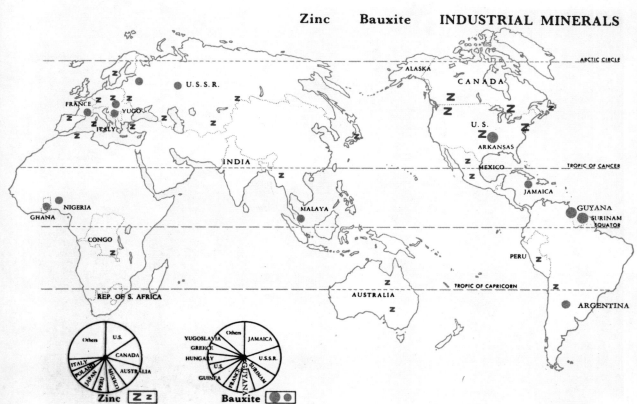

534

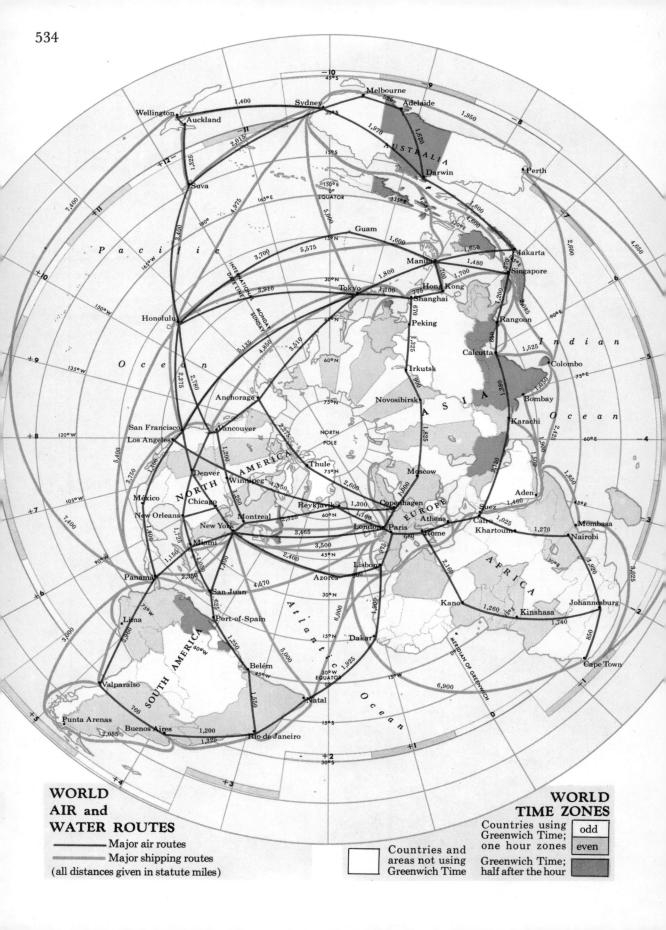

WORLD
AIR and
WATER ROUTES
——— Major air routes
——— Major shipping routes
(all distances given in statute miles)

Countries and
areas not using
Greenwich Time

WORLD
TIME ZONES
Countries using
Greenwich Time;   odd
one hour zones   even
Greenwich Time;
half after the hour

INDEX